# Devising Critically Engaged Theatre with Youth

*Devising Critically Engaged Theatre with Youth: The Performing Justice Project* offers accessible frameworks for devising original theatre, developing critical understandings of racial and gender justice, and supporting youth to imagine, create, and perform possibilities for a more just and equitable society.

Working at the intersections of theory and practice, Alrutz and Hoare present their innovative model for devising critically engaged theatre with novice performers. Sharing why and how the Performing Justice Project (PJP) opens dialogue around challenging and necessary topics already facing young people, the authors bring together critical information about racial and gender justice with new and revised practices from applied theatre, storytelling, theatre, and education for social change. Their curated collection of PJP "performance actions" offers embodied and reflective approaches for building ensemble, devising and performing stories, and exploring and analyzing individual and systemic oppression. This work begins to confront oppressive narratives and disrupt patriarchal systems—including white supremacy, racism, sexism, and homophobia.

*Devising Critically Engaged Theatre with Youth* invites artists, teaching artists, educators, and youth-workers to collaborate bravely with young people to imagine and enact racial and gender justice in their lives and communities. Drawing on examples from PJP residencies in juvenile justice settings, high schools, foster care facilities, and community-based organizations, this book offers flexible and responsive ways for considering experiences of racism and sexism and performing visions of justice.

Visit performingjusticeproject.org for additional information and documentation of PJP performances with youth.

**Dr. Megan Alrutz** (she/her) is a professor at the University of Texas at Austin, where she heads the Drama and Theatre for Youth and Communities area. She works nationally and internationally as a theatre-maker, as well as an applied theatre facilitator focused on gender and racial justice.

**Lynn Hoare** (she/her) is a nationally recognized facilitator in applied theatre, Theatre in Education, and theatre for dialogue. She is the Senior Director of School-Based Programs at Creative Action, a creative youth development organization, where she uses theatre to activate youth and communities around issues relevant to their lives.

# Devising Critically Engaged Theatre with Youth

## The Performing Justice Project

Megan Alrutz and Lynn Hoare

Routledge
Taylor & Francis Group

NEW YORK AND LONDON

First published 2020
by Routledge
52 Vanderbilt Avenue, New York, NY 10017

and by Routledge
2 Park Square, Milton Park, Abingdon, Oxon, OX14 4RN

*Routledge is an imprint of the Taylor & Francis Group, an informa business*

© 2020 Megan Alrutz and Lynn Hoare

*Library of Congress Cataloging-in-Publication Data*
Names: Alrutz, Megan, author. | Hoare, Lynn, author.
Title: Devising critically engaged theatre with youth: the Performing Justice Project / Megan Alrutz and Lynn Hoare.
Description: New York: Routledge, 2020. |
Includes bibliographical references and index.
Identifiers: LCCN 2019059015 (print) | LCCN 2019059016 (ebook) |
ISBN 9781138104266 (hardback) | ISBN 9781138104273 (paperback) |
ISBN 9781315102283 (ebook)
Subjects: LCSH: Children's theater–Production and direction. |
Amateur theater–Production and direction. |
Theater–Political aspects–United States–History–21st century. |
Race in the theater. | Sex role in the theater. |
Performing Justice Project. | Children's theater–Production and direction.
Classification: LCC PN3157 .A468 2020 (print) |
LCC PN3157 (ebook) | DDC 792.02/26–dc23
LC record available at https://lccn.loc.gov/2019059015
LC ebook record available at https://lccn.loc.gov/2019059016

ISBN: 978-1-138-10426-6 (hbk)
ISBN: 978-1-138-10427-3 (pbk)
ISBN: 978-1-315-10228-3 (ebk)

Typeset in Gill Sans
by Newgen Publishing UK

We dedicate this book to young people

who do the work of racial and gender justice.

We walk with you.

#WePushWeReachWeRise

# Contents

# Illustrations

## Figures

# Tables

# Performance Actions: The Performing Justice Project

## 2.3.1  Performance Actions: What Is Ensemble?

### 2.3.3 Performance Actions: What Is (In)Justice and How Does it Show Up in My Life?

### 2.3.4 Performance Actions: How Do I Perform Justice?

# Doing Justice Author Biographies

**Briana Barner** (she/her) is a PhD candidate in Media Studies at UT Austin, and is also a graduate of the Center for Women's and Gender Studies at UT, where she wrote her award-winning Master's thesis on the power of the #BlackGirlMagic hashtag. Her research interests include digital and Black feminism, new media, social media as a tool for social justice and activism, podcasts hosted by people who hold marginalized identities, and the representation of marginalized people, specifically Black girls and women, in popular culture and media.

**Laura Epperson** (she/her) is an actor, director, and teaching artist who explores the potential for artistic processes to create community-driven social change. Laura develops multi-disciplinary artistic collaborations that aim to intentionally engage with community and expand who and how people are invited into creative spaces. Originally from Iowa, Laura holds a BS in Theatre Performance from the University of Evansville and is currently an MFA candidate in Drama and Theatre for Youth and Communities at the University of Texas, Austin.

**Natalie Goodnow** (she/her) is a nationally recognized theatre artist from Austin, Texas who creates and directs activist performance for stages, streets, and class-rooms. She's collaborated with organizations such as Creative Action, Voices Against Violence, and Youth Rise Texas to make new work; and her solo play *Mud Offerings* was the 2011 winner of the Jane Chambers Award for feminist plays and performance texts. She holds a M.F.A. in Performance as Public Practice from the University of Texas at Austin.

**Tameika L. Hannah** (she/her) is a sound designer and screen-printer. She uses sound as narration for documentaries, film, theatre and other performance arenas. As a screen-printer, Tameika has facilitated screen-printing workshops with youth, printed t-shirts for conferences, created original designs with family and friends and is currently focused on designing and printing t-shirts from her personal collection.

**Faith A. Hillis** (she/her) is an actor, teaching artist and spoken word performer from Houston, Texas. Faith holds a BFA in Acting and Directing from Sam Houston State University. At the University of Texas at Austin (UT), Faith is a third-year MFA candidate in the Drama and Theatre for Youth and Communities program. Faith is passionate about continuously working in community to promote justice and equity as an embodied practice.

**Cortney McEniry** (she/her) is the artistic director and program manager of UVa Acts, an educational theatre program promoting equitable, vibrant spaces for working and learning at the University of Virginia. Her practice centers on facilitating agentive, asset-based artistic processes with and for communities, and her research focuses on grassroots practices in institutional contexts. Cortney received her MFA from UT Austin, where she was privileged to work with artists in the Performing Justice Project from 2015 to 2017.

**Sidney Monroe Williams** (he/they series) is a community-based theatre artist whose work is situated at the intersections of race, gender, and class. Through creative strategies, Sidney facilitates art-making and conversations with communities to spark dialogue, raise visibility, and celebrate marginalized bodies. Sidney is an assistant professor at the University of Louisville in the African American Theatre Program.

# Acknowledgments

The content of this book was developed over the course of several years and in collaboration with many critical voices. Our first appreciation goes to Dr. Kristen Hogan whose knowledge of and experience with gender and racial equity and advocacy, coupled with her justice-based approach to leadership, helped shape and grow PJP from a three-week theatre project, to a multi-year performance program, to a critically engaged performance framework. Her vision, experience, and encouragement underpin the PJP model and continue to inspire us to practice toward possibility. We are also grateful to all of the young people who have participated in PJP and challenged us to acknowledge our politics and name that PJP *is* in fact part of a movement, while lifting each other up and performing justice. Thank you to the Center for Women's and Gender Studies at University of Texas at Austin for the long-term and logistical support of this project: Pat Heisler, Molly Marchione, Nancy Ewert, Jackie Salcedo, Susan Heinzelman. Our deepest gratitude goes to Lauren and Gayle Embrey and the Embrey Family Foundation whose commitment to justice-based arts initiatives ensure that young people in the state of Texas have opportunities to perform justice and that the PJP model moves beyond the walls of our university campus.

The Department of Theatre and Dance and the College of Fine Arts at UT Austin supported the research and development of this book in critical ways. Thank you to Dean Doug Dempster for recognizing the value of critically engaged theatre with youth and for supporting this research through a Summer Research Fellowship, the Walter and Gina Ducloux Fine Arts Faculty Fellowship, and support from the Theatre for Youth Chair. Thank you to Brant Pope and Robert Ramirez for honoring the intersections of research and practice in critical and marginalized spaces; their support helps make room in the academy for theatre with and for youth and community-engaged research. Sincere appreciation to the Theatre and Dance faculty at UT for ongoing dialogues about teaching and racial and gender justice. Thank you to the DTYC faculty, Michael Avila, Katie Dawson, Lara Dossett, Amissa Miller, Roxanne Schroeder-Arce, and Sara Simons—colleagues whose work challenges us to imagine more just systems for young people and their allies. Thank you to Omi Osun Joni L. Jones, Gloria Gonzalez-Lopez, wura-Natasha Ogunji, Matt Richardson, Jennifer Adair, Andrew Carlson, Charles Anderson, Cherise Smith, Jesse O'Rear, Siri Gurudev, and Lyn Wilshire, whose critical wisdom and endless work and heart are also woven into the fabric of PJP and this book. We are grateful to Jane Bost and Karen LaShelle for their support of artistic work outside the office that creates reverberations inside the office; to Heather Davies, Erin Burrows, Natalie Goodnow, Florinda Bryant, Frank

Nappi and Matrex Kilgore for their commitment to art and activism as a part of daily life. You all inspire the Performing Justice Project.

Our heartfelt thanks to our publishing editors Stacey Walker and Lucia Accorsi, for believing in this project and supporting us at every step. Our deep appreciation also goes to zakia brown and Shane Whalley for their critical editorial support. Meg Greene and Lena Barnard played an essential role in the creation of this book. Their keen eye, honest feedback, significant editorial support, and deep generosity made this book stronger. Thank you to the brilliant group of resident teaching artists and guest artists who, alongside the young participants, remain the heartbeat of PJP: Kristen Hogan and Tameika L. Hannah, Victoria Dominguez-Edington and Emily Freeman, Patena Key and Meg Greene, Natalie Goodnow and Jenny Arffmann, Sidney Monroe Williams and Kaitlyn Newman, Briana Barner and Cortney McEniry, Tamara Carroll, Faith Hillis and Lara Epperson, Emily Aguilar and Megan Nevels, Jada Cadena and Becca Drew Ramsey. Thank you also to Britney, Malin, Laura, and Julia—for always saying "yes, and..." and for seeing the arts as a pathway to justice. We are grateful to the many graduate students in theatre and dance who explored this content with us—their participation in this developing program continues to deepen our work and lives. Thank you to Routledge, GLSEN, Clark Baim, Race Forward, Stylus Publishing, Renée Watson, and Michele Norris and the Race Card Project™ for allowing us to build on previously published material and to reprint several figures that deepen our relationship to this work and strengthen the practical applications of this book.

Heartfelt thanks to the many important teachers who encouraged us to pay attention to (our) power and privilege and to not take our platforms for granted. We are grateful for their efforts to bring race and gender and identity politics to the center of our education. Sincere gratitude to the many teachers we haven't met but whose words and actions remain a loud whisper in our hearts and minds as we learn and grow as critically engaged advocates, educators, and artists: bell hooks, Aimee Carrillo Rowe, adrienne maree brown, Patricia Hill Collins, Robin DiAngelo, Kimberlé Williams Crenshaw, Tony Morrison, Audrey Lorde, Mary Stone Hanley, Lee Ann Bell, Ijeoma Oluo, Alok Vaid-Menon, and Pigeon. We hope to inspire and challenge young people in the ways that these artists, educators, scholars, and activists inspire and challenge us.

Finally, much love and appreciation to our friends and family who showed up to PJP performances and supported our efforts to move theory and practice into this book. We are deeply grateful to Carrie Kenny and Sarah Sloan for sharing their beautiful Deadwood retreat; your magical space inspired many deep dives, especially as we inched toward the finish line. To Ted and Daniel, who remain our think partners and spirit lifters and who are committed to gender and racial justice in their own ways—we are most grateful for all of the ways they hold space for us and encourage us to walk bravely. Thank you to Lilah, Izzy, Sally, Maggie, Sonny, Joaquin, Raleigh, David and Hannah, "our" baby Lewis and the gaggle of Texas kiddos, they are why we do this work. To our fierce siblings, *Goodness* and *besties-for-life*, and our web of chosen family, we are ever grateful for your daily reminders of why this work matters, that this work is now, and that this work only happens in community, *together*, with you.

# Authors' Note

As we prepare to move this book out into the world, to share the Performing Justice Project with academic, artistic, and activist circles, we are deeply inspired by the ways that writer, organizational healer, and pleasure activist adrienne maree brown names truths that have something critical to teach us all.

> We are in an imagination battle.
>
> Trayvon Martin and Mike Brown and Renisha McBride and so many others are dead because, in some white imagination, they were dangerous. And that imagination is so respected that those who kill, based on an imagined, radicalized fear of Black people, are rarely held accountable.
>
> Imagination has people thinking they can go from being poor to a millionaire as part of a shared American dream. Imagination turns Brown bombers into terrorists and white bombers into mentally ill victims. Imagination gives us borders, gives us superiority, gives us race as an indicator of ability. I often feel I am trapped inside someone else's capability. I often feel I am trapped inside someone else's imagination, and I must engage my own imagination in order to break free.
>
> (brown 2017, p. 18)

> Our radical imagination is a tool for decolonization, for reclaiming our right to shape our lived reality.
>
> (brown 2019, p. 10)

brown's words echo in our ears, reminding us that imagination, our collective imagination, has the power to create freedom *and* fear, life *and* death.

> We are in an **imagination** battle.

brown's words echo in our ears, reminding us that our collective imagination has the power to will thoughts into action, to manifest realities.

> We are in an imagination **battle.**

brown's words echo in our ears, reminding us that imagination gives birth to images, words, and actions—each an individual prayer—calling in a future, the future that is now.

As theatre artists and makers, we dance with this thing called imagination, dangling our feet off the edge of its possibility. This edge, our dangling, allows us see something before it exists, to dream something into the present, and as brown writes, to decolonize our existence.

This book grows out of the absolute necessity to end gender- and race-based violence facing young people, our country, and our global communities. It also grows out of our belief in the possibility of freedom—of creating safe and brave communities where young people are free from constructs of race and gender and where they dance at the edge of their own imaginations. As white women, we know that we have a deep and long legacy of complicity in the ways that patriarchy and white supremacy have and continue to dehumanize and take the lives of Black and Brown youth, trans youth, lesbian, gay, bisexual, queer, and intersex youth, girls and women. Binary and oppressive constructs of race and gender are woven into the fabric of our beings, into what we know, and how we know it. Our creative and representational practices, then, run the risk of restricting opportunities to radically imagine new paradigms for dismantling the systems that oppress young people. For us, this means that we have a responsibility to actively disrupt internalized and systemic white supremacy, racism, sexism, homophobia, and patriarchal systems in our lives and work. It also means we must work against and through the easy excuses of perfectionism, fear, and the pain of failure, excuses that often keep white women and those with the privilege of safety from doing the work. After all, meaningful change is rarely gained without risk or failure. This book—the PJP model—is one of our efforts to engage at the edge of our collective imagination, and to collaborate with young people to break free of oppressive and limiting constructs. This is one of our efforts to manifest love and belonging as the practice of freedom (hooks 2006).

We (Megan and Lynn) are white, cisgendered, adult women, and in this book we propose and write about racial and gender justice work with youth. It is not lost on us that writing a book and directing a program about race-, gender-, and youth-related oppression raises important tensions and questions around our white identity and other privileges. As we work to disrupt the harmful practices of white supremacy, we remain aware of our responsibility to face the questions and tensions head-on. And while we continue to have personal fears and reservations about writing and publishing this book (Who are we to write about this topic—to write at all? Are we once again centering white, cisgender privilege by writing this book?), we know that retreating from the discomfort of gender and racial (in)justice is not the repair or the remedy to oppression. Retreating from gender and racial justice is not an option for many of the young people with whom we work; it is not a choice for Black or Brown youth and/or trans youth and/or queer youth. Our commitment to young people and to the loving world we want to live in, as well as our accountability to the people we know and love, requires that we do this work. It requires that we become even stronger advocates and that we become lifelong students of gender and racial justice in our organizations, and communities, and our homes. It requires that we center race and gender and acknowledgment of power in our ways of thinking, relating, and making art. It requires that if we write and make theatre, we write and make theatre that performs justice.

For some readers, this book will not go far enough, and for others, this book will be too radical. We (and the work in this book) will and should be critiqued—not simply for engaging in this work, but for how we show up for and engage others around gender and race and justice. Amidst the critiques, we must and will continue to examine the ways that we become critically engaged allies, advocates, and facilitators of social justice work. We must and will continue to learn from young people and community partners. We must and will continue to learn that failed efforts at justice require acknowledgment and reparations; intention is not the same as impact. In writing this book, we sit with deep privileges of time, funding, academic support, and freedom from the daily violence of systemic, racialized oppression targeting our bodies. These privileges afford us the opportunity to engage with youth, to make theatre, and to imagine that multi-racial and gender diverse ensembles can build gender and racial justice.

Given your own relationships to privilege, "what is it you plan to do / with your one wild and precious life?" (Oliver 1992, p. 94). What will you do to imagine and perform justice? Will you learn more about patriarchy and white supremacy? Will you try out some of the performance actions in this text? Will you bring gender and racial justice language to conversations and actions at work or the kitchen table or city hall? How will you listen to and amplify youth voices—even when their experiences differ from your own or threaten your power? How will you deepen your work as an artist, youth advocate, ally, or organizer? What does it mean for you to sit at the edge of your imagination, to do the work of facing your fear, of unlearning racism and sexism?

We wrote this book as one action, one way of showing up, listening, and learning. We share this book now as a way of lifting up our/your radical imaginations and creating a pathway to engage in the collective work of love, change, and art. We are in an imagination battle.

—Megan and Lynn

# References

brown, a. m. (2017) *Emergent strategy: Shaping change, changing worlds*, Chico, CA: AK Press.

brown, a. m. (2019) *Pleasure activism: The politics of feeling good*, Chico, CA: AK Press.

hooks, b. (2006) 'Love as the practice of freedom,' in *Outlaw culture: Resisting representations*, New York: Routledge, pp. 289–298, viewed July 4, 2019, https://ebookcentral-proquest-com.ezproxy.lib.utexas.edu/lib/utxa/detail.action?docID=1024684

Oliver, M. (1992) 'The summer day,' in *New and selected poems*, vol. 1, Boston: Beacon Press, p. 94.

**Figure 0.1** *The Good in Me/In My Skin* stage design represents participants' ideas of freedom. Set design by Becca Drew Ramsey with PJP ensemble. Lighting design by Tameika L. Hannah
Source: Photo by Lynn Hoare.

# Part One

# Performing Justice Project as Critically Engaged Theatre

## 1.0 Introduction

A novice, teenaged performer stands confidently in the makeshift staging area of the concrete gym of a juvenile justice facility. She faces a small audience of family members (not her own), social workers, teaching artists, and juvenile justice staff. Her peers watch attentively from seated rows on either side of the staging area as she comes to the end of a solo performance piece, a monologue about her experience as a young woman in the system. She details efforts to navigate life when a parent is incarcerated and nods to the ways systemic injustice plays out differently for her and her racially diverse group of friends. The performance piece includes a powerful critique of the juvenile justice system and her year-long incarceration: "I have a question for the whole juvenile justice system. When are you going to give me the real help I need? When I think about what I've done, I am not sure boot camp is it," she says, looking directly at the audience.

This book invites you to intentionally think through the use of theatre and performance to address issues of gender and racial justice with young people. The school-to-prison pipeline, identity-based violence directed at youth, inequities across employment, income, housing, healthcare, climate change, and education demonstrate that identity-based injustices remain central to the experiences of young people in the US. Media attention to systemic racial and gender violence in the US has resulted in a renewal of youth activism and increased public consciousness around race, gender, police brutality, and gun control, among other issues. As young people organize for social change through walkouts, marches, and social media campaigns, theatre and performance texts need to address how theatre-makers and teaching artists can similarly engage with and respond to current events impacting the lives of young people. To this end, *Devising Critically Engaged Theatre with Youth: The Performing Justice Project* considers performance-making with youth as part of larger conversations about theatre and society. Drawing on our own theatre work with youth, and informed by our commitment to gender and racial justice, this book presents practical performance actions and a flexible framework for creating original theatre with youth—theatre that supports young people as they imagine, create, and perform their individual and collective stories, and their vision(s) for more just and equitable communities.

The Performing Justice Project (PJP) is a highly structured performance-making program designed to engage young people in creating original theatre about their lives as a way of moving toward gender and racial justice. The PJP process is one model of engaging the arts to reflect on and dismantle systems of oppression with youth. Through PJP, we offer short-term residency programs and performance-based workshops for groups of young people. Each residency takes place over 12 to 15 sessions and invites young people to examine and name the connections between their individual experiences and systemic (in)justice. In turn, participants then imagine and perform new and more just possibilities for themselves and their communities. PJP directors and teaching artists guide the project, working with youth—who may or may not have experience with theatre or performance—in a variety of sites, including schools, juvenile justice facilities, and foster care settings. Each PJP residency culminates in a produced performance in which young people share their points of view about living in a racist, sexist, and patriarchal society, as well as their vision for fair, accessible, and equitable spaces for youth. By lifting up and amplifying the stories of young people, PJP illuminates some of the ways that identity, power and privilege, and systems of oppression significantly shape youths' lives and experiences.

As artists, teachers, and scholars, we—Megan and Lynn, the authors of this text—know that it is essential for young people to have the knowledge and resources to reflect on and name their gendered and racialized experiences. We also understand that society as a whole needs to hear from and reflect on youth's experiences; young people are critical members of our communities. To this end, PJP directors collaborate with teaching artists, partner sites, and young people to identify and understand intersecting power systems. In this book, we share a collection of what we call performance actions, namely theatre and performance practices and pedagogies designed to engage young people around concepts of personal power and privilege, as well as the ways that systemic and institutional racism and sexism impact every aspect of our lives. By devising original theatre that intentionally examines how our experiences are connected to identities, we aim to build alliances with and among young people and ultimately to foster creative pathways for building systemic change.

*Devising Critically Engaged Theatre with Youth: The Performing Justice Project* presents a performance-making model that:

1. builds ensemble and fosters a sense of belonging with and among young people;
2. engages young people in addressing critical social justice issues related to their lives and communities;
3. devises and shares original performance work that addresses and imagines gender and racial justice.

*Devising Critically Engaged Theatre with Youth* includes detailed maps and plans that we use for facilitating, devising, and staging original theatre about gender and racial justice. However, we hope this book encourages theatre directors, facilitators, teaching artists, and groups of youth participants to use and adapt the PJP model to fit their specific context(s). To this end, we organize the book into three major parts, offering a detailed picture of the PJP model and inviting readers to develop their own justice-oriented performance practices, residencies, and program models.

Part One, Performing Justice Project as Critically Engaged Theatre, outlines the purpose and rationale of the book, proposing an urgent need for creative and embodied approaches to addressing identity-based inequities with and among youth. Part One also introduces the PJP model, providing the history and background of the project, as well as the core values, beliefs, and theories that underpin our practice. PJP is part of many ongoing conversations and movements and this part of the book outlines theoretical and practical frameworks, such as storytelling, intersectionality, social justice education, and racial justice, that we draw on and remain in conversation with as we facilitate critically engaged theatre-making.

Part Two, Preparing Participants and Performing Justice, presents our approach to creating and staging original performance work with young people. We include detailed descriptions of how we work and how we devise. The bulk of Part Two includes a collection of performance actions that we use for devising critically engaged theatre with youth. PJP performance actions introduce embodied approaches to building ensemble, performing and staging small bits of performance, analyzing systemic oppression, and applying theatre as a tool to explore and disrupt patriarchal systems including white supremacy and racism, sexism, and homophobia.

We organize and codify our collection of performance actions based on three core questions that serve as the foundation of PJP:

- Who am I?
- What is (in)justice and how does it show up in my life?
- How do I perform justice?

Using these questions as our organizational framework, we scaffold performance actions in each section to engage participants in PJP's core questions and build toward performance. The performance actions are laid out as facilitator guides, including step by step instructions for leading the action and supporting participants to name and perform their visions for justice.

Part Three, Producing a Performing Justice Project, considers many of the practical elements and steps we rely on to build and produce a PJP residency, script, and performance. We reflect on the roles and responsibilities of the leadership team, logistical frameworks for producing a public performance, and partnership development and maintenance. This part also offers sample session plans and program outlines that our team has piloted with multiple groups of youth, many of whom were incarcerated, in foster care, or attending under-resourced middle and high schools. We end this part of the book with a reflection on the practice of belonging and accountability, and the ways that that this necessary work requires a commitment to each other, imagination, and above all, action.

Woven throughout the three parts of this text are original essays that we call Doing Justice. These essays were written by PJP resident teaching artists and speak to their experiences of facilitating PJP residencies and address what it means to "do justice" when working with youth participants. The authors of these essays employ autobiographical stories, reflection, and other research to frame their ideas and questions about what this work does, what it requires, and what it leaves behind. The essays dance with other parts of the book, offering insight into and questions about struggles with anti-racism and gender justice, facilitator identity, youth agency, healing, and respectability politics. The authors of these pieces have significantly shaped the PJP model, and the inclusion of their voices in these pages serve as a reminder that this work comes with tensions and questions and that it never happens in isolation.

As you move through this book, you may notice that we share only a few samples of script work, photographs, and stories from the PJP rehearsal room. With these select examples, we try to represent the energy, movement, and aesthetics of PJP. However, representing our work with youth often comes into conflict with institutional efforts to "protect" youth identity by restricting research with vulnerable populations and prohibiting the use of any identifying information about the youth participants in our writing. As a result, this book does not include our direct interviews or evaluations conducted with young people. Rather, as we share the PJP model, participants' voices are foregrounded through the small bits of performance material that were performed for larger publics, as well as animation, video, and audio recordings of participants' work and experiences in PJP. We encourage you to visit the PJP Gallery pages on our website for further visual and audio documentation of this work.[1] The performances and stories that are included in this book and on our website are shared with written permission, represent our own experiences in PJP, and/or come from public performances.

Taken together, the three parts of this book invite you to devise original performance work that lifts up youth voices, inspires critical dialogues around identity and justice, and imagines and performs a more just society. As young people experience and witness racialized and gendered oppression in the US, *Devising Critically Engaged Theatre with Youth: The Performing Justice Project* offers a blueprint—a possibility—for creating original, critically engaged theatre with young people in a variety of contexts and settings.

There is not one way to move through this book. If you are interested in the contexts and theoretical framings underpinning PJP, we encourage you to begin by reading Part One first. If you are looking for facilitation strategies and a practical approach to devising, you might begin with Part Two, which explores how to devise with youth and includes our collection of PJP performance actions focused specifically on gender and racial justice. And if you are looking for how to build or produce critically engaged theatre with youth in your context, you might turn to Part Three and the Appendices, both of which address many of the logistical, administrative, and relational practices that help develop a community-engaged performance program and produce a public performance. Megan recommends reading this book from front to back, suggesting that readers will gain a sense of the larger contexts, theories, and content that shape PJP before getting into the details of devising of performance. Lynn prefers to move through this book with a bit more freedom, knowing that readers might begin with Part Two to understand how PJP works in practice before reading Parts One and Three in search of theories on social justice education, autobiographical devising, or samples of PJP script outlines. No matter how you use this book, we hope it will inspire you to do justice—to support young people in critically engaged devising and to recognize the role that theatre and creative practices can and do play in imagining and performing justice.

# 1.1 Why the Performing Justice Project?

In our work with young people, the process is just as important as the product. We chose the name Performing Justice Project (PJP)[2] to reflect our intentional focus on *performing* as a way of presenting or staging something for an audience, and *performing* as a way of working, bringing about knowledge, or carrying something out. We imagine theatre as both a way to perform and practice justice. Participants in PJP embody their vision for justice, including opportunities for systems, communities, and actions to become just, impartial, or fair. Therefore, participants in PJP are both *performing* justice and performing *justice*.

We designed the PJP model as a way of working towards justice while also acknowledging that justice is not a fixed state, an agreed-upon set of outcomes, or even an achievable outcome within the limited structure of our process. Rather, we understand performing justice as ongoing work—always a project, intentionally being constructed and performed individually, together, and within systems. Within any given PJP residency, there are moments where an act of justice is performed. However, we also understand that those moments do not create a state in which justice continues to exist. Rather, the ongoing, daily need to work on, pay attention to, and perform justice remains.

The Performing Justice Project grew out of an already existing and dynamic partnership between the Center for Women's and Gender Studies at the University of Texas at Austin, a tier-one research university, the Embrey Family Foundation, a socially-engaged family foundation, and Gonzalo Garza Independence High School, an alternative high school in Austin, TX. All three institutions recognized a distinct need for high school curricula that paid more attention to the role of women in society. These three institutions partnered to create the first ever state accredited high school course on Women's History—a course that both recognizes and centers women. The course included student-driven research about women's history and women's rights as human rights. Importantly, the approved curriculum also called for a three-week performance unit that would conclude the course with a creative approach to reflecting on and sharing knowledge. Theatre became the chosen medium for the last unit of the history course.

As a result, PJP was founded in 2010 by faculty and staff at the University of Texas at Austin. Megan Alrutz, Lynn Hoare, and Kristen Hogan created and piloted PJP in 2011 as the theatre component of the high school's innovative Women's History course.[3] The school decided early on to restrict the course to students who they identified as "young women," and we ended up working with a racially and ethnically diverse group of 20 students, ranging in age from 16 to 21, along with two of their teachers.

During this PJP pilot, students devised and performed original monologues, scene work, poetry, and movement pieces. Their performance content grew out of their own life experiences with gender expectations and oppression, as well as their research on global issues related to women's human rights. While many members of the group initially struggled to imagine how their own life experiences might matter to an outside audience, the students eventually shared their work in public performances that invited and provoked audiences to consider women's rights as human rights in the US and their own local communities. Some of the larger themes in their performance included what it means to be a woman (and challenges with the question itself), international efforts to support the rights of women, children, and girls, and how human rights violations disproportionately impact women, children, and people of color. The performance included music, sound, and lighting design and took place in a small black box theatre at the University of Texas at Austin.

This pilot project taught us a lot about theatre as a tool for engaging young people in discussions about gender-based rights and oppression. We learned that while many participants did not always believe they had stories worth telling, they expressed the desire to write and perform stories about their own life experiences. We learned that telling stories and devising performance work about one's own lived experience raises questions about the relationship between identity and experience. Many young people in our pilot project were eager to talk about their experiences and to lift up their racial and gender identities at the center of those experiences. We also learned that many of the students in the course came to PJP with the belief that they did not experience oppression based on their identities as girls, women, and/or as people of color. For many of the students in PJP, this belief remained intact despite their own shared experiences to the contrary, including their own research documenting the ways that women and people of color are systematically disadvantaged by laws and justice systems, schools, and employment practices. We were surprised to learn that most of the young women in the project resisted the idea that sexism, patriarchy, and racism shaped their own experiences with schooling, family structures, and cultural norms. In our theatre devising process, they focused instead on their sense of—and perhaps desire for—personal agency or autonomy. They were able to discuss how "other women" might be oppressed while at the same time believing that their own lives were somehow free from these same systems of oppression. These kinds of beliefs highlighted an important tension that exists for many of the participants in PJP, namely that their beliefs about their own personal agency and abilities can make it difficult to acknowledge that systemic oppression is real and present, even their own lives. In this project, the participants often equated an acknowledgment of oppression in their lives as a personal weakness. In response to these tensions, we began to develop performance actions or theatre strategies that encourage young people to recognize the reality of systemic oppressions while also supporting and acknowledging their personal agency and individual empowerment.

This pilot project, including the tensions and questions it raised, prompted us to experiment with performance as a tool for exposing the often-invisible mechanisms of inequality. We began to pull apart and name ways that individual empowerment exists within systems of oppression, and some of the ways that agency and oppression might prove fluid within given scenarios, contexts, and relationships. Performance-making became a medium for embodying the ways that oppression works and a way to see and build opportunities to disrupt it and to imagine alternatives. When the PJP pilot ended, we decided to focus PJP more intentionally on gender and racial justice rather than on the broad category of women's human rights. Our original focus on women's rights as human rights sometimes failed to address what lawyer and critical race scholar Kimberlé Williams Crenshaw (1989) calls *intersectionality*, or the critical differences in women's experiences of oppression across multiple identity markers. The performance content of the pilot project focused largely on gender without a deep analysis or acknowledgment of how gender and ability, for example, are also racialized. As white women who often facilitate performance work with multi-racial, gender-diverse groups of participants, we needed to be more intentional about centering the intersectional impacts of race and gender on participants' experiences with oppression. Performing justice requires us to hold ourselves, PJP participants, and PJP itself accountable to the fact that injustice is systematically racialized and gendered in the US and around the world.

While the PJP model offers an intersectional approach to making theatre, our primary entry points into devising and performing justice now begins with and comes back to constructs of gender and race. In this way, we aim to ensure that within our practice inequities faced by women of color are not eclipsed by categorical discussions around class or socioeconomics (Race Forward 2014).[4]

Following our pilot project with Gonzalo Garza Independence High School, we continued to develop and revise PJP over the course of six years. We engaged youth and community partners in a variety of contexts throughout Texas. We also garnered critical feedback on the PJP model through national presentations at universities around the US and through Facing Race, the national conference of Race Forward, which is described as the largest multi-racial, intergenerational gathering for organizers, educators, creatives, and other leaders in the US. The Performing Justice Project now offers short-term theatre-making residencies (about 30 hours each) that focus on gender and racial justice content. PJP teaching artists partner with schools, juvenile justice facilities, and other community partners to engage youth ages 14 to 25. A PJP residency typically serves 5 to 30 young people at a time, and although we work with gender-diverse groups, most of our residencies engage groups of young people who are already labeled by the state or partnering institutions as girls, women, or females (an issue of injustice that we return to in later parts of the book).

Importantly, insight from a diverse team of teaching artists, community partners, and young performance-makers continues to deeply inform the PJP model. Moreover, we've established ongoing partnerships with juvenile justice centers, foster care facilities, and high schools. In these ways, the PJP model represents a set of collaboratively built practices that continue to evolve and respond to current and past events.[5]

The Performing Justice Project was named a signature program of the University of Texas at Austin's Center for Women's and Gender Studies (CWGS) in 2011 and was generously supported by the Embrey Family Foundation from 2011 to 2017.

## 1.2 Why We Do this Work

Four young women stand in front of a packed house. They divide and share lines as they speak directly to the audience:

My skin looks like I been through pain
like the caramel on top of an apple I used to eat
like mini pieces of chocolate, bittersweet or sour kinds
**ALL: My skin color**
is brown (touch) and I'm proud of it
and because my skin is brown (touch) and I am proud
I'm treated differently
(Performing Justice Project 2015)

As the youth perform this poem, they speak with confidence and awareness. They understand the impact of having skin the color of chocolate, caramel, or brown. They gently touch the skin on their arms while they acknowledge the violence done to them because of its color. The audience, if they didn't already understand, gains some insight into what identity-based oppression looks like for these young people, what it means, how it lives in the performers' bodies, and perhaps, in their own bodies. Audience members who already understood provide witness and solidarity.

In many ways, the Performing Justice Project model has evolved (and continues to evolve) as a response to deeply held knowledge and truths in our own lives. As artists and community members, we (Megan and Lynn) live and work in multi-racial and gender-diverse families and communities. In these everyday contexts, we work to undo our own learned biases and unearned privilege and to imagine how our tools as artists can help create pathways for undoing and unlearning racism, sexism, and patriarchal ways of living and working, relating, and making. We see the impacts of interpersonal, institutional, and systemic bias in our own lives and in the lives of people we know, love, and interact with. Moreover, we understand that women, LGBTQIA folks, and people of color in our lives and communities are disproportionately impacted by these systems of oppression that we participate in both knowingly and unknowingly.

Race Forward's *Race Reporting Guide* acknowledges that "There are deep racial disparities and divisions across our society, and some are even widening. Much like the notion of 'colorblindness,' the idea of a 'post-racial' society does not acknowledge that racism and inequity sit at the core of many of our nation's deepest challenges" (2015, p. 30). In other words, to meet and overcome our challenges as a country, we must continue to challenge the notion that we live in a post-racial world. We believe that attention must be paid to identity-based oppression, specifically systemic racism and sexism, in order to address the many issues of inequity and access that impact youth and their communities in the US. Given these beliefs, as well as our own privileged and marginalized identities, we are compelled to use our skills as artists to work alongside young people in unlearning oppressive narratives and enacting possibilities for justice and equity. As adults, we facilitate and participate in the work of PJP in an effort to support and encourage, as well as learn from, young people's critical consciousness. As artists, we aim to celebrate youth voices and help to amplify the experience and wisdom of young people.

We choose the PJP model as a way of working toward change because we know that embodied performance and reflection is a way of knowing that helps both imagine and create possibility. Working from our own tools for creatively addressing the world, we center PJP around the making and sharing of original theatre and performance about and by the participants themselves. Embodied performance offers a way of seeing, feeling, critiquing, and understanding that relies on visceral and personal ways of knowing and absorbing our own and others' experiences. Drawing on the feminist work of Elizabeth Grosz, Hui Niu Wilcox writes about the "body's capacity to know" and the ways that "embodied knowledges can be foregrounded [through] lived experiences, cultural performance, and bodily intelligence" (2009, p.106). By physicalizing or trying on one's own and each other's stories—through gestures, song, and poetry, or a collage of tableaux that represents a shared moment—youth in PJP share their experiences and explore ways of knowing that move beyond only an intellectual or verbal experience. Building on Grosz's (1994) understanding that our lived experiences are embodied, PJP engages live performance as one way to confront the systemic racism and sexism that bodies have experienced and already know.

We believe that devising original theatre with youth can activate spaces for critical consciousness and critical engagement, and thus possibilities for change (see Section 1.3 for a discussion on transgression [hooks 1994], transportation, and transformation

[Nicholson 2005; Schechner 2003]). PJP and the practices outlined in this book are underpinned by our belief that performance work can amplify youth voices and create critical opportunities for speaking up and back to systems of oppression. Many young people are already actively engaged in creating the kind of world in which they will thrive, while many others are ready and willing to jump in when the opportunity arises. PJP works with young people to build on their own cultural capital and assets; we believe that young people's stories and experiences, when scripted and performed by youth, can expose systemic oppression and remind participants and audiences alike of how inequities and injustices are maintained and can hopefully be disrupted.

We devise original theatre with young people, specifically leaning into experiences with and visions for racial and gender justice. Our process creates opportunities for understanding, naming and grappling with internalized, interpersonal, institutional, and systemic oppressions. In our experience, young people often believe their experiences of oppression are unique to them, are isolated events, and/or are not worth talking about. And yet, we know that sharing experiences with others often reveals patterns of oppression, inspires conversations about building alternative realities, and fosters a sense of belonging. As artists and activists, we want to use our skills and tools to amplify the voices and desires of young people, to support them in speaking back to a system that often dismisses or disenfranchises them. Moreover, we do this work because we believe that young people are essential partners in building a more just world. We are confident in the potential of young people to develop their own critical consciousness and to build and enact their capacities to make change. We do this work because it is absolutely necessary.

## 1.3 Part of a Discourse

### 1.3.1 Engaging in a Movement

Our voices echoed in the space, bouncing off of the gray, concrete walls. It was day four of a three-week-long PJP residency. We were working with 25 youth, sentenced to a juvenile detention center, living in a lock-up facility away from friends and family. In this moment, the youth were sitting in rows on the floor and our every word and action, the participants' every word and action, was highly surveilled by guards in army fatigues. We finished a long round of the Great Game of Power, an image-based theatre exercise developed by theatre director Augusto Boal as a way to make systems of power visible and name how oppression shows up in our everyday lives (Boal 2002). We began to transition from this image work into a PJP performance action called Six-Word Stories (adapted from Norris 2010). We were about to share examples of six-word stories and then offer the group a series of writing prompts to create their own: "Write a six-word story about a moment or experience that made you aware of gender. Write a six-word story about a time that someone suggested you couldn't do something or had to do something because of your gender. Write about a time you were treated differently because of gender."

A hand went up in the air. Megan made eye contact with a participant in the back of the space and the rest of the group looked back to the young person with a hand in the air, an individual whose gender identity and expression had been highly restricted by the staff and systems in place at the facility. "Can I ask you a question?"

they asked, and then launched a series of questions into the cavernous room—just loud enough for the guards in the back of the room to hear: "What are you about anyway? Why are you here? What do you stand for? Are you part of a movement or something?" (Alrutz 2015).

This moment called us (Megan and Lynn) to participate in what social justice and community educators Brian Arao and Kristi Clemens (2013, pp. 135–150) call "brave space," to bravely lean into what may feel like a difficult but necessary conversation. As Megan wrote about in *Digital Storytelling, Applied Theatre, and Youth* (Alrutz 2015), this young person invited us to name our politics within a highly contested space and to locate the Performing Justice Project as an intentionally political and activist effort. Or not. These critical questions, coming from a young person in this space, made us think deeply about the connections between the Performing Justice Project and larger social justice movements that our work is already in conversation with. The questions also prompted us to reconsider the role of transparency, accountability, and risk in PJP. Years later, we often return to this moment and this young person's provocation as reminders to clearly state what we are about, what we stand for, and the ways that PJP is part of a larger discourse related to youth experiences with race and gender. Moreover, it reminds us that PJP *is* decidedly part of a movement.

In the introduction to this book, we maintain that PJP is part of a movement to confront identity-based oppression with and for young people. We built this performance project from an understanding that identity is both fluid and intersectional. Critical race scholar and law professor Kimberlé Williams Crenshaw, who coined the term "intersectional" in her seminal article about anti-racist politics and justice for Black women, reminds us that "[b]ecause the intersectional experience is greater than the sum of racism and sexism, any analysis that does not take intersectionality into account cannot sufficiently address the particular manner in which Black women are subordinated" (1989, p.140). Crenshaw's argument applies across many dimensions of identity and demonstrates the necessity of seeing and naming how oppression differently impacts people with multiple, marginalized identities. "Intersectionality is not primarily about identity," Crenshaw says.

> It's about how structures make certain identities the consequence of and the vehicle for vulnerability. So if you want to know how many intersections matter, you've got to look at the contexts. What's happening? What kind of discrimination is going on? What are the policies? What are the institutional structures that play a role in contributing to the exclusion of some people and not others?
>
> (Crenshaw 2016, min. 7:00)

In PJP, we support youth to name and analyze structures of inequity and the resulting patterns of marginalization, erasure, and oppression. For example, participants might research and embody statistics about the wage gap in the US, seeing that while white women in the US are paid less than men, Black, Latinx and Native American women are paid even less than white women, and women with these different racial identities are paid differently from one another. Intersectional discussions of the wage gap require systemic analyses that address the historical and current contexts and experiences of women who carry multiple marginalized dimensions of identity. Building from Crenshaw's arguments, PJP residencies invite youth to consider the different and related dimensions of their identities, and the ways that identity-based oppression plays out through and across their experiences. We identify and build performance actions, namely critically engaged approaches to making and sharing performance, that support young people to name their own identity markers, while also unpacking how their identities are read by others and how systemic oppression uniquely impacts their experiences in the world. Any act of performing justice requires attention to intersectionality—both the various dimensions of identity and the contexts that allow certain intersecting identities to be oppressed and marginalized to the benefit of others.

Our approach to acknowledging and speaking back to intersectional oppression is through our curated collection of performance actions. Cultural studies and performance scholar Della Pollack writes: "Performance is a promissory act. Not because it can only promise possible change but because it catches its participants—often by surprise—in a contract with possibility: with imagining what might be, could be, should be" (2005, p. 2). As we engage youth participants in performance actions and the process of devising theatre, we attend to both lived experience and imagined possibilities.

PJP also builds on the work of feminist director and performance scholar Jill Dolan. Dolan's writing on performance and utopia urges theatre-makers to imagine and enact a better future, in spite of the seemingly impossible task of achieving utopia. Dolan writes,

> I have faith in the possibility that we can imagine such a place, even though I know that we can only imagine it, that we'll never achieve it in our lifetimes. But that knowledge doesn't prevent me from desiring a theater in which an image of a better future can be articulated and even embodied, however fleetingly.
>
> (2005, p. 37)

Dolan further articulates the importance of seeing, naming, and performing the now. Dolan quotes philosopher Ruth Levitas and performance theorist Rustom Bharucha when she says, "What is needed are not better 'maps of the future,' but more 'adequate maps of the present,' which can inspire the most effective means of activating the desire for a more humane world" (2005, p. 38).[6] This is what we hope to build with the Performing Justice Project—more adequate maps that reflect youth experiences now and offer radically new visions for today and tomorrow.

We have come to know that PJP is part of a movement—a movement to map the present and build more equitable and loving futures with and for young people. It is a movement of performance-makers who believe in the power of story and aesthetics to inch us toward utopia. The systems that shape the lives of young people remain stacked against youth of color, against trans, intersex, and non-binary youth, and against women and girls. We acknowledge the prevalence of violence associated with racism, sexism, colonialism, and patriarchy, and also believe in theatre as a site of seeing, resisting, and intervening in the narratives that shape our lives and our futures.

We are not alone in this work or in our ideals. We build on the writings and theories of Black, Brown, and Native feminist and queer scholars, as well as applied theatre-makers and youth workers. This section outlines how PJP grows from and participates in multiple discourses related to performance, pedagogy, social change, and identity. PJP—specifically the teaching artists and youth who participate—is part of a long history of artists, scholars, educators, activists, and youth working toward justice. Our work is part of many movements, of recognized discourses that engage the intersections of art with social and political change efforts. These various and intersecting discourses help us locate Pollack's promise of possibility at the center of critically engaged devising and at the center of each PJP residency.

Young people in the US have been deeply engaged in movement work and social change efforts throughout history. Youth now are challenging people and systems around them to center race, gender, and other dimensions of identity in order to dismantle oppressive systems that shape their lives. Moreover, young people are leaders and/or participants in the #blacklivesmatter movement, the #metoo movement and the #metooK12 movement, as well as the #neveragain movement.[7] And although much of this work has been celebrated and supported by the media and public figures, it has not been uniform across racial lines. For example, the #neveragain movement, which was largely led by white youth, has been highly celebrated, and generally avoided public critique. The mostly Black youth of #blacklivesmatter, on the other hand, were labeled "trouble-makers and even terrorists" by the media and public (Glanton 2018). This stark difference in the country's response to white and Black youths' activism speaks to our country's history and continued legacy of systemic racism. It also reinforces the need to critique identity-based injustice and imagine pathways to a more just and equitable society.

While some people argue that political and social progress has been made since the violent and racist inception of our country and that the work is mostly done, PJP works from the perspective that there is a deep and ongoing need to disrupt structural and institutional oppression. PJP acknowledges the systemic oppressions that impact the experiences of young people, and offers a performance model that lifts up identity-positive discourse and supports social change. PJP acknowledges and moves away from colorblind and gender binary frameworks for talking and collaborating with young people. Race Forward, a national organization that promotes racial justice, highlights the widening racial disparities and divisions in the US. Acknowledging this history, we ask PJP participants to name their own racial and gender identities and lean into discussions about how their own social locations impact their experiences of living and working in the US. Moreover, in PJP, we support a performance process and product that values and celebrates all gender and racial identities.

To this end, as directors in PJP, we strive to be reflective and transparent about the work we are doing and our connection to it. We are open with participants about the limits of our own knowledge, expertise, and experiences as cisgender, white women. We focus on normalizing and promoting identity-positive vocabulary and meaningful discussions about the ways that constructs of race and gender shape our standpoint and experiences. While our own backgrounds, education, and experiences are rooted in theory and practices from theatre with and for young people, our PJP work remains in conversation with multiple discourses related to theatre and drama education, social justice paradigms, creative and embodied pedagogical models, and work in community-based settings. We outline some of those discourses here—both to share where our PJP work comes from, as well as to encourage readers to explore additional resources and to bring one's own background and expertise to this work.

Finally, it is important to note that discourses around race, gender, and identity politics are rapidly shifting. We have no doubt that the ways that we name and talk about race and gender, including some of the theoretical and practical language of this book, may prove outdated in a short time. This reality does not hinder us from doing the work; we encourage you to also do the work—to engage in the most up-to-date language and theories as possible, to know that the landscape and languages around social justice are alive and changing. Changes in how we talk about race and gender reflect the work that has been done and the work yet to be done. Our job is to engage in the change as we participate in the movement to foster that change. At the same time, we believe that the underlying premise and underpinnings of PJP will remain relevant over time. We encourage you to collaborate with young people to explore gender and racial justice and necessary vocabularies for imagining new paradigms and ways of living. Creating a Performing Justice Project requires that we attend to ever-changing contexts and communities.

In the following subsections, we lay out some of the engaged performance practices, pedagogies, and content frames that underpin PJP. We discuss applied theatre and community-based arts, Theatre in Education (TIE), Theatre of the Oppressed (TO), theatre with and for youth, story-sharing, storytelling, and autobiographical performance. We then explore critically engaged pedagogies, such as social justice education, building connections to our creative and responsive process for making theatre with youth. Finally, we offer content-based resources to help artists and facilitators anchor their own PJP residencies in critically engaged, drama-based pedagogies and practices.

## 1.3.2 Performance
### Applied Theatre

PJP borrows heavily from theoretical and practical frameworks from the field of applied theatre and drama. Applied theatre scholars Tim Prentki and Sheila Preston define *applied theatre* as "a broad set of theatrical practices and creative processes that take participants and audiences beyond the scope of conventional, mainstream theatre into the realm of a theatre that is responsive to ordinary people and their stories, local settings and priorities" (2009, p. 9). Applied theatre is an umbrella term widely used to describe a variety of theatre practices that take place in educational, social, and community-based settings with aims that extend beyond a theatre production itself (Alrutz 2015). Many applied theatre projects engage performance as a means for social, cultural, political, educational, or personal change.[8] Prentki and Preston write that although theatre processes are applied in the service of self-development, well-being, and social change within applied theatre, the "intent is subject to differing interpretation and understanding by practitioners, and is influenced by context and the social, cultural or political landscapes which shape the artistic interventions that are created" (2009, p.14). Applied theatre often focuses on local participants and community interests, and tends to engage individuals and groups with little to no formal training in the arts. According to applied theatre scholars Monica Prendergast and Juliana Saxton, across this wide range of practices, participants, and intentions, applied theatre-makers guide participants through a collaborative and interactive process of examining questions, themes, or concerns within and through performance and embodied self-expression. These contexts support a performance practice that is simultaneously engaged, social, and artistic (Prendergast and Saxton 2009).

Importantly, applied theatre has roots in the community arts movement. Like community arts, applied theatre works to democratize social and cultural production by inviting direct participation in art-making and a critically engaged, reflective process. As social and collaborative art forms, community-based theatre and applied theatre often invite participants to perform and present stories of their own making. Applied theatre scholar Helen Nicholson argues that in theatre, knowledge—or meaning-making—is inherently "embodied, culturally located and socially distributed" (2005, p. 39). In other words, performance puts forward ideas about our bodies, our lived experiences, and ultimately our communities. In PJP, we embrace this notion by intentionally weaving participants' perspectives and experiences into the performance text, blocking, dramaturgy, and design. While community arts and applied theatre draw on individual experiences and cultures, they also rely on group participation and the building of an intentional community of collaborators.

In applied theatre settings, young artists are invited to participate as creators, decision-makers, and leaders. Rooted in Brazilian educator Paulo Freire's critical pedagogy, applied theatre often welcomes youth to explore and reflect on how their choices and actions affect themselves and others, and ultimately shape outcomes, including the creative process, group dynamics, community dialogue, and performance pieces or products (Freire 2018). Theatre education scholar Bethany Nelson writes, "The community-rich environment of [applied theatre] is uniquely well-positioned to facilitate the development of a sense of power in students and a capacity to act on and change their world" (2011, p. 166). As part of a collaborative and creative community, young people learn that they can and do impact, possibly even transform, themselves, the group, and sometimes society at large.

We use the term "applied theatre" to reference a way of working and an intentionality around the use of performance actions aimed at social justice. We borrow, revise, and/or reframe practices from improvisation, storytelling, creative writing, devising, and image work to engage youth participants in actions that explore and enact gender and racial justice. We also emphasize a process-oriented approach to theatre that ultimately works toward a collaboratively built and performed script. Like many community-based arts practices, PJP weaves the performance-making process together with guided reflection and ongoing dialogue with participants and the partnering organizations.

## Theatre in Education

Theatre in Education (TIE) began in Britain in the mid-1960s as an effort to use theatre as a force for social and educational change. As a significant movement in public schools in Britain and beyond up through the 1990s, TIE inspired and continues to inform many current practices and forms of socially relevant and "applied" theatre practices today. TIE's form, content, and function can be found in a wide range of contexts and locations, including schools, prisons, and museums.[9] Similar to applied theatre, TIE practices also shift and change in response to community needs and access to funding.

A specific form of interactive and participatory theatre, TIE tends to rely heavily on theatrical or performative frames and scenes to engage audiences and work toward an educational or social goal, such as solving a real-world problem about the environment and public resources. Applied theatre scholar Helen Nicholson argues that "[t]aking theatre into schools, encouraging active learning and energetic debate, allowed radical young theatre-makers to engage with the politics of both theatre and education" (2005, p. 58). In this way, TIE was born of a desire to engage young people in critically examining issues that shape their own lives. Anthony Jackson, seminal TIE scholar and co-editor of *Learning Through Theatre*, discusses how TIE uses theatre and performance work to put participants at the "centre of their own learning, pressing home challenges while simultaneously communicating the belief—and trust—that they are sufficiently intelligent and sensitive ... to think and act autonomously to find their own solutions" (Jackson and Vine 2013, p. 6). In "Challenging facilitation: Training facilitators for theatre for dialogue programmes" in Jackson and Vine's *Learning Through Theatre*, Lynn discusses a TIE program that she ran at the University of Texas at Austin. She emphasizes that TIE "creates opportunities for difficult discussions that help participants confront assumptions, gather information and make meaning around a topic or question – through the theatrical frame" (Hoare 2013, p. 143).

Drawing on these theories from TIE, we attempt to create spaces in PJP for discussion and reflection on racial and gender identities, making meaning with youth ensembles and engaging participants around local and global problems through theatre-making. PJP also strives to center youth in the process and product, offering language and structures for reflection, writing, and performance of their stories as they work toward solutions. PJP works toward developing critical consciousness of young performance-makers, their audiences, and the facilitators, further utilizing theatre as a sociopolitical framework for learning about and responding to systems of oppression.

## Theatre of the Oppressed

The founder and visionary of Theatre of the Oppressed (TO), Augusto Boal, developed his approach to theatre in an effort to democratize both who attends theatre and who participates in decision-making and change in society. TO breaks the fourth wall between actors and audiences, encouraging a collective approach to solving problems and an opportunity to rehearse interventions and strategies for revolution. Boal writes:

> Theatre should be happiness, it should help us learn about ourselves and our times. We should know the world we live in, the better to change it. Theatre is a form of knowledge; it should and can also be a means of transforming society. Theatre can help us build our future, instead of just waiting for it.
>
> (2002, p. 16)

As a Brazilian theatre practitioner, theorist, and activist, Boal's work began as a direct response to war and oppression in his home country. He drew heavily from fellow Brazilian educator Paulo Freire's work in *Pedagogy of the Oppressed* (2018) to build a theatre practice aimed at consciousness-raising—a practice that locates marginalized groups as active subjects rather than objects in social debates and political reform. To this end, Boal's well-known collection of theatre games and theatre forms, including Forum Theatre, Legislative Theatre, Rainbow of Desire, and Image Theatre, focus on heightening participants' awareness of their bodies and senses as pathways to building trust, activating dialogue, and disrupting moments of oppression.

While our work in PJP is not defined as Theatre of the Oppressed, we borrow philosophical ideas and practical devising strategies from TO. We adapt many of Boal's theatre games into performance actions that engage with gender and racial justice. Boal's TO work is particularly helpful in supporting non-actors and novice performers to begin building images with their bodies, generating content from their experiences, understanding different perspectives, and devising scenes. Specifically, Boal's embodied theatre games work to "de-mechanize"[10] the body and help participants see and name every day, but the nonetheless oppressive, actions and images in our lives. Boal reminds us to center actions of play and improvisation within the work of investigating oppression. His work helps participants generate ideas, embodied images, symbols, and metaphors about the topics at hand. It also illuminates key ideas and perspectives about power through those images, symbols, and metaphors. Boal's exercise, the Great Game of Power (2002, p. 163), for example, offers a way to investigate how ensemble members see and experience power in their lives, and invites participants to reflect on how constructions of gender and race function in their lives. In the Great Game of Power, participants describe and analyze statues made up of chairs and a water bottle. By naming which chair in the sculpture they believe holds the most power, participants also describe how power looks from different perspectives, how they see or recognize power, and how power shows up in their own lives and communities. Participants might describe and name who in their own lives represents the "power chair"— a teacher, parent, police officer, judge, etc. In this process of describing, analyzing, reflecting, and relating to a sculpture made of chairs, participants often see how power, and who holds it, may be perceived differently from various perspectives or vantage points, both in the performance action as well as in life.

We rely heavily on Boal's use of theatre as a strategy for promoting dialogue, specifically in the use of Image Theatre to create and perform new stories, relationships, and ways of knowing. Many of our performance actions are inspired by the practice of TO and function as pathways for illuminating complex systems and personal stories, and opening up dialogue about power and oppression.

## Creative Drama and Theatre for Young Audiences

Our approach to facilitating and directing PJP also grows out of our training and experience in both creative drama and theatre for young audiences. Jed H. Davis and Tom Behm define *creative drama* as "an improvisational, non-exhibitional, process-centered form of drama in which participants are guided by a leader to imagine, enact, and reflect upon human experiences" (1978, p. 10).[11] While creative drama is highly process- and participation-oriented and improvisational in nature, theatre for young audiences refers to more formal or "produced" plays or performances for young people. Theatre for young audiences (TYA) often involves adult artists performing for young people and adult artists attending to design and aesthetic elements such as lighting, set, costumes, and sound. Creative drama invites young people to play out stories in the classroom and see where they go; the work is often playful, imaginative, improvisational, and fun. Theatre for young audiences tends to be scripted, rehearsed, and then performed in a theatre or another similarly deemed space. Although the boundaries are sometimes blurred between these practices, creative drama is often considered more process-centered than theatre for young audiences, which offers a performance product created and performed for a public audience. In the best-case scenario, both creative drama and theatre for young audiences include meaningful opportunities for young people to reflect on and make-meaning about their experiences. Both practices tend to center the experiences of young people by exploring and/or representing characters, stories, and experiences that are relatable or relevant to them.

For PJP, we draw on the priorities and practices of creative drama and theatre for young audiences. We design performance experiences for young people that are improvisational and intentionally facilitated *and* that move into a produced performance and piece of theatre. Our PJP performance actions are adapted from both creative drama games and theatre devising and rehearsal practices. Our focus on creating a devised and performed theatre product also requires a dramaturgical focus that we learned from scripting and directing new work and theatre for young audiences.

## Story-sharing and Storytelling

Story-sharing, an informal exchange of experiences, and storytelling, the art and craft of creating stories to be shared more publicly, have a history of being used to connect people and catalyze social change efforts, particularly among marginalized groups of people.[12] According to Clark Baim, psychotherapist, author, and practitioner of theatre-based approaches with offenders and youth at risk, "During the past one hundred years, and more particularly in the past several decades, there has been a rapid expansion in the use of people's personal stories in the theatre, in both applied and commercial theatre contexts" (2017, p. 79). PJP builds on and contributes to this history, adapting storytelling prompts and structures from nationally recognized storytelling projects such as National Public Radio's *This I Believe* series,[13] journalist and NPR reporter, Michelle Norris and the Race Card Project,[14] digital storytelling efforts from the StoryCenter[15] (formerly the Center for Digital Storytelling), and Lee Ann Bell's Storytelling Project model as practiced in schools and educational settings (2010a).[16] Inspired by theory and practices from each these programs, PJP employs story-sharing to illuminate how bias and oppression show up in our daily lives, and then engages participants in rewriting narratives to create more just ways of living with one another. Distinct from these other nationally recognized groups, our approach to storytelling is embodied and performed for public audiences. Participants in PJP use storytelling to amplify their experiences, making often hidden patterns of bias, discrimination, and oppression visible. These stories also serve as counter-narratives, speaking back to the many negative and narrow stories, images, and reports about the lives and experiences of young people.

The work of PJP remains in conversation with critical scholar, artist, and pedagogue bell hooks who argues that telling and exchanging stories is necessary for building connections, deepening understanding, and thinking critically (2010a). hooks writes that, "A powerful way we connect with a diverse world is by listening to the different stories we are told. These stories are a way of knowing. Therefore, they contain both power and the art of possibility. We need more stories" (2010a, p. 53). Sharing her own personal experiences, hooks demonstrates how stories are often the bedrock of learning. She argues that listening to stories is both a necessary part of the process of self-actualization and critical to understanding across difference (2010a, p. 52). Like hooks, culturally responsive educator Lee Ann Bell emphasizes the value of sharing personal stories in classroom settings, offering up the practice of "counter-storytelling" as a way of teaching and learning about race (2010a). In *Storytelling for Social Justice: Connecting Narrative and the Arts in Antiracist Teaching*, Bell writes about the Storytelling Project and her efforts to engage youth in analyzing and re-envisioning stories that reify oppressive narratives and action.

> We examine ... the power *in* stories and the power dynamics *around* stories to help
> us understand how social location (our racial [and other intersecting identity mark-
> ers] position in society) affects storytelling and to consider ways to generate new
> stories that account for power, privilege and position in discussing and acting on
> racial and other social justice issues.
>
> (2010a, pp. 11–12)

Taken together, the story-work practiced and theorized by hooks and Bell urge directors and teaching artists in PJP to facilitate an exchange and analysis of stories as a
way to see and change not simply knowledge content, but also ways of thinking, seeing, and knowing. They emphasize the critical notion of experiences as knowledge
and wisdom.

## Autobiographical Performance

In her writing about digital storytelling with youth, Megan (Alrutz) draws on the work
of contemporary performance scholar of Deirdre Heddon to point out that theatre
artists and activists with marginalized identity markers have a significant history of
devising and performing autobiographical stories in an effort to diversify what stories
get told (Alrutz 2015). Autobiographical storytelling and performance point to the
importance of paying attention to issues of authorship and truth, such as who has
agency or subjectivity to write, preserve, and share histories and which ideas and
experiences move into the public consciousness as real, valued, and trusted.

In *Autobiography and Performance*, Heddon reminds readers of the history of autobiography in social justice movements, such as in the second-wave feminist movement:

> Autobiographical performance was regarded by women as a means to reveal oth-
> erwise invisible lives, to resist marginalization and objectification and to become,
> instead, speaking subjects with self-agency; performance, then, as a way to bring
> into a being a self.
>
> (2008, p. 3)

Heddon's research helps to position PJP, particularly our emphasis on personal stories and patterns of oppression, within existing efforts among artists to democratize representational practices and center the experiences of women, trans folks,
and people of color. By writing and performing their everyday experiences in public
spaces, youth participants in PJP control how their stories are told, providing them
with agency and legacy. Through the creative process of authoring and performing
stories, Bell suggests that storytellers and listeners might begin to see new ways of
moving through the world. Drawing on education theorists Rosemarie Roberts, Elliot
Eisner, and Maxine Greene, Bell states:

> The aesthetic experiences of stories told through visual arts, theater, spoken word
> and poetry, can help us think more creatively, intimately and deeply about racism
> and other challenging social justice issues. The arts provide a realm where charged
> topics can be encountered and engaged on an embodied level (Roberts, 2005) and
> thus stimulate deeper learning (Eisner, 2002).
>
> (Bell 2010a, p. 17)

Through that experience, Green argues, "we begin moving between immediacies and general categories ... [and] participate in some dimensions that we could not know if imagination were not aroused" (1995 cited in Bell 2010a, p. 17).

As a performance project, PJP participates in the politics of representation; we build meaning through words and embodied images. Our focus on autobiographical stories and self-representation in PJP stems in large part from our desire to diversify whose and what stories are shared with the public—an act of performing justice. We pair this individual work with reflections on privilege and oppression, as well as larger connections to systemic racism and sexism. Building on the legacies mentioned here, we understand that there is power in self-representation and we build PJP residencies to create opportunities for sharing and directing one's own stories and narratives.

Focusing on personal and autobiographical stories, particularly when devising with young people, sometimes raises tensions and concerns. We hear fears from adult educators, activists, and artists that inviting young people to share personal stories about their experiences of race and gender could bring up traumatic experiences, trigger negative emotions, and prove harmful.[17] Adults also sometimes worry that autobiographical story-work exploits the experiences of young people in an effort to make audiences consider a political point of view. In addition, concerned adult artists sometimes worry that devised, autobiographical performance does not connect to "general audiences," meaning anyone outside of the youth's small circle of friends, family, and supporters. In our work with court- and state-involved youth we raise our own concerns about how this work can blur lines between performance practices that feel therapeutic and practices that cross into drama therapy—namely, the intentional, therapeutic use of theatre and drama practices with the goal of healing and recovery. Responding to these concerns, we make it clear to PJP participants, teaching artists, and community partners that while working with an ensemble to address gender and racial justice can build feelings of solidarity and belonging—and may even feel therapeutic at times—this work is not therapy. In addition, we often partner with counselors and youth workers whose job is to provide that particular type of critical care and support. As we hold this range of adult questions and concerns with seriousness, the young people who participate in PJP continue to express a desire and need to share their personal experiences and stories with each other and with a public. They remind us that young people remain hungry for adults, allies, and advocates to witness, listen to, and uplift their stories. Moreover, they are often eager to understand how their individual experiences and stories sit in relationship to the systems and people around them. They want tools for engaging in the mess and working toward change. They want adults to bravely listen, witness, and act.

In an effort to remain both responsive to the interests of young people as well as the concerns surrounding personal story-work, we turn to Clark Baim's article "The Drama Spiral: A decision-making model for safe, ethical, and flexible practice when incorporating personal stories in applied theatre and performance" (see Figure 1.1).

As an applied theatre scholar, drama therapist, and psychotherapist, Baim's research explores "the ethics, risks, and responsibilities associated with applied theatre when personal stories are used" (Baim 2017, p. 80). Baim explains:

> While there are many positive reasons for incorporating personal stories in theatre and drama workshops, and indeed many examples of good practice, such work has

inherent risks because it is often conducted with vulnerable groups ... Therefore, there are important issues in relation to duty of care, reflexive practice, transparency, and structure, which are important aspects of the drama process when personal stories are used.

(2017, pp. 79–80)

In an effort to help practitioners negotiate these positive reasons and inherent risks in story-work, Baim offers the Drama Spiral (see Figure 1.1) as a tool for paying attention to the various power dynamics surrounding invitations for personal disclosure,

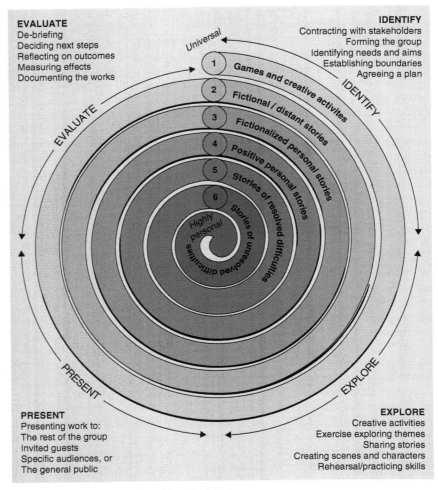

**EVALUATE**
De-briefing
Deciding next steps
Reflecting on outcomes
Measuring effects
Documenting the works

**IDENTIFY**
Contracting with stakeholders
Forming the group
Identifying needs and aims
Establishing boundaries
Agreeing a plan

Universal

1 Games and creative activites

2 Fictional / distant stories

3 Fictionalized personal stories

4 Positive personal stories

5 Stories of resolved difficulties

6 Stories of unresolved difficulties

Highly personal

EVALUATE

IDENTIFY

PRESENT

EXPLORE

**PRESENT**
Presenting work to:
The rest of the group
Invited guests
Specific audiences, or
The general public

**EXPLORE**
Creative activities
Exercise exploring themes
Sharing stories
Creating scenes and characters
Rehearsal/practicing skills

**Figure 1.1** The Drama Spiral by Clark Baim
Source: Reprinted with permission from Clark Baim (2017, fig. 2; 2018, fig. 3.2).

particularly in public performance work. Baim draws on the work of arts educator, Stella Barnes (2009) to suggest that

> The theatre of real stories certainly has the power to transform and heal, but it can also be a form of theatre that can do harm, by worsening the vulnerability of injured participants and also by passing on unresolved and uncontained (and typically unacknowledged) pain to audiences and performers.
>
> (Baim 2017, p. 90)[18]

The Drama Spiral demonstrates how applied theatre practitioners often work within a continuum of story-work, from the fictional to the highly personal. Baim offers frameworks for considering and regulating what he calls "distance," specifically how personal or vulnerable the story-work becomes. "In the outer rings, participants are involved in creative activities and work at the metaphorical and fictional level. As one 'spirals in' towards the centre, the rings represent stories that are increasingly personal and sensitive for the participants" (Baim 2017, p. 96). This spiraled continuum outlines practical examples and ways of working while also offering a concrete vocabulary for discussing the intentions and impact of the story-work at hand. Baim argues,

> When we elicit participants' stories and work with them in a drama process, what is crucial is not really whether or not we focus on injury and risk or on only positive stories; what is crucial is the skill of the practitioner in staying focused on ethical processes, working collaboratively in transparently negotiated processes with groups. For some groups, staying metaphorical will be where they feel able to work. Other groups may wish to portray their story in direct terms. With appropriate precautions and processes in place and with a reflexive, nuanced approach, skilled applied theatre practitioners ought to be able to operate across the full spectrum of theatrical forms, from fourth-wall, fictional stories to the up-close-and-personal forms that include autobiographical performances around even the most vulnerable and risky topics.
>
> (2017, p. 102)

Baim's figure also includes four important steps for building ethical story-work at any given place in on the Drama Spiral, namely *Identify, Explore, Present, and Evaluate*. With these processes (and their suggested actions, such as contracting with stakeholders and agreeing to a plan), Baim demonstrates practical steps for working toward safe, transparent, and effective story-work within an applied theatre activity, session, or project (Baim 2017, pp. 95–98).

## 1.3.3 Pedagogy
### Social Justice Programs with Youth

The challenges facing youth require multiple and diverse approaches to imagining and enacting justice. In building and facilitating PJP, we have learned from many youth and social-change organizations and programs, some engaged in arts-based frameworks and others whose pedagogies stem from theory and practices in education, literacy, political organizing, activism, positive youth development, and creative youth development. No matter the pedagogical frameworks employed, social change programs with and for young people remind us (again and again) that young people are already deeply engaged in significant, ongoing change efforts. Young people are not a singular group and they require and deserve multiple avenues, venues, pedagogical frameworks, and choices for how to participate in and make change in their lives and communities.

While PJP focuses on performance actions to explore and disrupt gendered and racialized oppression, we work alongside many organizations that engage youth differently. Some organizations center youth voices to end detention and deportation, developing collective strategies for healing, cultivating a sense of community, and working toward direct action in schools and neighborhoods. Other programs, such as Urban Roots in Austin, TX, focus on developing youth leadership in general, while still others, like Creative Action in Austin, TX, put resources specifically into training socially, politically, and civically engaged artists.[19] In addition to service and arts-based organizations that work with youth, many individual artists, as well as membership and policy organizations, also support arts and social justice work with young people. Critically engaged membership organizations focused on the social justice, such as Race Forward[20] and Alternate ROOTS,[21] offer publications, practices, and dialogues that continue to shape the ways that we think about and facilitate PJP residencies. Remaining in touch with youth arts and activist movements, as well as the artists, leaders, and organizations supporting them, is critical in the ongoing work of the Performing Justice Project.

We understand that social change requires many and varied approaches to the challenges and oppressions facing youth and communities. To this end, PJP offers an approach—not *the* approach—to lifting up youth voices and working toward racial and gender justice. With school shootings on the rise and climate crisis coming to a head, with the increased attention to the murder of Black and Brown and trans youth, young people are creating new ways to speak up and activate change. Within these efforts, one of the greatest assets of the PJP model is its ability to remain flexible and responsive to the lives and interests of young people. In PJP, supporting youth action means remaining responsive to ongoing changes in youth priorities, as well as shifts in culture and language related to identity and oppression.[22]

## Social Justice Education Frameworks

PJP also borrows frameworks from social justice educators and theorists. Books such as *The Art of Effective Facilitation: Reflections from Social Justice Educators* edited by Lisa M. Landreman, *Teaching for Diversity and Social Justice: A Source Book* edited by Maurianne Adams, Lee Ann Bell, and Pat Griffin, and *Is Everyone Really Equal? An Introduction to Key Concepts in Social Justice Education* by Özlem Sensoy and Robin DiAngelo are just a few texts that that have introduced us to social justice education and pedagogical approaches. In a chapter called "The evolution of social justice education and facilitation," Landreman and Christopher MacDonald-Dennis trace an evolution of social justice education in higher education[23] in the US, highlighting different ways that social justice education has impacted the participation of marginalized student populations in higher education. Their chapter lays out how social justice education began in the US as an "inclusion model" which came with expectations for students with minoritized identities to assimilate to the primarily white, western forms and content already in place within colleges and universities (Landreman and MacDonald-Dennis 2013, pp. 4–7). These inclusion models later gave way to multi-cultural approaches to education where social justice educators attempted to value identity and culture-based differences in the classroom. Many social justice educators argue that inclusion strategies and multicultural education frameworks are not enough to address the unequal social conditions that impact access and equity within education (Landreman 2013). Contemporary efforts in social justice education focus on systemic change and the ways that teaching and learning can disrupt dominant cultural norms and narratives that simply recreate oppressive schooling in the US. These three approaches to social justice education—inclusion, multiculturalism, and systems change—point to different goals and outcomes when working toward socially just reforms in schools and other educational settings. Seeing this evolution mapped out helps us shape PJP with attention to the ways that systemic oppression shapes teaching and learning.

For social justice educator and scholar Lee Ann Bell:

> Social justice includes a vision of society in which the distribution of resources is equitable and all members are physically and psychologically safe and secure ... Social justice involves social actors who have a sense of their own agency as well as a sense of social responsibility toward and with others and the society as a whole.
>
> (1997, p. 3)

In following this definition, social justice education often includes a focus on individuals' safety, security, and agency, as well as a focus on systemic equity and societal well-being. Landreman and MacDonald-Dennis draw similar connections between social justice education and critically engaged pedagogy, writing that "Good multicultural education asks students to critically examine social practices, reflect on what they learn, and put that learning into action ... this type of critical multicultural education *is* social justice education" (2013, p. 9). In this way, Bell, Landreman, and MacDonald-Dennis focus on the cyclical and necessary relationship between reflection and action in the process of learning and making change. These authors also draw heavily on critical pedagogues such bell hooks and Paulo Freire as they center identity and culture within education as an act of social justice and social change. By foregrounding the relationship between social justice education and critically and culturally engaged pedagogies, these authors remind us to continually examine how power and privilege show up in our program content and pedagogy.

Social justice educator and theorist Annemarie Vaccaro draws on critical theory from a variety of disciplines to demonstrate the ways that power and identity relate to equity and inclusion. She writes that "[c]ritical perspectives inspire individuals to question why society is structured in a way that privileges some and oppresses others" (Vaccaro 2013, p. 24). In reflecting on her own spaces of privilege and oppression, Vaccaro offers a pedagogical framework for social justice education that addresses three key factors: facilitator development, learning environment, and core content for participants (see Figure 1.2). Vaccaro situates "facilitator self-awareness and growth" as the outermost layer of her framework, signaling that effective social justice educators always engage in critical self-reflection and

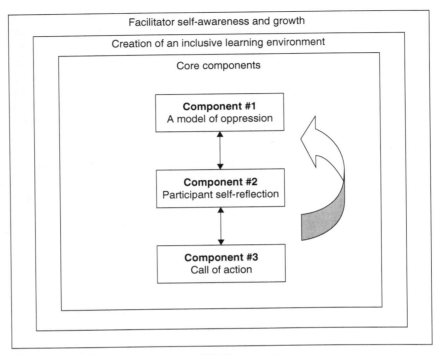

**Figure 1.2** Social Justice Education (SJE) framework
Source: Reprinted from Vaccaro (2013, fig. 2.1) with permission of the publisher. Copyright © 2013, Stylus Publishing, LLC.

opportunities for personal growth before and during work with students. Related to PJP, Vaccaro reminds us that successful social justice educators are committed to their own growth and ongoing efforts to gain knowledge around social justice, issues of diversity and multiculturalism, history, interpersonal dialogue, and facilitation (Vaccaro 2013, pp. 26–27).

The second layer of Vaccaro's model focuses on the creation of an inclusive learning environment. She draws on writing from Paulo Freire, bell hooks, and Frank Tuitt to demonstrate that strong social justice educators employ inclusive pedagogies that are "rooted in trust and respect," always aiming to "share the power of knowledge construction with learners" (Vaccaro 2013, p. 28). Her vision for an inclusive learning environment includes efforts to invite, value, and affirm students' personal experiences. She also emphasizes the role of compassion and making space for multiple perspectives. Moreover, she writes "Inclusive educators are willing to learn from participants and admit their challenges (e.g., unseen weaknesses, unconscious fears, shortcomings)" (Vaccaro 2013, p. 29). In her SJE model, Vaccaro situates the "Creation of an Inclusive Learning Environment" between "Facilitator Self-awareness and Growth" and the three "Core Components," or content areas, for students to learn or consider. This physical arrangement in the chart reminds us that creating an inclusive learning environment and beginning to address social justice content within PJP requires us to engage in ongoing personal reflection and growth.

The outer rings of Vaccaro's model focus on the facilitator's personal preparation and the preparation of the learning environment, while the center of Vaccaro's SJE framework includes three "Core Components," or content areas, namely a model of oppression, participant self-reflection, and a clear call to action. Vaccaro offers students concrete and relatable examples of systemic oppression, invites them to reflect on their relationship to the example of oppression, and then offers a call to action or an opportunity to seed change. Each of the three content areas may spark students' engagement in another she says. For example, a call to action might prompt students to reflect on their own experiences of privilege and oppression or reveal a different example of systemic oppression for another group or individual. Similarly, reflecting on one's own experiences with social (in)justice can reveal additional models of oppression and lead students to see or create a call to action.

While Vaccaro's framework suggests introducing a model of oppression to students before moving into personal reflection, we begin PJP residencies with a series of performance actions focused on personal reflection (see Section 2.3.2, who Am I?) before introducing a model of oppression (see Section 2.3.3, what Is (In)Justice?). Both PJP and Vaccaro's social justice education frameworks introduce or perform a call to action (see Section 2.3.4, How Do I Perform Justice?) after participants self-reflect and engage with a model of oppression. Our two models share the three content areas but move through the material in a different order. These different pathways toward justice education remind us that there are multiple ways of exploring individual and systemic oppression with young people, as well as imagining and performing change.

With a keen awareness of different entry points or pathways to justice, we approach social justice education in PJP through a critically engaged lens. Özlem Sensoy and Robin DiAngelo write that

A critical approach to social justice refers to specific theoretical perspectives that recognize that society is *stratified* (i.e., divided and unequal) in significant and far-reaching ways along social group lines that include race, class, gender, sexuality, and ability. Critical social justice recognizes inequality as deeply embedded in the fabric of society (i.e., as structural), and actively seeks to change this.

(2012, p. xviii)

In other words, critical social justice educators and artists attend to issues of inequity and make visible the often normalized and unseen relationships between identity and power, relationships that privilege certain groups of people and oppress others. Sensoy and DiAngelo similarly argue for the necessity of what they call *critical social justice literacy*, namely the ability to integrate both an understanding of social justice with actions toward change (2012, p. xix).

In PJP, critical social justice literacy requires an investigation into the nature of oppression, specifically the ways that racism and sexism both structure and impact the lives of young people. Our process for developing a social justice practice in a society and world steeped in oppression begins by asking participants to define and reflect on their own identities, as well as structures of racism and sexism, in order to understand how identity and oppression operate at individual, institutional, and systemic levels. To this end, in PJP we attend to gendered and racialized experiences of participants as a way into understanding systemic, identity-based oppression or what Vaccaro calls models of oppression. Inspired by culturally responsive pedagogy (Hanley 2013), we invite participants to bring their cultural experiences with and expertise around gender and race into our performance project. We begin broadly by introducing participants to the concept of social locations or identities that shape our relationship to power and our ability to impact change. We then move into concepts and ideas about equity and justice in society at large. Performing justice and talking about justice (both actions) require that we acknowledge our own many and intersecting identities and how oppression works across many intersecting power lines.

## Critically Engaged Pedagogies

As theatre artists and educators working toward racial and gender justice, we draw on several critically engaged pedagogical frameworks to address identity and inter-secting power lines. We understand that our choices as facilitators in PJP, about both form (how we lead, teach, and create) and content (the ideas, theatre structures, and practices we emphasize), directly shape the conditions of teaching, learning, and the type of performance actions we use. Our pedagogical choices shape how knowl-edge is shared and built, the messages young people receive about who and what is important, and the possibilities for changing narratives about ourselves, each other, and the world. In addition to rooting PJP in culturally responsive and social justice education models, we draw on elements of transgressive pedagogy (hooks 1994) and engaged pedagogy and performance (hooks 1994; Cohen-Cruz 2010). Moreover, we practice pedagogical approaches that support critical consciousness-raising (Freire 2018) and image and justice-based literacy (Freire 2018; Goodman 2003; Sensoy and DiAngelo 2012). Taken together, these critical theories and frameworks on teaching and learning shape the form and content of PJP and underpin the critically engaged performance process laid out in this book.

As discussed earlier, many of the pedagogies and practices associated with applied theatre and Theatre of the Oppressed build directly on the thinking of Brazilian edu-cator and theorist Paulo Freire and his writing in *Pedagogy of the Oppressed* (2018). Freire and later bell hooks emphasize education as the practice of freedom, arguing that knowledge building and critical reflection are required for making meaningful personal and/or systemic change.[24] Freire and hooks' writings about liberatory educa-tion deeply inform the goals and practices of PJP. Their focus on critical literacy—the ability to analyze images and texts for underlying messages about power, inequal-ity, and justice—and consciousness-raising—the ability to reflect on, understand, and take action to change power structures and social reality—are central to disrupting systems of oppression and achieving a more just and equitable society. As we imagine and enact justice with youth, we actively weave these concepts of critical literacy and consciousness-raising throughout PJP and our collection of performance actions, considerations, and practices.

In her earlier publication on critically engaged performance practices, Megan turns to media literacy theorists for insight on power and representation in visual arts practices (Alrutz 2015). With an interest in semiotics and meaning-making through visual representation, she engages with the work of Steven Goodman, author of *Teaching Youth Media: A Critical Guide to Literacy, Video Production and Social Change* (2003). Goodman suggests that critical literacy, or the ability to analyze, evaluate, and produce print, aural, and visual forms of communication is a human right. He writes that "learning about the world is directly linked to the possibility of changing it" (Goodman 2003, p. 3). Moreover, he argues that visual literacy and self-representation are directly tied to agency and the ability to fully participate in and impact society. Goodman reminds readers that "Command of literacy in this sense is not only a matter of performing well on standardized tests; it is a prerequisite for self-representation and autonomous citizenship" (2003, p. 3). Similar to Freire's ideas about generative themes (2018, pp. 87–124), Goodman emphasizes the importance of supporting young people's efforts to "defamiliarize the familiar taken for granted conditions of life" (2003, p. 3) and actively participate in the production of new knowledge. For Goodman, media literacy helps develop individual consciousness, liberating students from the narrative, image-based, and symbolic messages assigned to them by those in power. In PJP, we use performance actions to engage young people in naming and representing, analyzing, and reflecting on images, actions, and experiences, and more specifically on hegemonic narratives and images about themselves, youth in general, and their communities at large. Participants in PJP are invited to reflect on the connections between identity, power, privilege, and oppression. Afterward, they create performance pieces—their own embodied and narrated (re)presentations—that work to disrupt images and narratives, and actions of injustice and inequity.

Theories on applied drama and theatre often discuss the transformative potential of arts-based pedagogies, particularly when working with youth. PJP is built on the belief that arts-based social justice work has the potential to make systemic and long-term impacts on society; however, rather than focus on grand goals of societal or individual transformation within short-term performance residencies, we aim for what Megan refers to as opportunities for "transgressive transportation" (Alrutz 2015, p. 89). Borrowing from the work of bell hooks, Helen Nicholson, and Richard Schechner, Megan imagines how critical pedagogies and performance practices might in fact plant seeds of change or moments of perspective-building with and for participants and their audiences. Megan takes up the notion of transportation from Nicholson (2005) and Richard Schechner (2003) as a way to move away from transformational outcomes of theatre, suggesting instead that theatre-making and performance offer opportunities for moments of "transportation," meaning opportunities to move temporarily into another world and to experience something new. Nicholson argues that "transportation … is less fixed [than transformation]—performers are 'taken somewhere,' actors are even temporarily transformed, but they are returned more or less to their starting places at the end of the drama or performance" (2005, p. 12). Megan combines this notion of transportation with hooks' (1994) writing on transgressive pedagogy to imagine opportunities for a more critically engaged experience of "transportation." Like Nicholson, hooks critiques traditional expectations of transformation, calling instead for "teaching that enables transgressions—a movement against and beyond boundaries … movement which makes education the practice of freedom" (1994, p. 12). Specifically, hooks points to critically engaged pedagogies as pathways for transgression through and against racism, sexism, and classism. For Megan, hooks' notion of transgression and Nicholson's notion of transportation each signify an experience, a feeling, a movement, and an encounter, rather than simply a measurable change or outcome (Alrutz

2015, p. 89). To invite and support opportunities for "transgressive transportation," we take up critically engaged pedagogies as a core element of PJP. We call on participants to actively engage and participate in their own learning and theatre-making as an act of justice.

Critical pedagogies work to disrupt traditional hierarchies between youth participants and adult facilitators. In PJP we move away from what Freire (2018) calls the banking model of education and toward a co-constructed creative process with the youth participants. By sharing power in the room and collaborating to name and enact a process for democratic participation, we strive to foster mutual exchange and begin to develop opportunities for shared risk-taking. This process continues to be informed by the fact that taking risks and performing justice look different and have different consequences for people of color, women, and trans folks than they do for white men or white women, for example.

Our PJP work is also underpinned by a strong commitment to participant engagement, another tenet of critical pedagogy. bell hooks' (1994) writing on transgressive pedagogy and Jan Cohen-Cruz's (2010) writing on community-based performance each put forth frameworks for building dialogic and socially just practices in education and applied theatre respectively. In *Teaching to Transgress*, hooks (1994) suggests that in addition to addressing individual and systemic oppression, engaged pedagogy specifically attends to emotion and feelings, supporting the passion, interests, and excitement of students and welcoming these often-excluded forms of knowledge into teaching and learning spaces. hooks argues for integrating the public and private lives of students, engaging personal experiences in formal learning settings, and building connections between the two (1994, p. 16). Cohen-Cruz (2010) similarly focuses on the centrality of individuals' lived experiences, as well as the circumstances shaping those experiences, to what she calls engaging performance. She contends that truly engaged performance practices, and we argue performance pedagogies, enact the notion of call and response—both responding and contributing to social questions and contexts (Cohen-Cruz 2010, p. 1).

For both hooks and Cohen-Cruz, engaged practices—teaching and performance respectively—rely on dialogue and interaction among participating individuals. Both scholars emphasize the role of personal relationships, and the need for teachers and practitioners to bring themselves fully to an engaged process. Moreover, they suggest that engaged practices require teaching artists and facilitators to commit to one's own self-actualization (Cohen-Cruz 2010, p. 3; hooks 1994, p. 15), in addition to the well-being of their students, participants, and collaborators. Cohen-Cruz further emphasizes the importance of aesthetics in engaged practices, arguing that "engaged art is still art" (2010, p. 9). "What distinguishes engaged theatre from the mainstream is not a lack of technique ... but rather the artists' actively committed relationship to the people most affected by their subject matter" (Cohen-Cruz 2010, p. 9). Critically engaged pedagogies necessarily value the relationship between critical thinking and personal narratives and experiences. hooks argues that "Without the capacity to think critically about ourselves and our lives, none of us would be able to move forward, to change, to grow" (1994, p. 202). Creating critically engaged contexts within in PJP requires facilitators (and participants) to attend to pedagogical content and language that actively points to the constructed relationships between power, privilege, and identity. It is within this process that PJP participants begin to undo racism, sexism, and other forms of oppression.

## 1.3.4 Content

If social justice refers to equitable distribution of wealth, opportunities, access, and privileges within a society, as defined by Bell (2010b, pp. 21–26), working toward justice and equity requires acknowledging and naming dominant identities (those with power) and target identities (those without or with less access to power) in order to understand systemic oppressions that impact each person's ability to access equity. As noted above in Goodman's writing, one first has to develop the lens of critical literacy before being able to make change (2003).

PJP is based in the belief—validated by stories, statistics and historic trends—that access to our country's resources and opportunities remains inequitable in ways that are directly connected to constructs of race and gender. The construction and legacy of racism in the US—stemming from colonialism, the adoption and perpetuation of slavery, "pseudo-science," and capitalism—sustains institutions and systems that uphold both visible and invisible acts of oppression against people of color. Income levels, as well as disparities in access to affordable and safe housing and water, medical care, quality education, jobs that pay a living wage, and generational wealth are directly linked to one's racial identity. Additionally, women, trans and non-binary folks, and children are fundamentally not treated equally to men. Sexism and gender-bias also show up in wage gaps, access to basic human rights, the objectification of women, and sexual harassment and assault.

PJP functions as an investigation of and response to structural and institutionalized racism and sexism. In order to address these systems and resulting inequities, we must raise our own consciousness as well as the consciousness of young people and our communities around gender and racial (in)justices. Encouraging reflection and story-sharing is one way to acknowledge how youth are impacted by oppression and to offer youth opportunities to connect through lived experiences (Landreman 2013, p. 9). Seeing how strict constructs of race and gender, resulting from systemic racism and sexism, inform and direct our experiences supports an understanding that the personal is, indeed, political. Moreover, it lays bare the misconception that each of us is at fault for what is happening to us based on our race/ethnicity or our gender identity or birth assigned sex.

Youth arrive to a PJP process at different points of knowing, naming, and understanding their own identities and systems of power. In order to support their learning and lift up all stories in the room, we offer vocabulary and definitions to participants, providing a common language for the ensemble to explore racial and gender justice. We are keenly aware, however, that dialogue and language around race and gender is changing rapidly; what is forward-thinking today may be outdated in few short months.

### Race and Racial Justice

PJP and all racial justice work require an understanding that race is a not a genetic or biological truth; rather, race is a socially constructed system for dividing and categorizing people to the benefit of white people. To examine race and racism with PJP participants, we offer a historical analysis of race as a sociopolitical rather than biological construct, "one that is created and reinforced by social and institutional norms and practices, as well as individual attitudes and behaviors" (Bell, Castañeda, and Zúñiga 2010, p. 60). In PJP, we acknowledge that race science or "pseudo-science" was originally created to serve social and economic interests of white men, which in turn established cultural norms and legal rulings. We name how race emerged in the US as a way to justify domination by those defined as "white" over those defined as "non-white" including indigenous, First Nations peoples, enslaved Africans, and later Mexicans, Chinese, and others racialized as non-white (Bell, Castañeda, and Zúñiga 2010, p. 60). Understanding that the construct of race has evolved over time, and has been defined and redefined by those in power, is a critical step in undoing racism. Sharing historical truths helps situate the development of racialized oppression in the US; the first Naturalization Act of 1790 stated that only a "free white person" could be granted citizenship, which in turn built the foundation for excluding laborers from China (and, later, other parts of Asia) in the Chinese Exclusion Act 1882 (Public Broadcasting Service 2001).[25] In the case of the *United States v Bhagat Singh Thind* (1923), the Supreme Court stated that whiteness was based on the common understanding of the white man as understood by the framers of the Constitution. This document demonstrates how those who identify as white get to decide who else is white and thereby deny citizenship to others (History Matters 2018). A critical analysis of how definitions of whiteness came about and have changed over time shows how categories of race and ethnicity are used in political systems and as political capital. As Ta-Nehisi Coates demonstrates in his book *Between the World and Me*, "race is the child of racism, not the father" (Coates 2015, p. 7). In PJP, we strive to communicate how images and understandings of race have been constructed to justify racist systems and actions and to validate and normalize the ongoing privilege and supremacy of white people.

As we develop a PJP residency or workshop, we look to a range of sources for definitions of race and racism and how racism functions. One of our most trusted sources is Race Forward, a national organization that works for racial justice through research, media, and practice. Race Forward publishes Colorlines, a daily news site that focuses on race and the media, and presents Facing Race, the largest multi-racial conference and conversation about race and racial justice in the US. Race Forward defines racism as a "historically rooted system of power hierarchies based on race—infused in our institutions, policies and culture—that benefit white people and hurt people of color" (2015, p. 33). In PJP, we also rely on Race Forward's description of how racism impacts our lives in four different ways: structural, institutional, interpersonal, and internalized (see Figure 1.3).

At the individual level, racism includes experiences of internalized racism and interpersonal racism. When messages about race and racism become private beliefs and biases that we hold—subconsciously or consciously—they result in internalized racism or dominance, the adoption of messages that we do not realize we are taking in and might be surprised to find that we hold deep in our consciousness and daily patterns. Interpersonal racism refers to ways we act with others based on our racial beliefs, conscious or subconscious. Culturally, many of us—particularly if we identify as white—have been taught to think of racism as an interpersonal event: racism is when someone is *consciously* biased against another because of their race, ethnicity, or color, and *intentionally* acts on this bias (Sensoy and DiAngelo 2012). In *Is Everyone Really Equal?*, anti-racist educators Özlem Sensoy and Robin DiAngelo acknowledge the structural and institutional levels of racism that everyone in the US experiences as part of the "water we all swim in" (2012, pp. 16–17). They argue that because we all swim in the same water, we are all impacted, whether or not we actually notice

## Race Forward's Levels of Racism

During the course of our three decades of in-person trainings and consulting for clients of various backgrounds and fields of work, Race Forward has developed definitions for "Four Levels of Racism" – two within the individual level of racism and two within the systemic level – that we re-introduce here. The key distinction is between the two levels of racism, individual and systemic. While we acknowledge the impact of individual acts of racial discrimination, we believe that it is critical to do so within a deeper analysis of systemic racial injustice.

### Individual-Level Racism

| | |
|---|---|
| INTERNALIZED RACISM lies within individuals. These are our private beliefs and biases about race and racism, influenced by our culture. Internalized racism can take many different forms including racial prejudice toward other people of a different race; internalized oppression, the negative beliefs about oneself by people of color; or internalized privilege, beliefs about superiority or entitlement by white people. An example is a belief that you or others are more or less intelligent, or beautiful, because of your race. | INTERPERSONAL RACISM occurs between individuals. These are biases that occur when individuals interact with others and their private racial beliefs affect their public interactions. Examples include racial slurs, bigotry, hate crimes, and racial violence. |

### Systemic-Level Racism

| | |
|---|---|
| INSTITUTIONAL RACISM occurs within institutions and systems of power. It is the unfair policies and discriminatory practices of particular institutions (schools, work-places, etc.) that routinely produce racially inequitable outcomes for people of color and advantages for white people. Individuals within institutions take on the power of the institution when they reinforce racial inequities. An example is a school system that concentrates people of color in the most overcrowded schools, the least-challenging classes, and the least-qualified teachers, resulting in higher dropout rates and disciplinary rates compared with that of white students. | STRUCTURAL RACISM is racial bias among institutions and across society. It involves the cumulative and compounding effects of an array of societal factors including the history, culture, ideology, and interactions of institutions and policies that systematically privilege white people and disadvantage people of color. An example is the over-whelming number of depictions of people of color as criminals in mainstream media, which can influence how various institutions and individuals treat people of color with suspicion when they are shopping, traveling, or seeking housing and employment – all of which can result in discriminatory treatment and unequal outcomes. |

**Figure 1.3** Levels of oppression
Source: Reprinted with permission from Race Forward (2014, p. 3).

racism at work. "Swimming in the water" speaks to the systemic levels of racism, which are institutional and structural, and which we may be unaccustomed to noticing, particularly if we identify as or are read and treated by others as white.

Institutional racism refers to the unfair policies and discriminatory practices of institutions, as reinforced by individuals. Examples include red-lining, lack of access to bank loans for people of color, and ongoing segregation within schools. Structural racism refers to racial bias across institutions and society, such as the school-to-prison pipeline, higher dropout rates for youth of color as connected to educational access, poverty and punishment, racial profiling and sentencing that contributes to and upholds mass incarceration. In PJP we encourage an analysis of race with youth that acknowledges the impact of interpersonal and internalized racism *and* identifies and explores systemic racism as a way to understand that racism is not simply the fault or product of individual acts of prejudice and discrimination. Experiences of race are built through ongoing, systemic dynamics which are often invisible and over which we may have little individual control.

In PJP, we emphasize that although there is no genetic or biological basis to race, there is an undeniable impact of the social construction of racial identity and the ongoing oppression of people of color. For example, although the youth incarceration rate in the US has dropped since 2001, African American youth are five times more likely than white youth to be detained or incarcerated despite the fact that African Americans comprise only 16 percent of all youth in the US (Sentencing Project 2017). The impact of racism in the US has been well substantiated through research and data about wealth, health, incarceration, housing and education. Data that demonstrates inequities based on race overwhelmingly creates a picture of who is succeeding in the US, and has been extensively documented by a wide range of agencies, including federal (US Census Bureau) and nonprofit agencies (NAACP, Colorlines, Anti-Defamation League, Southern Poverty Law Center) among others (Sensoy and DiAngelo 2012, p. 127). To promote an understanding of the institutional and structural levels of racism in the US, the PJP process asks youth to analyze statistics about racial disparities and to engage a systemic view of their individual experiences.

As part of the PJP process, we spend time talking with participants about definitions of race and ethnicity. Because race is a constructed, manipulated, and continually changing concept, we support youth in determining and naming their own identity markers connected to race, ethnicity, and the color of their skin. As they name their own racial markers, they also articulate personal stories connected to their identities. PJP asks participants to explore these experiences through a lens of individual and systemic oppression as a way to build capacity for working towards racial justice, defined as "systematic fair treatment of people of all races, that results in equitable opportunities and outcomes for everyone" by the *Race Reporting Guide* by Race Forward (2015, p. 31). PJP ensembles begin to perform racial justice by naming experiences and impacts of individual and systemic racism and imagining radical alternatives for our lives.

## Gender and Gender Justice

Similarly, the PJP process asks youth to examine constructs of gender and sex, and to reflect on how these identity markers impact people's experiences in the world. In discussing various aspects of gender, we examine the effect of living within systems in which men hold power to the exclusion and subordination of women, trans people, and gender non-conforming people. Social justice educator Heather Hackman examines the intersection of sexism and patriarchy: "The importance of interrogating gender when studying sexism becomes clear ... when we realize how the structures of sexism in this society feed into and are nourished by the maintenance of hierarchies of power based on gender" (2010, p. 315). Exploring sexism requires an understanding of the social construction of gender and sex, which in turn requires attention to the differences between gender and birth-assigned sex, identities that are often conflated in ways that oppress people who do not fit neatly into a gender binary.

The saturation of messages we receive about gender roles and expectations can make it challenging to separate concepts of sex and gender. Foundational theorist on the social construction of gender, Judith Lorber, discusses ways that "a sex category becomes a gender statute through naming, dress and the use of other gender markers" (1994, p.14). In other words, strict constructions of gender are tied closely to societal expectations of people based on their sex assigned at birth. In PJP, we explore how the social performance and repetition of how we "do gender" starts at birth; we might create scenes about how when a baby is born the medical establishment assigns a sex of male or female based almost exclusively on visible genitalia at birth (assuming that these biological traits are also on a binary). Once assigned, this sex marker presumes gender; a baby assigned male sex quickly becomes gendered as a boy through dress, naming, and other social conditioning related to constructions of masculinity and femininity. Lorber writes:

> Gender is such a familiar part of daily life that it usually takes a deliberate disruption of our expectations of how women and men are supposed to act to pay attention to how it [gender] is produced. Gender signs and signals are so ubiquitous that we usually fail to note them unless they are missing or ambiguous. Then we are uncomfortable until we have successfully placed the other person in a gender status.
>
> (Lorber 1994, p. 14)

Gender roles and binary expectations, then, both reinforce and are reinforced by social, cultural, or familial constructs of how women and men should look, behave, dress, speak, and emote, as well as the roles they are assumed and encouraged to play in family, work, and community. In PJP, we examine the harmful impacts of strict gender binaries and gendered expectations on participants' experiences, and support participants to name their own identities related to gender and sex. Gender Spectrum, a website devoted to understanding the dimensions of gender, explains:

> Basic gender literacy is essential for children to understand their own gender, engage in healthy relationships, identify and place media and social messages in context, and have agency in determining aspects of their gender now and in the future. Societal ideas about gender will affect every critical aspect of their lives, from education to career, finances, relationships and more.
>
> (Gender Spectrum 2019)

As two cisgender women leading PJP, we actively listen to and learn from the youth and teaching artists with whom we work. We also rely on the ongoing work of GLSEN, a national education and advocacy organization which evolved to support K-12 students who identify as lesbian, gay, bisexual, transgender, queer, and questioning (LGBTQ). GLSEN provides language and other resources specifically for K-12 teachers and youth workers, arguing that "We all have the right to have language to define ourselves" (GLSEN 2019a). We also follow the work of advocacy organizations such as the Gay and Lesbian Alliance Against Defamation (GLAAD); the Human Rights Campaign (HRC) which advocates for the civil rights of LGBTQ folks; and InterACT, an advocacy organization for youth who identify as intersex. These organizations offer resources and education materials that promote inclusiveness, allyship, and understanding of gender-related issues and underpin many of the performance actions and pedagogical approaches we use in PJP.

# GLSEN®

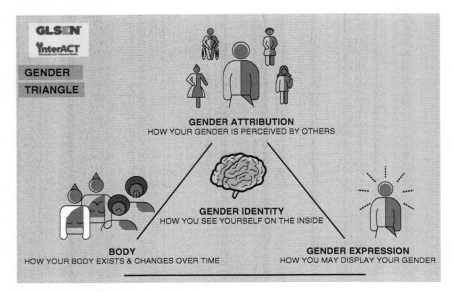

**Figure 1.4** GLSEN Gender Triangle
Source: Reprinted with permission from GLSEN (2019b).

We rely on the GLSEN Gender Triangle as a framework for understanding and exploring the ways that various aspects of gender and sex often get conflated.

**Gender attribution**[26] describes how others perceive the gender of a person. Although we are taught to read signs and signals of gender in certain ways, it is important to allow people to identify themselves, and to use and affirm the identities they name, and the language and pronouns they use.

**Gender identity** refers to how someone sees themselves on the inside. Gender might be described by terms such as man, woman, non-binary, gender fluid, gender non-conforming, cisgender, intersex, and transgender or trans, among other terms that will continue to develop in response to specific identities. Cisgender, meaning "on the same side of," refers to the matching up of birth-assigned sex, gender identity, and gender expression. For example, when someone who is assigned female sex at birth also identifies as and expresses herself as a woman, she is a cisgender woman. Transgender, defined literally as "on the other side of," means that these identity markers may not line up in the same way; someone with a birth-assigned sex of female may identify and/or express himself as a man, or may express themselves as genderqueer, trans, or non-binary.

**Gender expression** describes how someone may express gender to the world, which may or may not line up with how one feels inside or with sex assigned at birth. A person may have a birth-assigned sex of female, but identify as gender non-conforming, gender non-binary, or male, yet be unable to safely express their gender, or not have access to the particular clothes to express gender in the way they desire. Some people may also feel pressured to express gender in a specific way due to family or societal expectations, while others may express gender fluidly, combining markers of what society typically associates with female and male and moving between expressions of gender along a continuum.

**Gender and the body** acknowledges that gender identity is different from gender expression, which is also separate from what might be happening visibly or invisibly on/in the body, at birth but also over time. While many PJP participants and facilitators have been taught that babies—and people—are limited to the binary sex identity of male or female, about 1.7 percent babies are born intersex (Blackless et al., 2000). This statistic is often equated with the percentage of people in the world who are born with red hair. As a category, intersex includes a range of sex characteristics that do not fit a medical category of typically female or male. Not all intersex babies are identifiable at birth—intersex also includes variations that do not appear until puberty. interACT has excellent resources on their website, and adds this information:

> Intersex is different from gender or sexual orientation. Like anyone, intersex people can have any orientation or identity. Intersex people, like all people, may identify as male, female, with no gender, or with multiple genders—and they may express their gender in different ways. Similarly, intersex people may be straight, gay, lesbian, bisexual, asexual, or identify in another way.
>
> (interACT 2018, p. 2)

**Sexual orientation** is also sometimes confused with gender and sex. Sexual orientation describes who we are attracted to, and is separate from both sex and gender identity, although societal messages and media representation often inform assumptions about heteronormative connections between birth-assigned sex and sexual orientation. Sexual orientation is often named as heterosexual, asexual, lesbian, gay, bisexual or pansexual (among other language that will continue to develop to represent specific and non-binary identities). Neither transgender nor intersex is a sexual orientation, and trans and intersex folks have many different sexual orientations. Separating sexual orientation from gender and sex also helps to deconstruct heteronormativity—the assumption that birth assigned sex assumes a hetero (opposite) sexual attraction or sexual orientation. It is critical to not make assumptions about the way that any of these markers line up or are related to each other.

Throughout PJP, we stress the importance of not assuming someone's gender based on their name, how they look, or how they express themselves. As part of this intention, we invite each person in PJP to identify and name themselves. We introduce conversations around identity in many ways, but we often begin by modeling and then inviting participants to share their pronouns[27] and the name they use, both connected to expressing gender in the world. Recognizing that for some people the name given to them at birth doesn't accurately represent who they are, we often ask PJP participants to share their chosen name, or a name that authentically represents their gender identity and expression. The practice of sharing names and pronouns might sound like: "My name is Lynn, and I use she, her, hers," or "My name is Lynn and I use they and them pronouns," or "My name is Lynn, and I use ze, hir, and hirs," or "My name is Lynn and I use he/they pronouns." Rather than making assumptions about the gender identity of those around us and the pronouns they use,[28] this practice of naming ourselves can work against cis-normativity, the assumption that everyone's gender identity matches their birth-assigned sex. Regardless of who is in a PJP residency, the regular practice of introducing oneself with pronouns[29] can begin to build more inclusive and affirming spaces that acknowledge gender and sex as different categories and as identities defined by each of us for ourselves.

As part of the PJP process, we invite young people to identify and name their gender identities and share their thoughts and experiences around gender roles and constructs. We make efforts to lift up the stories and experiences of youth who identify beyond or in the margins of gender norms and expectations. And we remain mindful of the fact that naming gender identities remains highly political and at times dangerous, especially when someone identifies outside of the gender binary or fails to adhere to rigid gender roles. As a gender-justice program, PJP practices and advocates for inclusion, access, and equity for women and all people who hold marginalized identities, such as trans, non-binary, and genderqueer. Performing justice means imagining and enacting the possibility for all youth, regardless of gender identity, to access their full potential, agency, and power in the world. It also means imagining and enacting that youth will no longer be conditioned to a particular beauty ideal or be objectified or valued by their look/physicality; and that women and gender non-binary and trans youth and adults feel safe and develop a sense of belonging in all communities.

Understanding that knowledge can impact power, we draw on statistics and other data as one way to illuminate some of the impacts of systemic sexism in the US, including statistics on the gender pay gap, the impacts of sex trafficking, violence against women, trans, and non-binary folks, and the pervasiveness of sexual harassment and sexual assault. Developing a nuanced understanding of sex, gender, and identity is one of ways the PJP process works toward gender justice and promotes a "movement to end sexist oppression" (hooks 2010b, p. 337). How young people use language to describe their gender is inextricably linked to context and power, and PJP is built on the understanding that content knowledge remains critical to the possibility of performing justice.

## 1.3.5 Devised Theatre as Our Approach to Critically Engaged Performance, Pedagogy, and Content

There are several reasons that we choose theatre as a tool for addressing gender and racial justice with young people. First, our backgrounds and experiences grow out of theatre, specifically making theatre with young people. Theatre invites participants to move beyond reading and discussing ideas and toward embodied ways of knowing and sharing knowledge. Social justice educator Lee Ann Bell draws on

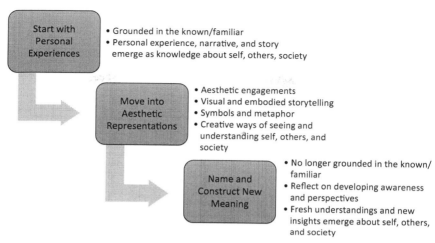

**Figure 1.5** A process for building new knowledge
Source: Alrutz (2015, p. 63, fig. 3.1).

Audrey Thompson as she writes about the critical nature of embodied storytelling in anti-racism work:

> Recognizing that racism is "embodied and ideational" as well as "structural and institutional" (Thompson, 1997) the arts provide a way to engage body, heart and mind to open up learning and develop a critical perspective that affords broader understanding of cultural patterns and practices.
>
> (2010a, p 17)[30]

In other words, devising and sharing stories offers a pathway to seeing and understanding the connections between identity and individual and systemic oppression. Second, devised theatre supports collaborative practices in which hierarchies between participants and facilitators are somewhat flattened through shared decision-making. Ensemble-based theatre practices also invite participants to contribute various forms of knowledge to a devised performance and to deepen their understanding of a given topic. The practice of devising theatre also offers participants an opportunity to integrate their lived experiences with information about systemic inequities. Lastly, we choose devised theatre because it supports ensembles to create and perform new stories, ideas, and images; representation matters. As we aim to build equitable and just narratives, representations, and systems, we know that embodied expression, collectively devised performance, and creative writing for theatre invite participants and audience members to reflect on the past and present, and bring something new into being.

More specifically, devising theatre holds the possibility of creating new knowledge—for makers, performers, and audiences. As a process for building new knowledge (see Figure 1.5), we ground our theatre-making first in the personal and familiar. We then move into aesthetic and embodied representations as a way of seeing and understanding through metaphor and symbol and creative expression. Finally, we move into reflections on unknown/unfamiliar territories, further supporting the development of new perspectives, awareness, and insight about ourselves, each other, and society.

We believe that the arts, and theatre in particular, have a critical role in change-making. In "Imagining otherwise: Connecting the arts and social change to envision and act for change," Lee Ann Bell and Dipti Desai argue that:

> The arts can help us remember, imagine, create, and transform the practices that sustain oppression as it endures across history and locality. When tuned to that purpose, the arts play a vital role in making visible the stories, voices, and experiences of people who are rendered invisible by structures of dominance. Equally important, the arts confront how we have learned to see and provide new lenses for looking at the world and ourselves in relation to it.
>
> (2011, p. 288)

In other words, as performance-makers, we are equipped with tools for foregrounding and backgrounding stories, voices, and experiences. Participating in performance actions—devising and structuring theatre work through a critically engaged lens—can confront personal bias, as well as systemic racism and sexism that impact the lives of young people. For these reasons, we choose devised theatre as our approach to critically engaged pedagogy and content.

## Doing Justice

### Why Talk About Race? Because We Deserve Happiness

*Natalie M. Goodnow*

Although I was drawn to the Performing Justice Project in part because of my passion for racial justice education, I found—much to my surprise—that I dreaded bringing up race during a PJP residency at a group home for girls and young women. The young people I was working with had been through so much already. I felt apprehension about introducing a topic that might make the multi-racial group feel less connected with one another, or that might cause pain. Why not preserve their innocence as long as possible?

I wonder now if that's what the adults in my life thought when they avoided talking to me about race and racism when I was a child. When I did hear about racism, it was in the past tense, as if it was a problem solved long ago. Although I had numerous opportunities to witness the inequities between my middle-class white family members' lives and those of my working-class Mexican American family, I didn't recognize them as such. I saw that the people of color in my family seemed to struggle more to finish school, secure stable employment and housing, stay healthy, stay sober, and stay out of jail; but, if racism was supposedly solved long ago, then no explanation was available to me other than the implication that one side of my family was just less able, more irreversibly broken than the other. Family, friends, and teachers never, or rarely, said this out loud, but the message landed just the same. Without racial justice education to help me understand the shape and contours of the new racism—mass incarceration, also called "The New Jim Crow" in Michelle Alexander's book by the same name (2012)—I thought what I was seeing was the result of individual moral failings. My family and my community were systematically dismantled all around me, and we were taught that we had brought it on ourselves. Furthermore, if we'd brought our struggles on ourselves, the implication seemed to be that we didn't deserve help, compassion, or happiness. Soon after learning to recognize this new racism as a young adult, I developed a passion for sharing racial justice education with young people.

For me, participating in racial justice education has been painful at times, but also deeply healing and empowering. Research suggests that this is the case for other young people of color as well. In a comprehensive review of research on culturally responsive pedagogy, positive ethnic socialization, resilience and academic success conducted in 2009, Drs. Mary Stone Hanley and George W. Noblit found compelling evidence that explicitly teaching about racism, the challenges it might present in a person's life, and strategies for overcoming such challenges, contributes significantly to young people's resilience (2009, p. 8). More recently, education scholars including Dr. Jeff Duncan-Andrade are exploring research in public health[31] which suggests that having space to talk about shared challenges can put years back onto the lives of people enduring chronic, toxic stress and trauma (2015). For young people of color, particularly in the USA, racial justice education cannot wait. This life raft helps young people navigate successfully and healthily through their current circumstances and towards adulthood.

I also continue to teach about race and racism despite the pain it can cause because I want young people of color to know that the struggles they and their community will inevitably face in a racist world order are not all their fault. I want to remind youth that their lives are worth fighting for, and that they do deserve happiness.

Despite the initial concern I felt during the PJP process, bringing up race and racism didn't seem to overly distress any participants, and it didn't appear to tear the group apart. I have faith that, for some, their time with us will be one stepping stone on a path to deep healing and renewal.

**Figure 1.6** PJP participants celebrate following a public performance
Source: Photo by Lynn Hoare.

## References

Alexander, M. (2012) *The new Jim Crow: Mass incarceration in the age of colorblindness*, New York: The New Press.

Duncan-Andrade, J. (2015) *"Only a fool would let their enemy teach their children": A license to be community responsive*, Oakland, CA: Scottish Rite Center.

Hanley, M. S. and Noblit, G. W. (2009) 'Cultural responsiveness, racial identity and academic success: A review of literature,' *Heinz Endowments*, viewed July 7, 2019, www.heinz.org/userfiles/library/culture-report_final.pdf

## Doing Justice

## Pushing Past Fear, Asking the Tough Questions

*Laura Epperson and Faith A. Hillis*

Before starting our Performing Justice Project (PJP) with a residential organization for young people living within the foster care system, the organization shared some of their "rules"—guidelines we quickly understood would impact our work. We—Laura and Faith—did not inquire further about the rules; it was our first PJP and we were not sure what we could, or should, ask of our community partners. Instead, we discussed how we planned to move through tricky moments with flexibility and integrity, knowing that such moments are often difficult to anticipate.

Our first unanticipated moment came in the first rehearsal. We asked each person to share "the name you want to use in this space," intentional language to offer participants choice in how they would be addressed. When the final young person said their name, an adult staff member from our partner organization rebuked the participant for using that name, vaguely mentioning "the rules" related to names and gender. The young person pushed back by referencing our invitation to share a name they *wanted* to use. Although we immediately recognized tension between the institutional policies in place and our understanding of gender justice, we did not directly address the situation in the moment. Instead, fear of conflict with the staff and uncertainty in how to resolve the situation took over, propelling us to move forward to the next activity and miss an opportunity to understand what was really going on.

Several rehearsals later, after our discussion on gender and sexuality, the staff member approached us privately to share that while they appreciated our efforts to honor participants' gender identity and expression, all name and pronoun "changes" had to be approved by a case worker before being implemented at the site. While this information illuminated why some participants in our group were being discouraged from using certain names and pronouns and others were not, this policy raised important questions about how to perform gender justice within an institution whose rules actively push against the work of PJP.

We understood that the staff might feel obligated to follow the institutional rules even if it went against a young person's right to self-identify. But where do we as PJP teaching artists stand when it comes to policies that explicitly enact gender oppression? We felt strongly that we did not want to call a person by a name they asked not be called, but we also felt pressure to follow "the rules" in order to maintain our developing relationship with our community partner. Throughout the residency, we used this person's chosen name and stated pronouns when out of earshot of the staff, but we never discussed the issue with the young person or the staff. Due to our own fear and uncertainty surrounding how to advocate for gender justice with our community partners, we missed an opportunity to have critical conversations in this residency concerning gender justice in the youths' lives. By reflecting on this experience we learned the importance of pushing past fear and uncertainty to ask questions—of participants, community partners, ourselves. As we prepare to begin a second residency at this site, we are asking ourselves: How can we create a radical space for youth voice that doesn't risk participants' safety within an institution when they leave rehearsal? How do we perform justice, and support youth in performing justice, when the values and/or rules of an institution oppose our own beliefs about gender and/or racial equity? What is our role as teaching artists to push against oppressive systems while also operating within (potentially) oppressive institutions? In seeking the answers to these questions, we must push past our fear of conflict and discomfort in order to take the time to have justice-centered dialogue with our institutional partners and youth ensemble. Moving forward, we hope that our developing relationship with our community partner will allow us to ask tough questions that serve the youth whose everyday experiences with justice are on the line.

**Figure 1.7** PJP participants build a dynamic embodied image for a public performance
Source: Photo by Megan Alrutz.

## Notes

1    While we include a small selection of photos in this book, the PJP website archives video, animation, and audio-recorded selections of PJP performances from various residencies with youth in schools, juvenile justice facilities, and foster-care sites. Visit our gallery page to see documentation of the work (Performing Justice Project 2019).

2    This title—Performing Justice Project—was developed by Megan Alrutz, Lynn Hoare, and Kristen Hogan prior to the first project.

3    In 2010, Kristen Hogan, then Associate Director of the Center for Women's and Gender Studies at the University of Texas at Austin, approached us, Megan

Alrutz and Lynn Hoare, faculty and staff respectively at the University of Texas at Austin, about creating a performance component for Texas's first accredited high school course on Women's History. The high school course had been previously developed by faculty at UT Austin and several high school teachers at Gonzalo Garza Independence High School. The curriculum was developed with the support of UT's Center for Women and Gender Studies and the Embrey Family Foundation, a foundation with a commitment to fostering the intersections of arts and women's human rights work. Kristen invited us to create a three-week performance component for the course that would extend and deepen students' study of women's rights as human rights, and together the three of us developed and piloted PJP with students from Gonzalo Garza Independence High School in Austin, TX. The project has also been supported by UT faculty and staff members Susan Heinzelman, Mollie Marchione, Pat Heisler, Matt Richardson, wura-Natasha Ogunji, and Lisa Moore.

4    We borrow heavily from Race Forward's online publication *Moving the Race Conversation Forward* (2014). This publication discusses the challenges associated with efforts to divert dialogue away from race and toward other dimensions of identity and identity-based oppression. The publication reminds us that diverting from race is "the practice of asserting that other social identities besides race, such as class, gender or sexual orientation, are the real determining factors behind a given social inequity" (2014, p. 16). "Its effect on racial discourse" is that it "ranks systems of power and dismisses racism as a primary, or even legitimate, determinant of social inequity. This logic inhibits an understanding of intersectionality, promoting an either/or instead of a both/and framework, which is more sociologically and historically accurate than a single identity or non-racial analysis" (2014, p. 16). PJP often works with groups of girls, women, and non-binary youth, and thus an intersectional approach has resulted in our focus on both gender and race. However, PJP has been criticized for a lack of focus on class. Taking that critique, we build on social justice education theory and remain committed to gender and race as the primary, although not only, entry points for addressing justice with young people.

5    The Performing Justice Project model and much of the work you will read about in this book grew out of the authors' collective research and practice in the areas of theatre for dialogue, theatre in education, applied theatre, and theatre for youth. The PJP also grew with knowledge, inspiration, and guidance from Kristen Hogan and her research and experience in critical and cultural studies, gender and sexuality studies, queer and feminist studies, and liberatory and embodied pedagogies. Moreover, the ideas and questions now guiding PJP were developed in early and ongoing conversations with Matt Richardson and Wura-Natasha Ogunji, colleagues whose work in arts and social justice-based pedagogies continues to inspire the PJP model.

6    In her book, *Utopia and Performance: Finding Hope at the Theater*, Jill Dolan builds on the ideas of Rustom Bharucha from his article "Contextualizing utopias: Reflections on remapping the present" (1995) in which he responds to Ruth Levitas' ideas on mapping future utopias from her article "The future of

thinking about the future" printed in *Mapping the Future: Local Cultures, Global Change* (2005).

7    These hashtags represent social justice movements that arose in response to particular instances of violence and became large-scale efforts to combat the ongoing and systemic violence perpetuated against people of color, women, and youth. #Blacklivesmatter represents the Black Lives Matter Global Network, "a chapter-based, member-led organization whose mission is to build local power and to intervene in violence inflicted on Black communities by the state and vigilantes" (Black Lives Matter 2019). This movement was launched by activists Alicia Garza, Patrisse Cullors, and Opal Tometi in response to the acquittal of Trayvon Martin's murderer, George Zimmerman. #Neveragain represents an American student-led political campaign and social movement for gun control and regulations to prevent gun violence. This movement was launched by students in response to the mass shooting at their school, Marjory Stoneman Douglas High School in Parkland, FL (Never Again MSD 2019). The movement was covered by Emily Witt in *The New Yorker* (2018). The #metoo movement was founded in 2006 by Tarana Burke "to help survivors of sexual violence, particularly Black women and girls, and other young women of color from low wealth communities, find pathways to healing" (Me Too Movement 2018). This hashtag and movement work brings global attention to sexual violence prevention efforts and supports survivor healing and promotes community-based action to interrupt sexual violence (Me Too Movement 2018).

8    For more information, see works by these authors: Cohen-Cruz (2005), Nicholson (2005), Prendergast and Saxton (2009), Prentki and Preston (2009), Taylor (2003), Thompson (2003).

9    Anthony Jackson, early scholar of TIE and co-editor of *Learning Through Theatre*, a seminal text describing TIE history and practices, argues that although the term "applied theatre" includes TIE, it is also derived from TIE: "TIE sits comfortably under the umbrella of applied theatre but at the same time can lay claim to playing a significant, if often unrecognised, part in shaping its various educational, social and political aspirations, its theoretical frameworks and its wide range of eclectic practices" (Jackson and Vine 2013, p. 2).

10    Boal posits that our bodies and senses become mechanized through patterned use. If we are to activate our senses fully in order to both create theatre and challenge our understandings of the systems in which we live, we must work to de-mechanize our bodies. Boal's theatre games present opportunities to move in different and sustained ways that may be challenging and uncomfortable as a way to awake our senses (Boal 2002, pp. 29–46).

11    This definition of creative drama evolved out of the work of Ann M. Shaw, Frank Harland, and Anne Thurman at the 1972 Conference of the International Association of Theatre for Children and Young People (Davis and Behm, 1978, p. 11, note 7).

12    For more information about storytelling as social justice efforts, see hooks (1994), Heddon (2008), Nicholson (2005), Jones, Moore, and Bridgforth (2010).

13    *This I Believe* was a radio program hosted by journalist Edward R. Murrow from 1951 to 1955, which invited stories about deeply held beliefs from well-known

figures and everyday people. We use this prompt as a PJP action when examining experiences of justice and injustice.

14    The Race Card Project is a widely available public conversation project that invites anyone to submit a six-word story of an experience of race (Norris 2010). It is also referred to in Section 2.3.3 as a foundational performance action in the PJP process.

15    The StoryCenter uses storytelling to democratize media making and promote self-representation.

16    *Storytelling for Social Justice* "examines ways to teach and learn about race by creating counter-storytelling communities that can promote more critical and thoughtful dialogue about racism" (Bell 2010a, back cover).

17    PJP teaching artist Natalie Goodnow discusses this concern further in her essay "Doing Justice: Why Talk About Race?" immediately following Section 1.3.

18    Through her work with refugee populations, Stella Barnes developed a table of personal and creative risk in theater-making. For more information Barnes (2009, p. 38).

19    Urban Roots is a youth leadership organization based in Austin, TX, that uses "food and farming to transform the lives of young people and inspire, engage, and nourish the community" (Urban Roots 2018). Creative Action, also based in Austin, works to spark and support the "academic, social, and emotional development of young people through the arts" (Creative Action 2019).

20    Race Forward: The Center for Racial Justice Innovation is a racial justice organization that "catalyzes racial justice movement building. In partnership with communities, organizations, and sectors, we build strategies to advance racial justice in our policies, institutions, and culture" (Race Forward 2019).

21    Alternate ROOTS is an arts organization based in the Southern United States that "supports the creation and presentation of original art that is rooted in community, place, tradition or spirit" (Alternate ROOTS 2019).

22    In working to be responsive we draw on approaches outlined by Lisa M. Landreman and Christopher MacDonald-Dennis in *The Art of Effective Facilitation*, "Multicultural education began as a radical approach to education toward greater equity and is now seen by social justice educators as an approach that was ineffective at challenging oppression and inequality. To these critics, key components of a social justice approach include movement away from becoming an expert of a particular culture but instead toward raising one's own and others' critical consciousness. This process involves gaining complex knowledge of history, contemporary issues, cultures and experiences, and engaging in relationship building, reflection, and action" (2013, pp. 14–15).

23    In Landreman and MacDonald-Dennis' chapter, they touch on diversity in American higher education starting as early as 1790, but spend the bulk of the section detailing the evolution of social justice education in higher education from the 1960s to the present. Their timeline details shifting attitudes within higher education from assimilation-based strategies to curriculums that centered more on multiculturalism and look toward challenging "the assumptions, practices, and norms embedded in the notion that we live in a homogeneous society" (Landreman and MacDonald-Dennis 2013, p 7).

24    Paulo Freire and bell hooks explore education as the practice of free-dom in several books: *Pedagogy of the Oppressed* (Freire 2018), *Teaching to Transgress: Education as the Practice of Freedom* (hooks 1994), and *Teaching Community: A Pedagogy of Hope* (hooks 2003).

25    The Chinese Exclusion Act of 1882 was signed into law by Chester Arthur and prohibited all Chinese immigration to the United States. For more information, see *Archives of the West from 1877–1887: Documents on Anti-Chinese Immigration Policy* (PBS 2001).

26    The definitions and explanations of "Gender attribution," "Gender identity," and "Gender expression" have been developed using resources provided by GLSEN (2019d).

27    Gender pronouns are sometimes referred to as "preferred" gender pronouns. We do not use the language of preferred as it indicates a choice rather than an authentic representation of one's individual and personal identity. Someone who is cisgender also does not have preferred pronouns – pronouns describe our gender and are not a preference, they reflect who we are.

28    Misgendering is the act of referring to someone by using the wrong pronouns—either in front of the person or in reference to them when they are not present. When someone is misgendered, it is important to acknowledge the mistake, shift to appropriate pronouns, and move on. Spending too much time apologiz-ing or explaining why a mistake was made can become embarrassing for the person impacted, drawing more attention than they desire. Similarly, when we hear the wrong pronouns being used for someone not present, the best way to be an ally to the person not present is to gently and consistently remind and shift to the correct pronouns.

29    GLSEN publishes a range of resources about pronouns for educators and youth. For more information see *Pronouns: A Resource for Education* (GLSEN 2019c).

30    In her book, *Storytelling for Social Justice*, Lee Ann Bell draws on the con-cepts developed by Audrey Thompson in her 1997 article, "For: Anti-Racist Education." Thompson's article addresses the need for anti-racist pedagogy to include elements of art and performance. Bell uses Thompson's ideas about art and performance as tools for combatting racism to expand on how the arts give us a unique perspective for addressing the pervasiveness of racism (Bell 1997).

31    In his presentations to educators, Duncan-Andrade references conclusions that can be drawn from the work of Robert M. Sapolsky, Brené Brown, Nadine Burke-Harris, David Williams, Bruce McEwen, and Elizabeth Blackburn, among others.

## References for Part One

Adams, M., Bell, L. A. and Griffin, P. (1997) *Teaching for diversity and social justice: A source book*, New York: Routledge.

Alrutz, M. (2015) *Digital storytelling, applied theatre, & youth: Performing possibility*, New York: Routledge.

Alternate ROOTS (2019) viewed June 10, 2019, https://alternateroots.org/about-us/

Arao, B. and Clemens, K. (2013) 'From safe spaces to brave spaces: A new way to frame dialogue around diversity and social justice,' in L. Landreman (ed.), The art of effective facilitation: Reflections from social justice educators, Sterling: Stylus Publishing LLC, pp. 135–150.

Baim, C. (2017) 'The Drama Spiral: A decision-making model for safe, ethical, and flexible practice when incorporating personal stories in applied theatre and performance,' in A. O'Grady (ed.), Risk, participation, and performance practice: Critical vulnerabilities in a precarious world, Cham: Palgrave Macmillan, pp. 79–109.

Baim, C. (2018) Theatre, therapy and personal narrative: Developing a framework for safe, ethical, flexible and intentional practice in the theatre of personal stories, doctoral thesis, University of Exeter, Exeter.

Barnes, S. (2009) 'Drawing a line: A discussion of ethics in participatory arts with young refugees,' in S. Barnes (ed.), Participatory arts with young refugees, London: Arts in Education, Oval House Theatre, pp. 34–40, viewed June 10, 2019, https://baringfoundation.org.uk/wp-content/uploads/2009/05/YoungRefugee.pdf

Bell, L. A. (1997) 'Theoretical foundations for social justice education,' in M. Adams, L. A. Bell and P. Griffin (eds.), Teaching for diversity and social justice: A source book, New York: Routledge, pp. 3–15.

Bell, L. A. (2010a) Storytelling for social justice: Connecting narrative and the arts in antiracist teaching, New York: Routledge.

Bell, L. A. (2010b) 'Theoretical foundations,' in M. Adams, w. Blumenfeld, C. (R.) Castañeda, H. Hackman, M. Peters, and X. Zúñiga (eds.), Readings for diversity and social justice, 2nd ed., New York: Routledge, pp. 21–26.

Bell, L. A., Castañeda, C. (R.), and Zúñiga X. (2010) 'Racism: Introduction,' in M. Adams, w. Blumenfeld, C. (R.) Castañeda, H. Hackman, M. Peters, and X. Zúñiga (eds.), Readings for diversity and social justice, 2nd ed., New York: Routledge, pp. 59–66.

Bell, L. A. and Desai, D (2011) 'Imagining otherwise: Connecting the arts and social justice to envision and act for chance: Special issue introduction,' Equity & Excellence in Education, vol. 44, no. 3, pp. 287–295, viewed June 18, 2019, https://doi-org.ezproxy.lib.utexas.edu/10.1080/10665684.2011.591672

Bharucha, R. (1995) 'Contextualizing utopias: Reflections on remapping the present,' Theater, vol. 26, no. 1–2, pp 32–49, viewed June 9, 2019, https://doi-org.ezproxy.lib.utexas.edu/10.1215/01610775-26-1_and_2-32

Black Lives Matter (2019) viewed May 9, 2019, https://blacklivesmatter.com/about/

Blackless, M., Charuvastra, A., Derryck, A., Fausto-Sterling, A., Lauzanne, K., et al. (2000) 'How sexually dimorphic are we? Review and synthesis,' American Journal of Human Biology, vol.12, pp. 151–166.

Boal, A. (2002) Games for actors and non-actors, 2nd ed., trans. A. Jackson, London: Routledge.

Coates, T.-N. (2015) Between the world and me, New York: Spiegel & Grau.

Cohen-Cruz, J. (2005) Local acts: Community-based performance in the United States, New Brunswick: Rutgers University Press.

Cohen-Cruz J. (2010) Engaging performance: Theatre as call and response, New York: Routledge.

Creative Action (2019) viewed June 10, 2019, https://creativeaction.org/

Crenshaw, K. W. (1989) 'Demarginalizing the intersection of race and sex: A Black feminist critique of antidiscrimination doctrine, feminist theory and antiracist politics,' University of Chicago Legal Forum, vol. 1989, no. 1, pp. 139–167, viewed

June 9, 2019, https://chicagounbound.uchicago.edu/cgi/viewcontent.cgi?article=1 052&context=uclf

Crenshaw, K. W. (2016) *WOW keynote: On intersectionality*, viewed June 9, 2019, www. youtube.com/watch?v=-DW4HLgYPlA

Davis, J. H. and Behm, T. (1978) 'Terminology of drama/theatre with and for children: A redefinition,' *Children's Theater Review*, vol. 27, no. 1, pp. 10–11.

Dolan, J. (2005) *Utopia and performance: Finding hope at the theater*, Ann Arbor: University of Michigan Press.

Eisner, E. (2002) *The arts of the creation of mind*, New Haven: Yale University Press.

Freire, P. (2018) *Pedagogy of the oppressed*, 50th anniversary ed., trans. M. Bergman Ramos, New York: Bloomsbury Academic.

Gender Spectrum (2019) *Understanding gender*, viewed June 18, 2019, www. genderspectrum.org/quick-links/understanding-gender/

Glanton, D. (2018) 'As country listens to Florida teens, Black Lives Matter youths feel ignored,' *Chicago Tribune*, February 28, viewed June 9, 2019 www.chicagotribune. com/columns/dahleen-glanton/ct-met-florida-teens-black-lives-matter-dahleen-glanton-20180223-story.html

GLSEN (2019a) *Gender terminology: Discussion guide*, viewed June 18, 2019, www. glsen.org/sites/default/files/Gender%20Terminology%20Guide.pdf

GLSEN (2019b) *Gender terminology visual*, viewed June 18, 2019, www.glsen.org/sites/ default/files/Gender%20Terminology%20Visual.png

GLSEN (2019c) *Pronouns: A resource for education*, viewed June 18, 2019, www.glsen. org/article/pronouns-resource-educators

GLSEN (2019d) viewed June 19, 2019, www.glsen.org

Goodman, S. (2003) *Teaching youth media: A critical guide to literacy, video production, and social change*, New York: Teachers College Press.

Greene, M. (1995) *Releasing the imagination: Essays on education, the arts, and social change*, San Francisco: Jossey-Bass.

Grosz, E. (1994) *Volatile bodes: Toward a corporeal feminism*, Bloomington, IN: Indiana University Press.

Hackman, H. (2010) 'Sexism: Introduction,' in M. Adams, w. Blumenfeld, C. (R.) Castañeda, H. Hackman, M. Peters, and X. Zúñiga (eds.) *Readings for diversity and social justice*, 2nd ed., New York: Routledge, pp. 315–320.

Hanley, M. S. (2013) 'Introduction: Culturally relevant arts education for social justice,' in M.S. Hanley, G. Noblit, G. Sheppard, and T. Barone (eds.), *Culturally relevant arts education for social justice: A way out of no way*, New York: Routledge, pp. 1–11.

Heddon, D. (2008) *Autobiography and performance*, New York: Palgrave Macmillan.

History Matters: The U.S. Survey Course on the Web (2018) *Not all Caucasians are white: The Supreme Court rejects citizenship for Asian Indians*, viewed June 10, 2019, http://historymatters.gmu.edu/d/5076/

Hoare, L. (2013) 'Challenging facilitation: Training facilitators for Theatre for Dialogue programmes,' in A. Jackson and C. Vine (eds.), *Learning through theatre: The changing face of Theatre in Education*, 3rd ed., London: Routledge, pp. 142–154.

hooks, b. (1994) *Teaching to transgress: Education as the practice of freedom*, New York: Routledge.

hooks, b. (2003) *Teaching community: A pedagogy of hope*, New York: Routledge.

hooks, b. (2010a) *Teaching critical thinking: Practical wisdom*, New York: Routledge.

hooks, b. (2010b) 'Feminism: A movement to end sexist oppression,' in M. Adams, w. Blumenfeld, C. (R.) Castañeda, H. Hackman, M. Peters, and X. Zúñiga (eds.), *Readings for diversity and social justice*, 2nd ed., New York: Routledge, pp. 337–339.

interACT (2018) *Intersex 101: Everything you need to know*, viewed June 18, 2019, http://4intersex.org/wp-content/uploads/2018/07/4intersex-101.pdf

Jackson, A. and Vine, C. (2013) 'Introduction,' in A. Jackson and C. Vine (eds.), *Learning through theatre: The changing face of Theatre in Education*, 3rd ed., London: Routledge, pp. 1–17.

Jones, O. O. J. L., Moore, L. and Bridgforth, S. (eds.) (2010) *Experiments in a jazz aesthetic: Art, activism, academia, and the Austin Project*, Austin: University of Texas Press.

Landreman, L. (ed.) (2013) *The art of effective facilitation: Reflections from social justice educators*, Sterling: Stylus Publishing, LLC.

Landreman, L. and MacDonald-Dennis, C. (2013) 'The evolution of social justice education and facilitation,' in L. Landreman (ed.), *The art of effective facilitation: Reflections from social justice educators*, Sterling: Stylus Publishing, LLC.

Levitas, R. (2005) 'The future of thinking about the future,' in J. Bird, B. Curtis, T. Putnam, G. Robertson, and L. Tickner (eds.), *Mapping the future: Local cultures, global change*, New York: Routledge, pp. 256–265.

Lorber, J. (1994) *Paradoxes of gender*. New Haven: Yale University Press, viewed June 17, 2019, http://search.ebscohost.com.ezproxy.lib.utexas.edu/login.aspx?direct=true&db=nlebk&AN=52870&site=ehost-live

Me Too Movement (2018) *History & vision*, viewed June 9, 2019, https://metoomvmt.org/about/#history

Nelson, B. (2011) '"I made myself": Playmaking as a pedagogy of change with urban youth,' *Research in Drama Education: The Journal of Applied Theatre and Performance*, vol. 16, no. 2, pp. 157–172.

Never Again MSD (2019) viewed June 9, 2019, www.facebook.com/NeverAgainMSD

Nicholson, H. (2005) *Applied drama: The gift of theatre*, New York: Palgrave Macmillan.

Norris, M. (2010) *The race card project*, viewed May 15, 2019, https://theracecardproject.com

Performing Justice Project (2015) *The good in me/In my skin*, devised performance, Central Texas.

Performing Justice Project (2019) *PJP performance gallery*, viewed July 6, 2019, https://performingjusticeproject.org/project-category/gallery/Pollock, D. (2005) 'Introduction: Remembering,' in D. Pollock (ed.), *Remembering: Oral history performance*, New York: Palgrave Macmillan, pp. 1–18.

Prendergast, M. and Saxton, J. (eds.) (2009) *Applied theatre: International case studies and challenges for practice*, Bristol: Intellect.

Prentki, T. and Preston, S. (2009) 'Applied theatre: An introduction,' in T. Prentki and S. Preston (eds.), *The Applied theatre reader*, New York: Routledge, pp. 9–16.

Public Broadcasting Service (2001) *Archives of the west from 1877–1887: Documents on anti-Chinese immigration policy*, viewed June 10, 2019, www.pbs.org/weta/thewest/resources/archives/seven/chinxact.htm#act

Race Forward (2014) *Moving the race conversation forward: How the media covers racism, and other barriers to productive racial discourse*, viewed June 9, 2019, http://act.colorlines.com/acton/attachment/1069/f-0114/1/-/-/-/-/Racial_Discourse_Part_1.PDFwww.raceforward.org/research/reports/moving-race-conversation-forward

Race Forward (2015) *Race reporting guide*, viewed June 9, 2019, www.raceforward.org/sites/default/files/Race%20Reporting%20Guide%20by%20Race%20Forward_V1.1.pdf

Race Forward (2019) *New mission, new look* [email].

Roberts, R. A. (2005) *Radical movements: Katherine Dunham and Ronald K. Brown teaching toward critical consciousness*, New York: City University of New York Graduate Center.

Schechner, R. (2003) 'Performers and spectators transported and transformed,' in P. Auslander (ed.), *Performance: Critical concepts in literary and cultural studies*, vol. 1, London: Routledge, p. 270.

Sensoy, Ö. and DiAngelo, R. (2012) *Is everyone really equal? An introduction to key concepts in social justice education*, New York: Teachers College Press.

Sentencing Project (2017) *Fact sheet: Black disparities in youth incarceration*, viewed June 10, 2019, www.sentencingproject.org/publications/black-disparities-youth-incarceration/

Storycenter (2019) viewed June 9, 2019 www.storycenter.org/about

Taylor, P. (2003) *Applied theatre: Creating transformative encounters in the community*, Portsmouth, NH: Heinemann.

Thompson, A. (1997) 'For: Anti-racist education', *Curriculum Inquiry*, vol. 27, no. 1, pp. 7–44, viewed June 18, 2019, www-jstor-org.ezproxy.lib.utexas.edu/stable/1180053

Thompson, J. (2003) *Applied theatre: Bewilderment and beyond*, Oxford: Peter Lang Ltd.Urban Roots (2018) viewed June 10, 2019, https://urbanrootsatx.org/

Vaccaro, A. (2013) 'Building a framework for social justice education: One educator's journey,' in L. Landreman (ed.), T*he art of effective facilitation: Reflections from social justice educators*, Sterling: Stylus Publishing, LLC, pp. 23–44.

Wilcox, H. N. (2009) 'Embodied ways of knowing, pedagogies, and social justice: Inclusive science and beyond,' *NWSA Journal*, vol. 21, no 2, pp. 104–120, viewed June 9, 2019, www.jstor.org/stable/20628176

Witt, E. (2018) 'How the survivors of Parkland began the Never Again Movement,' *The New Yorker*, February 19, viewed June 9, 2019, www.newyorker.com/news/news-desk/how-the-survivors-of-parkland-began-the-never-again-movement

# Part Two

# Preparing Participants and Performing Justice

## 2.0 Introduction

A group of 26 young people take the stage and perform choreographed, overlapping eight-count movements that demonstrate the overwhelming roles and responsibilities already expected of them as people identified by their families and society as "young women." As the young artists embody the physical and emotional labor of "women's work" on stage, they also vocally perform a list of gendered expectations they experience from society:

> **In society, women are expected to...**
> Keep your legs crossed
> Keep your legs closed
> Have the food ready
> Take care of laundry & children
> Stay at home
> Go to work
> Have babies
> Take care of family
> Talk respectful & proper
> Dress nicely
> Be & stay sexy...
> (Performing Justice Project 2015)

Part Two of this book offers details about our process of working with youth to create and perform content that addresses racial and gender justice. We begin with an overview of how we work and how we devise, followed by detailed descriptions of and steps for facilitating performance actions that build toward an original, devised performance. Section 2.1, How We Work, is about how we show up to a Performing Justice Project. We describe many of the beliefs, values, and considerations that underpin our critically engaged and embodied approach to collaborating with youth. Section 2.2, How We Devise, details our process for creating original theatre work with young people, including our scaffolded and intentional design for making ensemble-based theatre with novice performers. Section 2.3, Performing Actions, Performing Justice, lays out our collection of performance actions, all of which details PJP's critically engaged approach to theatre games, devising, writing, storytelling, and movement improvisation. The performance actions are designed and curated to support the building of ensemble, as well as the exploration of PJP's core questions. Section 2.3.1 offers performance actions that build ensemble and work toward trust and belonging as a foundation for more challenging identity-based performance actions. Section 2.3.2 asks young people to dive into the question *Who Am I?* as a way to name their own identity markers and explore positionality. The performance actions in Section 2.3.3 investigate the question *What is (In)Justice?* and explore the ways that individual experiences of injustice are related to identity-based, systemic oppression. Finally, Section 2.3.4, How Do I Perform Justice?, explores individual and ensemble-driven performance work as pathways for action and justice, offering concrete possibilities for publicly performing gender and racial justice through theatre.

With a focus on preparing to devise, producing small bits of performance (Johnston and Brownrigg 2019), and performing justice, our approach to devising and our collection of performance actions presents facilitators with ideas for creating visually dynamic and critically engaged theatre with novice performers.

## 2.1 How We Work

THIS I BELIEVE
This I believe.
That laws should be enforced to protect the equal rights for women.
Not to break families apart.
I am 20 years old and have a 4 year old son and I am 7 months pregnant. My babies are not an accident. They are wanted and they are my motivation to keep reaching up higher in life.
Therefore, I believe every woman should have the right to plan her parenthood with the same opportunities as any other human being.
I believe women should have the power to rule and state their authority. In my relationship we both rule when we feel we have to and I am respected as he is. Neither one of us put down the other because we are aware that we both have the ability to provide for our family.
I believe no woman should judge, disrespect or put down another woman.
I believe that as a woman I should do something when another woman is getting hurt.
I believe we all should get together and start fighting for what we really want which is "equal rights" for all of us.

(Performing Justice Project 2011)

We built the Performing Justice Project as a participatory and embodied way of reflecting on and working toward justice. While PJP is adult-led, it is also youth-informed. By listening closely to the experience and wisdom of young people, as well as the ways in which they wish to work, we aim to foster a sense of belonging and accountability among members of a youth ensemble and later with an audience. When developing this program, we identified core values and shared beliefs that guide our performance practices or ways of working in PJP. Over time, our relationship to these values and beliefs has shifted, often in response to our direct work with young people, different institutions, and community partners. Table 2.1 outlines some of the values and beliefs currently at the heart of PJP, as well as an overview of how they practically play out in our PJP work with youth. It informs both the form and content of our PJP residencies. Taken together, these values, beliefs and practices offer an approach to performing justice with young people. We hope the information in this section inspires your own intentional ways of creating, facilitating, and directing justice-oriented theatre that amplifies the voices of young people.

## Values: What Are the Shared, Core Values that Inform Our PJP Process?

The first column of Table 2.1 outlines five key values that inform both our process and products in PJP. These values signal what is important to us and ultimately help us prioritize practices and resources as we plan a residency, as well as who and what is centered in our creative practices. Our first core value is collaboration, or the intentional practice of working together as an ensemble to complete a task or create something new. We also value hard work and serious play. While PJP addresses critical and difficult topics of injustice, every session with youth includes theatre warm-ups, games, or tasks that are physically engaging and hopefully feel playful and fun. We choose performance actions with the intention of fostering moments of joy and

Table 2.1 How we work: PJP values, beliefs, and practices

| Values | Beliefs | How we work (practices that arise from values and beliefs) |
|---|---|---|
| Collaboration | Possibilities for change arise out of working with others to imagine and create something new. | Facilitator self-actualization (pre-work, and ongoing work) |
| Hard work and serious play | Ensemble-based play supports and sustains difficult work. | Flexibility and adaptability |
| Experience and wisdom of young people | Young people have abilities and capacities to make change. | Shared power |
| Opportunities for belonging | Ensemble-based theatre and sharing stories can create a sense of connection and belonging. | Ethos of play, participation, and exchange |
| Gender and racial justice | Devised theatre, namely the sharing and performing of stories, can reimagine narratives and enact justice. | Reflection and dialogue  ·  Devised performance |

laughter. We also value the experience and wisdom of young people as a necessary component of PJP and the process of achieving justice. We work from the belief that young people are not simply future assets or contributors to society once they reach adulthood. Rather, we understand and prioritize the notion that young people are necessary members of our communities *now* with critical perspectives on the world. Like adults, they deserve arts experiences as a part of daily life and they contribute meaningful knowledge about what justice looks like in our communities. We value opportunities to foster belonging by building positive relationships and feelings of connection with and to a group. This includes discovering similarities, but also finding opportunities to connect across difference. Finally, we value gender and racial justice, including but not limited to a focus on inclusion, equity, access, and belonging. We understand that our own liberation and freedom, particularly as white cis-women, is bound to the liberation and freedom of all women, trans and non-binary people, people of color, and any person or group of people that experiences identity-based oppression and marginalization.

## Beliefs: What Are the Shared, Core Beliefs that Underpin Our PJP Process?

The middle column in Table 2.1 details some of our shared, core beliefs that grow out of our PJP values. By reading the chart from left to right, you can see that we value collaboration, which is directly linked to our belief that possibilities for change arise out of working together to share and perform one's own and others' stories. We also believe that ensemble-based play supports and sustains difficult work. We combine playful, embodied theatre actions with the exploration of serious and often challenging topics that come up around racial and gender (in)justice. We value the experience and wisdom of young people, honoring their abilities, capacities, and ideas as an essential component of making positive change in the world today. We also believe that a sense of belonging is critical for everyone, and specifically young people, to thrive in their schools and communities. We trust that participating in ensemble-based theatre and sharing stories and experiences can help create a sense of belonging and connection to others for youth participants. Finally, our values of gender and racial justice underpin our belief that devised theatre can and does reimagine narratives about our lives, supporting the conditions to imagine change and enact justice.

## Practices: What are the Central Practices that Reflect Our Values and Beliefs?

Our values are evident in the beliefs listed above and also manifest as specific practices in the room. Rather than moving straight into a list of performance actions, here we attempt to think through practices that are central to the what and how of PJP. What are the specific practices that allow us to work as youth-allied adults? How does one create a piece of highly personal, original performance with young people? How can we hold space to examine the lived stories of racial injustice and sexism and still move forward at the end of the day, together? "How We Work" acknowledges our practices at the very center of how we run a Performing Justice Project. We have identified the following practices as intrinsic to any PJP process:

- Facilitator self-actualization
- Flexibility and adaptability
- Shared power
- Ethos of play, participation, and exchange
- Reflection and dialogue
- Devised performance

These practices are informed by and activated through all of the values and beliefs we have identified. For example, the way we share power informs how we collaborate, how we play together, how we value youth voice and experience, how we cultivate opportunities for belonging, and how we envision racial and gender justice. Because how we work is central to what the Performing Justice Project is and what it does, we discuss each practice individually below.

## Facilitator Self-actualization

We believe that working with youth around gender and racial justice requires and calls artists and facilitators to do their own work around self-actualization. In *Teaching to Transgress*, bell hooks reminds readers that "Teachers must be actively committed to a process of self-actualization that promotes their own well-being if they are to teach in the manner that empowers students" (1994, p. 15). In other words, prior to and throughout facilitating a PJP residency, facilitators must take on the personal work of actively reflecting on our own identities, privileges, and biases. How do racism, sexism, and other oppressive thinking/behavior show up in our ways of working, interacting, and creating? How does our access to power, based on our personal identity markers, inform how we collaborate, share leadership, and value youth voice? Gender and racial justice work necessitates that facilitators actively undo and (especially for those who benefit from white privilege) unlearn white supremacy in our daily lives, not simply in rehearsal with young people. Without this ongoing work toward self-actualization, we can damage relationships we are attempting to build and subconsciously—or even consciously— recreate oppressive structures and situations that impact the lives of young people.

As facilitators/directors, we have grown up within structures that often mask systemic racism and sexism. At times, this has meant that we fail to notice oppression because we are acculturated to such systems and often benefit from them. We have learned that we must be willing to continually interrogate our own ideas, choices, and assumptions and hold ourselves and each other accountable for messy and dangerous spots that arise. Without continual interrogation, transparency, and well-placed questions to assess one's own unconscious bias, a PJP project can reify power and privilege, leaving youth disconnected and marginalized. Doing political/social/civically engaged work means we have to grapple with the same questions we ask youth to grapple with:

- Who am I?
- What is (in)justice and how does it show up in my life?
- How do I perform justice?

This work necessarily digs into identity/identities, and if we, as directors/facilitators, enter a PJP process believing we have nothing to learn about ourselves and have done all of our own necessary work, we close ourselves off from opportunities to reflect on and realize the impact of our words, actions, and beliefs. PJP requires everyone involved to remain curious and open to learning—about oneself and about each other. Drawing on social justice education models (see Section 1.3), we understand that we can't move towards justice if we haven't examined how we each benefit from our own identity markers; how we resist, participate in, or collude with systems of power actively or passively; and how we prohibit justice by our own lack of awareness, resistance to change, or unwillingness to speak up.

As two white, cisgender, adult women engaged in racial and gender justice work with youth, we believe it is necessary to model open, frank conversation about our own racial and gender identities, coupled with the ways our privilege and power show up in both the world and PJP. Young people, no matter their identities, don't necessarily come to PJP believing in an adult commitment to thinking about race and gender, or an adult willingness to acknowledge their power in authentic and meaningful ways with youth. In acknowledging our own racial identities as white women, we talk about the unearned privileges that come with that whiteness in our racist society. While acknowledging our racial identities and unearned privilege is important, we also work to move discussions on race beyond a focus on whiteness or the experiences of white people. We believe that demonstrating an active commitment to critically conscious conversations means moving beyond talking about diversity, difference, or tolerance and toward the ways that systemic racism functions to give white people power at the expense of non-white people. In addition, we acknowledge to youth how our white privilege intersects with our cisgender privilege (and specifically name ways that we benefit in our daily lives from those privileged identities). These acknowledgments often prompt participants to think about their own gender and racial identities and expressions, including the ways that gender is narrowly constructed in school, family settings, and society at large, and/or the unearned privileges they or those around them might hold. As we invite young people to respond to writing prompts and engage in performance-making about their relationships to gendered and racialized constructs, we share examples from our own lives and work, as well as examples from artists of color, trans and non-binary folks. Finally, as our adult privilege intersects with our racial and gender privilege, we aim to be transparent about the fact that PJP is adult-led and youth-informed. In most cases, youth already see and understand many of the ways we, specifically as white adults, hold power and privilege in the world. As we acknowledge our own identities and privileges, we make an active commitment to work toward gender and racial justice in our PJP practices and in our daily lives. We've learned that both within the structure of PJP and the larger contexts of social justice work "constant vigilance and courage are required to challenge patterns of domination and subordination" (Bell 2010, p. 110). To prepare for this work, we have included suggestions and questions for facilitators, directors, and teaching artists in Section 3.1, Director/Facilitator Preparation. Making these commitments visible and making them together with PJP participants helps build group action and accountability to one another.

## Flexibility and Adaptability

The Performing Justice Project reminds us that working thoughtfully toward gender and racial justice requires an ongoing commitment to flexibility and adaptability. For us, practicing flexibility means a willingness and ability to make short-term and long-term changes or alterations to a PJP process based on the needs/desires of people in the room or the needs of a community partner. This often means having to balance priorities such as achieving high production values while also responding to the skills of participants and the limitations of any given partnership or project. It also means cultivating practices that remain responsive to current events in the room and in society. This may mean making time to record youth voiceovers for a performance in case young people struggle to be present (physically or emotionally) in rehearsal each day or in case anyone finds it too challenging or too risky to perform lines out loud or participate in live, embodied work. Practicing adaptability also means attending to longer-term or systemic needs for program changes, such as putting more resources and attention toward trauma-informed pedagogy and "healing-centered practices" (Ginwright 2018), as well as responding to changing vocabularies around gender identity, or leaning into alternate models of leadership for an ensemble or partnership. We plan each daily session and PJP residency in great detail knowing that many things will change once we are in the room. We ask ourselves if and how we can be responsive and responsible to the young people in PJP and to the critical content, engaged pedagogy, and performance frames that inform our process. While PJP is informed by a set of core values and beliefs, we are doing our jobs well when participants in the room drive the conversations, the questions, and the performance work. bell hooks writes in *Teaching to Transgress* that "the engaged classroom is always changing. Yet this notion of engagement threatens the institutionalized practices of domination. When the classroom is truly engaged, it's dynamic. It's fluid. It's *always* changing" (hooks 1994, p. 158). We know that who is in the room matters. Lived experience matters. Listening to what is called for in any given moment matters. PJP asks us to grow and learn, to flex and adapt in each moment and throughout a project.

## Shared Power

Social justice education, engaged pedagogy, and feminist pedagogy underpin the Performing Justice Project. Stephani Etheridge Woodson writes about community-based theatre models that move away from two prominent ways of working: (1) skills-based residencies led by teaching artists with little focus on a product, and (2) the often hierarchical and strictly defined relationships between directors and actors supported by many regional theatres, often focused largely on a performance product (2015, pp. 85–86). In conversation with Woodson's theories about ways of working that might transcend this binary, we strive to be youth-allied adults,[1] namely creative partners who understand that our own (adult) liberation is bound to the liberation of youth. We acknowledge to participants that PJP is adult-led and within that model we are committed to facilitating youth-informed and youth-responsive projects. This means that although PJP facilitators and teaching artists create partnership models, identify program goals, and plan sessions, they also create opportunities for young people to shape the performance, influence decisions in the room, and offer feedback to peers and adults in the project. Woodson reminds us that "Adult facilitators walk into the studio with specific knowledge of benefit to the ensemble, but everyone in the room holds knowledge and ability—capital—no matter their age" (2015, p. 85). In other words, we strive to acknowledge the assets and skill sets that both youth participants and adult facilitators bring to each Performing Justice Project. We begin from a practice of inquiry around identity, experience, and justice. We share decision-making with youth participants and locate creative control of their performance materials in their hands. Guest artists often lead workshops that explore singing, spoken word, or other skills and performance forms requested by the group. Responding to participants' curiosities, questions, and lived experiences, we bring in material and information about gender and racial justice from a variety of people and sources. We couple the ensemble's interests with our own stories, knowledge, and skills, creating a shared space for creativity and reciprocity. This means that every Performing Justice Project looks different, employing a variety of performance forms and inquiries related to aspects of gender and racial justice.

With these efforts to share power among adults and youth, PJP activates our commitment to work as youth-allied adults within a co-intentional practice: facilitators and students are both teachers and learners in various moments, deepening the knowledge of all involved. As directors, our major task becomes to listen intently to participants in order to inform the work and create a reciprocal process in the room. We work to disrupt top-down power dynamics between adults and youth in PJP by centering the experience and wisdom of young people and focusing on what it looks like for adult facilitators to actively create in alliance with young people. "Our view of young people and our relationship to their identity and development directly underpins how and to what end we (adult practitioners—and the likely reader of this book) facilitate performance practices with them" (Alrutz 2015, p. 24). In PJP, this means remaining constant learners and curious and responsive partners in the room. Building on theory and practice from Paulo Freire and bell hooks, we look for multiple ways to open youth access to language and other tools that support critical engagements with the world.

## Ethos of Play, Participation, and Exchange

Young people often find themselves in positions of responsibility, facing deep challenges at home, in school, and in their communities. As systemic oppressions impact their lives, it becomes an act of justice to make space for play, physical activities/actions/games, group participation, and an exchange of knowledge and experience. Therefore, we intentionally choose and create performance actions with an ethos of play and participation.

As laid out in Table 2.1, we believe that possibilities for change arise out of working with others to imagine and create something new. In the Performing Justice Project, this means that we center play and a sense of playfulness to help move away from self-conscious participation and toward opportunities for imaginative creation. We begin each session by inviting young people to engage in theatre games and interactive actions even when it might feel silly or embarrassing. The PJP process asks young people to explore their own boundaries as they build comfort in using their bodies and voices in new ways or in ways that are often reserved for younger children. Expressing playfulness requires a deep level of vulnerability for many of the teens with whom we work, and in the beginning of a PJP residency, many participants resist our invitation to play and practice joy and silliness in our program setting. We work to build the group's capacity to be playful together, as a way to access laughter, build joyful connections within the group, and to relate to one another in ways that society discourages as we get older. Many of the performance actions in PJP ask young people to practice full use of their bodies and we notice that the physical work results in laughter, exchange, and connection. Through the invitation to participate in a playful group experience, to see and be seen by one another, young people often experience a sense of belonging, even if only temporarily. We find that building the capacity to play, laugh, and share experiences as a group lays a necessary foundation for creating theatre and performing justice together. While the work and content of gender and racial justice is serious, we know that group play—ensemble-based play as laid out in PJP actions—supports and helps sustain the difficult work of imagining and performing justice.

## Reflection and Dialogue

As a matter of practice, we weave reflection and opportunities for dialogue through-out the PJP process and occasionally within a PJP performance itself. In addition to reflecting on one's own experiences and identities throughout the process, we struc-ture opportunities for youth participants to engage in reflection and reflexivity—reflection on self—through creative writing, journaling, drawing, and improvised movement and embodied tableaux. Our performance actions invite participants to reflect on their beliefs and experiences, as well as the contexts and systems that shape those experiences. We intentionally end each daily PJP session with reflection actions and questions designed to build connections among participants and adult facilitators. These reflection actions and questions are also designed to deepen par-ticipants' knowledge of gender and racial justice, and theatre and performance.

Within the PJP process, reflection often occurs in moments of active dialogue. Communication scholars Kenneth N. Cissna and Rob Anderson address the nature and value of public dialogue, suggesting that authentic dialogue requires "settings and attitudes that enable unique 'moments of meeting,'" or opportunities to connect, listen, and be changed by an exchange with someone else (2002, back cover). PJP aims to sup-port the conditions for such "moments of meeting" by structuring opportunities for conversation, debate, and group problem-solving. Through performance actions such as Vote with Your Feet (Section 2.3.2), participants reflect on their own lives, share a point of view about gender or race, and then talk with each other about the connections and points of departure between various perspectives, beliefs, and understandings sur-rounding a particular topic or issue in society. In addition, PJP sometimes builds direct dialogue between the performers and the audience through pre- and/or post-show discussions, talk-backs, and moments of audience interaction. Finally, the performance itself presents a performed dialogue of sorts, illustrating how specific issues and per-spectives are in conversation with each other in society and in the youths' lives. For example, movement improvisation, scene work, and a series of poems or monologues come together to demonstrate how racial injustice intersects with educational access and binary gender expectations of young people. Drawing on the work of Buber and Rogers, Cissna and Anderson remind us again that "dialogue is neither an ongoing state nor an empty aspiration, but instead a matter of momentary insight that is hard-won and ephemeral but at the same time potentially life-changing" (2002, xviii). In other words, the practices of dialogue and reflection in a PJP residency prove critical to creat-ing the necessary conditions for personal insights and systemic change.

## Devised Performance

While staging and performing scripted plays can certainly support gender and racial justice efforts, PJP focuses on the practice of devising original performance material as a way of imagining and enacting justice. By inviting young people to create and per-form original performance material about their lives and communities, PJP works to center their often silenced or marginalized experiences and perspectives. We believe that possibilities for change in society arise out of working with others to imagine and perform something new. The practice of devising in PJP, and specifically working as an ensemble to create original performance material, invites and values the experience and wisdom of young people as critical to justice efforts.

In the US, the titles of artist, story-maker, or writer are reserved largely for adults. In *Culturally Relevant Arts Education for Social Justice*, Mary Stone Hanley reminds us that the capacity to create culture belongs to everyone.

> The capacities of imagination, creativity, and agency are ways of knowing and doing that belie the powerlessness of the oppressed; subjugated people, whether because of race, national origin, class, gender, language, age, or sexual orientation, have in their hands and minds the power to create like those with privilege because all humans create culture.
>
> (Hanley 2013, pp. 3–4)

Devising performance similarly offers "ways of knowing and doing that belie the powerlessness of the oppressed" (Hanley 2013, p. 3). Making original theatre then serves as a pathway to naming the present, imagining possibilities for change, and enacting justice. Devised theatre is a central practice for us in our work alongside youth to perform justice. It produces critically engaged and critically conscious theatre that both comments on racial and gender (in)justice and imagines and performs the specific conditions of justice for all.

## 2.2 How We Devise

It was week two of a PJP residency in a juvenile detention facility. We were working with 15 young people, ages 14 to 20. The ensemble was finalizing individual bits of writing—poems, scenes, and stories—and each participant was invited to choose a piece of their work to put forward for the performance script. One of the youth was struggling with a particularly violent narrative—she wanted to include it in the performance, but she didn't want to perform it herself. She also felt certain the story was "too much" and that no one else would want to perform it either. We scanned her journal as she held it in her hands. The story began playfully with "Once upon a time..." and then quickly began to detail the story of a young girl who was kidnapped and sex trafficked as she tried to escape a family situation that was crumbling around her. She knew the story well. Her words on the page ended with two big ideas: a solemn recognition that life is far from being a fairytale and a call to action for all of the "princes" of the world to "get their shit together." Ultimately, this young writer decided to read her story to a small group of peers and get some feedback on whether or not to include it in the larger script. As the last words of the story rolled off her tongue, several hands went up in the air:

> "I'll perform that story..."
> "I want to perform this one..."
> "What if we perform this one as a group?"

This story illustrates one of the ways that the PJP devising process focuses on relational practice as a pathway to justice. Moisés Kaufman and Barbara Pitts McAdams, authors of *Moment Work: Tectonic Theater Project's Process of Devising Theater*, explain that "The popular term *devised theater* is used to describe creative processes in which a script is developed through improvisation and collaborative group work" (2018, 20). In this section of the book, we detail our approach to improvising and collaboratively devising a script with an ensemble of 5 to 30 young people. We include some of our overarching practices, such as daily rituals and an emphasis on story-sharing, as well as our step-by-step process for devising (preparing, producing, and performing) original theatre with young people. While the PJP process remains organic and situationally responsive, we offer a solid framework for both facilitating and directing ensemble-based devising with groups of novice performers.

Leading a PJP devising process often requires fluid movement between facilitating the creative process and directing the performance for a public audience. In this way, our devising practices resonate with those of longstanding ensemble-based theatre companies that are similarly interested in socially engaged theatre. In *Ensemble-Made Chicago: A Guide to Devised Theater*, Chloe Johnston and Coy Paz Brownrigg remind us that many of our documented ensemble-based theatre practices grow out of work from Neva Boyd and Viola Spolin, both of whom were connected to the Settlement House movement in Chicago (2019, xi–xvi).

> Ensemble-based or devised process is a way of creating theater that welcomes the ideas and contributions of everyone in the room, that relies on a collective vision rather than the singular vision of a playwright or a director. Ensemble process rejects a predetermined hierarchy in favor of figuring out what works best *this* time, with *these* particular people. It happens in the spaces between people, it responds to the space, it responds to the world outside the space because the people in the room can't help but bring it in. It models a world where people are valued equally and welcomed as they are, for what they are able to give. Ensemble-created work models democracy in inspiring ways.
>
> (Johnston and Brownrigg 2019, p. x)

To this end, PJP residencies begin with a series of performance actions that help build relationships in the room. We scaffold youth engagement from lower-risk group participation to brave(r) spaces for autobiographical writing and staging of individual and group narratives. We invite young people to share, reflect on, and stage what theatre-makers Chloe Johnston and Coy Paz Brownrigg call small "bits of performance" (2019, p. xviii), such as a poem, a short scene, a movement improvisation, or a titled tableau. Simultaneously, we work toward a curated frame and arrangement of those bits of performance into a larger script, a performance treatment, or a performance outline. In thinking about a larger performance arc for the devised pieces, we explore several possibilities for how to arrange, sequence, and connect everything together. We consider the relationships between form and function and ask if and how the devised pieces suggest a collage-style script, a linear narrative script, moments of non-realism, or another shape or form altogether.

The shape of the performance remains open-ended at first and we facilitate a series of actions to begin the devising process. We invite and encourage participants to respond to prompts and provocations through creative writing, embodied stage pictures, improvisational scenes, gestures or movement phrases, and other small bits of performance. They then share those bits of writing and performance with each other—combining, arranging, building on, and refining each other's work. Participants continue to develop select pieces, working in small groups to explore different ways to vocalize, physicalize, and otherwise represent their small segments of performance. Toward the end of a PJP residency, the directors work with the youth participants to determine which bits will move into the larger performance for an audience, as well as how the bits might be linked together to form a more cohesive whole.

## Our Approach to Ensemble-based Devising

When facilitating PJP, we focus on a creative process for devising small bits of performance and a dramaturgical practice for structuring and staging those elements into a cohesive whole. The Tectonic Theater Project, known for devising original work that invites social and political engagement with audiences, divides their devising process into two similar tasks which they call "creating sequences" and "editing sequences" (Kaufman and McAdams 2018). The Tectonic Theater Project directors suggest a clear divide between their generative process and their editorial process:

> In rehearsal, we have discovered that it is imperative that each process be given its own time and kept separate ... The two sets of priorities conflict if they're addressed at the same time, and that's why each process must be religiously guarded from the other. First, we create narrative; *then* we sculpt it.
>
> (Kaufman and McAdams 2018, 125)

Unlike Tectonic Theater Project and many other devising ensembles, we weave these steps together, both creating and editing narratives throughout each step of the PJP devising process. While we understand the potential tension at play in addressing the generative process and the refinement of product at the same time, devising with novice performers has taught us the value of simultaneously attending to the performance process and the final performance product. We support young participants by attending to and structuring their creative process as a place of discovery and creativity, while always following opportunities to move bits of performance into fully realized or sculpted performances pieces. Waiting until the end of a process to sculpt or begin to refine and stage the work can prove challenging when devising with large groups, preparing young artists to perform, and working on a restricted timeline. In PJP, participants need to see examples of how the text and movements they are generating can move into small bits of performance in order to understand what they are working toward.

## Creative Process

While the content varies with each residency, our daily PJP sessions follow a fairly standard creative practice. We love to set up routines and rituals so that participants can anticipate the flow of a PJP session.

**Table 2.2** PJP framework for daily creative process

| Check in | PERFORMANCE ACTIONS |
|---|---|
| | Invite participants to share how they are doing before engaging in devising work. |
| | Choose actions from: |
| | 2.3.1 What Is Ensemble? |
| Session overview | POST INFORMATION |
| | Offer participants a clear picture of the daily plan. |
| | Review a visual map or outline of the day's actions, including when breaks will occur. |
| Warm up | PERFORMANCE ACTIONS |
| | Invite participants to warm up their body, voice, and imagination. |
| | Choose actions from: |
| | 2.3.1 What Is Ensemble? |
| | 2.3.2 Who Am I? |
| Write/devise/embody/stage | PERFORMANCE ACTIONS |
| | Invite participants to create original bits of performance material. |
| | Choose actions from: |
| | 2.3.2 Who Am I? |
| | 2.3.3 What Is (In)Justice? |
| | 2.3.4 How Do I Perform Justice in My Daily Life? |
| Relate part to whole | DISCUSSION |
| | Support participants to work toward the unknown, build connections between performance actions and justice, and stay connected and motivated to complete something new. |
| | Discussion questions address: |
| | How small bits of performance relate to larger performance |
| | How the day's actions and reflections relate to participants' lives and society |
| Close with reflection | PERFORMANCE ACTIONS or DISCUSSION |
| | Invite participants to cement their own meaning-making, building connections and deepening understanding of the work at hand. |
| | Choose actions from: |
| | 2.3.4 How Do I Perform Justice in My Daily Life? (see Action and Reflection section) |
| | 2.3.4 How Do I Perform Justice? |

We usually begin by standing in a circle and engaging participants in Creative Introductions or a Check-In Circle (see Section 2.3.1, What Is Ensemble?). We offer transparency about the daily session plan by posting and reviewing an outline of the day's actions and noting where breaks will take place. We then move into warm-up actions focused on a particular performance skill such as warming up the body and voice or working as an ensemble. Following the warm-up, we engage participants in both individual and ensemble-based performance actions to imagine, improvise, write, and devise small bits of performance material. We draw on performance actions that create performative material such as poems, stories, and movement sequences. Before ending a session, we look for opportunities to notice and survey the work that has been created to cement big ideas, "ah-ha" moments, and other connection points.

We often end PJP sessions by reflecting on the day's work and building connections between the day's performance work and gender and racial justice. We help participants imagine how their bits of devised performance could later move into a larger performance or script. Many of our PJP participants have never participated in or seen devised theatre. Since the form is often new for them, we continually describe how their creative work is building toward a larger performance piece for a public audience. Our sessions usually end with a closing or a check-out action, such as It Made Me Think or a journaling prompt that invites reflection on the day's work.

This daily routine repeats throughout our residency process. Once a script draft is developed, we move into a rehearsal process during which bits of performance material get refined, expanded, or staged. Even in the rehearsal phase of PJP, we begin with a check-in and a warm up and end with an intentional and reflective closing action. Although not always necessary, we often include a snack break in our PJP sessions. We bring (or ask the community partner to provide) food and beverages, encouraging less-formal social time and extended opportunities to foster connections and conversations between participants. These rituals and routines offer a creative process which, over time, builds to a performance.

## Individual Experiences and Systems

As discussed in Section 1.3, our devising process focuses heavily on autobiographical story-sharing and storytelling as a way to witness and validate the experiences of young people. Performance actions focused on naming and developing stories are included throughout Part Two of this book. We often begin a PJP residency with an invitation to everyone to share something about themselves with the group. We offer open-ended prompts such as "what is something people might not know about you by looking?", inviting participants to share something personal and to practice putting their voice into the room. We use a variety of performance actions to invite young people to bring their individual lived experiences into the PJP process and to reflect on and name aspects of their identity. We like open-ended prompts that allow participants to control what and how much they share about themselves. We also move back and forth between provocations to respond to alone and invitations to share stories out loud with a partner or small group, as participants have different thresholds for sharing personal information and respond differently to written and oral modes of storytelling and story-sharing. Performance actions that access individual experiences and stories, through writing, talking, or embodiment, lay a foundation for deeper inquiries about identity and (in)justice later in the residency.

Importantly, we couple our process of devising from personal stories with an examination of systemic oppression. This means that we devise scenes and other bits of performance that speak to the ways that sexism and racism are reflected in participants' stories and how they play out in patterns that move beyond an individual experience. For example, to bring systems frameworks into our devising process, we introduce statistics and historical contexts that speak to the origins and impacts of gender and racial injustice in our communities. We sometimes bring in an info-graphic that shows statistics on how LGBTQIA youth and women of color are disproportionately impacted by school discipline policies and incarcerated at higher rates than their white, heterosexual, male counterparts. Working from the statistics and the group's dialogue about the systemic impacts of racism and sexism, participants then devise scenes, record voiceovers, and create movement/dance pieces that illuminate how power and oppression function. They devise bits of performance material that imagine a disruption or offer a response to systemic oppression. By making small bits of performance based in personal experience and/or systemic patterns of oppression, our devising process works to build an understanding of how systemic privilege and oppression show up in our lived experiences. Importantly, as young people share identity-based experiences with each other and simultaneously learn how systems work, they often make discoveries about how gender and racial injustice remain intact—not simply through individual actions, but also through systemic bias and seemingly invisible structures of power.

While we focus on the relationship between personal experiences, histories, and statistics in PJP, we also emphasize a practice of sharing and learning from patterns of experience among participants in the room. Statistics and histories demonstrate patterns that impact across identities, while personal story-sharing can reveal where and how sexism and racism gets perpetuated. Both systems and individual experiences reveal places where oppression might be disrupted. For example, statistics show that gender non-binary youth and youth of color often experience harsher disciplinary sentences in school than their white, cisgender peers. Story-sharing and devising among PJP participants might then reveal the bias inherent in many school dress-code policies or the kinds of racially biased comments and expectations that many students of color experience in school settings. The process of making and sharing performance on this issue can offer opportunities to imagine, name, and embody alternative ways of living and interacting and creative supportive learning environments regardless of one's identities.

Our devising process aims to place young people's stories in conversation with each other, and, at the same time, in conversation with historical patterns and current statistics about the large-scale impacts of gender and racial bias. By engaging participants around where and how oppression shows up in their lives and the world, we aim to make visible and reimagine some of the hidden and insidious ways that oppression functions.

## Participation and Agency

In each PJP residency, we ask that all ensemble members participate in the performance actions. At the same time, we practice flexibility in reaching this goal and in what that means or looks like for each participant to engage in the performance-making process. We try to vary our performance actions each day and create opportunities for youth to actively participate, witness, or support the process in ways that are possible and enjoyable for them.

As a way of centering youth participation and agency, we also pay close attention to casting and staging decisions throughout the devising process. Youth are encouraged to choose which of their stories and bits of performance they would like to include in the final performance, and to take an active role in casting and staging their own stories with other members of the ensemble. Throughout our devising process, we encourage youth to create work that is personal and meaningful to them. We then focus on maintaining each author's creative control over the performance of their stories, experiences, and theatrical work. We remind participants that their work can be anonymous and/or fictionalized. We offer strategies for moving from a personal experience into a creative performance text, a piece of poetic writing, or a movement piece, any of which might move away from realism or an obvious connection to a single participant's life story. We also remind PJP audiences that each story or performance piece may or may not belong to the individual who performs it. In fact, more often than not, multiple participants are writing about similar events—sex trafficking in their lives, racial profiling, learned racism and sexism from family and teachers. As a way of moving toward anonymity with the audience and communicating the widespread nature of particular racialized and gendered experiences, we offer PJP participants various ways to cast and stage each bit of performance; we support participants to make choices about their level of anonymity, about the visual representation of their experiences, and about if and how their life stories move into performance contexts or not.

Early on in PJP residencies, participants often imagine their stories are unique to them; they sometimes blame themselves for experiences of gender and racial injustice. However, as groups of youth work together to stage a scene, story, or monologue, they often begin to see how their different experiences share patterns of oppression with others in the group or in society at large. This reflection on the relationship between self and others can reveal the ways in which racial and gender bias play out as familial, cultural, and societal norms. Centering creative control with the youth participants—by supporting their casting and staging decisions—enacts justice. It can also activate new pathways for youth to perform justice, such as writing, vocalizing, performing movement, and/or directing their performance work for a public.

## Grouping Strategies for Devising

Making theatre with large groups of youth requires careful attention to grouping strategies throughout the devising and rehearsal process. We constantly strive to balance participants' desires around who they want to work with, who is interested to perform what material, and practical considerations that allow for efficiency in devising and rehearsing. At the risk of stating the obvious, if one participant is cast in three different scenes, those three scenes cannot all rehearse at the same time. To address this challenge, we remind participants that groups and casting may shift as we move into a final script or performance outline and we practice a lot of different groupings before we land on final performance groups and casting for any given piece of text. We borrow some of our logistical thinking on grouping from Johnny Saldaña's book *Drama of Color*, in which he outlines casting terms such as whole group, split halves, small groups, pairs, and individual roleplaying (1995, pp. 8–9). As we devise and move toward a performance, we structure our session plans with his grouping strategies in mind. We know, for example, that we will often begin and end the performance with a whole group performance piece such as a song, dance, or movement piece. We also aim to have one or two days where we focus on small group performance pieces, and we try to avoid double casting any one participant in more than one small group. If we have some pair work and some individual work, we might schedule pairs to rehearse at the same time as the solo work, ensuring that participants are either in a pair or working solo, but not both. When working with a large group, we might also split the group into halves. Small groups or pairs are then created within each split half and we avoid having small groups that include participants from both halves. Thinking ahead on the logistics of grouping and casting helps keep everyone involved at all times and has become a key organizational strategy for us as theatre-makers, and directors.

## Memorization

Within a three-week PJP residency, we do not focus on or ask youth to memorize lines. Instead, we focus our time and attention on gaining comfort with embodied movement, practicing physical and vocal expression of their ideas and stories, and making brave choices about how to put one's stories into public spaces as an action toward justice. Many of the youth in PJP do not have access to scripts outside of our designated PJP time and we also find that a fear of forgetting lines can prohibit youth from participating in theatre and performance work altogether. Given these realities, we often make an intentional choice to include small black binders containing the PJP script in every public performance. The small, hand-held scripts become part of the PJP aesthetic and we work to include poetic ways of holding and turning the pages as needed. For example, some participants might perform a poem from the page while other participants focus on movement improvisation that gets performed while text of the poem is shared. In addition, we often record and play audio of youth reading/performing poems, statistics, songs, dialogues, or stories. Playing recorded voiceovers through speakers can free participants to perform visual and physical scores with their bodies while not worrying about holding a script or memorizing lines. Our choice to move away from required memorization speaks both to our focus on process and our desire to support young people to perform for a public audience without the added anxiety of learning or forgetting lines. That being said, many youth ultimately learn or know their lines through the process of embodying and rehearsing their work again and again throughout our PJP process.

## Activate Material Early

We take the stance that everything we invite participants to do in PJP has the potential to become performance material, whether it is a warm-up action, a transition moment, a conversation about hashtags, or a writing exercise. Activating moments from the PJP process into performance requires that we constantly invite participants to bring their words to life, or more specifically to get on our feet and imagine how to share moments and materials with an imagined audience. By sharing, performing, or embodying at least one thing each day, we help participants see the impact and power that their stories and conversations contain for a witness. We model simple ways to layer vocal text and movement, or physical images and music. As directors and facilitators, we constantly guide participants to imagine new ways of activating or embodying their stories and experiences as they are being developed. We want participants to imagine their ideas and experiences as potential performance material, borrowing lines, sounds, images, and performance techniques/tools/frames from what is happening around them. (For example, participants have staged social media debates about Beyoncé's feminism, created hashtag activism stories, and played with masks as a representation of public/private and masculine/feminine selves.) By activating or embodying material early and often in the PJP process, we continue to blur the lines between creating and editing performance material. This process both prepares young people to perform and ensures that the materials created are performing justice, not simply presenting ideas about justice.

## Reflection and Reflexivity

Our devising process moves beyond creating a performance and sharing it with an audience. We also focus heavily on participant reflection and reflexivity as pathways toward developing critical consciousness and creating a critically engaged performance. Each of our performance actions include reflection questions that invite participants to reflect on the work they've created or participated in. In addition, our devising process includes reflection on the relationships between self and society, as well as individual experiences and systemic oppression. Finally, we devise with a focus on self-reflexivity, or a process of looking at and considering the implications of one's own relationships to gender and racial (in)justice. In practice, this might mean acknowledging cisgender and/or white privilege, looking at how white supremacy creates internalized messages of oppression for people of color, or figuring out how and why oppressive narratives shape beliefs about our racial and gender identity, ability, and access. We intentionally work to weave reflection and reflexivity into our daily devising practice, as well as the performance and the residency as a whole.

## Dramaturgical Weaving

The dramaturgy, namely the organization and structure of a PJP performance, grows out of our devising process and practices. In other words, we figure out the overall shape of the performance as we work on a particular project. Our devising process focuses on three things: (1) developing single elements of performance (such as text, movement, or sound); (2) imagining ways to move those bits or elements into fully realized performance pieces (such as scenes and movement pieces); and (3) determining how best to organize, group, and layer those elements into a larger performance structure and script. For example, we often begin devising with a focus on individual creative writing actions. Once a bit of text is written, we explore ways to activate the text, perhaps first through vocal performance and later through a physical score, embodied images, or choreographed movement phrases. In another approach, we might start with the creation of three tableaux or embodied images, and afterward move to oral storytelling or scene work with activated dialogue.

The dramaturgical process for creating a script becomes a practice of weaving—of going forward and then back, forward and then back again. We might move from written text to vocalization to staging through movement improvisation, or a physical score consisting of gesture work or choreography. After this initial work, we might revisit and revise the text or vocalization to better dance with the physical movement score. This process of weaving has many possible starting places. Our larger devising process similarly extends to the script as a whole. While we build a performance script from the bits of material devised in the room, putting the material together also reveals gaps in the performance script as a whole, suggesting places to go back and devise new bits of performance to fill out the performance arc or content as a whole.

## Supporting Novice Artists

We structure the PJP devising process specifically to support young artists, many of whom are new to creating and performing original performance work. In addition to scaffolding our devising process from lower to higher risk participation, supporting youth agency and decision-making, and responding to youth's interests and experiences in the room, we lean into aesthetics and artistry as yet another critical way of supporting novice performers. First, we attempt to learn about the aesthetic preferences of the participants—what music or artists inspire them, what kinds of images and symbols are important to them, what colors they are drawn to, and how they want their performance to make the audience feel. These initial conversations help us collect and bring music options into the creative process, as well as to narrow a color palette for t-shirts/costumes, and hone in on images to inspire a simple backdrop, environment, or set design. Grounding our project with elements of a youth aesthetic becomes not only a pathway for building relationships and trust with the group, but also produces design elements for the performance that both reflect the interests of and inspire the participants to imagine and perform something new.

Intentionality around design elements and movement in the space can also uplift the work of novice performers and draw audiences into the content at hand. For example, a strong sound design can enhance the emotional impact of a movement sequence by participants with little dance experience. Similarly, a beautiful scenic element can lift up a novice performer or writer, framing their work as important or special. Adding synchronized or choreographed movement on stage can make transitions engaging and/or amplify a simple gesture phrase by an ensemble that might otherwise feel self-conscious performing for the first time. As novice performers bravely share their performance work about gender and racial (in)justice, an often challenging topic for public audiences, lighting, sound/music, costumes, and scenic elements become important theatrical tools for unifying a novice ensemble and moving the performance beyond the ordinary experiences of the participants and the audience.

While small budgets and site/location rules often limit our choices around costumes, lighting, and sets, we continue to challenge our own creativity in these areas as a way of performing possibility and thus justice; building an aesthetic world that moves beyond the everyday experiences of both the participants and the audience proves an important pathway for imagining new ways of being, for enacting possibility, for performing justice.

## PJP Devising Structure

In addition to our daily rituals and devising practices outlined above, we also have an overarching devising process that is guided by our core PJP questions and is

**Table 2.3** PJP devising process

| Devising Phases | Goals | Performance Actions |
|---|---|---|
| Preparing to devise | Develop group agreements<br>Develop relational practices<br>Introduce project vocabularies<br>Play, write, create<br>Exchange stories | 2.3.1 What Is Ensemble?<br>2.3.2 Who Am I? |
| Producing small bits of performance | Write, create, stage, and perform bits of material<br>Explore constructs of race and gender<br>Explore power and oppression<br>Stage relationships between experiences and systems | 2.3.1 What Is Ensemble?<br>2.3.2 Who Am I?<br>2.3.3 What Is (In)Justice and How Does it Show Up in My Life? |
| Performing original ensemble-based performance | Develop script outline<br>Stage scripted material and transitions<br>Devise new material as needed<br>Solidify visual vocabulary<br>Consider audience engagement | 2.3.4 How Do I Perform Justice?<br>*Return to 2.3.1, 2.3.2, 2.3.3 as needed. |

structured into a three step process: *preparing* to devise, *producing* bits of original devised performance, and *performing* an original ensemble-based work.

In preparing to devise, which takes place over the first few days of a PJP residency, we employ performance actions from Sections 2.3.1, what Is Ensemble?, and 2.3.2, who Am I? These actions support building an ensemble and developing relationships that support a collaborative devising practice. We write group agreements as well as introduce vocabularies for exploring gender and racial (in)justice. Preparing to devise involves intentional efforts to play games, reflect on our identities, exchange stories, and begin writing and sharing short bits of performance.

To produce devised performance material, which is the middle piece of a PJP residency, we continue to lead performance actions from Section 2.3.2, who Am I?, and we delve into performance actions from Section 2.3.3, what Is (In)Justice and How Does it Show Up in My Life? In this phase of devising, we invite participants to individually and collectively write and perform short bits of performance. We lean into reflection and self-reflexivity to explore power and oppression, and to stage various relationships between individual experiences and systemic (in)justice. In this middle phase, we begin staging scenes, monologues, dance or movement sequences, and look for songs that speak to gender and racial justice. We also stage statistics and examine historical contexts that demonstrate the ways that systemic and institutionalized racism and sexism become seemingly fixed. Producing devised work also means weaving together and making sense of the relationships between individual stories and experiences from the participants and systemic, identity-based oppression.

As we move into performing original devised material, we employ actions from Section 2.3.4 How Do I Perform Justice? In this phase, we develop a script outline, organizing small bits of performance material into a larger performance arc with an intentional beginning and end. We also devise transitions and develop an emotional and visual heartbeat for the performance piece. At this time, we focus more on staging and design, and consider the performer/audience relationship. Once a preliminary script outline is agreed upon by the group (we usually create an outline, present it to the youth, and revise it based on their suggestions), we work as an ensemble to finalize casting and begin staging the discrete bits of performance (whole group pieces, scenes, monologues, pair work, etc.). We spend several days rehearsing and refining each bit of performance. We also add transitions and sound cues to create a cohesive performance from all of the small bits and pieces developed by the ensemble. This part of the process, performing original material, often reveals the need for some new performance material, such as a poem or scene that speaks to a current event or a performance piece that offers alternatives to a current injustice. Thus, this last phase of PJP often requires some last-minute devising with a keen focus on the already determined dramaturgy, or arc of the performance. Finally, at this point in the process, we also begin to plan how the audience will be invited to engage with the ensemble—possibly through a pre-show gallery walk, a post-show discussion, an invitation to join performers on stage, or moments of interaction during the performance itself.

Because we know young people's lives are steeped in inequities, we structure our devising process to focus first on their experiences and interests. We begin with reflections on self, then explore power and relationships with others, and finally address identity-based bias and relationships between self, others, and society. These three phases—namely preparing, producing, and performing—combined with the PJP performance actions, offer a framework for moving toward a critically engaged, hopeful theatre-making process.

## Doing Justice

## Snapping into Agency, Trust, and Craft

*Cortney McEniry*

My experiences as a teaching artist taught me that agency, trust, and craft are crucial to a process that honors and amplifies participants' artistic voices. One of my favorite ways to cultivate agency, trust, and craft in a devising process is to use a simple theatre game in several different ways. Over time, the game changes from an exercise that I teach to the group to a ritual that is owned and shaped by the group collaboratively.

One of my favorite theatre games is Pass the Snap. Participants pass a snap around and across a standing circle, keeping a rhythm of accepting and sending the snap from one to another. Pass the Snap provides an easy-to-learn baseline that strengthens soft skills like eye contact and listening, but it can also be built upon and used to meet specific goals around agency, trust, and craft.

Before beginning our PJP residency, my co-teaching artist Briana and I held an introductory session for interested participants at a detention center where we would be creating a PJP residency. I facilitated a game of Pass the Snap. The students mastered it quickly, and we began to use the game as a platform for more nuanced artistry and skills. I asked the students to make an aesthetic choice within the game, manipulating the shape, tempo, scale, or velocity of their snap to create a full-body movement rather than a single, simple snap. Snaps were sent around the circle like bowling balls, like whispers, like hot potatoes, and they were received as such, too.

Throughout the residency, we returned to this exercise. Some days, we would use it as a check-in, a trust-building ritual; when the snap was passed, participants would say one word to describe what they were bringing into the room emotionally and physically (i.e., a hurt knee, a hard day, a big hope). On other days, we used Pass the Snap as a word-association strategy to activate dialogue, asking participants to pass the snap and say a new word that came to mind when they heard activating words such as "justice" or "peace." When reflecting on a round of a word-association iteration of the game, one of the participants said, "We should do this for our play."

"That sounds like an interesting idea," I responded. "How do you envision that?"

"We'll do it [Pass the Snap] with the audience. They'll respond, too."

"Okay! So it will be interactive?" I said.

"Yeah, they'll do it with us, around the words we want, and we'll tell them how."

Briana and I worked with the students to craft clear language for the audience invitation and instructions for participation, and to determine what words would be used to prompt associative audience responses. The youth practiced this element of the play—the invitation and interaction with the audience—as much as any other, and when the performance day came, Pass the Snap became a powerful, unifying moment between artists and audience. Through repetition, revision, and reflection, Pass the Snap moved from an introductory exercise to an ensemble-building game, and then to a dialogue activator for an interactive performance moment. The young artists moved from learning the game structure to rewriting the rules, and finally to teaching it to others. What began as a silly game became a tool for supporting agency, trust, and craft in our Performing Justice Project.

Since this residency, my thinking around session planning has changed. I often joke that I have my MFA in theatre games; I know dozens and dozens of them, and I can easily fill a residency with new games for each session. But if I do that, each session requires that the young artists start over again as students (rather than generative artists), learning the game for just a moment before they no longer need it. I now push myself to use the least amount of games with the greatest amount of variations and ample time for revisions and reflection. After all, this work is not about my voice as a facilitator, or my skill as a teaching artist. PJP is about providing platforms for young artists' expressions to be heard—and sometimes, a simple snap is all you need.

**Figure 2.1a** PJP participants weave an embodied movement sequence with poetic text to perform their vision of a world free from violence against women
Source: Photo by Lynn Hoare.

**Figure 2.1b** PJP participants use physical imagery and metaphor to communicate their belief that "women have the right to feel safe from physical violence"
Source: Photo by Lynn Hoare.

# 2.3 Performing Actions, Performing Justice

Section 2.3 is organized into four categories of performance actions. Taken together, the collection of performance actions in Part Two reimagines commonly used theatre strategies, games, and exercises to offer critically engaged ways of exploring and performing racial and gender justice specifically. Many of the performance actions in Section 2.3 are inspired by and adapted from the work of theatre artists and educators such as Viola Spolin, Michael Rohd, and Augusto Boal. Notably, many of our mentors, colleagues, and students have been influenced by the work of artists from Dance Exchange, as well as artists trained in the Viewpoints philosophy and technique. While we have not worked in depth with these approaches, some of our performance actions have resonances with, and probably roots in, the work of Anne Bogart, Tina Landau, and Liz Lerman. In this section of the book, we codify, design, and adapt what we've seen, read, and learned into actions that specifically explore power and privilege, racism and sexism, and racial and gender-based equity and belonging with young people. We also include many performance actions that are original to PJP and specifically reflect our critically engaged approach to devising with youth.

The first category, Section 2.3.1, addresses What Is Ensemble? and outlines performance actions that help build a working ensemble and prepare groups of novice participants to devise original pieces of theatre. The actions included here are some of our favorites for building ensemble, but we encourage teaching artists to facilitate warm-ups and performance actions from their own training in theatre and devising as well. The actions in this category invite participants to begin expressing themselves to the group, build connection and trust with each other and the adults in the room, and explore specific theatre and performance skills.

The remainder of our performance actions are organized into three categories that address PJP's core questions:

2.3.2 Who Am I?
2.3.3 What Is (In)Justice and How Does it Show Up in My Life?
2.3.4 How Do I Perform Justice?

These categories include performance actions designed to engage young people in reflecting on their experiences and identities, analyzing systemic injustice in their lives and communities, and imagining and performing their ideas for a more just society. The performance actions in Sections 2.3.2 and 2.3.3 move beyond preparing an ensemble and toward creative approaches to devising short pieces of original text, movement work, and performance pieces that address identity, power, and privilege. The last category, 2.3.4, focuses on performance actions that move from personal stories and small bits of performance into collaborative scenes, a series of monologues, movement and dance pieces, songs, and other forms creative expression that imagine and enact youth's vision of justice. This section supports directors and performers in their efforts to collaboratively develop a collage-style and episodic performance piece that reflects the experiences and wisdom of the ensemble. Taken as a whole, the performance actions in Section 2.3 work toward a movement to perform justice. We hope that you find these performance actions helpful as you explore, experiment, and adapt your own work to question and disrupt the social constructs and lived implications of gender and racial oppression.

## 2.3.1 Performance Actions: What Is Ensemble?

This section offers a collection of performance actions that invite youth participants to begin working together, building relationships, and fostering trust as a performance ensemble. Specifically, the performance actions in this section help groups learn each other's names, as well as practice vulnerability with and accountability to one another. At their core, the actions in this section invite participants to use their bodies and voices to express themselves. Moreover, these actions support collaboration and aim to bolster group-centered creative practices. These skills are essential to most performance-making processes, but even more so when asking young people to share personal experiences as they develop critically consciousness and autobiographical performance material. In our experience, belonging to an ensemble may be a new and sometimes uncomfortable experience for PJP participants. Cultivating a sense of belonging through embodied performance actions can support the sometimes emotional and vulnerable work of performing justice and can begin to prepare the ensemble for devising.

In this section, we outline performance actions that we facilitate early in a PJP residency. We often return to these actions throughout the performance-making process. For example, ensemble-building actions may become warm-ups for rehearsals later in the process, as well as performance actions for exploring more personal questions, developing script material, or preparing for performance after a script has been developed. For ease of use, these ensemble-building actions are organized into four categories or subsections: Building Community, Strengthening Teamwork, Engaging Voice and Body, and Activating Group Focus. However, one could argue that any of the following actions fit within multiple categories. In Building Community, the actions focus on cultivating trust, connection, and a sense of belonging among participants. The actions in Strengthening Teamwork require participants to work together toward a common goal or outcome, while those in Engaging Voice and Body are designed to develop an awareness of body and comfort with physical and vocal expression. In Activating Group Focus, we offer performance actions that develop listening and focus skills, a sense of timing, and group awareness. These actions are often repeated over time and become favorite strategies for warming up the body and voice for performance and/or building energy in the group.

Below is an overview of the performance actions included in each subsection, followed by a facilitation guide for each action. These short facilitation guides begin with a basic description of each action—which might be a theatre activity, game, or strategy—followed by an overview of how the performance action is adapted for or directly connected to the Performing Justice Project.

## Building Community

- Creative Introductions
- Check-In Circle
- Thumb Grab
- Heads Up
- Name and Gesture
- The Truth About Me
- Groupings
- Two Truths and a Lie
- Group Agreements
- What is Ensemble?

## Strengthening Teamwork

- Your Greatest Fan
- On the Line
- People, Shelter, Storm
- Round of Applause
- Number Up
- Keep 'Em Standing

## Engaging Body and Voice

- Cover the Space
- Go-Stop/Name-Jump/Knees-Arms
- Hey!
- Everyone's It Tag
- People to People
- Statues and Sculpting

## Activating Group Focus

- Zip, Zap, Zop
- Ta-Da-Da
- Group Rhythms
- Flocking

# What Is Ensemble?

## Building Community: Creative Introductions

*This action offers a playful way to share names and introductions with a new group of people.*

### PJP Connection

Offering a silly or thoughtful question along with an introduction offers participants a way to connect with others and practice bringing themselves and their voice into a semi-public space. We use this action when participants are meeting each other or participating in storytelling and performance work for the first time. Because young people are often silenced in society, making space for them to voice their names and experiences creates conditions for performing justice. Moreover, sharing names and experiences with a group in and of itself becomes an act of racial and/or gender justice in some settings.

**Time**: 8–12 minutes, depending on size of the group

**Materials**: None

### Directing the Action

1. Invite participants to sit or stand in a circle.
2. Choose one question to frame the introduction circle. Examples might include:
   a. What is one thing we can't tell by looking at you?
   b. If you were something that belonged in a kitchen, what would you be and why?
   c. Tell us where you are from by describing a sound, smell, or sight. For example: I am from loud sirens on Saturday night; I am from the smell of wood fire in my clothes; or, I am from rain drizzling outside my window.
   d. If you could travel anywhere, where would you go and who would you take with you?
   e. What is one thing that is unique about you?
   f. What or who is inspiring you right now?
3. Explain to participants:
   a. One at a time, we will go around the circle and introduce ourselves to the group.
   b. Please introduce your name, the pronouns you use (share examples: she/her/hers, he/him/his, they/them, ze/hir), and your answer to our question at hand (see above for examples).

### Guiding Reflection

• Ask the group to reflect on themes, surprises, and images that came to mind during this action.

### In Our Experience

Although we commonly ask participants to introduce their name and pronouns, this practice can be risky, particularly for non-binary, gender-fluid, and gender non-conforming youth. In addition, while inviting youth to share where they are from has worked to build connections among participants with strong place-based allegiances, this prompt sometimes illuminates conflicts across neighborhood gang rivalries and reveals significant gaps among participants' socioeconomic status. Given the risk of even basic introductions for some participants, we often invite young people to think about their own comfort level in the room and with each other, as well as the possible consequences of sharing (and not sharing) identifying information about themselves (such as non-binary pronouns). We often model this action by sharing our own creative or silly introductions first, supporting participants to take time to consider how they will bring themselves into the action.

### Connecting to Performance

Learning names is essential to collaboration and ensemble-based devising. Creative introductions help participants quickly identify basic commonalities and differences in a playful circle. This action asks participants to share a bit about themselves and sets a personal and engaged tone for collaborative practices and devising performance.

**Source**: We have played this game in multiple contexts. The original source is unknown.

# What Is Ensemble?

## Building Community: Check-In Circle

*Check-in circles offer structured routines for the ensemble to share how they are doing as they enter or close the ensemble work each day.*

### PJP Connection

The PJP process requires building trust, connection, and relationships. Having some space—even if brief—at the top of a session to share how you are communicates that PJP directors and teaching artists care about participants and are interested in how they are doing. Additionally, knowing how students are feeling or what they are grappling with as they enter the room allows PJP staff to assess what individuals and the group may need to fully participate in the day's actions and adapt as necessary within the session plan.

**Time**: 3–10 minutes, depending on size of the group

**Materials**: None

## Directing the Action

1.  Invite the group to sit or stand in a circle.
2.  Explain to participants:
    a.  We will start our sessions each day with a check-in. This is an opportunity for you to tell us how you are doing or feeling today.
    b.  Sometimes we might ask a specific question for you to respond to and other times we might ask you to indicate with a thumbs-up or thumbs-down how you are feeling. Sometimes we might ask you to use your face, a gesture, or one word to communicate how you are feeling.
    c.  During the check-in circle, we will ask everyone to listen carefully to each other without any side-conversations. Please don't ask any questions or comment on what is shared. For this ritual, we are simply listening and witnessing, except when it is our turn.
    d.  We will share out by going around the circle (unless you decide the group can "popcorn" meaning pop out their contribution when they are ready), and if you aren't ready to speak or don't wish to share, you can say pass. We will return to you at the end of the circle to allow you to share at that point, and if you still want to pass, you can.
3.  There are multiple ways to "check-in." Choose an option and direct participants with one of the following prompts (or create your own):
    a.  Use your thumb to share how you are feeling as we get started today. You might show a thumbs-up if things are good, a thumbs-down if you're not feeling great, or a thumbs-sideways if things are so-so. (Everyone in the circle can share simultaneously.)
    b.  Today we are going to check in with one phrase or word that sums up your morning before you arrived here.
    c.  Today we are going to check in by using our faces (or a gesture) and a sound to communicate how we are feeling. While we are checking in, we are also rehearsing tools for expression, which are necessary for performing.

d.   Today we are going to check in with one word that describes what you are bringing into our session today. Everyone take a moment to think about what you are bringing in: an emotion, an energy, an experience. If someone else says your word, you can still use it or think of a different one.

e.   Today we are going to check in by going around the circle and briefly sharing how we are feeling at the start of this session. This is an opportunity to share your thoughts, questions, or concerns about this process that we are in together, or just a chance to let us know how you are feeling. Please keep your check in to one minute or less.

## Guiding Reflection

- We don't tend to ask reflection questions after check-ins. However, we pay attention to themes that come up around the circle, in order to address them at the end of the round if necessary.

## In Our Experience

Although a check-in circle can feel awkward in the beginning of a process, the practice builds trust and connection throughout a process. We have found it invaluable for hearing everyone's voice, for helping participants feel seen and validated, and for sometimes clearing the air after a difficult previous day. Although it may feel tempting to cut a check-in to save time, it is essential in building ensemble and understanding the energy of the group. Seeing that adults are willing to share can open up participation in the group. We try to model sharing with honesty and vulnerability without over-sharing. We also use this action to close daily sessions with a check-in, question, or take-away.

## Connecting to Performance

Bringing everyone into the circle is essential to creating a strong ensemble. A check-in offers participants an opportunity to transition between whatever came before the session began into ensemble work where they may need to set aside complicated feelings or outside conflicts in order to fully present for making and performing theatre.

**Source**: We have played this game in multiple contexts. The original source is unknown.

# What Is Ensemble?

## Building Community: Thumb Grab

*This physical warm-up and ice-breaker includes an element of light touch and relatively low-stakes competition.*

### PJP Connection

We often use this action as a way to begin playing with a new group. We invite participants to draw connections between the physical action in this activity and personally held ideas about theatre and performance. The action requires that youth stand near each other, respectfully engage in light touch, and listen closely. It also requires simultaneous actions, offering a powerful metaphor for considering the intersection of multiple identities and multiple goals, as well as the ways that theatre and justice-oriented work requires multi-tasking.

**Time**: 5–8 minutes

**Materials**: None

### Directing the Action

1. Invite participants to stand in a circle. Instruct everyone to create the "thumbs-up" sign with their right hand and to hold their left palm out to their side and open, facing upwards. Invite participants to then turn their right thumb down and place it gently on their neighbor's open palm (to their right).
2. Explain: Following the count of "One, two, three, go!", each participant simultaneously tries to escape the person's palm to their right and grab the person's thumb on their left. Playfully hold the participants accountable for not moving until the facilitator says "go."
3. Play the game a few times, switching sides (Place the left thumb down and the right palm open, gently grabbing a thumb with the right hand, and escaping a grabbed thumb on the left.)

### Guiding Reflection

- What was challenging about this game?
- What strategies did you have to use to succeed?
- What does this activity have to do with theatre or performance?

### In Our Experience

This strategy energizes a group quickly and invites participants into a playful space; youth groups often respond with laughter and surprise. We sometimes point out that this action is not about winning or losing. Rather it focuses attention on a challenging and slightly competitive task. Youth love that we participate in the game with them and groups tend to improve their focus and success in the action over time.

### Connecting to Performance

Thumb Grab introduces basic theatre skills such as listening, focus, multitasking, and respectful touch. This action provides a metaphor for listening and not anticipating lines in scenes and performance work.

**Source**: We learned this game from Michael Rohd, who learned it at a Physical Education Conference.

# What Is Ensemble?

## Building Community: Heads Up

*This action offers a gentle and connected way to begin building trust in the ensemble, as participants are asked to look each other in the eyes with intention.*

### PJP Connection

The visual and physical connections required in this action support a group in working together and developing a sense of ensemble. The ritual and structure of the action is somewhat performative and invites the group to practice seeing each other. These steps lay the foundation for later actions that directly engage around race and gender constructs.

**Time**: 5–8 minutes

**Materials**: None

### Directing the Action

1.  Invite participants to stand in a tight circle with you. Make sure that you can see everyone in the circle without moving.
2.  Explain to participants:
    a.  Everyone will look down at their feet, and when I say "heads up," raise your eyes to look directly at someone in the circle.

    b.   When we look up, if two people are looking at each other, they will both quickly move into the center of the circle, give each other a double high five, and quickly return to their place in the circle.

    c.   We will then quickly reset for another round by stepping back into our tight circle and lowering our heads when I say, "heads down."

3.   Play the action several times, keeping the game moving quickly, until most participants have connected with at least one other participant across the circle.

## Guiding Reflection

- What did it feel like to meet someone else's eyes?
- What did you notice about yourself, your identity, or your participation in this action?
- What does this action have to do with creating an ensemble or performing theatre?

## In Our Experience

This action works well when it moves quickly and when the ensemble includes approximately 6–12 people. Participants are sometimes reluctant to make eye contact with each other. In this case, we support group members to participate at their comfort level. We love to facilitate this action as a follow-up to Thumb Grab.

## Connecting to Performance

This activity calls on participants to connect quickly and to allow themselves to experience vulnerability through eye contact. These skills support collaboration and promote comfort with scene partners.

**Source**: We learned this game from Michael Rohd, who learned it at a Physical Education Conference.

# What Is Ensemble?

# Building Community: Name and Gesture

*This action invites participants to express themselves physically and begin to embody or physicalize ideas for an audience.*

## PJP Connection

Name and Gesture invites youth to begin thinking about the various identities they occupy in their lives. Participants create a simple "text" about themselves and perform it through movement and voice. This is the beginning of lifting up the voices, identities, and experiences of the people in the room.

**Time**: 8–15 minutes, depending on size of the group

**Materials**: None

## Directing the Action

1.  Encourage participants to think about something they like to do or an action that is significant to their daily lives. After each participant decides on their action, invite them to create a gesture or movement that represents their chosen action.
2.  Model for participants how to introduce themselves with their name and their embodied action. For example, "My name is Sam, and I like to play soccer" (show a kicking gesture).
3.  Invite the group to turn their backs to the circle so that they each have a "private studio" to develop and rehearse what they will say and do.
4.  After one minute, invite the group to turn back toward each other. Go around the circle and ask each participant to share their name and gesture/action.
5.  Encourage participants to listen and watch carefully so that they can repeat the name and gesture back to the performer, "Sam, soccer" (while repeating gesture with their body).
6.  This can be repeated by those in the circle a second and third time as a way to get to know names and as a way to work together as a group. Gestures should stay the same when repeating.

## Guiding Reflection

-   What did you learn about someone else, us as a group, or yourself through this activity?
-   How are identities and actions related?

## In Our Experience

This action flows well when we provide the group with time to consider their identity or action first, and then instruct them to create a gesture. We keep the creation time short so that participants do not have time to second-guess their choices, or get too complex with their gestures. If participants get stuck coming up with a gesture, we ask them to name a favorite activity and gather ideas from the group for a physical expression of that activity.

### Connecting to Performance

We often use this activity as a way to learn names at the beginning of our process. It serves as a tiny snapshot of what we will do in our time together: think about who we are, create original text (name, description), activate text with an embodied movement (gesture), and share the creation with an audience (the ensemble). This activity provides a simple and clear structure for creating a short performative moment. It supports participants to follow their impulses and make a quick choice rather than planning ahead.

**Source**: We have played this game in multiple contexts. The original source is unknown.

# What Is Ensemble?

# Building Community: The Truth About Me

*This action helps participants identify others with whom they have similarities and differences. It is sometimes called Big Wind Blows On Those Who... or All My Neighbors Who...*

### PJP Connection

In this action, youth are to consider the question "Who am I?" as they begin to map their various identities with the ensemble. Naming personal identities, experiences, and affinities in this action requires self-reflection and vulnerability—two skills that support the work of racial and gender justice.

**Time**: 10 minutes

**Materials**: None, although pieces of tape, sticky notes, or chairs can be helpful in marking "places" in the circle

### Directing the Action

1.  Invite youth to stand in a large circle. Stand in the middle of the circle to give directions for the action.
2.  Encourage participants to look around and note that everyone in the circle has a spot, except for the leader of the round, who is standing in the center.

3. Explain to participants:
   a. As the person in the middle of the circle, I will offer a statement to the group about something that is true for me: "The truth about me is that I am the oldest in my family" or "The truth about me is that I have a cat."
   b. If the statement is also true for you, you will leave your spot and quickly find a new spot across the circle.
   c. Ultimately, one person will be left without a spot in the circle. Whoever is left in the middle offers a new statement to the group—something that is true for them.
   d. You have control over what you would like to share and when you would like to move.
4. The action continues until everyone has had a turn in the middle or time ends.

## Guiding Reflection

- What did you notice or learn about our group?
- Were you surprised by any of our truths? Which statements and our movement made an impact on you?
- What is the benefit to sharing truths with one another in this setting/context? What are the challenges?

## In Our Experience

This performance action can be played standing in a circle or sitting in a circle of chairs so the spots are clearly defined. If one person repeatedly gets stuck in the middle (either by accident or on purpose), invite someone who hasn't had a turn to sub in for them. Sometimes participants offer a statement and no one else moves from their spot. Sometimes this offers a powerful message to the group around identity. In other times, we encourage the person in the middle to imagine a statement that that might invite others to move as well. Additionally, everyone who moves can be invited to share more information as a way to continue building community and creating space for youth to individually claim their truth among the group consensus.

## Connecting to Performance

This activity can function solely as an ensemble game, or as a quick warm-up for rehearsal. We also use this action to stimulate the writing for the performance script. Each "truth" might become a line in the script, or we may use the activity's premise as a writing prompt to stimulate deeper thinking about personal truths as related to identify.

**Source**: Developed by Matt Weinstein and Joel Goodman and published in *Playfair: Everybody's guide to noncompetitive play* (1980, p. 54).

# What Is Ensemble?

# Building Community: Groupings

*This action asks group members to quickly sort themselves by categories, finding similarities and differences.*

## PJP Connection

In this performance action, participants quickly work together to sort, categorize, and name things about themselves. Guiding a group to sort themselves by various likes and dislikes lays important groundwork for playful interactions and more vulnerable discussion around identity that happen later in the process.

**Time**: 3–10 minutes

**Materials**: None

## Directing the Action

1. Invite participants to stand up and move into an open area. Explain to participants:
   a. When I announce a category, please find others who are similar to you in this category. Common categories may include: something you are wearing, your favorite type of music, what you had for breakfast today, your favorite dessert, what you like to do on the weekend, and where you are from (part of town, country, state), or where your parents are from.
   b. Respond to the category by deciding your own answer and milling about with the group to find others who have a similar answer.
2. Encourage groups to flex on their category a bit in order to incorporate others. For example, if the category is shoes, and a group has divided into "black sneakers" but there is someone with black sandals that wants to join, the category might change to black shoes with rubber bottoms.
3. Once small groups have been formed, invite each group to come up with a descriptive name or title for their group.
4. Invite each group to share out their group names.
5. Mix up the groups and play again with a different category.

## Guiding Reflection

- What was difficult about this exercise? What was easy?
- What did you learn from this exercise?

- What surprised you?
- Describe a moment where teamwork was important for the group.
- What does this process of grouping and naming have to do with gender and racial justice?

## In Our Experience

This action provides a fun way for participants to get to know each other. If it is early in a residency, we invite participants to share their names and pronouns with everyone in their "grouping." Categories, or grouping topics, can also be sourced from the group. What does the ensemble want to know about each other?

## Connecting to Performance

Working quickly to build and name groupings supports intuitive decision-making and can foster relationships between ensemble members. This action is also fun to facilitate with an audience prior to or after a performance.

**Source**: We have played this game in multiple theatre classes and contexts. It is also outlined under the name "Incorporations" in Weinstein and Goodman, *Playfair: Everybody's guide to noncompetitive play* (1980, pp. 40–41).

# What Is Ensemble?

# Building Community: Two Truths and a Lie

*This ice-breaker provides a space for participants to share fun facts about themselves and to see what they may have in common with others.*

## PJP Connection

Two Truths and a Lie offers a short structure for sharing personal experiences with a group. This action offers a metaphor for thinking about first impressions and snap judgments, and can lead to a larger conversation about prejudice and oppression. This action also fosters discussions about what truths/lies we see portrayed in the media and how we internalize, recognize, and/or disrupt them.

**Time**: 10 minutes

**Materials** (optional): A notecard for each person, writing utensils

## Directing the Action

1.  Pass out a notecard and writing utensil to each participant. Ask them to write three statements about themselves on their notecard. Two of the statements must be true and one must be a lie.
2.  After everyone has written their statements, invite each participant to share them out as an introduction of themselves. For example: "My name is Tyler and I have been to Spain. I have written a novel. And I have never seen *Star Wars*."
3.  After each person shares two truths and a lie, ask the group to guess which statement is a lie. For larger groups, take a vote.

## Guiding Reflection

*   How did you know when someone was telling the truth or sharing the lie?
*   What kind of body language or delivery made you *think* something was true when it was a lie?
*   When thinking about the things you hear or see in the media, how do you know what is truth and what are lies (or mistruths)? What steps might you take to find out more?

## In Our Experience

This action allows youth to push some boundaries around truth-telling in creative way. As participants imagine ways to communicate or perform their ideas, they often think fantastically and critically about what things in their lives are noteworthy or might be interesting to an outside observer. Youth also tend to share mundane and exciting facts about themselves with the group, allowing the ensemble to know or see them on multiple levels.

## Connecting to Performance

We sometimes extend this action into a writing or devising prompt where youth imagine two truths and a lie about racial or gender justice. Short bits of writing might then get incorporated into the script as transitions between larger performance pieces or might become performance pieces in their own right.

**Source**: We have played this action in multiple contexts. The original source is unknown.

# What Is Ensemble?

## Building Community: Group Agreements

*This action invites participants to name and clarify group expectations and set guidelines for the PJP working environment.*

### PJP Connection

Building a clear contract or guidelines for participation offers participants ownership of the PJP process and a way to build accountability toward group expectations. Writing down participants' suggestions and expectations creates a physical contract for participants and facilitators to sign on to and a touchstone to return to as needed. Group agreements support opportunities to bring up ways of moving through conflict such as racism and sexism that might come up during the residency.

**Time**: 10–20 minutes, depending on size of the group and depth of discussion

**Materials**: Large paper for recording group agreement suggestions. Ideally, this can be posted in the working space every day that participants work together (writing on a chalkboard or whiteboard is not ideal for this reason).

### Directing the Action

1. Invite the group to respond to some or all of the following questions:
    a. What are some things we need to do our best work together?
    b. In order to collaborate well as a group, and to do our best work—work that is sometimes scary or difficult or challenging—we need to feel like we are safe or brave enough to try new and different things. What group agreements would help create a supportive environment for participating in difficult dialogues?
    c. How do you need and want to be treated by others in the space in order to do brave work?
2. Work with the group to get as specific as possible with the list of agreements so the group has a clear understanding of what each idea looks like in action. For example, what does showing respect look like or mean to people in the ensemble?
3. After the group identifies their main ideas and needs, ask if everyone can agree to the ideas on the list. If there are still statements that need revision, take time to discuss where the tensions lie and possible language to address hopes and concerns of the group.
4. Optional: Invite everyone to sign the actual paper, including adults/facilitators in the room.

### Guiding Reflection

- Why are group agreements important?
- What happens if an agreement is broken?
- How might our identities and experiences shape the kinds of agreements we each want for our residency?

### In Our Experience

The list of group agreements becomes important for setting expectations about how we will work together. The list of agreements becomes critical if and when participants' behavior does not align with the group's list. If this occurs, we revisit the document and identify where the moment or behavior violates or fails to support the group's way of working.

### Connecting to Performance

Creating group agreements and articulating guidelines for engagement help build participants' agency and communication skills for the collaborative devising process. Identifying how we will all work together also supports the performance-making process.

**Source**: We have experienced this action in multiple contexts. The original source is unknown.

# What Is Ensemble?

# Building Community: What Is Ensemble?

*This intentional discussion with participants helps define what it means to participate in a performance ensemble.*

### PJP Connection

PJP necessitates the intentional development of an ensemble in order to create an original piece of theatre together. Because PJP often engages youth with little to no theatre experience, facilitators intentionally discuss, define, and reflect on notions of ensemble. Understanding how groups work together to build something greater than themselves is part of enacting justice.

**Time**: 10 minutes

**Materials**: None

## Directing the Action

1. Invite the ensemble to sit in a circle or in a configuration where everyone can see each other.
2. Use this list of discussion questions to help youth reflect on and consider the notion of ensemble:
   a. What performance actions have we participated in so far? What did these actions require to be successful?
   b. What does the word "ensemble" mean to you?
   c. What does it mean or require to be part of an ensemble?
   d. Why might ensemble be important to the PJP process?
3. Share some core ideas around ensemble that are important to you or the particular site/context, or community partners. Some examples might include:
   a. Challenge yourself to take risks, and know that we will do everything we can to support you.
   b. Notice opportunities to "shine and let shine" (to talk more or to listen more).

## Guiding Reflection

The idea of ensemble is not always familiar to youth. Offer affirmation when you see ensemble in action to help illustrate the benefit and necessity of working together.

## In Our Experience

As PJP residencies come to an end, youth often reflect on the significance of their developed connections and relationships with each other. Although unfamiliar at first, young people experience the benefits of working collaboratively and feeling supported and valued with an ensemble. Taking time to discuss what make an ensemble sets the groundwork for ongoing efforts to build communities of practice and committed collaborators.

## Connecting to Performance

As we work to create original performance material, the notion of ensemble remains critical. We use this discussion to name how youth will participate and to help them understand that devising requires collaborative relationships and practices.

**Source**: This action was developed as part of the Performing Justice Project.

# What Is Ensemble?

## Strengthening Teamwork: Your Greatest Fan

*This fast-paced, playful action asks participants to shift quickly from competition to support.*

### PJP Connection

PJP residencies require participants to support others and at times allow someone else's ideas to take center stage. This performance action offers a structure for practicing these skills. It helps build group energy, group agreement, and participation, which can be essential in the beginning of a process that addresses gender and racial justice. Moreover, this action models group cohesion and offers a practice of lifting each other up which, over time, translates to performance.

**Time**: 5–8 minutes, depending on size of the group

**Materials**: None

### Directing the Action

1. Ask everyone to find a partner and stand with them in their own space in the room.
2. Introduce the rhythm and hand motions for a traditional game of Rock, Paper, Scissors.
   a. We typically play this action with a call of "1-2-3-go!"
      i. Rock is expressed by balling the hand into a fist.
      ii. Paper is expressed by laying the hand out flat.
      iii. Scissors is expressed by extending two peace fingers (pointer and middle) of one hand, held sideways in the shape of a pair of scissors.
3. Explain to participants:
   a. When the group plays Rock, Paper, Scissors (in pairs), one person will win. Whoever loses the game of chance automatically becomes the biggest fan for the person who won. The "biggest fan" follows the "winner" around, cheering them on as they look for another Rock, Paper, Scissors challenger.
   b. In each round, the loser and their fans become fans for the new "winner" until their leader loses a round of the game, at which time they all become fans for whoever has won next.

4. This action continues until a final challenge between the last two players (with many fans behind each person). Fans are encouraged to express their love and support for their "person."
5. Eventually, the game ends with one winner.

## Guiding Reflection

- What does this action have to do with ensemble?
- What does it mean to be a "fan" and where might this be helpful in our theatre-making process?
- What could it look like to lovingly dissent as a fan in this game?

## In Our Experience

Once this performance action begins it moves quickly and the room gets loud! This action is best learned by trying it out. We avoid sharing too many directions and instead jump in with a few practice rounds.

## Connecting to Performance

This action encourages youth to perform a role (biggest fan!) with relatively low stakes. Youth think about a familiar role from life (being a fan of something) and embody that role in a performative setting.

**Source**: We have played this game in multiple contexts. The original source is unknown.

# What Is Ensemble?

# Strengthening Teamwork: On the Line

*This performance action asks participants to negotiate and work as an ensemble through non-verbal communication.*

## PJP Connection

Participants work together and get to know each other in this performance action. The challenge of working non-verbally creates interesting opportunities for physical communication as the group tries various ways to accomplish the task at hand. This action sets the groundwork for later action that includes greater stakes around identity and oppression.

**Time**: 3–10 minutes

**Materials**: None

## Directing the Action

1. Tape out a long line on the floor. Ask participants to put their toes on the line.
2. Invite participants to then silently arrange themselves on this line in a particular way, while always keeping one foot on the line. Prompts for arranging themselves might include: line up by birthdate, height, or alphabetical order based on first name.
3. After participants have arranged themselves on the line, check in to determine if the arrangement is accurate.

## Guiding Reflection

- What was difficult about this exercise? What was easy?
- What strategies did you use to achieve your outcome while following the guidelines?
- Describe a moment where teamwork was central to your success.
- What might this action have to do with performance? With making change in the world? With gender and racial justice?

## In Our Experience

This performance action gives youth experience in non-verbal communication, working as an ensemble, and focusing during physical movement. We often remind participants that while an important part of non-verbal communication might include touch, they must remain conscientious of those around them and about their use of touch in this exercise. We often repeat this exercise multiple times, quickly reflecting on each "round" and making the prompt increasingly difficult. Groups also enjoy being timed—working to beat their previous times as the action gets repeated.

## Connecting to Performance

Non-verbal communication is a critical skill for participating in groups, reading subtext, and performing. This action also invites participants to collaboratively problem-solve, a skill that serves the devising and performance-making process.

**Source**: We have played this game in multiple theatre classes and contexts. It is also outlined under the name "Data Processing" in *Drama-based Pedagogy: Activating Learning Across the Curriculum* by Kathryn Dawson and Bridget Kiger Lee (2018, pp. 119–121).

# What Is Ensemble?

## Strengthening Teamwork: People, Shelter, Storm

*This fun and high energy action invites participants to work together to create frozen images with their bodies as they race to be part of a group.*

### PJP Connection

This action offers a playful approach to teamwork and using the body to express an idea. Participants have to work with multiple people and the fast pace of the activity disrupts cliques. This action offers a metaphor for working together and also speaks to justice issues such as housing insecurity and climate change.

**Time**: 10 minutes

**Materials**: None

### Directing the Action:

1. Invite youth to begin moving around the room, silently and in their own space. Ask them to find a group of three people and to move their group into their own space in the room. All groups of three should be spread out in the space.
2. Explain to participants:
   a. Two people in your group will face each other about two feet apart. They will make a "shelter" by holding their hands above their heads and touching them together in a triangular shape, like a peaked roof.
   b. The third member of the trio will stand inside the "shelter" as a "person."
3. Once each group has established this frozen image, slowly introduce the next instructions, practicing each one a few times.
4. Explain to participants:

   a. When the leader calls "shelter," those who are creating shelters with their arms in the air will break away from their "shelter" partner and their "people" (inside the shelter) and find a new partner to make a shelter over a different "person." When "shelter" is called, "people" always stay where they are while "shelter" people move and create new shelters over a new people. Each group will break apart quickly and new groups will be formed as quickly as possible.

b.  When the leader calls "people," those creating "shelter" will stay frozen in place while the "people" move away from their group and quickly and find a new "shelter" to stand underneath. Only one person may occupy a "shelter" at a time.

c.  When the leader calls "storm," everyone leaves their group and can switch roles, if desired, creating a new trio of person under a shelter. During a "storm," participants may switch roles or stay in the same role, but they all must form new groups.

## Guiding Reflection

- What does this action tell us about ensembles?
- What happened when the leader called "storm"? How does this connect to our creative process so far?
- What issues in society does this action bring up for you? How might these issues be connected to race, gender, or justice?

## In Our Experience

This action provides a fun way to begin a rehearsal or energize the ensemble. The action is suited for a group size that is divisible by three (9 or 12 players for example). If this isn't possible, we sometimes play this game with "outs," where anyone who is left out of a group joins the leader and facilitates the action while trying to gain a spot in one of the trios.

## Connecting to Performance

This action builds theatre skills such as focus, listening, and improvised action.

**Source**: We have played this game in multiple theatre classes and contexts. It is also outlined in *Teachers act up! Creating multicultural learning communities through theatre* by Melisa Cahnmann-Taylor and Mariana Souto-Manning (2010, pp. 50–53).

# What Is Ensemble?

## Strengthening Teamwork: Round of Applause

*This action invites participants to connect with each other through listening and working together.*

### PJP Connection:

This action provides a physical metaphor for the process of creating performance together, inviting the group to consider how everyone participates and the time needed to find or build group agreement and tempo. This ensemble action helps develop trust and a working vocabulary for collaborating toward racial and gender justice.

**Time**: 8–10 minutes

**Materials**: None

### Directing the Action

1. Invite participants to stand in a circle.
2. Explain to participants:
   a. In this performance action, our goal is to pass a clap around the circle. I will identify which way the clap will travel (clockwise or counter-clockwise).
   b. To pass the clap, person A turns toward their neighbor, B, makes eye contact, and both participants clap together at the exact same time. Next, B turns to the next neighbor, C, passes the clap in the same way to C, and so on.
3. Encourage participants to listen to one another and to set a clapping rhythm as a group.
4. If the group successfully focuses and develops a clear rhythm, challenge them to reverse the direction of the clap. To do this, the person receiving the clap will send the clap back towards the direction it came, resulting in a pair clapping twice to signal a reversal in the direction. Encourage the ensemble to keep the rhythm going even when they change directions.

### Guiding Reflection

- When were we most successful at this activity?
- What strategies did you use to keep the rhythm going?

### In Our Experience

This action is often harder than participants think it will be, but offers a great reward when the group finds a rhythm together. The group often struggles at first because this game sounds easy. Remind the group to not rush the exercise but to meet the goal of clapping together and finding a rhythm. Making eye contact as they pass the clap can help. Once the group finds a rhythm the speed will increase.

### Connecting to Performance

This game can be used as a warm-up, as a focusing activity, or for connecting with each other at the start of a day or after a difficult moment.

**Source**: Outlined under the name "Slap Pass" in *Training to imagine: Practical improvisational theatre techniques to enhance creativity, teamwork, leadership and learning* by Kat Koppett (2001, pp. 171–172).

# What Is Ensemble?

# Strengthening Teamwork: Number Up

*This action requires youth to work together toward a series of common goals, building ensemble and non-verbal communication skills.*

### PJP Connection

Number Up reminds participants that an ensemble must constantly adjust and respond in order to take care of each other; this is also true of sustaining gender and racial justice work. This action also builds group cohesion and helps youth identify if/when they tend to move back or move forward in group settings. Reflecting on this action provides a way to discuss how justice works and what support means given our own identities and context.

**Time**: 15 minutes

**Materials**: A chair for each participant

### Directing the Action

1. Invite youth to arrange the chairs in a circle and take a seat. The facilitator who calls the numbers also sits in the circle.
2. Explain to participants:
   a. This is a non-verbal, silent activity. When I call a number, the group is responsible for having that number of people standing. Anyone can stand or sit at any time to help achieve the goal.
3. Play a few rounds by calling out a number, waiting until the group achieves the correct number of people standing. Do not call a new number until the group has the correct number standing; from this point,

call a new number which can be bigger or smaller. Some people may continue to stand and others may sit, and this is fine. The work of the group is to fill in for any change until the correct number of people are standing. It is not necessary to have everyone sit or reset between calling new numbers. Ideally, the group finds a flow to sitting and standing so that as someone sits, someone else stands (if necessary) and the goal is achieved.

4. Once the group understands how the game works, introduce the "follow-through" rule: once someone begins to sit or stand, they must follow-through on their impulse or action and fully sit or fully stand. Help the group stay accountable to this rule by pointing out when participants start to sit/stand and asking them to follow-through in their movement.

5. The objective of this game is for the ensemble to constantly shift and respond to one another in order to achieve the correct number of people standing.

## Guiding Reflection

- What did you do to meet the group challenge—individually? As a group?
- How does this action mirror your experience with group or ensemble-based work?
- How might this action serve as a metaphor for making theatre or trying to make change in your communities?

## In Our Experience

This performance action pairs well with Keep 'Em Standing to support teamwork. Participants often begin counting out loud in this action and we gently encourage the group to find ways to solve the problem without talking. Sometimes participants blame themselves for their impulse to sit or stand, and we gently remind them that it is a group task, and success is not in the hands of any single person.

## Connecting to Performance

This action models the importance of group responsiveness and the notion that performance requires the cooperation and focus of the entire group. We often repeat this action as a warm-up throughout the residency and as we head into performance.

**Source**: Adapted from the game "Four Up" developed by Weinstein and Goodman and published in *Playfair: Everybody's guide to noncompetitive play* (1980, p. 107).

# What Is Ensemble?

# Strengthening Teamwork: Keep 'Em Standing

*This action offers a variation on "keep away" and tag games. It requires focus and promotes strategy, challenging youth to work together to keep their leader out of an empty chair.*

## PJP Connection

We facilitate this action after the group is familiar with each other and has begun to build ensemble. This action often inspires group cohesion, especially if the group is working against the facilitator/leader. It offers a powerful, physical metaphor for inclusion and exclusion and the strategies involved in blocking people from what they want or need.

**Time**: 10–15 minutes

**Materials**: One chair for each person

## Directing the Action

1.  Invite participants to arrange their chairs randomly, facing different directions, around an open space and to then take a seat in their chairs. Include one empty chair in the arrangement. Position one person in the room—standing—on the opposite side of the space from the open chair (as far from the chair as possible in the playing space). The standing person is usually the facilitator and we call this person "it."
2.  Explain to participants:
    a.  The objective of this game is to keep "it" from sitting in any open chair. "It" will walk toward whichever chair is empty to attempt to sit in it. "It" may not run in the space.
    b.  Seated participants may switch chairs as often as desired to keep the standing person from sitting. The open chair will constantly change (although actual chairs should never move in the room).
    c.  The goal for "it" is to try to sit in the open chair, wherever it is.
    d.  The group can talk to each other as much as you like to keep the "it" from sitting.
3.  "It" slowly begins to walk toward an empty chair while seated participants work together to switch seats and block "it" from getting an open chair. By moving into new chairs, the group continually changes the location of the empty chair and prevents "it" from sitting down. Participants can talk to each other, move quickly, and strategize. "It" may not run, although other participants may run if desired.

4. Once "it" sits in the empty chair successfully, the round is over and the action starts again.
5. After playing a few rounds, ask the group if they have any strategies they want to try. Give them a time limit (1–2 minutes depending on group size) to decide on a strategy together. The facilitator may choose to allow participants to move or rearrange the chairs in the space before beginning the action again. Play again, allowing the group to experiment with their strategy.

## Guiding Reflection

- What did you have to do to be successful in this game?
- What kinds of strategy helped keep "it" from sitting?
- What did you learn about yourself in this action? How did you end up participating?
- Is there anything in this action that reminds you of something happening in society right now?

## In Our Experience

This game is particularly powerful with a group who struggles to work together. When the facilitator plays "it," the entire group of participants works together to block them; this dynamic offers a playful way to unite the ensemble as they all work against an adult in the room rather than each other. If participants step into role as "it," we remind them to walk their regular pace to the empty chair. The bigger the space, the more spread out the chairs can be which creates a bigger challenge for the participants.

## Connecting to Performance

This action fosters ensemble and clear communication skills. Like performance, it invites everyone to work together to achieve a clear goal and requires the cooperation and focus of the ensemble as a whole.

**Source**: We have played this game in multiple contexts. The original source is unknown.

# What Is Ensemble?

# Engaging Body and Voice: Cover the Space

*This action energizes students through physical movement and invites them to be aware of their surroundings and ensemble members.*

## PJP Connection

This action provides an opportunity for youth to focus on their bodies in space. It helps raise their awareness of physicality in preparation for performance and begins to focus attention to their bodies, a site where racial and gender injustice often plays out or is held.

**Time**: 2–8 minutes

**Materials**: None

## Directing the Action

1. Set up an open and clutter-free playing space with a clear perimeter. Consider a minimum of 12 × 12 feet for about six participants.
2. Invite participants to walk around the space without interacting with other participants. Explain to participants:
   a. If you see a space where someone is not walking, or an area that is not "covered," walk to that space. You should be constantly moving your body to fill the empty spaces in the playing area.
   b. Your goal is to move and cover the space without communicating or interacting with others.
3. Call out "freeze" and ask participants to stop and notice where there are open gaps or clusters of people. Invite the group to take two steps each in an effort to even themselves out around the playing area.
4. Invite the group to begin moving again and to try to predict where clusters and gaps might happen. The goal of this action is to keeping the ensemble spread out evenly around the space while staying in motion.
5. As time passes, add different tasks and challenges, such as stopping and starting simultaneously when the facilitator claps or stops/starts moving. Each added challenge helps participants listen with their whole body.
6. Added challenges: ask participants to quickly make an internal and external circle; subdivide into (equal) groups, make three triangles, move to the perimeter of the room, find an ensemble speed together (speeding up or slowing down), etc.

### Guiding Reflection

- What did you have to do to cover the space?
- What helped you be more aware of the potential gaps and spaces?
- Where did you find yourself holding tension in your body (if anywhere)?

### In Our Experience

This action helps brings energy and fun into warm-ups and transitions—between writing actions and/or beginning again after a break. Cover the Space is deceivingly simple and often works best with a group that is already excited to develop performance skills. We use this action to achieve various goals, such as making eye contact, noticing breath, and seamlessly changing pace with the group.

### Connecting to Performance

Cover the Space fosters basic performance skills such as spatial awareness, an awareness of body, presence, and focus. This action can also be beautiful to watch and we sometime incorporate the movement improvisation from Cover the Space into the blocking of the performance.

**Source**: We have played this game in multiple theatre classes and contexts. The original source is unknown.

# What Is Ensemble?

# Engaging Body and Voice: Go-Stop/Name-Jump/Knees-Arms

*This action builds on Cover the Space, adding mind-benders that challenge, energize, and focus a group. This action also fosters a sense of community and ensemble among participants as they struggle simultaneously to meet the task at hand.*

### PJP Connection

The specific activities in this action challenge the brain to reverse commands, *a la* Simon Says, and to try something that doesn't feel intuitive. It encourages failing and continuing to play, and also provides a foundation for experimentation and failure around more difficult topics such as racial and gender justice.

**Time**: 10–15 minutes

**Materials**: None

## Directing the Action

1. Invite youth to begin walking around the room or open playing space, silently and on their own. Explain to participants:
   a. Listen for simple commands and respond with the appropriate action:
   b. When I say "stop" everyone should freeze in place. When I say "go," you can resume moving around the space.
   c. When I say "jump" everyone should jump in the air, land on their feet and continue moving around the space (tiny jumps are fine!).
   d. When I say "name" everyone will say their name out loud (at the same time), while continuing to move around the space.
   e. When I say "knees" everyone will tap your knees with your hands, while continuing to move around the space.
   f. When I say "arms" everyone will lift your arms up in the air and then return them to your sides, while continuing to move around the space.
1. Introduce each instruction slowly, giving participants time to master and practice each instruction a few times. Mix up the various commands to help participants get the actions in their bodies.
2. Once everyone has learned all of the "commands" slowly begin to reverse one set of instructions at a time. Explain to participants:
   a. I am going to add a layer of challenge. When I say "stop" you are going to go (and vice-versa). All other commands and actions will stay the same.
3. Give the group some time to practice the reversed direction, while continuing to use all other commands as well. After playing for a few minutes, reverse the next instruction. Explain to participants:
   a. Now, in addition to the reversal of stop and go, if I say "name" you are going to jump, and if I say "jump," you are going to say your name.
4. Continue to play with two of the three command sets reversed. After the group has practiced the pattern, reverse the last set of commands. Explain to participants:
   a. Let's add in the last reversal. When I say "knees" you are going to lift your arms in the air (and vice-versa).
5. Build the action to include a mix up of all the reversed directions. Play until the group becomes more confident and successful in following the multi-layered directives.

## Guiding Reflection

- What was most challenging aspect of this action? What strategies did you use to complete the tasks successfully?
- How does this action relate to the process of making theatre together?
- What aspects of this action relate to your ideas about justice or the justice system?

### In Our Experience

This action offers a playful challenge, requiring deep listening and focus. We offer participants time to adjust to each new instruction and slow down if the group is having trouble holding all of the reversals in their mind and body. In later rounds of this action, we sometimes invite youth to facilitate the game and call out the various instructions for their peers as we play alongside them in the ensemble, or to add new language to the action. Most groups love to tackle the mind/body challenge in this action.

### Connecting to Performance

This action helps a group begin to work in sync with one another. We use it prior to beginning a rehearsal session and repeat it often. It requires group focus, careful listening, and improvisation.

**Source**: We have played this game in multiple theatre classes and contexts. The original source is unknown.

# What Is Ensemble?

# Engaging Body and Voice: Hey!

*This action energizes the room and invites everyone to play together safely and with focus.*

### PJP Connection

PJP work is supported by non-competitive, energy-building actions. Hey! asks people to fully show up physically and verbally in the circle. It also serves as a critical discussion starter about the platform and visibility that comes with performance. As the ensemble aims to perform gender and racial justice, what are they calling attention to and whose attention are they aiming to get?

**Time**: 8–10 minutes

**Materials**: None

### Directing the Action

1. Invite everyone to stand in a spacious circle. Explain to participants:
   a. Someone in the circle (person A) will begin by making eye contact with someone else (person B) across the circle. Person A will then move quickly (slow jog is ideal) across the circle to person B.

b. When person A arrives in front of person B, the pair faces each other, jumps up in the air and gives a double high five while saying "Hey!" with great enthusiasm. The goal in this moment is for person A and person B to jump up and high five each other with both hands at the exact same time.

c. Once they jump, high-five, and say "Hey!", person A will switch into the spot of person B in the circle. Person B will make eye contact with someone new across the circle, jog toward them and repeat the process until everyone has a chance to say "Hey!"

d. Everyone around the circle needs to stay focused during this action in order to be ready to synchronize their movements with the person coming toward them.

2. Optional: Facilitator can begin a second and even third round as the first round continues to travel across and around the circle.

## Guiding Reflection

- What was experience of participating in this action?
- Were there any points that you noticed discomfort in your body?
- Performance is like saying "hey!" It draws attention and focus. What do you want to point people's attention toward with our performance?

## In Our Experience

This action is really fun but it can take time for participants to build their confidence to look each other in the eye and high five without missing. On the hand, it can also get a bit rowdy! We encourage participants to move toward the other person with enthusiasm, as if they are heading to see a long lost friend, while remaining mindful of the group. We ask participants to imagine how their approach could serve as an invitation to their high-five partner.

## Connecting to Performance

This action teaches commitment, cooperation, and unison play. It is an excellent energizer, but also requires everyone to work together.

**Source**: We learned this game from a Pig Iron Theatre Company workshop.

# What Is Ensemble?

# Engaging Body and Voice: Everyone's It Tag

*This action is a fast-paced energizer, where every person is engaged at all times, and the "it" constantly changes.*

## PJP Connection

Tag brings a playful energy to the group which can be used as a break from difficult dialogues or as a way to fully get into our bodies. We love playful games that change the energy and develop connections between participants.

**Time**: 10–15 minutes

**Materials**: None

## Directing the Action

1. Invite participant into a large, open playing space. Delineate the boundaries for the game. This action moves fast and it works well in a smaller room without furniture.
2. Explain to participants:
   a. In this action, everyone is "it." Once the game begins, each "it" will try to tag as many other people as possible without being tagged. When someone gets tagged, they must show they are "out" by squatting down in place. They also must notice who tagged them.
   b. The game continues around those who are "out" as they wait for their "tagger" to be tagged by anyone else in the game. When the "tagger" gets tagged out and squats down, suddenly anyone who was tagged by that person is now set free and is back in the game, ready to tag others.
3. This game has the potential to go on forever. End the round when the group is out of breath or tired from all of the running.

## Guiding Reflection

- How do you feel after playing this action?
- What happened in this action? What does this remind you of in your life or in society?
- What does this action teach us about being in an ensemble?

## In Our Experience

This action is high energy and exciting, with the added bonus that no one loses. It is a great way to begin rehearsal, or quickly pick-up the group when they are lacking energy. Because this action is so fast-paced, it can be difficult to track down who has tagged whom. Encourage participants to pay close attention to who tagged them and to then follow their movements with intense focus.

## Connecting to Performance

This action offers an opportunity to warm up the body for performance and to practice skills in close observation and focusing on many things at once.

**Source**: We have played this game in multiple contexts. It originates from the physical education field.

# What Is Ensemble?

# Engaging Body and Voice: People to People

*This action offers a surprising and physical way to prompt participants to work together and solve physical challenges.*

## PJP Connection

This action is a PJP favorite that is adapted for almost every piece of the program. It serves as a creative discussion starter, a framework for a physically engaged dialogue, and a fun way to mix up pairs. As participants work with a variety of people over a short period of time, they become more comfortable in the ensemble at large. They also rehearse safe physical touch, often required for theatre and performance work, and directly connected to gender and racial justice in the rehearsal room.

**Time**: 10–15 minutes

**Materials**: None

## Directing the Action

1.  Invite youth to begin moving around the room, silently and on their own. Explain to the participants:
    a.  When I say "people to people," each participant needs to find a partner as quickly as possible and stand back to back with your pair.

If we need to have one group of three that is okay. Whenever you hear me say "people to people," you will stop what you are doing and find a new partner as quickly as possible.

2. Once everyone has a partner, offer a prompt that invites each pair to solve a physical challenge—namely, connecting two parts of their body together (pinky fingers to pinky fingers or elbows to elbows). Encourage pairs to work together to lightly touch those parts of the body together. Sometimes the challenges require some physical experimentation and maneuvering.

3. Give pairs a few more challenges to solve with their current partner (wrist to wrist or hip to hip). Encourage pairs to get creative in how they respond to the prompt.

4. When the facilitator calls "people to people," participants will find a new partner and stand back to back. Repeat the same process of offering physical challenges but continue to increase the difficulty (wrist to foot, head to knee, shoulder to hip, bottom of feet to bottom of feet).

5. We often ask participants to hold a particular pose (elbows to thumbs) and discuss a question at the same time (i.e., Did any adults in your life talk to about gender while you were growing up? What do you think of when you hear the phrase "gender binary"?).

6. Variation: Invite participants to freeze and spotlight one of the pairs. Ask the ensemble to consider what the relationship could be between the two people. Ask everyone to imagine this is a scene with two people in it. What do you think could be happening here? Who has more power in the image and why? Emphasize that there is no right answer.

7. Variation: Layer emotions, relationships or themes onto the physical challenges. For example: wrist to forehead—parent and child, hand to hand—rage, or back to shoulder—enemies.

## Guiding Reflection

- What discoveries did you make during this action?
- How did you make decisions with your partner about how to connect and how to gain consent?
- What physical images did you make in this action that are sticking with you now that the action is complete? If that image was the start to a scene, who are the characters and what is going on?

## In Our Experience

This action requires a lot of trust among the group, but also builds trust, making it applicable at various points in the creative process. Because it requires ensemble members to literally connect to one another with their bodies, we carefully consider how to scaffold the risk associated with various part of the body. We often work with groups that have regulations on physical contact. When this is the case, we ask youth to participate in the action by standing across from each other on either side of an imaginary or taped-out line on the floor. By keeping space between bodies, we balance between our own goals in PJP and the rules of our site partners.

### Connecting to Performance

Making comfortable, trusting physical contact with another person is a valuable skill that serves youth as they continue to create movement and image work throughout the PJP process. This action requires participants to negotiate physical comfort and ideas with other people and come to a paired consensus. These practices support artistic collaboration among ensemble members.

**Source**: Developed by Augusto Boal and published in *Games for actors and non-actors* (1992, p. 78).

# What Is Ensemble?

## Engaging Body and Voice: Statues and Sculpting

*This action is important to building images and using the body expressively.*

### PJP Connection

Using the body to express an idea or concept or response is an essential skill when building performance and can also be uncomfortable for non-performers. This action scaffolds various ways to practice embodied response. We use statues and sculpting throughout our devising work—sometimes to respond to a story or idea, sometimes to create a group picture or tableaux, and often in performance to illustrate a piece of writing in a dynamic way. This is a foundational PJP action for addressing race and gender.

**Time**: 15–60 minutes

**Materials**: None

### Directing the Action

## STATUES

1. Invite participants to find a place to stand on their own, spread out across the room.

2. Explain to participants:
   a. I am going to give you a word, and I'd like you to respond physically. This might mean that you make a statue *of* that idea or word, or it could mean that you make a statue with your body that *reacts* to that word or *responds* to it. There is no right or wrong way to respond to the words I will give you, except that you must find a position and stay still, like a statue. I will count down from five—5-4-3-2-1—and then I will say "freeze." At this point, please hold your statue. Make sure you find a position you can hold without moving.
   b. Let's try one together. Everyone will create their own statue in their own space.
   c. Please make a statue that responds to the idea of JOY. 5-4-3-2-1. Freeze.
3. Comment on what participants are doing with their bodies without remarking on specific individuals: "I see hands raised up high, I see bodies at a variety of levels, I see eyes directed to the ceiling, I see people with their arms around themselves…"
4. Invite participants to relax from their statues and return to a neutral stance. Try a variety of words to provoke different images—freedom, loneliness, justice, anger, independence, belonging, etc.
5. If participants are confident and ready to share, ask half of the group to remember their statue and relax, and look at the other side of the room. Take a moment to discuss:
   a. Describe what you see: what is happening in bodies? What do you notice? What is similar or different? What words do these statues make you think of?
   b. Switch sides, letting statues relax, and counting observers back into their previous statues. Repeat discussion questions.

## SCULPTING

6. Explain to participants that we will now work in pairs to sculpt statues:
   a. Please find a partner (or pair participants as necessary)
   b. Decide who will be A and who will be B.
   c. A will be the first sculptor. This will work similarly to your own statues, except that you will be "sculpting" your partner, or your "clay," into your image instead of using your own body.
7. Sculpting tips: model for participants a few ways to sculpt their "clay" respectfully. We typically model this in these ways:
   a. Option one for sculpting: Silently use your own body to show your clay what to do with their body. Ask them to follow you. Be specific with each body part, and where energy and weight is held, where different body parts are directed, and how the different pieces of clay, or statues, interact with each other.

    b.   Option two for sculpting: Ask permission to touch someone else's body to help manipulate it. Let them tell you if this is okay or not, or to tell you which body parts they don't want touched (for example, the back of the neck can be very sensitive). If you have permission, silently sculpt, or move someone's body parts into the statue you want to illustrate.

    c.   Always use your own face to model facial expressions for your statue; do not try to sculpt someone's face. Consider all parts of the face to show expression, including eyebrows, lips, cheeks, direction of the eyes, whether the face is covered or not.

8. Offer clear prompts for sculpting. Words to explore include: injustice, activism, together, exclusion. Even in these early actions, it is productive to bring in terms and ideas related to identity, justice, and injustice.

9. Sculpting moves well into a statue gallery. After each sculptor has finished their statue, explain to participants:

    a.   We are going to look through our statue gallery. If you are a statue, please do your best to hold very still. If you need to direct your eyes so that you don't see people observing your statue, you can look past everyone, or direct them up or down if it doesn't interfere with how you have been sculpted.

    b.   Sculptors, let's take a walk through our statue gallery. Please don't touch or get too close to the statues. As you walk through, observing the different statues, what do you notice? What stands out to you? What words come to mind? How are these statues similar or different?

10. After walking through the statue gallery, invite statues to relax and switch participant roles so that B has a chance to sculpt A into an image (responding to a new prompt).

## Guiding Reflection

- Which role did you prefer – sculpting or being the clay? Why?
- Which statues made you think about the word or idea differently?
- What elements made effective and interesting statues?

## In Our Experience

Youth who are new to performance and not used to using their bodies are sometimes uncomfortable in this action, but gain confidence with time and repetition. It helps to lift up (without saying names) elements that made interesting statues (like an expressive face, or an interesting use of levels).

### Connecting to Performance

Statues and sculpting are a core component of building a PJP performance and will be used in combination with various PJP actions including activating six-word stories about race and gender. Through these actions statues may end up as a part of a performance as illustration of a monologue, or alongside live or recorded text.

**Source**: Developed by Augusto Boal and published in *Games for actors and non-actors* (1992, pp. 164–172).

# What Is Ensemble?

## Activating Group Focus: Zip, Zap, Zop

*This action support participants in warming up their bodies and voices, gaining focus, and sending and receiving energy. It is also fun and provides a great break.*

### PJP Connection

We introduce this action early in the PJP process and revisit it often as we move towards performance. This low-risk action invites participants to use their bodies and voices to build and send energy around the circle. It is useful for developing comfort in body and voice and also listening and connecting with an ensemble.

**Time**: 10–15 minutes

**Materials**: None

### Directing the Action

1. Invite participants to stand in a circle. Introduce the three words used in this game, which will always be used in this order: zip, zap, zop. Repeat these words a few times as a group. Explain to participants:
   a. Imagine that I have ball of energy between my hands. I will send this energy across the circle to someone else by sliding my hands together and then extending my arms outward toward the other person. Using my arm movements and intentional eye contact, I will send energy directly across the circle to a specific person as I say the word "zip!"

    b.    As soon as this other person receives my ball of my energy with the word "zip," they will quickly pass the energy on to another person in the circle by saying "zap" and sending it with a strong forward arm motion and clear eye contact.

    c.    This recipient will then pass the energy to someone else, in the same manner, by saying "zop."

    d.    Let's practice by putting the words and actions into our bodies. We want to work toward a sense of flow and rhythm as we move through the repeated sequence of zip, zap, zop, zip, zap, zop.

2.    The game continues as participations pass the energy around the circle, and until someone makes a mistake in the word sequencing or drops the rhythm. As a group, take a cheer break, shake out your bodies, and then continue.

3.    Encourage the group to stay in rhythm with one another and pick up the pace as they gain comfort with the words and the concept of passing energy.

## Guiding Reflection

- What did we have to do to be successful in this action?
- What individual efforts did you make to support the success of the entire group?
- How is the action similar to performing or making theatre?

## In Our Experience

This action becomes a fun, quick ritual for re-engaging the ensemble throughout the PJP process. It can also be played as an elimination game, where participants sit down in their spot when they miss a word or break the rhythm, and the action continues around them.

## Connecting to Performance

We introduce this action early in our process but play it often as a warm up for rehearsal and performance. As participants gain proficiency with zip, zap, zop, we focus on speed and articulation and sending the energy with a strong gesture and voice.

**Source**: We have played this game in multiple theatre classes and contexts. The original source is unknown. It is also outlined in *Theatre for community, conflict & dialogue: The hope is vital training manual* by Michael Rohd (1998, p. 22–23).

# What Is Ensemble?

## Activating Group Focus: Ta-Da-Da

*This action helps participants and facilitators learn each other's names while practicing group rhythms.*

### PJP Connection

In this action, participants work together to perform sound, names and movement through a complicated layering of rhythm and words. Participants experience what it feels like to rehearse and share something about themselves in a performative way.

**Time**: 8–15 minutes

**Materials**: None

### Directing the Action

1. Invite participants to stand in a circle.
2. With the participants, establish a group rhythm. We suggest finding this rhythm by clapping your hands together and then on your lap, making two even beats, and repeating (clap, lap, clap, lap...).
3. When the group rhythm has been established, invite participants to go around the circle and say their names in pairs. For example, Natasha might say her name, and then the person to her right will say her own name: Alma. Next, Alma will say her own name again, and the person to her right will follow by saying her own: Genesis. Each of these paired names will be followed by the phrase "ta-da-da."
   a. Here is an example of the order, with the above beat:
   Natasha: Natasha.
   *(clap, lap)*
   Alma: Alma.
   *(clap, lap)*
   Everyone: Natasha, Alma, ta-da-da.
   *(clap, lap, clap, lap)*
   Alma: Alma.
   *(clap, lap)*
   Genesis: Genesis.
   *(clap, lap)*
   Everyone: Alma, Genesis, ta-da-da.
   *(clap, lap, clap, lap)*

4. Go around the circle, building on the names and maintain the rhythm until everyone has said their name twice.

## Guiding Reflection

- What was challenging about this? When did this action feel most successful?
- What role does rhythm or music play in making a performance? What does rhythm or music add or bring to a performance of names?

## In Our Experience

This performance action can be challenging to teach in terms of rhythm, but worth it once the group gets going. Participants often begin to speed up the rhythm as they gain confidence in the strategy. We focus on maintaining a steady rhythm and moving at a pace that will allow for everyone to say their name clearly.

## Connecting to Performance

Learning the names of other members of the ensemble is critical to the PJP process, as it builds the means of effective communication and supports the idea of an intentional learning community. Group rhythms are a physical manifestation of an ensemble. This action provides a fun way to think about performance—joining voices and claps together, remembering everyone's name, and when successful, it becomes a moment of performance.

**Source**: We have played this game in multiple contexts. The original source is unknown.

# What Is Ensemble?

# Activating Group Focus: Group Rhythms

*This action invites participants to devise and perform an original sound-scape or rhythm together.*

## PJP Connection

This action moves directly into performance, inviting the ensemble to create and perform a rhythmic sequence together. The action demonstrates how repetition can support the learning of new actions and behaviors, an important aspect of sustaining justice work and building group cohesion across difference.

**Time**: 12–15 minutes

**Materials**: None

## Directing the Action

1. Gather the ensemble into a circle. Invite some volunteers (about one-third of the group) to sit on the floor. Invite some volunteers (a quarter of the group) to sit in chairs. The rest should remain standing, but the sitting, standing, and chairs should be distributed randomly around the circle.

2. Explain to participants:
   a. Each position (sitting on floor, sitting on chair, standing) signals a number of beats or a particular rhythm. Standing signals a triple beat or three count, sitting in a chair signals a double beat or two count, sitting on the floor signals a single beat, or whole note. Each count takes the same amount of time, however (as if each set of beats is within one measure).
   b. As a group, we are going to clap out the rhythm of our circle. The sound score we are creating together will be determined by the physical score that we have built with the levels of our bodies. We will hear a representation of our standing, chair, and floor positions around the circle.

3. Practice clapping out the circle's score. Everyone will clap simultaneously until the whole circle of standing, chair-sitting, and floor-sitting people are represented in the overall group rhythm. Practice until the group feels comfortable and everyone is performing the score together.

4. As the comfort levels grow, try reversing, or splitting into two groups that clap out the score of the circle from two different directions.

## Guiding Reflection

- What did you notice about this action? What skills did you use to complete the task?
- Working as an ensemble is not always easy. What did you learn about ensemble work in this action?
- How is this action related to issues of performance and representation?

## In Our Experience

This is a fun but challenging game that takes some time to accomplish. We tend to use it later in the process when youth already have started to feel a part of the ensemble.

**Source**: We learned this game from applied theatre practitioner and scholar Fiona Macbeth.

# What Is Ensemble?

# Activating Group Focus: Flocking

*This action asks participants to use their bodies in expressive ways, work together, and share leadership.*

## PJP Connection

This action invites participants to share leadership, as they might do in an ensemble-based performance process. During flocking, participants mirror and direct movement, both of which are excellent skills to stage and rehearse original performance. This action offers a way to explore and rehearse abstract movement which is often used to support the performance of personal stories and text.

**Time**: 10–15 minutes

**Materials**: None

## Directing the Action

1. Invite students to stand in groups of four or more, arranged in a diamond shape.
2. Explain and model for participants:
   a. The person in the front of the diamond will begin leading the group by performing a controlled, fluid movement. The rest of the group will mirror the leader with similar movements and the whole group will strive to move in unison.
   b. The leader of each diamond will eventually begin to turn to their right or left so that the group's line of sight is now focused in a different direction and there is a new leader in everyone's line of sight. The new lead will continue moving, offering the group a new set of movement phrases to follow or mirror.
   c. The goal is to move slowly enough that it is difficult for someone from the outside to know who is leading. If you are leading, it is up to you to make sure that you are moving slowly and fluidly enough that everyone else can keep up with you. Try to move as fluidly as possible when you hand off leadership.
3. Ask the group to continue rotating leadership until every participant has led the movement and each group is moving smoothly together.
4. This action can also be played by the whole group or half group. In this case, the leader is the person who cannot see anyone else around them. As the leader begins to shift to one side or another, the leadership shifts to a new leader.

### Guiding Reflection

- What skills did you draw on to participate in this action?
- What was difficult and why?
- Has your understanding of collaboration changed during this process? How so? How did you see collaboration show up in this exercise?

### In Our Experience

We find that music often inspires movement and keeps youth focused and can also help to create a particular meditative mood. This action helps participants regain a sense of peace after diving into difficult subject matter, and serves as practice for letting oneself follow and making oneself lead. Although we are sometimes tempted to "correct" a group that hasn't yet found the fluid, soft movement this exercise aims for, when we offer more time and space, we find that groups typically work this out on their own.

### Connecting to Performance

Flocking often becomes a movement-based performance or a set of transitions that we include as part of a public sharing. We have used this exercise to create beautiful, meditative ensemble-based movement pieces. Flocking builds collaboration, physical control, and specificity in performance, skills that will undoubtedly contribute to a PJP performance, even if the actual outcomes are not included.

**Source**: Although we've participated in this action in multiple settings, this version is adapted from the work of Ann Bogart and Tina Landau as published in *The viewpoints book* (2005, pp. 78–79).

## Doing Justice

## Visual Mapping + Embodied Agency

*Sidney Monroe Williams*

Admittedly, I was timid about stepping back into a classroom. My previous five years of teaching theatre in a secondary environment was laden with homophobia, racism, and classism. I did not have a problem with the teaching, but rather the fact that people were so concerned with policing my identity. The Performing Justice Project's (PJP) content focus on gender and racial justice amplified my anxiety as a queer, cis-man of color. On one hand, I was confident in my ability to design and execute the curriculum; on the other, I questioned if the curriculum would be received well coming from an identity that is not always affirmed in high schools—let alone Texas high schools. Here I reflect on how (re)membering the body can be an activist pedagogy within oppressive environments for youth and youth workers.

Kaitlyn Newman, co-facilitator, and I used "the body" as a framework for our curriculum. Here is an excerpt from a planning document we wrote on key terms:

> The body is a conduit of action and reaction, which allows for it to shift between active and passive functions. The body caries histories and is adorned with testaments of its journey. The body is wholistic and part of a whole. While our bodies share many commonalities, the body is also unique to each individual and their journey. How are our bodies (dis)membered? How do we (re)build our bodies? How is (re) membering the body an activist pedagogy.
>
> (Williams and Newman 2014)

With this foundation, we structured our eight-week residency to interrogate how the body accesses agency in contexts of community, race, gender, and justice. At the start of our residency we had each student outline their entire body on a large sheet of paper. We invited the youth to write/draw characteristics from their day-to-day world outside the body perimeter (i.e., hangout spots, role models, peers, social networks, etc.), followed by personal characteristics inside the body perimeter (i.e. identity markers, personality traits, familial background, aspirations, hidden qualities, etc.). Each week, we allotted time for the youth to return to their body maps and visually represent their agency (or lack of agency). Sometimes the youth documented this agency by drawing images/words relating to one's privilege inside the body perimeter. They also used images/words to locate oppressive influences/structures outside the body perimeter. We concluded this weekly exercise by analyzing how race, class, and gender impacts the agency a body can access within spaces like schools and communities. Sometimes, we depend on the agency of others when our own has been impacted by systems of oppression. Our body maps also suggested that we learn to use our agency and privilege if/when others cannot.

By the end of the residency, my initial anxieties around entering the classroom subsided because I realized that, in some respect, all of us were embattled in our journey towards liberation. No doubt, there were moments when the youth and I did not see eye-to-eye, or I felt like I could not bring my full self into the classroom. This became most evident during activities and discussions centered around the gender roles for Latinx women and sexual orientation amongst Black and Brown men. In these moments, I returned to the aforementioned framework, and focused on how the act of (re)membering the body—my body, their bodies—is an activist pedagogy. The process of mapping one's privilege(s) and the oppressive influence(s) affecting one's body highlighted how we can use our agency, not only to liberate ourselves, but also to lift others with us.

### Reference

Williams, S. M. and Newman, K (co-facilitators) (2014). *PJP key terms (Eastside memorial HS)*, Performing Justice Project.

**Figure 2.2** PJP participants bravely share and analyze personal stories about race, gender, and agency
Source: Photo by Lynn Hoare.

## 2.3.2 Performance Actions: Who Am I?

This section outlines reflective, writing, and performance-making actions that explore how we name and identify ourselves in the world, and how our intersecting identities are privileged or not by society. While many of these actions are commonly used to devise performances with young people, we specifically pair these actions with content, reflection and inquiry on gender and race. We include actions that ask young people to think deeply about their own identities and to reflect on the identity-based experiences of the group. Through writing prompts found in performance actions such as "I Am" Spoken Word, This I Believe, and I Come From a Place, participants often develop creative writing and performance materials that reflect complexities of identities, power, and access in our group and in society.

The performance actions in this section develop participants' consciousness about their own identities and experiences in the world while continuing to build a sense of ensemble. Many of these actions lead to a writing prompt or open writing time as a way to create text for performance. At this stage in the process, we are not focused on creating the specific pieces for performance, but rather on providing entry points for young people to consider and name their own identities, and on generating material to potentially return to later. These performance actions also establish systems for sharing bits of writing or storytelling with partners or small groups. Setting up systems for creating, sharing, and reflecting begins to prepare youth to later devise critically engaged performance pieces together in groups, including as scenes, embodied group images, spoken word pieces, or whole-ensemble movement pieces.

Many of the actions in this section relate to exploring justice and injustice and several of the actions found in the Who Am I? section could be interchanged with actions in Section 2.3.3, what Is (In)Justice? Here, we share our scaffolded process for exploring the relationships between identity, privilege, and power with a new group of participants, building from "Who Am I?" towards investigating "What Is (In) Justice?" However, when working with a group that is more familiar with each other or accustomed to discussing identity and oppression, we might try out a different set of performance actions, moving more fluidly between content or actions from "Who Am I?" and "What Is Justice?"

For ease of use, the performance actions in this section are organized into four categories or subsections: Naming My Identities, Understanding Race and Ethnicity, Understanding Sex and Gender, and Activating Intersectional Identities. The actions in Naming My Identities prepare young people to think critically about their own identities and name them out loud. The actions in Understanding Race and Ethnicity, as well as the actions in Understanding Sex and Gender,[2] offer opportunities to discuss race, ethnicity, and gender openly, while encouraging personal reflection on experiences related to these identities. Within Understanding Race and Ethnicity and Understanding Sex and Gender, we offer actions focused on sharing critical content, meaning content connected to power, and building common vocabulary (see the actions Defining Race and Ethnicity and Defining Sex, Gender, and Attraction). We have learned that is it necessary to take time to center content about race and gender and these actions offer one way to explicitly discuss vocabulary tied to these constructs. These two content-focused actions are not typically performative in the ways that others actions are; rather, we have found that they support focused conversations and provide essential information for the development of performance and critical consciousness. To prepare for these content-focused actions, we have found it necessary to draw on the theoretical underpinnings included in Section 1.3, as well as to acquaint ourselves with related vocabularies and theories (knowing that youth are often ahead of us in vocabulary and terminology [see Glossary, Appendix F]). The final performance action section included in "Who Am I?", Activating Intersectional Identities, acknowledges the many and varied identity markers that are in conversation with each other in ways that produce unique and sometimes resonant experiences and stories. While PJP focuses on experiences of race and gender, it is essential to also acknowledge that these experiences are also about race+gender, as well as age, sexual orientation, location, class and socioeconomics, religion, ability, and other identities.

Below we offer an overview of the performance actions included in this section, followed by a facilitation guide for each action. These short facilitation guides begin with a basic description of each performance action, followed by an overview of how the action is adapted for and connected specifically to our work in PJP.

## Naming My Identities

- Story of My Name
- Identity Gestures
- Writing the Truth About Me
- Who Am I? Word Web
- Mapping Geographies

## Understanding Race and Ethnicity

- Vote with Your Feet
- Defining Race and Ethnicity
- Six-Word Stories About Race
- Activating Text Through Image (Race)

## Understanding Sex and Gender

- Exploding Atom
- Alphabet Relay
- Defining Sex, Gender, and Attraction
- A Baby is Born
- Six-Word Stories About Gender
- Activating Text Through Image (Gender)

## Activating Intersectional Identities

- Identity Pie
- Body Maps
- I Come From a Place
- "I Am" Spoken Word

# Who Am I?

## Naming My Identities: Story of My Name

*This action asks participants to share a short, personal story about one of their names.*

### PJP Connection

This action demonstrates how a simple story about a name can reflect personal experience, knowledge and wisdom about our lives. Inviting participants to share a short story about one of their names provides an entry point for participants to learn about each other, and brings participants' lived experiences into the performance space early in the process. This action takes the focus off of performance and "acting," and instead models a practice of informal storytelling, which helps participants imagine storytelling as a tool for performing justice.

**Time**: 15–25 minutes, depending on size of the group

**Materials**: none

### Directing the Action

1. Invite participants to partner with someone of a different height.
2. Explain to participants:
   a. Choose who will be A and who will be B.
   b. "A" will begin by sharing a story about your name to your partner: your whole name, a name you almost had, a nickname, or whatever story about your name that is important to you. Fill in the details for your partner. What does your name mean? Why is it special? Who gave it to you or where does it come from? What do you like/dislike about your name? Don't rush your storytelling; you have two minutes to fill with description and content.
   c. "B"—your job is to listen carefully so that you can later introduce this storyteller to others. You will switch roles in two minutes.
3. Track time and let the group know when to switch storytellers/listeners.
4. From this point, the action might proceed in one of two ways, depending on the comfort and experience level of the group. The facilitator might invite the whole group to either return to a circle so each person can introduce their partner to the group *or* combine partners and ask pairs to introduce each other in a small group setting.
5. Whole group: After both pairs have shared, invite the group to come back to the full circle. Ask each partner to introduce their storyteller to the group by introducing their name, their pronouns, and a shortened version of the story of their name.

6. Small group: After both partners have shared, invite the groups of two to partner with a new group of two. Explain to participants:

   a. Each person will introduce their partner to the newly created group of four, sharing your partner's name, pronouns, and a one sentence version of the story of their name. You will have about four minutes for everyone in your group to complete your introductions.

   b. Bring your sharing to a close. Please split your group of four into two new pairs. With your new partner, find a new pair in the room. Introduce your new partner to the other two people in your new group, sharing their name, pronouns, and a one sentence version of the story of their name.

   c. After a few rounds of introductions, return to the large circle. At this point, each person can introduce their new partner to the entire group.

## Guiding Reflection

- What did you learn that surprised you?
- How is knowledge and wisdom related to stories and names?
- How and why might storytelling serve as a tool for imagining or enacting justice?

## In Our Experience

We facilitate this action near the beginning of a PJP residency to build trust and establish expectations around listening and sharing. This action invites participants to share something personal but offers options for what and how to share information about themselves. We encourage partners to listen carefully to details, so they can share back an accurate accounting of their partner's story. It is also important to encourage ensemble members to ask for and use names—for some people remembering names is easy, for others it takes longer.

## Connecting to Performance

This action serves as a first step in sharing stories, setting the groundwork for sharing further experiences with each other and considering storytelling structures. Although we use this action as a warm-up and trust-building exercise, the shared stories might later get adapted for performance. We also sometimes weave stories about names into writing actions such as "I Am" Spoken Word or I Come from a Place.

**Source**: Adapted from a game created by Bay Area Theatresports, via George Silides' ice-breaking activities for pastors, and outlined in *Training to imagine: Practical improvisational theatre techniques to enhance creativity, teamwork, leadership and learning* by Kat Koppett (2001, pp. 193–194).

# Who Am I?

## Naming My Identities: Identity Gestures

*This action invites participants to express themselves physically and to begin to name personal identities.*

### PJP Connection

This simple action invites youth to consider the various identities and roles they occupy in their lives. It also requires participants to consider how to create text and perform it through movement. This action begins to lift up the voices, identities, and experiences of the people in the room.

**Time**: 8–15 minutes, depending on size of the group

**Materials**: None

### Directing the Action

1. Invite participants to stand in a circle.
2. Encourage participants answer the prompt "I am…" with language that actively describes who they are.
3. After each participant decides on a word that names one of their identities, invite each to create a gesture or movement that represents their word.
4. Give the group a minute to think about their word and the movement they would like to pair with it. If needed, invite the group to turn their backs to the circle so that they each have a "private studio" to rehearse their name and gesture prior to sharing it with the whole group.
5. Model for participants how to introduce themselves with their name, identity, and gesture. For example, "My name is Lynn and I am a mother" (holding and rocking a baby).
6. When ready, go around the circle and ask each participant to share their name, gesture, and identity.
7. Encourage the group to listen and watch carefully so that they can repeat the name and gesture back to the performer, "Lynn" (while repeating gesture with their body).
8. This action can be repeated by those in the circle a second and third time as a way to get to know names and as a way to work together as a group. Gestures should stay the same when repeating.

## Guiding Reflection

- What did you learn about someone else, us as a group, or yourself through this activity?
- How are identities and actions related?
- What does this action have to do performing?

## In Our Experience

Participants need just a bit of time to consider their identity before we instruct them to create a gesture. Let participants know beforehand that the group will repeat each name and gesture back to the storyteller. Participants sometimes feel shy about coming up with and sharing a gesture. If participants get stuck coming up with a gesture, we ask them to name a favorite activity and gather ideas from the group for a physical expression of that activity.

## Connecting to Performance

We often use this action as a way to learn names at the beginning of our process. It serves as a tiny snapshot of what we will do in our time together: think critically about who we are, create original text (name, description), activate text with an embodied movement (gesture), and share the creation with an audience (the ensemble). This activity provides a simple and clear structure for creating a short performative moment.

**Source**: We have played this game in multiple contexts. The original source is unknown.

# Who Am I?

# Naming My Identities: Writing the Truth About Me

*This simple place-switching performance action can also be used to generate ideas for monologues.*

## PJP Connection

By asking students to go to a deeper level on this round of The Truth About Me, we begin to access the core content of PJP. Sometimes we move from The Truth About Me directly into journal writing to give participants time to reflect on which identities were easy to share, which were more difficult, which ones stood out, and what questions they are left with. Spending some time in a journal reflection writing a long list of "truths about me" can be a strong starting point for starting to write stories and scenes about identities and truths.

**Time**: 10 minutes

**Materials**: Paper and writing utensils

## Directing the Action

This action builds upon the exercise you may have already used as a warm-up, and can either begin with the same warm-up, or move directly into a writing exercise.

1. This action begins as outlined in the Ensemble section—see The Truth about Me for directions on facilitating the start of this action. As the group plays the action, encourage participants to share truths as a way to find similarities and differences with others. Be aware of how comfortable your group is sharing personal information, and allow participants to self-select whether they share or withhold information. Play long enough to generate many different answers to the prompt.

2. Next, invite participants to find a spot to sit alone and write. Pass out personal journals.

3. Explain to participants:
    a. We are going to take some time to work through a writing exercise that uses the idea of the personal truths about to generate writing about something that is important to you.
    b. Title your page "The Truth About Me Is…" and begin with a brainstorm of as many "truths" as you can think of in two minutes. You might consider "truths" in the circle that were true for you. You might consider truths about the world or your local community and the way they connect to you, or truths about your family or yourself. Which truths feel important to record?
    c. After you have written a list of truths, read back over your list. What is missing? What stands out? Circle the ones that feel most important to you.
    d. Now, take five minutes to write about one of the truths that feels important to you. What does this truth mean to you? Why is it important? What are the impacts or consequences of this truth? What do other people in your life think about your truth? Is this truth visible or invisible? What joys and/or challenges does this truth offer in your life?

4. When participants have mostly finished writing, invite them to gather into groups of 2–3 and share some of their writing. If participants prefer not to share their truth, they can discuss what they noticed when writing or what felt challenging about the exercise.

## Guiding Reflection

- What did you discover about yourself in this writing?
- In what ways does this truth impact your life?
- How do others respond to this truth?
- What ideas or themes came up in your group?

### In Our Experience

Depending on how participants respond to the challenge of sharing more personal information, we, as facilitators, also share our own identity markers and truths to model vulnerability, honesty and transparency. We might include statements such as "The truth about me is that I am white" or "The truth about me is that I don't spell very well." Sharing truths and writing about them can be a vulnerable experience for some participants; this action has the potential to build connection between youth but if the group does not trust each other yet, sharing truths may also be too vulnerable.

### Connecting to Performance

Some of our most powerful pieces in PJP performances have started with the line, "The truth about me is..." and have been developed into a monologue, poem or scene. The writing developed through this process can also be used for performance "acts" built around a specific identity or truth.

**Source**: This action (moving the exercise into writing) was developed as part of the Performing Justice Project.

# Who Am I?

## Naming My Identities: Who Am I? Word Web

*This action asks participants to brainstorm their own social locations, which include the identities we hold and what they mean in the context of power.*

### PJP Connection

The PJP process relies on interrogating identities in relationship to power, and we have found that many young people with whom we work have not had access to naming and thinking about identities and oppressions. This action asks them to think about their identities in terms of social categories—race, class, gender, religion, sexual orientation, ethnicity, and so on—as well as identity in terms of social roles which include experiences and relationships. By allowing students to name these categories themselves, they self-identify and claim a variety of identities that other people may not even know about them.

**Time**: 20–30 minutes

**Materials**: Paper, markers and/or pencil for all students

## Directing the Action

1. Invite participants to find a place to work on their own—at desks, tables or on the floor—as long as they can concentrate and write. Hand out paper and markers or pencils/pens.
2. Explain to participants:
   a. We are going to create webs of our own identities. When we look at a spider web, we can strands or threads individually but also the way that they are connected to other threads, and it takes many threads to hold up a web. For your web, you will put your own name in the center of your paper, and then think about all the different identities you hold—the different threads that make up who you are. Each identity will extend by a thread from your name in the center (model web or mapping for all to see).
   b. Think about all the different identities you hold in your lives. What roles do you play in your family? In your school or community? With your friends?
   c. How do others see you and describe you?
   d. Take some time to think through how you identify within the following categories and add to your web: age, sex, race, ethnicity, religion, gender, class/economic status, sexual orientation, ability or disability. How would you describe your identity in terms of these labels? (It helps to write these categories where everyone can see and reference them.)
   e. Map your identities into a visual web on the page.
3. If participants finish early, invite them to write in their journals about identity markers or social locations that stand out to them.
4. Invite participants to find a partner and share a few things they notice about their identity web. Depending on relationships and comfort level in the group, invite everyone to a circle and ask that each person share one thing they realized or that was surprising.

## Guiding Reflection

- Which identities are easy for you? Why?
- Which identities are more challenging? Why?
- Which identity or identities are things you think about every day? Which identities do you rarely think about?

## In Our Experience

This action offers a way into naming identities, after which we offer vocabulary and space for discussion about race, gender, and multiple oppressions (through the following actions). Allowing participants to name their own identities is a powerful exercise. This is not the time to correct vocabulary or language unless you have time to discuss language in detail. Sharing our personal web with participants sometimes helps to model both vocabulary and vulnerability.

## Connecting to Performance

This action is intended to be a building block toward exploring and naming identity, but can also be used to develop content for performance. We have also extended this action into visual body maps in which participants stretch out on a long piece of butcher paper and ask another participant (or facilitator) to trace around their body to create an outline (see Activating Intersectional Identities: Body Maps). Participants then use their social location words and webs to decorate, fill in, and design their body maps.

**Source**: Inspired by the work of Amanda Christy Brown and Holly Epstein Ojalvo in their article "Express yourself: Crafting social location maps and identity monologues" (2010), drawing on the ideas of Greg Hamilton in his article "English in the city" (2003, pp. 100–104).

# Who Am I?

# Naming My Identities: Mapping Geographies

*This action invites participants to physically represent and move between places that hold significance, as if creating an embodied map.*

## PJP Connection

This action is a powerful way to remember and embody stories related to our identities and our physical spaces. This action relies on favorite PJP components: using the body to express location and movement, solo and group devising experiences, and expressing story through gesture or image. After creating and staging this movement-improvisation piece, participants might be ready to write about significant experiences related to location and identity.

**Time**: 30–60 minutes

**Materials**: Open space and music with speaker if desired

## Directing the Action

1. Invite participants to imagine that the floor of the room is a personal map of important places in their lives. They can place things wherever they want in relation to one another, but they should try to use the entire space. Explain any necessary boundaries (if the space is large).
2. Invite participants to establish a representation of each important space or place on their map:
   a. Walk to the place where you were born.
   b. Walk to the place where you lived before coming here. (Note: This is most appropriate for spaces where youth are not living in a place they might consider home. An alternate phrasing is *Walk to the place you most consider home.*)
3. Invite youth to consider the following prompts and to respond physically (choose 3–4):
   a. Walk to the place where you have your earliest memory. Create a frozen image with your body and face to represent the essence of that memory.
   b. Walk to the place where you started school. Create a frozen image of how you felt in that place.
   c. Walk to the place where you are safest. Create a frozen image representing how this place makes you feel.
   d. Walk to the place where you are most challenged. Create a frozen image representing how this place makes you feel.
   e. Walk to the place where you are most loved. Create a frozen image representing how this place makes you feel.
4. Using these places on "stage" and these frozen images, create a sequence of images and movements (transitions from place to place). Rehearse these images and movements in order. Begin by calling out reminders (for example, "school," "safe," "challenge," "loved"). You may want to play music as the ensemble rehearses. Rehearse with the group until participants are confident and can move easily between locations. We often use a six-count to hold the frozen image and a six-count to move from location to location.
5. Invite youth to split in half to share their sequences with each other. Have one half perform while the other half observes, then switch. Ask the audience portion of the group for "appreciations" to give back to the performers.
6. We often invite pairs to teach each other their movement sequence and to combine two or three together into a performance piece.

## Guiding Reflection

- What did you realize about yourself through this sequence? What new information came up for you?

- What inspired you about the embodied work of your ensemble members?
- What is the value of sharing a visual, embodied representation of parts of your life with others?
- How might this connect to our performance?

### In Our Experience

This action can get to the heart of some deeply personal stories and experiences as related to the places and spaces of our lives. Inviting youth to connect to one another based on spatial relationships (as tied to geography) reveals interesting and surprising commonalities among them. This action also provides an opportunity to consider the ways that movement, image and sound are an important part of performance and storytelling, even without text, and how the vulnerability of the artist communicates something personal and meaningful to an audience.

### Connecting to Performance

The movement sequences from this action often move directly into a PJP performance. As we continue to rehearse, we ask the participants to become increasingly specific and to add music. We sometimes record the performers telling a story and then layer this movement action with music and recorded text. This action is great first step for using the body in performance and creating ensemble movement for performance.

**Source**: Learned from Omi Osun Joni L. Jones, Mady Schutzman, Jan Cohen-Cruz, and Lisa Barker in various workshops. A related version of this performance action is also outlined in *The viewpoints book: A practical guide to viewpoints and composition* by Anne Bogart and Tina Landau (2005, pp. 56–57).

# Who Am I?

# Understanding Race and Ethnicity: Vote with Your Feet

*This is a low-risk, embodied way to begin a dialogue that allows participants to see various responses through spatial relationships.*

### PJP Connection

As an embodied discussion strategy, this action invites participants to respond to a prompt physically without needing to explain their response. The group gains a sense of the similarities or differences without putting anyone on the spot. If youth have not had the opportunity to discuss race and racism openly, this action offers an excellent first step but also requires intentionality around developing statements that will encourage rich dialogue. We choose to engage youth through embodied responses to questions about race and then move into defining race and ethnicity in the following action, but this could also be reversed.

**Time**: 15–20 minutes

**Materials**: None

## Directing the Action

1. Invite participants to stand in an open space. Describe an imagined or taped line on the ground as our continuum. Indicate that one end of the line will mean "completely agree" and the opposite end will mean "completely disagree." Explain that the line illustrates a continuum, or spectrum, of opinions.
2. Explain to participants:
    a. In a moment, I will read a series of statements and you will use your bodies to respond to the statements non-verbally by arranging yourselves on the line.
    b. You will each move along your own continuum of agree to disagree. If you agree with a statement you will move towards the "agree" end of the spectrum, placing yourself according to how strongly you agree. If you disagree with a statement, you will move towards the "disagree" end of the spectrum depending on how strongly you disagree. If you are unsure, or ambivalent about the statement, you can choose a middle area on the continuum.
3. Invite the group to try out the action with an easy statement such as, "I love pizza." Remind them of the entire continuum and encourage them to actively (and silently) choose a place on the continuum by moving their bodies to a location that reflects their response.
4. Once they understand the idea, move onto the following statements. It helps to read the statement once and invite the participants to silently consider their answer. Then, read it again and ask them to respond by moving to their location:
    a. I grew up talking openly about race and ethnicity.
    b. Where I live/stay (in my neighborhood or community), there are a lot of people who look like me.
    c. I am clear on the differences between race and ethnicity.
    d. I am always aware of my race and ethnicity.
    e. I remember a time when someone said something or something happened that made me aware of my race/ethnicity.

5.  In response to each statement, encourage discussion through a variety of methods.
    a.  Ask participants to turn to someone near them to share why they chose this specific location.
    b.  Ask the whole group, why are you standing where you are? Invite people from different points on the continuum share out.
    c.  Ask people to pair up with someone in a very different location on the continuum and share about why they answered the way they did.

## Guiding Reflection (After Each Statement Is Read)

- As you place yourselves on the continuum, notice where you are in relationship to others. Where are most people standing? What do you notice?
- How is your experience similar or different to how others answered this question?
- Why are you standing where you are standing?

## In Our Experience

This action stimulates dialogue with participants. Seeing each other's physical "vote" can create opportunities for discussion, and may also provoke movement as people rethink their answers. Sometimes we ask: "Would anyone like to shift their position based on our discussion?" This is a great moment to discuss how hearing other perspectives can make us re-evaluate our own opinions and see things in a new light. We scaffold the statements in order of low-risk to higher-risk statements. While we attempt to support youth and nurture safe-enough spaces, we also think deeply about how to scaffold and create opportunities for in-depth dialogue about challenging topics such as race.

## Connecting to Performance

Stimulating conversations about social justice in an active, dialogic way lays the groundwork for the participatory, youth-driven nature of this program. It also asks youth to listen carefully and share focus with both the facilitator and each other—skills necessary to the collaborative devising process. Additionally, responding to statements about race introduces a central focus of PJP and begins to acclimate the group to examine issues that often go unaddressed in public spaces.

**Source**: We have played this game in multiple theatre classes and contexts. The original source is unknown. A version of the activity called "Values Clarification" is also outlined in *Theatre for community, conflict & dialogue: The hope is vital training manual* by Michael Rohd (1998, pp. 54–56).

# Who Am I?

# Understanding Race: Defining Race and Ethnicity

*This content-focused action offers some definitions we use in PJP, collected from various sources. For more definitions and related terms, see Glossary of Related Terms, Appendix F.*

## PJP Connection

A significant part of the PJP process involves looking at how race and ethnicity shape the ways we are treated or have been treated by others, and the ways we understand and view our own experiences. We have found that young people and the devising process benefit from interspersing some direct instruction and content throughout a PJP process. Many youth (and PJP teaching artists and directors) may have grown up avoiding the topic of race or have been taught to keep experiences and feelings about race private. However, devising critically engaged theatre requires an understanding of and comfort with talking about racial constructs; providing vocabulary and a structured way to discuss the construct of race can be beneficial in identifying and understanding our own experiences.

**Time**: 15–20 minutes

**Materials**: Something to write on (whiteboard, butcher paper) and markers, TV or video screen with ability to play video

## Directing the Action

1.  Explain to participants:
    a.  We started with Vote with Your Feet to explore our different ideas and experiences around race. As we start to center and lift up discussions and reflections on race, it is important that we have some common language to use together.
    b.  When we say the word *race*, what comes to mind? What are some examples of race? (Scribe all examples that come up, even if examples refer to ethnicity rather than race.)
2.  Invite participants to sit somewhere comfortable where they can see the TV/video screen. Watch the video "The Myth of Race Debunked in 3 Minutes" (or another similarly accessible video about race as a social construction): www.vox.com/2014/10/10/6943461/race-social-construct-origins-census.[3]
3.  Discuss with participants:
    a.  What surprised you? What is difficult to understand or believe? What questions come up for you?

4. Discuss with participants *(The following information is covered in the video. However, if you cannot access the Vox video, this summary offers important information to bring up, or to use as the basis for choosing a different video)*:
   a. *Race* is a social construction, not a biological identity, and refers to characteristics possessed by individuals and groups. The meaning of race is not fixed; meaning it can and does change because of the way it is related to a social, historical, and geographic context. For example, when Irish and Italians first started coming to the US they were not thought of or categorized as white. Today, people are often classified into different socially constructed categories of race attached to a variety of physical attributes including but not limited to skin and eye color, hair texture, and bone structure. The construct of race has a deep history of lifting up people identified as white and oppressing anyone outside current definitions of white. Although race does not actually signify a scientific or biological characteristic, these constructs significantly impact the ways people are treated in the world. In fact, genetically, there can be more difference in a group of people who identify as the same race than in a group of people who identify differently in terms of race (Desmond-Harris 2014b; Sensoy and DiAngelo 2012; Butler 2010).
5. Share current racial categories according to the US Census: White, Black or African American, American Indian and Alaska Native, Asian, Native Hawaiian, Pacific Islanders, and Other. Invite participants to reflect: What do you think about these categories? Do they represent the diversity of people in our country? Why or why not? How do these categories or constructions of race show up in our lives or narratives about our lives?
6. Discuss with participants:
   a. Let's talk about ethnicity. Ethnicity refers to the idea that someone is a member of a particular group that may share some of the following elements: culture, religion, race, language, or place of origin. Two people can share the same race and have different ethnicities. For example, among two Black individuals one may be African American and another may be African Caribbean (Sensoy and DiAngelo 2012; Butler 2010).
   b. Ethnicity often refers to a cultural, religious, or regional identity. We can't tell someone's ethnicity by their race, and vice versa. Ethnicity is not always identifiable from the outside—sometimes is it connected to the language we speak, or the religion we practice or the country we come from (Sensoy and DiAngelo 2012; Butler 2010). What are other examples of ethnic identities, or ethnicities?
   c. After reflecting on definitions of race and ethnicity, are there any identities on our list that refer to ethnic identities rather than racial identities? How do these identity markers relate to each other and how are they different? Why is it important to understand the differences between race and ethnicity in the US context? In our

communities? Nationality is sometimes conflated with ethnicity, but refers to a person's membership, or affiliation, to a country.

d. Let's talk about *racism*. Racism describes a situation in which people are excluded from and oppressed by institutions and systems because of their racial/ethnic identity. Sometimes we think about racism as something that happens interpersonally, just between a few people or groups of people, but we define racism as a form of oppression in which one racial group dominates over others. In the US, white people belong to the dominant group. People in dominant groups receive unearned privileges denied to and at the expense of peoples of color. The critical element that differentiates racism from racial prejudice and discrimination is the historical accumulation and ongoing use of institutional power and authority that supports discriminatory behaviors in systemic and far-reaching ways. Think about our laws—who created the government in our country? Who is allowed to vote and when did our laws support that right? Who were the universities and schools built by and for? All of these systems were built for white people, typically white boys and men. Institutions and systems built for white people were intended to exclude people of color (as well as LGBTQIA people and often all women). "Institutional racism" and "structural racism" refers to these types of systemic oppression.

e. Sometimes we hear people say "reverse racism." Because racism relies on having the power to exclude people from systems and institutions, reverse racism isn't a real dynamic. People of color may hold beliefs or prejudices that discriminate against white people, but as a group, they do not have the social and institutional power to categorically exclude white people from benefiting from systems of privilege, access, and belonging already in place. The impact of individual or personal prejudice on white people is temporary and contextual and does not override the systemic privileges enjoyed by white people. While white people may experience challenges in life, such as poverty, their challenges are not a direct result of their whiteness.

## Guiding Reflection

- Pay attention to your body and how you are feeling. What kinds of questions and feelings are coming up for you? What is uncomfortable and/or affirming?
- What is surprising to you? What is difficult to understand?
- Where do these ideas and definitions resonate with your life or the world around us?
- In what ways does racism show up in our schools and communities?

### In Our Experience

These conversations are not always easy to have because we are steeped in our own family cultures and lessons, some of which may include explicitly avoiding the topic of race or only talking about race in private spaces. We have sometimes found ourselves reluctant to have conversations with young people about race and identity because we fear upsetting participants or institutional partners, or we are worried we will not have the right answers. In these moments, we attempt to draw on participants' knowledge and understanding, by asking: "What do you think? How would you define this? And let's find out more and revisit this together." We try to model that we are always learning and remain open to changing or being changed by this work and each other. Sometimes we must leave a session to reflect, research, or challenge ourselves to find additional information to deepen our perspective and/or that of the group.

### Connecting to Performance

Offering young people specific language about race, ethnicity, and racism proves key to supporting self-identification and naming. Vocabulary explored through these performance actions may become the basis for how students write and talk about themselves in performance and in their lives. PJP residencies highlight racial and gender constructs and how they impact our experiences in the world. Therefore language and vocabulary proves an essential component of preparing for performance and performing justice.

**Source**: This action was developed as part of the Performing Justice Project.

# Who Am I?

## Understanding Race and Ethnicity: Six-Word Stories About Race

*This performance action is inspired by the Race Card Project™ which was created by Michele Norris. It encourages participants to consider their own identities as related to privilege, power, and cultural norms. Visit theracecardproject.com for additional inspiration.*

### PJP Connection

This action invites participants to succinctly name and articulate a personal story or opinion related to their experiences with race. Writing and sharing stories about personal experiences is a core component of the PJP devising process, particularly in response to PJP core questions of *Who am I?* and

*What does (in)justice look like?* Six-Word Stories succinctly highlight identity and oppression and help participants name the ways that individual and systemic oppressions show up in our lives.

**Time**: 20–25 minutes

**Materials**: Pen/pencil, journals or paper, notecards

## Directing the Action

1. Invite participants to find a solo spot for some reflective writing. Pass out a writing utensil and journal or paper to each participant.
2. Explain to participants:
   a. You will have some time to brainstorm and write about moments in your life when race and ethnicity came to the forefront of your experience. This is a free-write and you are welcome to write about whatever thoughts are coming up in response to race and ethnicity. Some questions to prompt your reflection:
      i. What is an assumption someone has made about you related to your race, ethnicity or color of your skin?
      ii. What is an experience you have had related to your race or ethnicity or the color of your skin?
      iii. What do you wish you could say to others about your race, ethnicity or color of your skin?
3. Allow participants time to brainstorm and write. Then invite participants to put their writing down for a moment. Share examples of six-word stories (pre-written by directors and teaching artists or collected from the Race Card Project website) and ask participants to reflect on what they notice about the form and content of the writing. Note that each story is exactly six words and they all express experiences related to racialized identities and experiences. Share examples (source: www.theracecardproject.com):
   a. You don't look like you're Chinese—Tucson, AZ
   b. My skin does not define me—Atlanta, GA
   c. Borderlands born. Always illegal. Always home—Houston, TX
   d. Native American. We are still here—Anchorage, AK
   e. Taxi took me, not black friend—Hollywood, CA
4. Explain to participants:
   a. We are going to give you some time to write six-word stories. This means that you only get six words to capture an experience, situation, response, message or phrase that explores a time when you felt very aware of your race, ethnicity, or the color of your skin.
   b. Look at your journal for ideas. How could you take your brainstorm writing about an experience and move it into a six-word story?

    c.   The six words might tell a story, but they do not have to be a complete sentence or even a single thought. The six words might offer a question, a list, a sentence, or a phrase.

    d.   Let's take some time to write a few different six-word stories.

5. Pass out notecards and ask participants to write at least one six-word story on a notecard. They are welcome to write more than one, but each six-word story should be written on a separate notecard. Let participants know that they will be sharing at least one of their stories with the group.

6. After participants finish writing (they might try several drafts), model how to activate or perform the six-word story through a movement or gesture. We, PJP directors or teaching artists, model the process by using our own six-word stories, pairing them with gestures, images, or movement improvisation. We find that sharing our own experiences helps to level the hierarchy in the room and can build connections as participants learn things about us.

7. Invite participants to choose just one six-word story notecard and stand in a circle.

8. Invite participants to face outward in the circle so that each person has their own "personal studio" in which to create and practice activating their six-word story. Ask participants to consider the emotions, feelings, or images in their six-word story and to then create a gesture or short movement phrase to accompany the text of their short story. Allow some time for the group to create. Encourage participants to try on various gestures or movements to find something they like or something that represents their text.

9. After a gesture has been created, ask students to practice saying their six-word story aloud while performing their gesture. The gesture may be repeated, performed in slow motion, etc. Finally, invite the group to participate in a simultaneous dress rehearsal, physically and vocally performing their six-word story in their "personal studio."

10. Ask the group to face inward toward the circle of participants and perform their six-word story, one at a time, for the group.

11. Offer participants a ritual or way to show their appreciation following each short performance (such as snapping, clapping, or sharing a one-word response).

## Guiding Reflection

- What did you see and hear in the performances? What is sticking with you? Did anything surprise you?
- What did you notice about race and ethnicity in these stories and gestures?
- How are our experiences with race and ethnicity related to ideas about justice?
- How might we expand, link, or stage these stories as a larger performance piece?

### In Our Experience

Participants often ask if they can write five or seven words. We love the creative challenge of sticking to six words, but if a participant is truly stuck, we are flexible about the structure. The key idea is to name the essence of an experience in a way that is meaningful to the participant. These stories are often rich, emotionally charged, and powerful. While multiple six-word stories might get woven together to create a collaged poem, they can also stand on their own and/or be used as text that helps transition between other pieces in the script. This structure invites participants to think about the importance of their word choices, while also activating storytelling and scene work. We use the structure of six-word stories to investigate experiences of gender as well as race.

### Connecting to Performance

After youth share their six-word stories, move into smaller groups of three to four to begin staging. Ask the groups to create a frozen image for each six-word story, with the author of each story in charge of shaping or directing the group image for their own story. Ask participants to create an order for sharing their three to four stories: How do the stories fit together to tell one story? Which story might offer a strong beginning? A strong ending? Also, ask participants to think about composition: How do the frozen images fit together, transition, or shift from one image and story into the next? Does the collection of frozen images or gestures include a variety of levels (high, medium and low)? This performance sequence may become a single piece of text or a small bit of performance for the larger PJP script. Alternately, six-word stories can be expanded into a scene with dialogue or a monologue (see next activity, Activating Text Through Image, for a way to begin this process).

**Source**: Adapted from Michele Norris and the Race Card Project™ (2010) as part of the Performing Justice Project.

# Who Am I?

# Understanding Race and Ethnicity: Activating Text Through Image (Race)

*In this action, participants use sculptor and clay techniques from Statues and Sculpting to create embodied images from the six-word stories they just generated.*

### PJP Connection

Writing six-word stories about race can be challenging for youth as they crystalize experiences of race and racism. Embodying these experiences with others in a small group is one way we begin to build connection between individuals and group experiences, to create a space of acknowledgment and witnessing.

**Time**: 15–20 minutes

**Materials**: None, possibly music to underscore movement

### Directing the Action

1. Divide participants into groups of three or four.
2. Invite participants to share their six-word story about race with their group, and then to share some information about the story that inspired it. Give each participant one to two minutes to share.
3. After each story, ask participants to brainstorm images that come to mind. Ask participants to consider:
   a. What does this story look like in pictures?
   b. What is reflected in the bodies of the people involved in this story?
   c. If you had to create pictures of this story with your bodies, what would that look like?
   d. What type of abstract shapes might represent the emotional landscape of your story?
4. After everyone has shared their stories, invite participants to create frozen pictures for each story. Each participant will be the sculptor for their six-word story and the other two or three participants will be the "clay."
5. Invite each storyteller/author to "sculpt" or guide the participants to physicalize an image with their bodies to represent their own story about race. The entire group should be involved in each image. Sculpting tips: model for participants a few ways to sculpt their "clay" respectfully. The performance action is detailed in Section 2.3.1, what Is Ensemble? We typically model this in these ways:
   a. Silently use your own body to show your clay what to do with their body or how to shape their bodies in space.
   b. Ask permission to gently touch or move someone else's body to help manipulate it or move it into the desired image or shape.
   c. Always use your own face to model what someone might do with their own face; never try to sculpt someone's face.
6. Once each sculptor has created a group tableau or frozen picture of their six-word story, invite the group to develop transitions from one story into the next. Each "sculptor" should share aloud their text as the sculpted images are performed.
7. Ask each group to perform for other groups in an audience/stage configuration.
8. After each mini-performance, ask the audience to offer three things they appreciated about the performance. Encourage them to be as specific as possible.

## Guiding Reflection

- What did you just do to create these performances? What steps did you go through?
- What skills did this process require?
- What surprised you, from your own group's work or another group's performance?
- What similarities and differences did you notice?
- How do the six-word stories about race change when they are performed by the group?

## In Our Experience

We find that groups often benefit if we visit each group to work with them and guide them for a few minutes. We also build in time for a "final rehearsal" for all of the groups before they perform for one another.

## Connecting to Performance

Moving the six-word stories into frozen images helps participants create a concrete representation of their experience, gaining experience with and working toward more animated performance. As a series of images and pieces of text, the stories could move into the final performance, or they could accompany another story, be expanded to create a scene, or become choreography with music.

**Source**: Adapted by Performing Justice Project from Boal (1992, pp. 164–172).

# Who Am I?

# Understanding Sex and Gender: Exploding Atom

*This action allows youth to think critically while responding to statements kinesthetically. Like Vote with Your Feet, this performance action encourages dialogue in a relatively low-risk manner.*

## PJP Connection

Exploding Atom gently introduces conversations about gender through careful scaffolding of statements and dialogue. Statements ask youth to respond to the idea of gender (i.e., woman) rather than sex (i.e., female).

We find it helpful to identify and briefly discuss the challenges of binary categories of gender (woman/man) before starting so that participants are clear about responding to messages about gender and gender roles, although the statements will not ask them to expose their own gender identity, nor will statements rely on a gender binary. Alternately, this exercise could be used to explore birth-assigned sex—female/male—instead of gender. We focus on gender because it is more closely tied to how people express themselves and are perceived by others, rather than sex, which cannot be assumed from the way one presents or expresses gender to the world. This performance action is meant to initiate an investigation and dialogue about gender constructs but could also follow the Defining Sex, Gender, and Attraction action.

**Time**: 8–15 minutes, depending on number of statements read and how many participants share

**Materials**: None

### Directing the Action

1. Invite youth to stand in a circle. Explain to participants:
   a. In a moment, I will read you a series of statements and you will use your bodies to respond to the statements non-verbally. All statements are related to our experiences of gender.
   b. Each person will move along their own continuum of agreement to disagreement. If you agree with a statement, you will move to the center of the circle. If you disagree with a statement, you will move as far away from the center as you want, indicating your level of disagreement on the continuum. If you are unsure, or ambivalent about the statement, find a middle area on your continuum.
2. Similar to Vote with Your Feet, this action asks participants to embody their response to the statement. However, the response options with this action are less linear and often identified on a more personal continuum.
3. Take a moment to invite the ensemble to try out the action with a low-stakes statement such as, "Strawberry ice cream is the best dessert of all." Remind the group of all response options and encourage them to silently respond to the statement by moving their bodies along their own "exploding atom" continuum. Read the statement aloud and invite the participants to silently consider their answer, then read it again and ask them to respond by moving to their answer.

4. Once the basics of this action are clear, move to more complex statements related to gender justice:
    a. My gender impacts how others see me or treat me.
    b. I am always aware of my gender.
    c. Other people have told me I should behave a certain way because of my gender.
    d. My gender has a direct relationship to my power in the world.
5. After participants have responded to each statement by choosing a location on the continuum, use one or more of the following prompts for reflection and/or discussion:
    a. Notice where you are in relation to the rest of the group.
    b. Turn to a neighbor and talk about why you are standing where you are.
    c. Who would like to share with the group why you are standing where you are?
    d. Would anyone like to change your position based on what you've heard?

## Guiding Reflection

- Which questions were most difficult to answer?
- Would your answers have differed if any of the questions were about race in combination with gender? Why or why not?
- Where do messages about gender and expectations around how we are supposed to behave because of our gender (or birth-assigned sex) come from?

## In Our Experience

This performance action provides an effective way to stimulate dialogue with participants on their own terms. Asking participants to respond to prompts about gender before discussing the difference between gender identity, gender expression and sex assigned at birth allows them to respond based on their own diverse gender identities and relationships to gender. However, questions or challenges to the idea of gender, such as "Do you mean gender identity or gender expression?" or "What if I don't identify as a man or woman/girl or guy?" may arise throughout the action; we encourage youth to respond from their own viewpoint and experience and remain responsive to discussion points raised within the performance action. At this point in the action, it is not necessary for the group to have an agreed-upon definition or specific use of the word. For some groups, it could be useful to employ Exploding Atom after participants move through the action Defining Sex, Gender, and Attraction.

### Connecting to Performance

This action exposes the many different experiences and understandings we have around gender and hopefully builds comfort in talking openly about sex, gender, and identity. We have also used this action as a way for youth to facilitate and engage the audience before and/or after a performance.

**Source**: We learned Exploding Atom from Jonathon Sullivan and adapted it significantly as part of the Performing Justice Project.

# Who Am I?

## Understanding Sex and Gender: Alphabet Relay

*This action offers a way for participants to brainstorm vocabulary around a topic in a non-didactic, playfully competitive, and team-oriented manner.*

### PJP Connection

This is a great way to source language from your group. What terms, slang, or other language do participants use to name different identities and issues related to identity? Asking the group to brainstorm a vocabulary list brings up terms that may need to be defined and/or challenged. This performance action is foundational in supporting later work on Six-Word Stories About Gender and examining (in)justice. Alphabet Relay could also be used to examine race/ethnicity.

**Time**: 30–60 minutes, depending on number of teams and how many terms need discussion

**Materials**: One poster per team (butcher paper works well) labeled with each letter of the alphabet with space next to the letter to write a word or phrase, markers, game show music (optional)

### Directing the Action

1.  Divide participants into two groups and have them line up, one behind the other, facing the front where a poster is taped to the wall. (If group is small, they can form one team and compete against the clock instead of competing against another team.) The poster is labeled with each letter of the alphabet, with space to write next to the letter.
2.  Explain that the task of the team is to fill in a word for each letter of the alphabet related to the idea of gender, which can include gender identity, gender expression, sex characteristics, words used to describe different genders (this could include slang), or even phrases or descriptions

related to gender. Anything they can defend as somehow connected to or associated with gender and assigned sex is acceptable.

3. This action is a relay. The person in the front of the line will approach the list and write their word/phrase for the first letter A. They will then pass their pen to the next person in the line, and then move to the end of the line. The second person will quickly approach the wall and add a word/phrase for B, and so on.

4. If someone doesn't know what to write, at any time, they can access the support of the group. Encourage the writer to call out to their team to ask for help. This should feel like a team competition with everyone supporting each other. The groups are competing for time against the other team, not against their own teammates.

5. Once the relay has been completed by one group (the entire alphabet filled in with gender-related words and phrases), give the other group 30 seconds to finish as much as they can.

6. Work through each alphabet relay list and talk about each term. Ask the groups for help defining terms. There may be language that adult facilitators are not familiar with; similarly, there may be vocabulary that is new to some participants. Additionally, there may be terms that are hurtful to people who hold specific identities. It is important to address why certain terms could be hurtful or oppressive. This dialogue is part of building justice and offers a way to clarify and establish boundaries in the PJP space around gendered language.

7. Speaking words aloud gives them power, and alternately can normalize them for the participants not used to speaking these things aloud. Decide where your boundaries are as facilitators so that you can identify which words you will not speak aloud because of the additional (sometimes violent) impact they may have on members of the group. This can be a delicate balance at times—words can be added to the list that may have or may not have been meant to be hurtful; the way we respond to words that feel violent or hateful sets important boundaries for the way the group will continue to work together.

8. After all words have been spoken/addressed and defined/identified, introduce the language of sex, gender identity, gender expression, and sexual orientation. This will require additional explanation of the differences in sex and gender identity and gender expression, which are often conflated. (See the performance action Defining Sex, Gender, and Attraction for definitions.)

9. With the entire group, decide which terms belong to each category of sex, gender identity, gender expression, or sexual orientation. This process of analyzing and grouping begins justice-based dialogues.

## Guiding Reflection

• This action should move directly into the next action where the ensemble offers definitions and supporting language for reflecting on the relay brainstorm.

### In Our Experience

This action helps to source language and vocabulary from the group without defaulting to adult-based language. As facilitators, if language comes up that we do not know, we ask participants to help us understand what it means. It is likely that some slang will be added to the list, possibly even words that don't feel appropriate for the location/space in which you are working. When young people ask us if they can use certain words in actions such as this, we default to a general response. "Please don't use any words that will get you in trouble, or get us in trouble [if we are guests in the space]. Please move away from words that you know could be hurtful to people." Generally, youth participants already know what is appropriate to use in their space. If they feel a word is the best fit for their letter, but know it isn't appropriate, we might suggest they use alternate signs in place of letters/vowels so that they refer to the word without writing it and possibly inviting conflict (sh!t or f*ck, etc.). We don't assume that these additions are meant to be hurtful, and at the same time, we don't assume they are *not* meant to be hurtful. Addressing language openly on the Alphabet Relay list is an invitation to discuss why language can be harmful or oppressive.

### Connecting to Performance

Establishing a common language and vocabulary helps create ensemble. Defining and clarifying language provides a common vocabulary base for devising scenes, dialogues, and images and also normalizes identities that are marginalized or rarely discussed and named.

**Source**: We have played this game in multiple contexts. The original source is unknown.

## Who Am I?

## Understanding Sex and Gender: Defining Sex, Gender, and Attraction

*This action provides specific language and definitions that allow participants to gain clarity about various terms they may or may not have used before. For more definitions, see Glossary in Appendix F.*

### PJP Connection

Alphabet Relay offers a strong foundation for engaging in this performance action. We find that young people and the devising process benefit from including some direct instruction and content throughout a

PJP process; this content-focused action offers information about birth-assigned sex and gender identity versus gender expression. Taking time to explicitly name and investigate gender binaries and gender assumptions deconstructs heteronormativity and supports inclusion of everyone in the space.

**Time**: 20–40 minutes; ideally this action directly follows Alphabet Relay and unpacks language that has come up on the relay poster, in addition to other terms essential to gender justice

**Materials**: Marker board or butcher paper and marker

## Directing the Action

1. Gather the ensemble in a circle or another position for a group conversation.
2. Discuss with participants:
   a. What are the different sexes babies are typically assigned at birth? (male, female). What does this assignment describe or mean?
   b. Offer a definition of assigned sex according to US medical establishments: anatomical characteristics of femaleness and maleness with which a person is born or that develop with physical maturity—internal and external genitalia, chromosomes, hormones, body shape. Sex assigned at birth is sometimes confused with gender, although they are not the same thing. Gender refers to both gender identity and gender expression.
   c. What do you know about the term *intersex*? How is intersex connected to sex assigned as birth? Intersex refers to having sex characteristics that do not adhere to strictly defined categories of male or female. The sex characteristics may be ambiguous, or a person may have qualities of multiple sexes, or have any number of variations that do not fall into a specific male or female category. Babies and people who are intersex are more common than many people realize. Research surveying medical data suggests that "this frequency may be as high as 2% of live births" (Blackless et al., 2000, p 151). Sometimes this is equated to the number of people who are born with red hair, which is thought to be 1–2 percent of the population.
   d. Gender identity refers to the feeling or sense of knowing that we have about our own identity internally. Do we feel like a woman, like a man, non-binary (not feeling strongly male or female or feeling male and female strongly), gender-fluid, or on a continuum of gender?
3. Draw a line and place male at one end and female at the other end and explain that these are binary (or polar) concepts and do not work for

everyone. Each end of the line represents how much of our society constructs gender and categorizes people into only two opposite, or binary,
genders.

4. Explain to participants:
   a. Gender identity is how we feel inside about our own identity. Some
      of the words associated with gender identity (and gender expres-
      sion) include:
      i. Woman, man, non-binary.
      ii. Genderqueer, gender-fluid, gender non-conforming, girl-boy,
          boy-girl: alternatives to restrictive or binary gender roles and
          presentation.
      iii. Agender: people who identify as having no gender.
      iv. Androgynous: a gender expression that includes elements of
          both femininity and masculinity.
      v. Cisgender (also cis): gender identity lines up with sex assigned
         at birth (cis means "on the same side of").
      vi. Transgender (also trans): umbrella term for folks whose gen-
          der identity doesn't match their sex assigned at birth—they
          might be transitioning from sex assigned at birth to a differ-
          ent gender identity (trans means "crossing over"), or they may
          have already transitioned.
   b. Gender expression refers to how we express our gender to the
      world. Think about how people express their femininity. Will two
      or three volunteers stand up and each create a frozen image of one
      way people express or think of femininity?
   c. Think about how people express masculinity. Will two or three
      volunteers stand up each create a frozen image of one way people
      express masculinity?
   d. Sometimes our gender expression matches our gender identity,
      and sometimes we don't feel comfortable or able to express our
      gender because of societal or family expectations (i.e., if someone
      is assigned female sex at birth, but identifies as a man, he may not
      be able to express this identity because family members expect him
      to behave and dress in a way that aligns with their ideas regarding
      female behavior and dress).
   e. Sexual orientation describes who we are attracted to romantically,
      or sexually. This is not related to our sex or our gender identity
      or our gender expression. Let's brainstorm different sexual ori-
      entations (heterosexual, bisexual, homosexual/same-sex attracted,
      pansexual, etc.). Scribe as participants share responses.
      i. Heterosexual means attracted to the opposite sex.
      ii. Lesbian or gay or homosexual means attracted to the same sex.
      iii. Bisexual means attracted to people of multiple sexes.
      iv. Pansexual means attracted to people regardless of sex or
          gender.

    v.   Asexual refers to someone who does not experience sexual attraction to people of any gender.

    vi.  Queer is an umbrella term that refers to non-heterosexual identities. (Queer is also an umbrella term for gender identities that don't align with the binary.)

    vii.  It is important to note that homosexual is often used as a derogatory expression. We encourage participants to use language such as gay, queer, or lesbian, depending on the person and circumstances.

5.  To review: Sex is assigned when we are born, according to anatomy (and often on a binary). Gender identity is the gender that a person feels inside. Gender expression is the gender that a person presents to the world. Gender expression and gender identity may correspond with sex, but this is not the case for all people. Sexual orientation refers to attraction.

6.  Identities and language must be claimed as one's own—not imposed on people. We encourage participants to consider why it is important to claim and name their own identities.

## Guiding Reflection

- What questions do these definitions and terms raise for you?
- In what ways does this information feel interesting? Useful? Uncomfortable?
- What is one thing you have learned today?
- Why is language important in justice work?

## In Our Experience

The facilitators in the room must be comfortable with the language and terms in order to decrease participant (and community partner) anxiety around conversations about gender/sex with youth. We find that young people rarely experience open conversations about identity-based language, although they may have heard some of the terminology. When given the opportunity, participants could often spend more time diving deep into identity-based vocabulary and definitions, both because they have much to say and they have often desire a deeper understanding of how to name themselves and their experiences. Discussing language openly can help build understanding and empathy; it can also provide opportunities to talk about ways that language is used to put people down. As facilitators, the way we talk about identity (around sex/gender and race) has a significant impact on the ways a young person understands identity and might feel validated. For this reason, we remind everyone of group agreements and the goal of creating a safe and brave space as we move through vocabularies connected to race and gender.

### Connecting to Performance

While this dialogue provides a way for young people to bring up terms they are familiar with and begin to name their own identities (if they have not done this yet), these discussions offer examples of dialogue that might later be scripted and included in a performance. Staging dialogues is one way to share information directly with an audience.

**Source**: This performance action was developed as part of the Performing Justice Project.

# Who Am I?

# Understanding Sex and Gender: A Baby is Born

*This action illustrates how quickly we jump to assigning sex and gender, starting with a brand-new baby, and how binary constructions of gender become a way we categorize and make assumptions about others.*

### PJP Connection

This action is one way to activate the sometimes lengthy discussions about differentiating sex, gender identity, and gender expression. The moment of a baby's birth, or even announcement of pregnancy, is a crystalizing moment of sex and gender assignment, reinforcing how quickly we assume that sex = gender, and gender = specific behaviors in the world.

**Time**: 10–15 minutes

**Materials**: Scripts of the text below

### Directing the Action

1. Invite participants to discuss: "When a baby is born, what is the first thing people ask?"
2. Ask participants to consider: Who decides the sex of a baby? This moment of birth is an excellent example of examining our assumptions about each other. Let's take a look at what people say about gender when a baby is born.
3. Explain to participants that we will bring a scene to life that illustrates some of this conversation about sex and gender.
   a. Let's get two volunteers to read a scene. One volunteer will play "society" in the role of an aunt of a newborn, and the other

volunteer will play the role of a doctor or a midwife who just helped deliver the newborn. Doctor/midwife, your line is the same each time. Volunteer playing "auntie," your job is to respond to the sex that the doctor mentions, keeping in mind what "society" says or assumes about boys and girls.

   b.  Choose volunteers, offer a script to read from, and decide who will play the doctor/midwife.

      1.  Dr/Mw: You're her aunt, right? Meet your new niece!
         Dr/Mw improvisation: What do you think? Isn't she beautiful? What wisdom do you want to share with your new niece?
         Auntie improvisation:_____

      2.  Dr/Mw: You're her aunt, right? Meet your new nephew!
         Dr/Mw improvisation: What do you think? Isn't he handsome? What wisdom do you want to share with your new nephew?
         Auntie improvisation: _____

      3.  Dr/Mw: You're one of the baby's aunties, right? Meet your new little one!
         Dr/Mw improvisation: What do you think? Aren't they beautiful? What wisdom do you want to share with your new dear little one?
         Auntie improvisation: _____

## Guiding Reflection

- What differences did you notice between the responses?
- Why do you think asking about a baby's sex is one of the first questions we ask?
- I wonder what the conversation sounds like if the doctor knows the baby is intersex?
- What questions can we ask when a pregnancy is announced or a baby is born that don't focus so heavily on sex and gender?

## In Our Experience

This simple scene, played three times, creates an opportunity to discuss how we step away from gendering others and towards more inclusive language right from birth.

## Connecting to Performance

This short scene has been added to a PJP performance in the past, and has also been recorded and played as a voiceover with live embodied images and statues on stage. A voice recording of this scene has also been played as a transition between other bits of material. Whether or not these scenes are used in performance, this action becomes a way to see and analyze some of the ways that we are both gendered, and make assumptions based on the gender assignments of others.

**Source**: This action was developed by Kristen Hogan and the Performing Justice Project.

# Who Am I?

# Understanding Sex and Gender: Six-Word Stories About Gender

*This performance action invites participants to succinctly name and articulate a personal story related to gender, and is inspired by the Race Card Project™ by Michele Norris. Find out more at theracecardproject.com.*

## PJP Connection
Similarly to creating six-word stories about race, six-word stories about gender crystalize messages, moments of experience, and realizations around our own gender identities. We find these six-word stories offer a powerful way to build alliances around similar experiences with gender expectations that dictate how we are allowed or encouraged to behave in different contexts.

**Time**: 20–25 minutes

**Materials**: Writing utensil, journals or paper, notecards

## Directing the Action

1. Pass out journals or paper.
2. Invite youth to think about how they might describe how gender (or sex) affects them and makes them feel, about their experiences, questions, observations. Some possible prompts to guide reflection might include:
   a. Think about a time around your sex or gender identity:
      i. That shaped your understanding of gender or was a moment of realization.
      ii. When you were treated differently because of your gender.

       iii.  That someone made an assumption about you or told you that you couldn't do something because of your gender, or told you that you should do something because of your gender.

    b.   What is an observation or question you have about gender?

3.   Give participants five minutes to write in response to these questions. Then ask them to choose one experience, story, or observation and capture it in six words. It doesn't have to be a complete sentence, or even one thought. It can be a question or a phrase. The six-word stories don't need to be narrative, or even necessarily make sense to anyone but the author.

4.   Share examples with the group. (The below examples were written by PJP teaching artists and directors.)

    a.   My body is not your business.

    b.   I never liked playing with Barbies.

    c.   Woman, girl, no. Who am I?

    d.   Nighttime defense: carry your pepper spray.

    e.   Little girls are more than dolls.

5.   Pass out notecards and ask participants to write their six-word stories on the notecards. They are welcome to write as many as they want, but ask participants to write only one six-word story per notecard.

6.   After participants have finished writing (they might try several drafts), invite them to consider how to perform or stage one of their six-word stories with a repeated gesture or series of gestures or a frozen image to accompany this story. (It is helpful to prepare a six-word story and gesture or image in advance to model for the participants.)

7.   Invite participants to stand in the circle and face outward, so they have their own "personal studio" in which to practice their gesture and the performance of their six-word story.

8.   Ask the ensemble to turn back to the circle, and go around the circle to share their six-word story performances with one another. You may want to provide participants with a way to show their appreciation (i.e., snapping or clapping).

## Guiding Reflection

- What did you notice in our performances? What is still sticking with you?
- How would you describe your experience of creating this story and performance?
- Which six-word stories made you think about gender in a new or challenging way?
- How might we move these stories and bits of performance material into a performance for an audience?

## In Our Experience

Almost always, participants will ask if they can have five or seven words. We encourage participants to keep their stories to six words, but if they can't move forward, we remain flexible with the form. These stories are often rich, emotionally charged, and powerful. While they can stand on their own as a collage poem, they are also excellent material to use during transitions between pieces of performance. We use this action to explore both gender and race, and it works well as a way for the participants to begin thinking about the importance of each word in sharing narratives publicly, and as a starting point for telling a story and building a scene.

## Connecting to Performance

This performance can become a piece of "text" that youth can perform as part of the script. If you need longer pieces for your script, invite youth to expand their six-word story into a scene, monologue, or poem.

**Source**: Adapted as part of the Performing Justice Project from Michele Norris and the Race Card Project™ (2010).

# Who Am I?

# Understanding Sex and Gender: Activating Text Through Image (Gender)

*Participants will use sculptor and clay techniques from Statues and Sculpting to create embodied images from the six-word stories on gender that they just generated.*

## PJP Connection:

Moving individual stories into images is a great way to explore performance-making before participants are aware that they are making performance. These images are often a first step towards creating scenes that will be used to perform racial and gender justice.

**Time**: 15–20 minutes

**Materials**: None, possibly music to underscore their movement

## Directing the Action

1. Move participants into groups of 3–4.
2. Invite participants to share their gender cards with their group, and then to share some information about the story that inspired it. Give each participant 1–2 minutes to share.

3. After each story, ask participants to brainstorm with their group about images and pictures that come to mind: What does this story look like in pictures? What is reflected in the bodies of the people involved in this story? If you had to create pictures of this story with your bodies, what would that look like?

4. After everyone has shared, tell participants that they will be doing more sculpting work in their groups. Each participant will be the sculptor for their six-word story, and the other two or three participants will be the "clay."

5. Each group should develop an image for each group member's story. The entire group should be involved in each image. The group then decides the order of the group's pieces to share out.

6. Develop transitions from one story into the next. Each image's "sculptor" should read their six-word story as the images are performed.

7. Ask each group to perform for other groups in an audience/stage configuration.

8. After each mini-performance, ask audience to offer three things they appreciated about the performance. Encourage them to be as specific as possible.

## Guiding Reflection

• What did you just do to create these performances? What steps did you go through?

• What skills did this process require?

• What surprised you, from your own group's work or another group's performance?

• What similarities and differences did you notice?

• Why are gender-based stories important to building justice?

## In Our Experience
Giving less time for this activity can actually help groups create content.

## Connecting to Performance
These short stories can be combined to be performed as a part of the final script, or they can accompany another story, expanded to create a scene, or become choreography set to music.

**Source**: Adapted by Performing Justice Project from Boal (1992, pp. 164–172).

# Who Am I?

## Activating Intersectional Identities: Identity Pie

*This action offers a list of various identities and invites participants to name their own identities as well as identify which groups hold power in our country and society.*

### PJP Connection

This action provides a framework for youth to name out their own identities and examine how they are similar to or different from identities that hold power in our country. Youth also have the opportunity to assign a weight to how important each identity has been in their experience. Identity pie provides a type of reflection that isn't just about writing, and when we encourage young people to decorate their own identity pie with color and symbols, they take pride in representing themselves visually.

**Time**: 45–60 minutes, depending on how much time allowed for decorating

**Materials**: Identity pie worksheets (blank sheet with large circle on it), colored pencils, pens

### Directing the Action

1.  Prepare a list of identity categories, which should include:
    - birth-assigned sex
    - gender identity/expression
    - race
    - ethnicity
    - religion
    - ability/disability
    - citizenship status *(undocumented, green card, citizen, etc.)*
    - socioeconomic status *(owning, middle, working class)*
    - age
    - sexual orientation
2.  Part one: As a whole group, invite participants to name the "dominant group" in the US for each identity marker, meaning the group that holds the most power. Work through each identity category, visually recording this list where can see the dominant group listed for each category.
    a.  As participants discuss which identity marker has the most power, it may sometimes be necessary to offer more information if the group doesn't have the language or critical analysis to identify the dominant group.

b. Groups can become distracted by considering who holds power in particular situations, as power can be contextual and local. In this case, we ask who holds the power financially and systemically in our country. If, in a particular context or community, women are believed to hold the power, it is important to delineate that women do not make up the majority in government, in CEO positions across large corporations, or in holding wealth.

3. Part two: Ask participants to record their own identities for each category in their journal or on a worksheet, and then give some time to reflect and write about which identities have more or less weight in their own experiences. Questions to think through include:
   - Which identities feel like a bigger or smaller part of who you are?
   - Which identities do you tend to think of more often or take more energy/attention?
   - Which identities do you tend to think about the least? Why?
   - Which identities are hard to separate out from each other?

4. Ask participants to use the circle (on their paper) and divide it up into pie slices according to how important different identities are to them, and how much these slices impact their experiences. They will use all the identity categories but decide the size of the pie slice according to how much a category shapes their daily experiences, or how much they tend to think about a particular identity marker. For example, Sex or Gender might take up a bigger slice, while Religion might be just a small sliver. There is no right or wrong in this action, but each slice should be labeled with a personal identity. If participants get caught up in percentages and are having a hard time fitting everything into 100 percent, discourage them from using percentages—this tends to stall the process. Instead, encourage them to find other ways to demonstrate the weight or impact of their identity slices.

5. Give participants time to fill in their identity pie with words, symbols, color. Give them a specific amount of time and work backward so they can get close to a final state.

6. Put all the identity pies on the floor or a wall and host a gallery walk (everyone walks around the pieces of art). Encourage everyone to look at the identity pies without talking or commenting until you move into a discussion.

## Guiding Reflection

- What did you have to think about in this performance action?
- How did you decide which identities to use? What was difficult or easy about this?
- Which identities do you think of more often? Less often?

### In Our Experience

We find that young people enjoy having time to decorate their "pie" with their own identities, creating a visual reflection of how they experience these various identity markers.

This action provides an organic way for participants to realize that they may take some identities for granted and may focus on some identities more than others. Often, the identities that hold more weight or focus tend to be ones where they hold less power or privilege. This is an interesting realization, particularly when thinking about race and gender. This action also provides a way to think about intersectionality; it can feel impossible to separate some categories of identity from other categories, because of the way they are connected to power and oppression and because we never experience them separately.

### Connecting to Performance

Through Identity Pie, participants name which of their identities carry more weight. This is important to pay attention to as material is developed for performance. If a participant has an identity they realize is a significant part of who they are, it may be important to draw this out in performance or support their exploration further. The work of creating the Identity Pie can become a starting point for writing monologues or "This I Believe" text.

**Source**: Developed by Cox and Beale (1997, p. 53).

# Who Am I?

## Activating Intersectional Identities: Body Maps

*This action allows participants to create a full-scale, hand-drawn map of their own bodies, locating identity and experience in different places on their body map.*

### PJP Connection

Creating a body map is one way to visually identify and demonstrate the impact of identity and identity-based oppressions on our lived experiences. This action helps participants acknowledge how their experiences impact them and where on their bodies the experiences and memories live. Connecting experience and body is one way to begin performing justice.

**Time**: 30–45 minutes

**Materials**: Large pieces of butcher paper, large enough for participants to lie down and have their bodies traced; markers, and possibly other art supplies

## Directing the Action

1.  In this action, participants create a full-size map of their bodies, naming their identities and reflecting on impactful experiences in their life.
2.  Explain to participants:
    a.  You will each receive a full-size piece of butcher paper to create your own body map. Lie down on the butcher paper in any shape you like, asking another participant (or director) to trace around your body to create an outline. Think about the outline shape—do you want an angel-in-the-snow shape? Do you want your outline to have hands outstretched? Feet jumping? Think about the position you create on your paper before you are outlined.
    b.  Once you have a body outline, think about how and why and where you will decorate your body. Think about using your Identity Pie to help you decide what is important to reflect in your body map. Is there a place in or on your body that is impacted, or that carries the weight of each of the identities you detailed in your Identity Pie or of significant life experiences? Which identities and experiences really live in your head? Your heart? Your gut? Your feet? Feel free to use words, symbols, colors, or whatever will help you convey your full body and identity map.
    c.  Hand out markers (and other art supplies, if using) and invite participants to decorate the map with the words and images they have come up with and any desired images related to their identity markers and social locations.
    d.  If these body maps are not completed in this session, they are a great reflection/quiet action to return to throughout the process.
    e.  Once the maps are relatively complete, hang them up in a gallery fashion.

## Guiding Reflection

*   What did you realize or notice about your body map as you made it?
*   What are you proud of on your body map?
*   Looking at our body map gallery, what do you notice?
*   How should we incorporate these into performance?

## In Our Experience

We often have to pull participants away from this project as they enjoy the relaxing, reflective time to create and are typically proud of what is reflected on their body maps. This work supports the performance of stories and experiences of racial and gender injustice—the more we lift up and share out our experiences of oppression, the more we build capacity for change. This includes finding a variety of ways to highlight experiences of oppression—text and movement is one way, and visual art projects are another method.

## Connecting to Performance

Body maps become an important part of the performance-making process, as they can lead to the development of performance material, providing a critical way to reflect silently and visually before choosing what will move into a performance piece. The maps sometimes become set backdrops or material for audiences to browse before and after a performance.

**Source**: This performance action is inspired by an activity led by Matt Richardson in a curriculum development circle at the University of Texas at Austin.

# Who Am I?

# Activating Intersectional Identities: I Come From a Place

*This action gives participants an opportunity to write personal stories from a prompt, producing content that is structurally different from much of the previous PJP writing.*

## PJP Connection

This writing produces dynamic group poems that focus on experiences related to identity and location. As the ensemble writes about where they come from, they have the opportunity to think through how a place influences and is tied to experiences of race and gender.

**Time**: 12–15 minutes

**Materials**: Notecards (five for each participant), writing utensil, butcher paper, markers

## Directing the Action

1.  Invite participants to find their own space to sit with five notecards and a writing utensil.
2.  Explain to participants:
    a.  I am going to ask you to reflect on places you come from. Remember the sensory language you have used in some of our PJP actions.

b. Use your notecard to respond to this prompt: "I come from a place...".

c. Please find five different ways to finish this prompt. (For example, I come from a place where the vacuum runs early and loud on Saturday mornings.) Write each idea on a separate notecard. Think less literally and more descriptively and through your senses. What images, sounds, sensations, feelings evoke the places you come from? Consider different places that you come from—it might be a literal place or a state of mind. It could be places you associate with right now or places from ten years ago. Here are some examples:

  i. I come from a place where loud voices were loving voices.

  ii. I come from a place where kids were responsible for doing the dishes.

  iii. I come from a place where dreams didn't always wake up in the morning.

3. When participants have finished writing 3–5 notecards, split them into groups of three.

4. Explain to participants:

a. You will each choose three of your notecards to share with your group. Take turns reading them out.

b. Work as a group to choose only one line from each person to now put together into a short poem. Spread out your three chosen notecards on the ground and arrange the three chosen lines into a specific, pleasing order.

c. Next, collaboratively write a final fourth line of text that begins with the words, "We imagine a place...".

d. Number your cards 1–4 so that you are clear on the order of the lines in your newly created poem.

e. Think about how you might share this poem out with the rest of the ensemble. Will one person read each line? Will you read all the lines together? Will you repeat any words or lines? Rehearse so that you can vocally perform your group poem with confidence.

5. Invite each group to share their poem with the rest of the ensemble.

6. Collect the notecard poems so that you have a record of the created text.

## Guiding Reflection

- What did you recall about your life that you hadn't thought about for a while?
- How did you decide how to combine lines?
- How did combining your line of text with others change the meaning or feeling?
- What do these poems have to do with justice?

### In Our Experience

These poems are typically moving and lyrical, particularly as participants use more sensory, evocative language. If a group is particularly invested in their poem, this action can also be extended, using more of the individual lines they have written moved into a full performance piece.

### Connecting to Performance

These poems can be used as transitions or put together to form a large group poem. Each small group poem can become one stanza in a longer group poem in which the same "We imagine a place" line repeats throughout. We have used these poems in combination with abstract ensemble movement and also very specific repeated gestures. The poems can come to life in realistic or abstract ways, and can be used as transitions, stories, or a central ensemble performative moment.

**Source**: We learned this writing prompt from storyteller Jon Spelman. A version of the prompt is also outlined at the I Am From Project by George Ella Lyon and Julie Landsman, inspired by George Ella Lyon's original poem "Where I'm From."

# Who Am I?

# Activating Intersectional Identities: "I Am" Spoken Word

*This action guides participants through writing, editing, rehearsing, and performing a spoken word piece. A version of this worksheet in both Spanish and English is included in Appendix A.*

### PJP Connection

Because of the ongoing focus on race and gender, this action often references experiences of race and gender without explicit prompts around these identity markers. The writing is often vulnerable and rich with metaphor and imagery. Participants thoroughly enjoy this process when given enough time to dive in. The format and worksheet support a thoughtful and interesting devising process.

**Time**: 50–60 minutes

**Materials**: Worksheet, writing utensils

## Directing the Action

1. Pass out worksheets with prompts and blank spaces for participants to fill in (see Appendix A). Ask that they take some time to fill in the blanks. Explain that there is no right or wrong, they should fill in the worksheet in a way that describes them.
2. Allow time for participants to fill in their worksheet; checking in with youth as they write/work.
3. Invite participants to create a final line by pulling any three words from the poem.
4. Ask participants to give their piece a title.
5. Allow time for participants to read their poems out loud three times to themselves. Ask them to reflect on how the piece feels, and to make any changes they'd like to make.
6. Invite them to stand with their piece in hand. Facing away from the ensemble, ask them to perform their revised piece. Encourage participants to find words, phrases or moments that can be reflected through gesture along with text.
7. Invite students to incorporate the following into their pieces:
   • one significant pause
   • one significant inhale or exhale
   • two gestures
8. Invite participants to try placing these elements in several different places before choosing where to add them. Remind them to notate all movements in their piece.
9. Once participants have marked where their movements belong, invite them to run through their entire piece.
10. Finally, invite participants to prepare to share with the rest of the ensemble, with one final rehearsal, reminding them that this is not a final performance, but just a sharing.

Spoken Word Sequence (provided in a worksheet format in Appendix A):

Line 1: My name is…
Line 2: My skin looks like…
Line 3: My body feels like…
Line 4: My voice tells me…
Repeat line 2 from above: My skin looks like…
Line 5: My mind thinks…
Repeat line 4 from above: My voice tells me…
Line 6: You should know…
Repeat line 5 from above: My mind thinks…

Line 7: My hands want…
Repeat Line 6 from above: You should know…
Line 8: My feet want…
Repeat line 7 from above: My hands want…
Line 9: The world says…
Repeat line 8 from above: My feet want…
Line 10: I say…
Repeat line 9 from above: The world says…
Line 11: Today I am…
Repeat line 10 from above: I say…
Line 12: Tomorrow I will be…

## Guiding Reflection

- What did you find out through this performance action?
- If you could choose one line that feels like it really describes you or your experiences, which line would it be?
- How is your poetry, and specifically this spoken word activity, working toward gender or racial justice?

## In Our Experience

These poems create rich imagery, providing powerful opportunities for devising and image work. They are also incredibly rewarding for participants, as the structure helps to create a product rather quickly. This action may require extra support if the ensemble struggles with writing quickly, and we recommend offering participants a worksheet if pressed for time or if this is the first time they try writing longer-form piece of text.

## Connecting to Performance

Sometimes when these pieces are performed for an audience they are accompanied by an image sequence or complete the image as a visual accompaniment. And sometimes the words are so powerful that they need to be performed alone with nothing else happening. It is also possible to bring together several different spoken word pieces to create one larger poem or performance piece.

**Source**: This action was developed by PJP guest artists Emily Aguilar and Megan Nevels as part of the Performing Justice Project.

## Doing Justice

# Challenging Respectability

*Briana Barner*

As a person of color working with majority youth of color during my time with PJP, I was always aware of the similarities that I saw between me and the young people. It often made me uncomfortable—sometimes I felt like the only difference between me and them was that I was lucky enough to be identified early on as "gifted," which meant extra, favorable attention from teachers and other adults. I was a respectable young woman and did everything the "right way." Ideally, I would be the kind of girl that didn't end up in a place like a South Texas juvenile detention center (JDC).

But realistically, that isn't true. One bad encounter could have led me right to a JDC. Being respectable helped me avoid—for the most part—interactions with the criminal system, and also probably made me a good candidate to work at the center. Respectability was a thread that ran through each and every session that we had at our particular JDC. After all, a program like PJP is part of the rehabilitation process to help the young people become respectable citizens, despite their criminal record. So their actions during each session should, in theory, reflect this. For people of color and other marginalized groups, respectability can be a tool to counter negative images and stereotypes. It can also be a way to assimilate into mainstream culture and society and in turn reap the benefits awarded to non-marginalized groups.

But we know that is not how power works. Individual actions alone cannot shift systemic oppression. There are people who have serious investments in respectability, and in teaching racial and sexual justice, it's something that we have to be aware of. Being respectable can be a tool for survival, a way to navigate oppressive systems. But we must keep in mind as facilitators that when possible, we should push back against this, even when the young people cannot. This can look like pushing back when the young people continuously referred to some girls as "trashy" versus "classy." This can look like not batting an eye when a young person curses while expressing themselves. This can look like letting the young people choose songs that truly reflect their experiences instead of forcing them to choose more "appropriate" songs.

These may seem like small actions, but they matter, particularly in a juvenile detention center where both participants and facilitators have little control. It is important to think about the role that respectability plays in the lives of these young people, because it will impact the lens through which they see racial and sexual justice. It's also important to think about how we can challenge respectability politics while avoiding reinforcing them.

**Figure 2.3a** PJP participants explore relationships between gender, power, and the workplace
Source: Photo by Lynn Hoare.

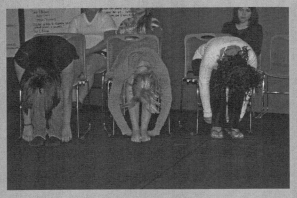

**Figure 2.3b** PJP participants perform an abstract movement sequence about the impacts of societal expectations on women
Source: Photo by Lynn Hoare.

## 2.3.3 Performance Actions: What Is (In)Justice and How Does it Show Up in My Life?

The actions described in this section support participants' evolving investigation of concepts of power, oppression, justice, and injustice. Specifically, the actions in this section invite participants to weave back and forth between concepts of interpersonal and systemic oppression. They support critical reflection on and visions of the ways that personal identities are connected to the ways (in)justice shows up in their daily lives. In this section, we describe and frame how performance actions that focus on devising, such as the Great Game of Power, Machines, and 8-Count Movement can generate performances themes, visual metaphors, and small bits of performance that show or make visible identity-based inequities. *

Performance actions in this section provide opportunities to name and identify personal identity markers. These actions help build an understanding of how identities impact access to power and privilege, as well as our relationships to institutional, interpersonal, and internalized oppression. Performance actions in this section are divided into three categories or subsections: What Is Power?, Understanding Oppression, and Exposing and Resisting Injustice. In the first category of performance actions, what Is Power?, participants have the opportunity to analyze power and privilege through nonverbal and physical actions to creating text together. The second category of actions, Understanding Oppression, offers various frameworks such as metaphor, embodiment, and reflection to understand oppression and examine how it is experienced at both individual and structural levels. Exposing and Resisting Injustice, the third category in this section, encourages young people to consider ways to speak back to structural oppression and take action through theatre and performance. These performance actions expose inequity, strengthen youth power, and build hope.

Below is an overview of the performance actions included in this section, followed by a facilitation guide for each action. These short facilitation guides begin with a basic description of each action, followed by an overview of how the action can be used to generate content and prepare young people for performance within a PJP residency.

## What Is Power?

- Columbian Hypnosis
- The Great Game of Power
- Creating Group Definitions
- The Bag Game
- Complete the Image

## Understanding Oppression

- Carnival in Rio
- The Four Levels of Oppression Through Dress-Coding
- Respectability Politics
- Machines
- Writing Prompt "In Society…"
- 8-Count Movement
- Writing Prompt "My Skin Is…"
- Injustice/Justice Creatures

## Exposing and Resisting Injustice

- Send a Snap
- Hashtag Activism
- Hashtag Stories
- Complete the Image—Resistance
- Still I Rise
- The Human Knot
- Justice for Women Means…
- Activating Statistics
- This I Believe
- Imagining Justice

## What Is (In)Justice?

## What Is Power? Columbian Hypnosis

*From the "arsenal" of Theatre of the Oppressed by Augusto Boal, this action is a partner exercise that examines how power and trust plays out in the practice of leading and following.*

### PJP Connection

This performance action raises critical questions about comfort and responsibilities connected to leading and following. This action supports reflection and discussion about how power and privilege show up in relationships and institutions in participants' lives.

**Time**: 15 minutes

**Materials**: Open playing space for moving around

### Directing the Action

1. Invite participants to find a partner. Once they are in pairs, ask them to designate one partner as A and one partner as B.
2. Explain to participants:
   a. Partner A will play the leader first by holding their open palm up in front of partner B's face, about 6–10 inches away. B, please imagine that there is an invisible string attached from your nose to the center of partner A's open palm. It is through this connection that the leader (A) will move the follower (B) around the space. This is a silent activity, so please move through the space without talking (it can help to model leading and following). Remember that when

you are the leader it is your job to take care of your partner—you are responsible for them.

3. As partners get comfortable moving and exploring the space as leader and follower, remind the leaders to explore speed, forward and backward movement, and different levels. Remind leaders that they are in charge of taking their partners on a physical journey, while also taking care of them.

4. After three to five minutes of exploration, ask the leaders to bring their partner to a safe stopping point. Invite them to cut the connection to the follower by closing their hand and moving it away from their partner's face.

5. Before the pairs begin talking, ask them to switch roles. Let them know that discussion will happen after both partners have experienced each role.

6. Repeat the exercise with similar reminders for Bs as they lead As through the space.

7. After everyone has tried out both roles, ask participants to share their experience of leading and following with their partner.

## Guiding Reflection

- What was your experience in leading? What was your experience in following?
- What strategies did you use to feel successful in leading/following?
- Which role was more comfortable for you, leading or following? Why?
- Who holds the power in this action? What makes you think that?
- Where do these power dynamics show up in your own lives and communities?

## In Our Experience

This action both requires and builds trust; it can take partners time to fully commit to playing. It offers an embodied way to explore power and reflect on our experiences, comfort, and patterns of behavior related to leading and following. Depending on the group's experience and focus, we provide detailed side coaching during this action, encouraging each leader to adjust to the needs of the follower and pay attention to speed, risk, and/or the physical comfort and abilities of their partner.

## Connecting to Performance

Like other forms of image work, the movement patterns in this action could be adapted as a physical score or background visual for a monologue, recorded voiceovers, or other performed text. This action proves interesting to watch from the outside, particularly as trust and focus are built between participants.

**Source**: Developed by Augusto Boal and published in *Games for actors and non-actors* (1992, p. 63).

# What Is (In)Justice?

# What Is Power? The Great Game of Power

*This action, from Theatre of the Oppressed, asks participants to use chairs and a water bottle to sculpt and analyze what power looks like in the world.*

### PJP Connection

This performance action invites participants to think symbolically and metaphorically about how power is projected, how we "read" power in the world, and where and how power and privilege show up in our lives. We use this action to begin talking about who holds power in our lives and communities and how power is related to identity.

**Time**: 20–25 minutes

**Materials**: 3–5 chairs (identical, light enough to move and stack), one water bottle

### Directing the Action

1. Set up a playing space with 3–5 chairs and water bottle. Ask for a volunteer to be the sculptor and silently arrange the chairs and water bottle so that one chair becomes the most powerful object in the sculpture. Explain to participants:
   a. Any of the objects can be moved or placed on top of each other, on their side, or in any other configuration. However, none of the objects may be completely removed from the space.
   b. Sculptor, you will not reveal your thinking behind the arrangement. Rather, you will be invited to listen to the group's multiple interpretations of what you create.
2. Provide 30–60 seconds for the sculptor to arrange the chairs and water bottle in the playing space. After the sculptor completes their task, invite the rest of the group to move around the 3D image, to see it from all angles and take it in silently.

3. The next part of this action relies on group reflection and participants "reading" the sculpture for meaning. This action isn't about everyone guessing the sculptor's intention; rather, it invites the group to consider how one image or sculpture can spark a multiplicity of stories and ideas about power.

4. Once everyone has viewed the image from all angles, invite the group to describe what they see in the image:
   a. How are the chairs arranged? How is the water bottle arranged?
   b. Describe what you see without naming what you think it means.

5. Next, invites the group to share what they notice about the image:
   a. Which chair do you think holds the most power in the image and why?
   b. How do the power dynamics in the sculpture change when you look at it from an angle or different sides?
   c. Why do you think there are multiple interpretations of which chair has the most power?

6. Encourage different readings of the sculpture from various people in the room. After everyone shares their ideas about what the sculpture means, invite the sculptor to share what they were thinking or imagining as they created it.

7. Invite someone new to rearrange the chairs and water bottle to create a new sculpture. Repeat the witnessing and reflection process, starting with "what do you see?" and following it with an analysis of power.

8. After a few rounds of this action, invite the group to consider how a sculpture tells a story.

## Guiding Reflection

- If the chairs represent character, who are they and where are they? What might the water bottle represent?
- What is happening in the sculpture? What happened in the moment before the action in this sculpture? What might happen next?
- How is power at play in the sculpture?
- How do your own or others' social locations or identity markers play into your perceptions, assumptions, readings of these images? Specifically, how does gender and/or race play into your perceptions, assumptions, reading of these images?
- What drew your attention or your eye in each of the sculptures? Pay attention to how we might craft images and sculptures to help an audience look at or notice something specific. We will continue to consider this as we move forward creating frozen images with our own bodies on stage.

- What kinds of power are we talking about as we look at these sculptures? Let's write these down to refer to later. *Encourage youth to articulate what kind of power they are referring to, such as personal agency, systemic power, the power of an institution that backs an individual, etc.*

### In Our Experience

This action allows youth to think deeply about social justice issues and push each other's thinking through the description and analysis of what they see in the chair sculptures. Since this action accesses metaphor and symbol, youth tend to dig into their own life experiences to make meaning of the images created. We rely on this process to invite a rich, layered dialogue and invites youth to deconstruct and analyze how images are crafted for meaning and relevance.

### Connecting to Performance

The Great Game of Power allows youth to connect metaphorically to ideas of power and oppression in a low-risk way, as they cognitively access ideas without embodying them. This action often inspires stories from participants' experiences and can be used to generate themes for devising or to inspire participants to write stories and scene.

**Source**: Developed by Augusto Boal and published in *Games for actors and non-actors* (1992, p. 150).

## What Is (In)Justice?

## What Is Power? Creating Group Definitions

*This action invites participants to grapple with different definitions of power, helping them to make visible the often invisible structures that impact their personal power.*

### PJP Connection

Young people often equate power with personal agency. In this action, youth consider various definitions of power that often extend beyond their own experiences. As participants locate their own identity markers and personal experiences within larger systems of power, they reflect on, analyze, and deepen their understandings of systemic oppression.

**Time**: 20 minutes

**Materials**: Journals, writing utensil, butcher paper, and markers

## Directing the Action

1. Invite participants to sit comfortably with their journal and a writing utensil. Explain to participants:
   a. In your journals, reflect on what the word *power* mean to you. What does power look like in the world? Where and how does it show up in your life?
   b. Next, use your journal to brainstorm multiple responses to the following prompts:
      i. Power is...
      ii. Power means...
   c. Looking at your brainstorm, write a definition of power that you are comfortable sharing with a small group.
   d. Move into a group of three with your journal. Share your definitions with each other. Discuss what is similar or different. What types of power are you leaving out? Expand your list of possibilities with your group members.
   e. In your trio, come up with one group definition of power together, using any parts of the definitions you each wrote. Write your definition on a piece of butcher paper, large enough for others to see from wherever they are sitting.
2. Invite the ensemble to return to a large circle and share their definitions. As participants share out, write down the different kinds of power being discussed. The following definitions of power can help guide facilitation:
   a. Social power—power within social groups and power to motivate and move social groups; power because of social location.
   b. Financial power—having money, resources, time, and/or access to money, resources and time; having access to whatever kind of currency grants more of what an individual desires (goods, services, attention, decisions, control).
   c. Institutional power—the power behind and connected to large institutions in our society, such as churches, educational systems, large corporations, governments, prison system, etc.
   d. Personal power—having agency to take action or to have elements of control where desired.
   e. Power of social movements—the conditions that provoke or allow the response of groups to shift from individual action to collective action.
3. Explain to participants:
   a. Now, we are going to return to your journals. Think about the different kinds of power that we have listed here and look at your writing. Are there experiences you wrote about that involve one or more of these kinds of power, or an absence of one of these kinds of power? Mark these pieces in your journal and let us know if you need help thinking this through or have any questions.

4.  Next, count the ensemble into groups of four and give each person one minute to share an example from their journal that demonstrates something about power.
5.  As an alternate closing, or next part of this activity, encourage participants to respond individually or as a group to the following prompts (coming up with as many ideas as possible for each prompt):
    a.  Power looks like…
    b.  Power smells like…
    c.  Power feels like…
    d.  Power sounds like…
    e.  Power says…

## Guiding Reflection

- Which definition of power are you most familiar with?
- Which category of power do you tend to think about most often? Which definition of power most influences the experiences you have in the world?
- How are power and privilege connected?

## In Our Experience

Young people often equate personal power, or agency, as the ability to do whatever they want in the world. As we hope to support the development of personal agency, we also want to illuminate institutional and systemic oppressions and the ways that they limit or impact access, particularly for those that hold visible markers of marginalized identities. Critical literacy and the ability to identify larger structures of power and oppression also shape our relationships to power and privilege.

## Connecting to Performance

We often turn definitions into recorded voiceovers which we then use in various places throughout a performance. Layering recorded voiceovers with the movement landscape from a "complete the image" sequence can be a powerful way to share or deepen text with the addition of an abstract image or movement sequence.

**Source**: This action was developed as part of the Performing Justice Project.

# What Is (In)Justice?

# What is Power? The Bag Game

*This action illuminates concepts of power and privilege. As the action unfolds, participants see the potential conflict and consequences that arise from unchecked privilege and limited resources.*

## PJP Connection

This action visually exposes challenges related to access, resource distribution, and privilege. We use this action early on to discuss access to resources before we delve into the connections between racial and gender identity and similar issues of access.

**Time**: 30 minutes, or more depending on size of the group

**Materials**: A clear plastic baggie or small see-through plastic container that is filled with random items, most of which do not appear to be valuable. Fill the bag with one-third to one-quarter fewer items than the number of people participating in the action. Items should include one to two valuable items (such as a $20 bill and chocolate bar), and one to two items that are desirable but less valuable (such as gum, mints, sunglasses or a nice tea bag), and a variety of everyday items that are less interesting, as well as some items that appear to be old, useless, or used. Examples of other items might include: a pen, cork, pompom, a rubber band, a sticker, a rock, a piece of string or yarn, a blank sticky note, an empty paper towel tube, etc.

## Directing the Action

1.  Ask participants to sit in a circle. Stand inside the circle and walk around the perimeter with the prepared bag of items, asking participants to look at what is in the bag.
2.  Explain to participants:
    a.  I will give this bag to someone in the circle. You can take whatever object you want out of the bag, and then pass it on.
3.  Hand the bag to someone and allow some time for the bag to move around the circle. At some point, it will arrive empty to someone before it has traveled around the entire circle. The final person who receives the empty bag may ask if they can just keep that.
4.  Ask the group a few reflection questions and allow time for several responses.
    a.  What happened in this game?
    b.  How do you feel about what you chose?

c. How do you feel if you weren't able to get anything—because the bag didn't even make it to your location in the circle?

d. At what point did you realize there wouldn't be enough things to make it around the circle? How did you feel about that? What were you thinking?

e. One of the words we are going to think about in PJP is *privilege*. Who had the privilege in this game? *(Facilitator might also offer a definition of privilege here.)*

f. Who had the power in this game? *(Facilitator might guide a short discussion about the differences between power and privilege. It is important for participants to realize that the facilitator, who filled the bag and chose where it would begin in the circle had power. Some groups forget that this person is also a player in the game.)*

g. Is there anything we could have done differently?

## Guiding Reflection

- Stepping outside of this game, how do you feel about what happened?
- Where do you see similar situations or systems playing out in your world?
- If we were to compare the "bag" to something in life, what could it be?
- How does power and privilege show up in your daily life?

## In Our Experience

The bag game produces rich discussion that lays the groundwork for later examinations of how privilege and power operate in our daily lives. We try to present the bag to someone with great ritual and attention, rather than handing it off casually. This gesture emphasizes the power of the facilitator to choose who first has access to the resources in the bag and how that plays out for those at the "end of the line."

## Connecting to Performance

This action offers an interesting metaphor to bring into performance. Audience members might replicate the action or participants might develop scenes, a series of images, or a dance piece that mirrors the practice of marginalization and the insidious nature of systemic injustice.

**Source**: This action has been adapted from a workshop with Renée Watson.

# What Is (In)Justice?

# What is Power? Complete the Image

*This action, from Augusto Boal's Theatre of the Oppressed, encourages embodied ways to know and communicate ideas, and offers a way to move beyond words and text. While simple and relatively low-risk, this performance action tends to generate stunning movement sequences.*

## PJP Connection

This action supports embodied movement for participants and helps cultivate an appreciation of the shapes bodies make. By creating physical images and small movements with a partner, participants begin to translate ideas and feeling and experiences into abstract but connected movement in their bodies. The work of justice includes valuing and lifting up the body as tool for knowing and communicating truth.

**Time**: 15–20 minutes

**Materials**: None

## Directing the Action

1. Invite participants to spread out around the room with a partner.
2. Explain to participants (and model as appropriate):
   a. Standing across from your partner, decide who is A and who is B.
   b. A and B will shake hands and freeze in that position.
   c. Partner A will then step out and away from the frozen image while B stays frozen in the handshake position.
   d. A will look at the shape of their partner's pose and notice how the frozen image creates negative space or empty space (such as under and over the arm or above the shoulders). A will re-enter the image, using their body to create a shape that fills in some of the negative space around the shape of B's body.
   e. B will now step out and away from the frozen image, leaving A in a frozen image. B will look at the shape and image created by A's body, find the negative space in the image, and fill it with their body to create a new image with their partner.
3. Encourage partners to alternate, filling the negative space with their bodies and completing the image.
4. Invite participants to create abstract images in response to some key words. Explain to participants:
   a. the image is not necessarily a direct representation of the idea, but rather a response to the idea. Your images might represent a feeling or an abstraction of these ideas.

    b.   Invite the group to respond to works such as:
        i.   Childhood
       ii.   Rage
      iii.   Safety
      iv.   Oppression

5.   After the pairs have explored the action and built a rhythm, ask pairs to move into small groups (combining 2–3 pairs). In these larger groups, they will continue the activity, adding one person at a time to the frozen image, and then continuing to rotate who moves out and in at any given moment.

6.   Once the groups are in a rhythm with Complete the Image, ask them to respond to the following words within the construct of the action:
    a.   Injustice
    b.   Justice

7.   Finally, bring all of the groups together so that the whole ensemble is completing the image together, with one participant moving at a time. Ask the group to respond to the following words:
    a.   Power
    b.   Empowerment

8.   As the group completes the images, you might play music, read a poem or story that has been generated by a participant, or add some other element of sound for the movement to play with or respond to.

9.   Variation: We sometimes invite a few people at a time to step out and watch the larger group complete the image. We sometimes play with different styles of music to demonstrate how music and movement influence each other and communicate emotion or knowledge.

## Guiding Reflection

- What stood out to you about this action?
- What did images of power look like? What did images of injustice/justice look like?
- How did it feel when you began to collaboratively work on communicating an idea?
- How did your movements change as the prompts or music shifted?

## In Our Experience

It is important for the facilitator to watch this action from outside of the group. If participants get stuck doing the same movements, remind them to try leading with different parts of their bodies, exploring levels, and thinking about their facial expressions. While it can take a group some time to settle into this action, we challenge participants to stick with it. As a group becomes more comfortable using their bodies to respond to ideas and build images, this action turns into visually dynamic staging.

### Connecting to Performance

Movement sequences created through Complete the Image offer visual material to support transitions, a longer story or monologue, or a song.

**Source**: Developed by Augusto Boal and published in *Games for actors and non-actors* (1992, p. 130).

# What Is (In)Justice?

# Understanding Oppression: Carnival in Rio

*This action, developed by Augusto Boal, helps to "de-mechanize" the body and make us aware of our daily routines and patterned behaviors.*

### PJP Connection

This is a high energy performance action, useful when trust already exists within the group. We use this action as metaphor and a tool to investigate the ways that dominant narratives (in this case rhythms) take up space and work to erase or marginalize important stories, experiences, and identities.

**Time**: 15–20 minutes, depending on size of the group

**Materials**: Open space for moving around the room

### Directing the Action

1.  Ask participants to form groups of three and number off by 1-2-3 in their group.
2.  Number 1 will create a sound and movement that is easy to share and repeat while moving throughout the room. Partners 2 and 3 will repeat this sound/movement while moving through the room with number 1. At a signal from the facilitator, partners 2 and 3 will repeat this process of developing and sharing a sound and movement that their group members repeat while moving around the space.
3.  Explain to participants:
    a.  You are going to stay together as a unit and move around the group. However, each person in your group will now return to their own sound/movement while you all move together through the room. The groups of three will move through the room as a unit while each person performs their own sound/movement solo.

4.  After about one minute, ask the groups of three to "Unify!" Explain to participants:

    a.  At this point, try to unify the sound/movements of your three group members—without talking and without stopping your movement/ sound/walking.

    b.  This may mean that you find a common sound/movement that arises out of the three different sound/movement sequences, or it may mean that you adopt one sound/movement from one group member. I am going to give you about one minute to find your unified version.

5.  Once they have found their unified sound/movement, groups should continue moving around the space as a unified trio.

6.  At various points, call out "You may change groups," at which point anyone who wants to change to a different group may do so. Even while changing groups, participants must continue moving. They may not stop their sound/movement, and will continue until they assimilated into a new group, adopting that group's sound/movement.

7.  If at any point, someone is left alone, they must join a different group. Let the action play out until there is a stasis in the sound/movement and groupings.

8.  Relax and form a circle for discussion.

## Guiding Reflection

- What happened in this performance action?
- How did you feel at any given point in the process?
- What steps did your group take to unify?
- If you changed groups, why did you change? Describe your experience of changing groups and/or having someone leave your group.
- Did any of sound/movement rhythms gain momentum over others, and if so, what was happening?
- For anyone who was left alone with a sound/movement, how did you feel?
- Who had the power in this action? Whose power influenced you in any given moment and why?
- How did assimilation happen in this action? Was it a choice?
- What does this performance action have to do with gender or racial justice?

## In Our Experience

This action is most enjoyable when people are excited about a rhythm they've created and are willing to play and improvise. We often use this action after we've had time to build a sense of ensemble and participants feel somewhat comfortable committing to a movement/sound rhythm.

### Connecting to Performance

Practicing sound and rhythm together can help build a sense of ensemble. We often use abstract movement at various places in PJP performances, and activities such as this build group capacity for movement improvisation and the use of body and voice on stage.

**Source**: Developed by Augusto Boal and published in *Games for actors and non-actors* (1992, p. 98).

# What Is (In)Justice?

## Understanding Oppression: The Four Levels of Oppression Through Dress-Coding

*This action asks youth to assign quotes from a report on dress-coding to the four levels of oppression as a way to begin situating personal experiences within larger systems of oppression.*

### PJP Connection

In this performance action, participants identify and name institutional and structural oppressions, exploring how power functions and deciding where to direct their change-making efforts. This action supports youth agency by engaging participants in an analysis of the very systems of power and privilege that often ignore or actively suppress youth voice and activism.

**Time**: 60 minutes

**Materials**: Poster paper and markers; copies of the chart detailing the four levels of oppression (see Section 1.3); notecards with quotes (see below); a large chart with four open squares or quadrants labeled Interpersonal, Internalized, Institutional, Structural. Quotes are taken directly from *DRESS CODED: Black Girls, Bodies, and Bias in D.C. schools* (Davis et al. 2018). Note: We have sorted quotes from the report into the four levels of oppression; however, some quotes reflect more than one type of oppression. On your notecards, include quotes that represent all four levels of oppression. Without labeling them, keep track of which quote describes which level(s) of oppression, in order to support participants as they work to assign each quote to a level of oppression.

## Directing the Action

1. Begin this action by sitting in a circle or another arrangement that supports discussion and direct instruction. Ask participants, "When you hear the word *oppression*, what comes to mind?" After hearing some responses from participants, guide the entire group to define the word together.

2. The following PJP notes are for reference when discussing oppression.

   a. Oppression means that one identity is exploited, excluded or dismissed while a dominant group receives preference, access, visibility.

   b. Oppression often shows up through cultural norms, laws and practices. Someone is treated a particular way because of an identity they hold. They might be treated this way by someone else, by the rules in a school, or by the law.

   c. Oppression is often thought of as the "isms," experiences of oppression linked to our own identities. (Sexism, racism, adultism, ableism, heterosexism are examples of oppression.)

3. Ask the group to provide some examples of sexism.

4. Ask the group to provide some examples of racism.

5. Following this initial discussion, invite participants to find a partner and brainstorm some examples of other types of oppression. (Examples might include: adultism, ageism, homophobia, ableism, heterosexism, etc.) Let participants know they have three minutes to brainstorm and decide one example of oppression to share with the rest of the group.

6. Give the pairs time to discuss and then invite them to share out one example per pair. On a piece of poster paper, scribe the oppressions ("isms") named by each group.

7. Explain to participants:

   a. There are four levels of oppression that we will talk through today. Two of them are considered individual-level oppressions: interpersonal oppression and internalized oppression.

      i. **Interpersonal** oppression describes what happens between people as the result of bias or exclusion because of identity. (Participants may have identified examples of interpersonal oppression related to sexism or racism in the first brainstorm, if so, bring examples in here.) We are often familiar with seeing oppression at this level, either through microaggressions (subtle or unconscious comments and actions that indicate prejudice and discrimination), or through overt comments that support oppressive frameworks such as slurs, hate crimes, and violence.

      ii. **Internalized** oppression is when we start to believe things about ourselves or others because of what we have been told, and/or the messages we have absorbed and witnessed through various aspects of society, such as family, media, faith, peers, music, culture. These beliefs and biases can show up as internalized oppression (adopting negative beliefs about oneself), and they can also show up as internalized privilege or dominance (believing in one's own superiority or entitlement).

b. The next two types of oppression are considered systemic-level oppressions:

   i. **Institutional** oppression refers to how institutions, such as schools, businesses or workplaces, and government agencies enforce unfair policies and practices built on bias or inequity. An example might be a school that doesn't allow someone to wear a hijab or headscarf, or enforces stricter rules for certain people based on their identities.

   ii. Structural oppression describes how institutions work together to oppress categories of people based on a particular identity. This type of oppression is built on cultural and ideological beliefs and biases that are often so embedded across systems and society that they become normalized and almost invisible despite their role in maintaining systems of oppression. Structural oppression "involves the cumulative and compounding effects of an array of societal factors including the history, culture, ideology, and interactions of institutions and policies" (Race Forward 2014, p. 3).

8. After introducing and reviewing these levels of oppression, ask participants to raise their hand if they have a dress code policy at school.

a. Ask for a few responses from those raising their hands:

   i. How do you feel about the dress code policy?

   ii. How does it get enforced?

   iii. Who is impacted by the policy and the enforcement?

9. Invite the ensemble to move into small groups of three or four people to take on the next part of this action. Explain to participants:

a. Now that you are in your groups, you will receive one or two quotes that we pulled from a report called DRESS CODED: *Black Girls, Bodies, and Bias in D.C. Schools* (Davis et al. 2018).

b. In your group, please read your quotes out loud and discuss which level of oppression they reflect and why. Assign them to one of these boxes on this quadrant that we have drawn on butcher paper.

   i. These two boxes represent individual oppression and you will put your quote into the box that says interpersonal if your quote describes oppression between individuals, or internalized if your quote describes oppression that makes us believe certain things about ourselves.

   ii. These two boxes represent systemic oppression and you will put your quote in the box that says institutional if your quote describes the oppression that someone might experience because of an institution, and you will put your quote in the box that says structural if your quote describes an experience someone might have because of the way institutions work together.

    iii. Questions?

10. After dividing into smaller groups, give each group two or three quotes to sort. Give small groups time to read, discuss and sort their quotes.

    a. Let's look at each quote and the level it has been assigned to. Does it fit here? Is there anywhere else it could fit? (Because this discussion can be lengthy, it is not necessary to use all report quotes included below, but it is important to have at least one, if not two, that represent each level of oppression.)

    b. Once you have decided which level of oppression your quote fits into, choose one of the quotes you placed, and work with your group to create a tableau, or frozen picture, with your bodies, of one of your quotes. Use your body and face to communicate who is in this picture, how each person is feeling, and what is happening.

    c. Finally, title your tableau.

11. Give each group about ten minutes to prepare their quote, tableau, and title. When two minutes remain, explain to participants:

    a. As you prepare to share your work with the group, consider how you will share your title and if you want to include some of the text from your quote. Figure out how to add any text or spoken language into the sharing of your tableau. Will one person read the quote? Will you share the title or quote before, during, or after sharing the tableau?

12. Finally, invite each group to perform their image and content for the entire ensemble.


## Guiding Reflection

- What information about the dress code was familiar or surprising to you?
- Which levels of oppression feel most familiar to you? Which feel least familiar?
- Which levels of oppression do you think most impact young people?
- Why should we care about these four levels of oppression? How does this knowledge help us perform justice?
- What are strategies for disrupting institutional and structural oppression? How do you think big systems get changed?


## PJP Notes
Prepare to give the following quotes from DRESS CODED: Black Girls, Bodies, and Bias in D.C. Schools out to participants.

## INTERPERSONAL

- "Dress codes also communicate to students that girls are to be blamed for 'distracting' boys, instead of teaching boys to respect girls, correct their behavior and be more responsible. This dangerous message promotes sexual harassment in schools" (Davis et al. 2018, p. 1).
- "Too many schools make it clear that girls need to cover up their bodies so as not to 'distract' or 'tempt' boys. That enforcement sends the clear message that boys are not responsible for their bad behavior. By blaming boys' misconduct on girls' choices, schools promote an environment where sexual harassment is excused. Students may think it is appropriate to comment on girls' bodies because they see their teachers do it, too, when they enforce the dress code" (Davis et al. 2018, p. 20).
- "This trend [sexual harassment] is reinforced by adults' comments that girls wearing tight or revealing clothing are 'asking for it'" (Davis et al. 2018, p. 27).
- "Adults also promote harassment when they focus on girls' bodies over their minds. When students see girls sent out of the classroom because they are out of dress code, they learn that how a girl looks is more important than her thoughts and actions. When students see educators talking about girls' bodies, they learn to 'sexualize' young women and view them as objects meant for others' pleasure rather than full human beings" (Davis et al. 2018, p. 27).
- "I in 5 girls ages 14–18 has been kissed or touched without her consent. In addition to perpetuating harassment, adults who exclude girls from class to avoid 'distracting' their male classmates prioritize boys' education over girls" (Davis et al. 2018, p. 27).

## INTERNALIZED

- "Girls who believe gender stereotypes are more likely to have low self-esteem, including negative feelings about their bodies" (Davis et al. 2018, p. 27).
- "[D]iscriminatory dress codes and unfair enforcement change how Black girls see themselves and how their classmates see them, too. Studies show school practices that draw distinctions between students cause young people to form biases based on how different groups of students are treated. Dress codes create distinctions both through different rules for girls and boys and through different enforcement based on race, sex, and body type. In these ways, dress codes are not only rooted in stereotypes, but also reinforce them" (Davis et al. 2018, p. 26).
- "Studies even show that girls who wear gender-specific clothing perform worse in math and science. Practices that put pressure on students to conform to sex stereotypes are especially damaging for girls

who do not conform to gendered expectations, like girls who prefer wearing traditionally masculine clothes, as well as transgender students of all genders and students who are gender-fluid or non-binary" (Davis et al. 2018, p. 27).

- "Plus, when educators say girls are 'distracting' boys or 'asking for it,' students get the message that boys are not responsible for how they behave, and girls who wear certain clothes or makeup deserve harassment and violence" (Davis et al. 2018, p. 27).

## INSTITUTIONAL

- "Many schools across the country have different dress codes for girls and boys based on sex stereotypes (i.e., notions about how people 'should' act based on their gender). For example, such stereotypes may presume that girls should wear feminine skirts, while boys should be active and athletic in pants. These rules also can present obstacles for transgender students whose schools do not respect their gender identity, as well as non-binary and gender-fluid students" (Davis et al. 2018, p. 12).
- "Dress codes also can encourage sexual harassment. Boys who believe in sex stereotypes like those promoted by many school rules are more likely to harass girls" (Davis et al. 2018, p. 27).
- "Black girls are 20.8 times more likely to be suspended from D.C. schools than white girls. One reason for this disproportionate punishment is that adults often see Black girls as older and more sexual than their white peers, and so in need of greater correction for minor misbehaviors like 'talking back' or wearing a skirt shorter than permitted" (Davis et al. 2018, p. 16).
- "Across the city, Black girls are missing out on class time because of dress and grooming codes. Some are suspended, while others are pulled out of the classroom informally. Both formal and informal classroom removals cause these girls to lose out on the opportunity to learn" (Davis et al. 2018, p. 26).
- "74 percent of D.C. public high school dress codes authorize disciplinary action that can lead to missed class or school" (Davis et al. 2018, p. 24).

## STRUCTURAL

- "Suspensions put students at risk for not graduating and going to college. This exclusionary discipline threatens girls' long-term earning potential. Black women without a high school degree made $7,631 less annually than Black women who graduated from high school, and $25,117 less each year than Black women with a college degree" (Davis et al. 2018, p. 26).

- "Harsh and discriminatory school discipline leads to pushout, lost future earnings, poorer health outcomes and increased likelihood of living in poverty. For example, a girl who misses three or more days of school in a month can fall a year behind her peers. And even short, informal removals—like when a student is sent to the front office to cover up with a sweatshirt from the lost and found box—can add up to hours of lost instruction" (Davis et al. 2018, p. 26).

- "Nationally, Black women who do not graduate from high school are 2.2 times more likely to be unemployed than white, non-Hispanic women" (Davis et al. 2018, p. 28).

- "Black women in D.C. who do find employment and who work full time, year round, are paid 52 cents for every dollar paid to white, non-Hispanic men. This amounts to more than $1.8 million dollars in lifetime losses" (Davis et al. 2018, p. 28).

## In Our Experience

This information often takes time to sink in and we have found that we need to continue unpacking the oppressive messages that we internalize about ourselves and others—often over multiple sessions. This framework clarifies that oppression/being oppressed is often not in one's own control nor is it something that occurs only between individuals or small groups of people. To be able to reflect on internalized, interpersonal, institutional or structural oppressions, beliefs and ideologies that impact our own access and power in the world is a powerful way to expose injustice and disrupt the systems that keep injustice in place.

## Connecting to Performance

The tableaux created in this action may provide visual or textual information for a short scene, or a series of embodied pictures that represent various levels of oppression for an audience. This action may also simply lay the groundwork for creating performance pieces that complicate racism and sexism and point to needed systems change.

**Source**: This action was developed as part of the Performing Justice Project and draws content from "Moving the Race Conversation Forward: How the Media Covers Racism, and Other Barriers to Productive Racial Discourse, Part 1" (Race Forward, 2014) and DRESS CODED: Black Girls, Bodies, and Bias in D.C. Schools (Davis et al., 2018).

# What Is (In)Justice?

# Understanding Oppression: Respectability Politics

*This action explores the belief that certain groups have to earn the respect of others in order to be treated fairly.*

## PJP Connection

This performance action exposes the constant social and political messages we receive about how to behave and become "respectable"—messages particularly aimed at people outside a white, male, heterosexual identity. In thinking through what constitutes respect in our society, participants begin to acknowledge the ways in which white, patriarchal society often confers privilege on bodies that match the dominant group and hold everyone else to a narrow and oppressive construct of respectability, namely the ability to garner respect. This action helps young people articulate why they often feel marginalized or invisibilized, and begins to make visible the often hidden messaging we receive around who is worthy and who is not worthy of respect.

**Time**: 35–45 minutes

**Materials**: None

## Directing the Action

1. Explain to participants: In this action, we are going to use embodied statues to reflect on ideas of respectability. How is respectability constructed? By and for whom? And how do ideas of respectability play out across racial and gender lines in dangerous ways?
2. Model how to create statues with the body. Demonstrate how to freeze safely with both feet on the ground, to use facial expressions to communicate emotion and subtext, and to employ levels.
3. Explain to participants that embodied statues might be literal or abstract. Literal statues create a realistic picture of an idea, action, or person, while abstract statues communicate the essence of an idea, emotion, person, or action through shape or line, texture, and/or relationships.
4. After modeling examples of literal and abstract statues, invite participants to find their own place in the room where they can work alone and have a bit of space to move their body.
5. Explain to participants:
   a. We will start with a practice round and this will be a silent activity.
   b. We will use a five-count to move into each statue. For this first round, use your body and face to create a statue of *hopeful*.

5-4-3-2-1, freeze. Hold your statue. Feel where your body is, notice how you responded to the word *hopeful*.

c. Relax your body. Let's make a second statue, and this time, try to make it even bigger and more expressive. On our five count, use your body and face to make a statue of *lonely*. 5-4-3-2-1, freeze. Hold it. Feel where your body is, notice how you responded.

d. Relax your body. This time, let's respond to the idea of *respectable*. Respectable—as in a respectable person, someone respected by others. Respond to whatever that means to you. Make your statue in 5-4-3-2-1, freeze. Hold it.

e. Take a moment to memorize this statue, remember where your bodies are and what they are doing.

6. Guide the group in reflection:

a. If you are in the back half of the room, go ahead and relax your body. Let go of your statue. From where you are standing, look at the statues in the front half of the room. What do you notice? What similar images or shapes to you see? What shapes or images stand out as different or unique?

b. Now, let's switch. Those of you who were holding your statue relax, and those of you observing, let's count you back into your last statue. 5-4-3-2-1, freeze. Those of you in the front of the room: What do you notice? What is similar? What is different?

7. Guide the group in another round of statues and reflection:

a. Statues, go ahead and relax. Let's all do another round. Shake out your bodies and find a new standing place in the room. This time, create a statue of what it looks like when someone is *not* respectable, or not respected by others. 5-4-3-2-1, freeze. Hold this statue.

b. If you are in the back half of the room, go ahead and relax your body. Let go of your statue. From where you are standing, look at the statues in the front half of the room. What do you notice? What similar images or shapes to you see? What shapes or images stand out as different or unique?

c. Let's now switch. Those of you who were holding your statue relax, and those of you observing, let's count you back into your last statue. 5-4-3-2-1, freeze. Those of you in the front of the room: What do you notice? What is similar? What is different?

d. Thank you for exploring these words and sharing your statues. Go ahead and relax and take a seat in one large circle.

8. Invite participants to discuss (either in pairs or whole group):

a. What did you notice in these statues about respectable/not respectable?

b. What does it mean to be respectable? Where do we learn rules about how to look, dress, act respectable? Who do these rules or messages come from? Who gets to decide what is respectable? Why?

c. Who are respectability politics targeting and why?

    d.  Adopting ideas of respectability can be an act of protecting oneself from real and present danger. If a person dresses a certain way, talks a certain away, or acts a certain way how might this help keep them from being mistreated, or protect them from specific "isms" such as racism, sexism, classism?

9.  Following this discussion, offer a short history of respectability politics to the ensemble:

    a.  Respectability politics (although it wasn't called this at the time) came about after the emancipation of slaves. One of the ways that slavery was justified was to support the idea of white supremacy over Black inferiority—the idea that Black people are biologically inferior to white people, are less than humans, and this is why it was okay to treat them as less than human, and why they needed to be enslaved.

    b.  Once former slaves were freed they had additional barriers to fight; they unjustly had to *earn* their status as humans in a society that normalized the supremacy of white people. Respectability politics, which is similar to racial uplift—or lifting as we climb—is one way that middle-class Black Americans tried to help lower-class Blacks have better lives. Many people believed that respectable behavior was behavior that mirrored that of "respectable white people." Any other ways of acting, dressing, and interacting might be considered "less than human," "barbaric," or "biologically inferior." This belief impacted what would become acceptable in terms of dress, hairstyles, language, food, and other daily practices for people of color. Respectability politics also became a way for Black people to protect themselves from the racial terror of the twentieth century by assimilating into white ideals of what it meant to be worthy of respect. Respectability politics remained "situated within the larger structural framework of America and its attendant social norms." (Higginbotham 1994, p. 189).[4] Respectability politics continues to play out today in harmful ways that oppress people of color and maintain white supremacy.

10.  Invite participants to discuss (whole group):

    a.  What are examples of how respectability politics shows up in our world right now?

    b.  I am going to read a series of statements. How are these are examples of respectability politics? Where do these harmful ideas come from and how do they impact the lives of young people and those with stereotyped identities?

- "Wearing a hoodie makes you look like a thug."
- "I can't wear my hair in locs. I won't get a job."
- "She had on a really short skirt. She was asking for it."
- "If she hadn't spoken back to the police, she wouldn't have gotten arrested."

## Guiding Reflection

- What messages did you receive or do you currently receive about respectability in your family, school, or community? What does respectability look like?
- What happens when people with identity markers that are outside the white, cis, male, upper-class paradigm do not attempt to be "respectable" as we have defined it? What is at risk? When and how are ideas of "respectable" dangerous for people with marginalized identities?
- How might we safely challenge the idea of having to be "respectable"? How does our identity impact levels of risks in challenging the status quo related to respectability?
- How are ideas about success tied to ideas about respectability?

## In Our Experience

This action touches on big and sometimes painful ideas that often need to be unpacked over multiple sessions. The term may not be familiar, but the foundational ideas are often more than familiar—young people understand that they have to act a certain way in order to be accepted, to get a job, or to stay "safe." The harsh truth is that controlled behavior can't stop racism, sexism, homophobia, transphobia, ableism, classism, etc. We can't talk about racial and gender justice without acknowledging the critical role that respectability politics plays in the lives of those of us at the margins.

## Connecting to Performance

Exploring the idea of respectability politics offers a critical theme to draw into scene work in both abstract and literal moments. Once participants understand this concept, invite them to think about how it relates to each piece they create and to expectations of them in every area of their lives.

**Source**: This action was developed by Briana Barner and Cortney McEniry as part of the Performing Justice Project.

# What Is (In)Justice?

# Understanding Oppression: Machines

*This action offers a way to develop collaboration skills and activate specific themes and ideas as an ensemble.*

## PJP Connection

This action invites youth to think literally/realistically and abstractly as they translate ideas into movement and sound. Creating machines offers an embodied framework for examining our perspectives and responses to a particular concept and to expose systems that impact us on a daily basis. In PJP, we often create machines to make physical and visible representations of theoretical ideas.

**Time:** 15–20 minutes

**Materials:** None

## Directing the Action

1. Invite participants to join a standing circle or to sit in a U-shape facing the performance space.
2. Explain to participants:
   a. In this action, you will use your bodies and voices to create a machine. What is a machine? What are some examples of machines?
   b. We need one volunteer to begin this action by choosing and performing a simple sound and movement combination, something simple that you can comfortably repeat for the duration of the performance action.
   c. After this first person has started our machine with their sound/movement combination, others can add on to the machine one by one, until we have 8–10 participants performing their sound/movements as part of one large machine. To add on to the machine, you will volunteer to join the first person in the playing space and add a repeating movement/gesture working off of or in connection to someone already part of the machine. In this way, each performer will be doing individual motions (like a single machine part) that connect to a larger ecosystem or machine.
3. Once the group has built a machine, try conducting the machine or various parts of the machine by raising or lowering your hand to signal faster/louder or slower/quieter movements and sounds. After a moment of collaborative performance, turn off the machine by saying "stop" (or pushing a pretend off button).
4. Once the participants understand how to create a simple machine, you can layer on more complex challenges, such as: build a machine that makes something specific, such as "non-binary clothes," or build a machine that a metaphorical, emotional, or ephemeral thing such as "justice" or "joy."
5. For an additional challenge, ask participants to think about what the machine would look or sound like if it broke down.

a.  We recommend making several types of machines—in this order:
    i.  Freestyle (use this type of machine to model what happens in this action—this is a simple machine and does not need to be in response to a prompt)
    ii.  Carwash machine
    iii.  School machine
    iv.  Justice machine/injustice machine
    v.  Hope machine

## Guiding Reflection

- Describe moments that we worked well together during this action.
- How could we have been more cohesive in our performance?
- What would have happened if we took one piece of our machine away?
- If we are thinking about in/justice in society, who or what are the "machines" that make or build justice and injustice? Who distributes injustice and justice?
- How are our machines similar to or different from the different levels of oppression?
- What kind of machines are needed to build racial and gender justice in our communities? What machines need to be discontinued?

## In Our Experience

This action reminds participants to think about how they are all working together as parts of a whole to create something new. How do the sounds and movements of each person relate to one another and communicate a larger idea or truth? Before anyone joins the machine, encourage participants to look carefully at what is happening on stage and to notice the spatial layout of the machine. Where might a space need to be filled or gesture included? Encourage participants to walk all the way around a machine, and to add themselves into the machine from any side and facing any direction.

## Connecting to Performance

Machines can be used to create movement-based performance pieces, which can stand alone as a beginning or ending of a performance, or might become a movement sequence that pairs with a group poem or voiceover.

**Source**: We first encountered this game in Viola Spolin's book *Theater games for the classroom: A teacher's handbook* (1986, p. 68) and later in Augusto Boal's book *Games for actors and non-actors* (1992, p. 90).

# What Is (In)Justice?

## Understanding Oppression: Writing Prompt "In Society..."

*This action prepares participants for the 8-Count Movement and also captures ideas and questions that might be used for later devising strategies.*

### PJP Connection

This action generates a list of behaviors that can be used in "In Society..." and "8-Count Movement." By naming the messages and expectations that we receive from society, we are able to see and disrupt patterns of oppressive narratives and who they impact in what ways. Gender and racial justice requires systemic change and systemic change requires an understanding of what exactly needs attention or needs to be changed.

**Time**: 5–8 minutes

**Materials**: Journal and writing utensil

### Directing the Action

1.  Pass out journals to each participant. Invite participants to review their earlier written reflections and six-word stories about gender.
2.  Ask participants to respond to the following prompt:
    a.  **In society, women** *(men, trans folks, Black and Brown youth, etc.— choose one to brainstorm at a time)* **are expected to_____.**
    b.  PJP Note: We have explored different versions of this prompt, settling on this one—for now. It is important to reflect on the fact that we all receive very different messages from society based on our intersectional identities. While there is no one set of messages that all women receive, we also believe that women (including and inclusive of trans women) are subjected to a cacophony of messages about bodies, clothing, emotions, relationships, etc. In this torrent of messages, young people are able to name very specific and contradictory directives. This prompt can be applied to the gender binary (women/men) as a way of showing how restrictive and constructed the binary is or it can be adapted toward a statement that proves more productive for a specific context, group, or intention. The point is to illuminate the barrage of oppressive messages about strict gender roles, regardless of the gender identities/sexes in the room. And, it is also okay to ask or encourage young people to add other specific identity markers to their prompt, as we realize that separating gender from race is not actually possible in our lived experiences.

3. Explain to participants:
   a. Generate as many responses to the prompt as you can in five minutes. Play with length, rhythm, poetry, direct address, metaphor, etc. Consider all the things you think "women" are expected to do/say. What are the messages from society about what it means to be a woman, what it looks like to be successful woman, and who gets to be a woman? Invite participants to add intersecting identity markers to their prompt if they want (*In society, Asian/Latina/Black/white women are expected to...*)
   b. If students are struggling, not writing, or have many questions, this list could also be generated verbally as a whole group, or as a brainstorm in small groups. Side-coaching questions can help participants dig a little deeper and may include: Think about what family members or teachers say to you about how women or girls are supposed to behave. Think about moments when you have been corrected or told to do something a specific way because of your gender or other identity markers. Think about the images you see in the media—from video games to advertising to movies to magazines and social media. How are these images promoting messages or directives to and about women?

4. After a list has been generated, guide the group to make connections between societal messages and oppression of women.

5. Ask participants to look at their list and identify the following:
   a. Which messages on your list are internalized—things that you have been told and things you hear yourself accepting or believing to be true?
   b. Which messages are interpersonal—things you can imagine or hear someone telling you, whether it's a relative or even a stranger?
   c. Which messages are larger than you and relate to institutions of education, or family roles, or the workplace? What messages on your list suggest where women belong or should be spending their time or are messages about how women are supposed to participate in our society?

## Guiding Reflection

- At what points did you struggle with this writing? At what points did it feel easy?
- What surprised you and what did you discover in this action?
- As you brainstormed your list, when did racial locations in combination with the gender location come up for you? (For example, in brainstorming "women are expected to..." were you actually thinking more specifically to "white women are expected to..." or "Latina women are expected to...," etc.)?

- Is it possible to separate the societal expectations of women from the societal expectations of gender and race in combination with each other?
- Why are societal expectations an important part of gender and racial justice work?

### In Our Experience

This is a rich exercise for people of all identities. Participants often expose the dichotomy of messages directed at young women: "be sexy/don't be a prude", "be nice/be assertive/don't be a bitch," revealing the impossibility of meeting all social expectations. Trans and gender non-binary youth have access to and are impacted by many of these same messages, as well others that are specific to the gender binary. Young men are also familiar with these messages, but may understand them as "how women do/should act" rather than as harmful and restrictive constructs.

### Connecting to Performance

We use this writing to generate text that informs the 8-Count Movement and the performance of a group poem titled "In Society…". We don't typically use the text after the movement has been generated, but it can be used as background text—read during the embodied performance, or pre-recorded by participants and layered over sound and movement.

**Source**: This action was developed as part of the Performing Justice Project.

---

# What Is (In)Justice?

# Understanding Oppression: 8-Count Movement

*This action generates gestures and embodied images that demonstrate the multiplicity of messages constantly directed at women's lives and bodies.*

### PJP Connection

This action asks participants to craft short movement pieces that focus on gender roles, sexism, and oppression, often regardless of one's own gender/sex. The 8-Count sequence often becomes a core movement piece in a PJP performance; sometimes with spoken or recorded text layered over the repetition of an 8-Count Movement sequence. The repetition of simple, daily movements and actions illuminates some of the "normalized" gender expectations coming from society.

**Time**: 25–30 minutes

**Materials**: Pre-written responses to "In society, women are expected to…" or alternate prompt.

## Directing the Action

1.  Ask participants to choose one idea from the "In society, women are expected to…" list (see action called Writing Prompt "In Society…"). Alternately, participants could respond to other prompts, including:
    a.  Choose one action people do on a daily basis that is specific to gender expectations.
    b.  Choose one specific stereotype of a man or woman.
    c.  Or an original prompt that accesses particular messages about gender expectations and behavior.
2.  Invite participants to choose one specific activity/gesture that represents an answer to the prompt. Explain to participants:
    a.  Once you choose your specific action, you are going to break that action into an 8-Count Movement sequence. For example, if your text is: "Being a woman means wearing lipstick," you might break down an action into eight counts as follows:
        Count 1: Take cap off of lipstick
        Count 2: Roll up lipstick
        Count 3: Lean into mirror
        Count 4: Apply to bottom lip
        Count 5: Apply to top lip
        Count 6: Rub lips together
        Count 7: Smack lips
        Count 8: Smile in mirror
    b.  Please find your own small rehearsal space in the room, away from others.
    c.  As you rehearse, try to be specific and clear in each of part of your action. Don't try to do too much in any one 8-Count sequence.
3.  Give the ensemble five minutes to rehearse with the goal of performing each count of their movement exactly the same way each time.
4.  Next, invite everyone to rehearse their 8-Count Movement simultaneously as part of a large group (still in their own spaces). Count to eight slowly and evenly so the whole group performs their movement sequences on the same count. Ask the group to reset to neutral, and begin their movement sequence again. Rehearse a few times as a large group, helping the ensemble to repeat their 8-Count Movement four or five times in a row without a break or stop in-between. We sometimes rehearse this with music as well, noticing that an 8-Count sequence moves well into a movement improvisation or dance.

5.  Next, assign each participant a partner or a group of three. Explain to participants:
    a.  As a group, your goal is to teach and learn all of your group's 8-Count Movements. You will have ten minutes to teach and learn each movement sequence in the group.
    b.  Once you have learned all of your group's movements, you will order the two or three 8-Counts into a short performance piece. As you work, think about how the individual 8-Count Movements might flow together into a 16-Count or two 8-Counts, and which piece should go first, second or third (if working in groups of three). Please take a few minutes to rehearse your pieces all together, one right after the other.
    c.  Next, you and your partner are going to spread out in the playing space, away from each other. This means that pairs are going to be all mixed up in the space and you may be standing next to someone else's pair. Rehearse your full sequence of 8-Count Movements again, working to stay synchronized in your movements with your partner and fluid in the transition between the two 8-Count Movements, despite the physical distance between you.
6.  To share out these movements, divide the entire ensemble into split halves (two big groups that keep pairs together). One half will become the audience. The other half will all simultaneously perform their movements three times in a row as the facilitator counts for them (if working in pairs, they will perform three repetitions of each 16-Count). Ask the performers to remain spread out, away from their partners. Performers may need to adjust their placement slightly so as to avoid bumping into another pair as they perform.
7.  Finally, ask the performers to become the audience and the audience to perform. We often play music as the youth perform these sequences, and we slowly move away from counting out loud as the youth gain confidence with moving to and silently counting their own 8-Counts.

## Guiding Reflection

- What did you see in these 8-Count Movements? Which actions do you relate to and why?
- What actions made you think more deeply about what society thinks about or dictates for women?
- What issues of justice does this performance action bring up for you?
- How are the ideas in your 8-Count Movements related to other areas of identity, such as race, ethnicity, culture, birth order, religion?
- When you see all of these movements performed together, what do you think about society's expectations of women?

### In Our Experience

Youth often need direct support to sharpen and clarify their 8-Count actions and movements. We side-coach participants to consider: How might you adjust your body position so that you are more visible to an audience member? How can you make each beat of your movement more crisp, active, or expressive? How might you engage more of your body or face to communicate what you are doing in your 8-Count Movement? With only eight counts to perform the details of a single action, it is important to use each count to convey an action clearly to an audience.

### Connecting to Performance

We often combine this type of pair work and small group movements into one larger movement piece in which everyone performs on stage at the same time. 8-Count Movements can also be added to the physical staging of a final performance moment, set to music, or performed during a voice over of a youth-written group poem.

**Source**: We learned this action from PJP teaching artist Emily Freeman. It has roots in the work of the Dance Exchange and devising workshops led by Michel Rohd.

# What Is (In)Justice?

## Understanding Oppression: Writing Prompt "My Skin Is..."

*This action asks participants to acknowledge their experience of being racialized as they move through the world.*

### PJP Connection

Just as we ask youth to develop their lens of experiences related to gender and sex, we also invite them to focus on their experiences connected to race, ethnicity and skin color. Through this writing prompt, participants reflect on their daily lives through the lens of race and generate text that can be integrated with other content.

**Time**: 8–10 minutes

**Materials**: Journal and writing utensil

## Directing the Activity

1.  Pass out journals. Invite participants to review their reflections and six-word stories about race.
2.  Ask participants to answer the following prompt with as much writing as they can for the next five minutes. Encourage them to write whatever comes up without censoring themselves. It may help to post prompts where they can be seen easily:
    a.  My skin is... *(What are all the ways you can describe your skin, through color, feeling, smell, touch?)*
    b.  In society, the color of my skin means...
    c.  In my family, my skin is...
    d.  In my school, the color of my skin means...
    e.  In my neighborhood or city, my skin is...
3.  Questions to encourage deeper writing:
    a.  What are messages you have been told directly or indirectly by those close to you about your racial identity and/or your skin color?
    b.  What messages do you receive from society about your racial identity and/or your skin color?
    c.  What messages do you receive from the institutions and systems around you?
4.  Find a partner, and share some of the things you wrote.
5.  Return to the circle as a whole group for reflection and discussion.

## Guiding Reflection

- Where did you struggle with this writing? Where did it feel easy?
- What surprised you? What did you discover?
- Why do you think race and ethnicity play a role in our experiences?

## In Our Experience

We find that youth have few opportunities to talk openly about their racial identity and how it impacts their experiences in the world, and once they are invited to do this they have much to say. Although brainstorming based on the color of one's skin may feel superficial, it can open avenues for discussion about how identity shapes our experiences in the world. Sometimes youth are reluctant to discuss race because they have received the message that it is preferable to be colorblind—that to acknowledge race is, in itself, racist. We take time to unpack these beliefs when they arise in order to lift up the necessity of acknowledging race.

### Connecting to Performance

This writing generates text that can inform a variety of other actions. We use these lines to shape spoken word pieces, justice and injustice creatures, and scenes. We have also found this writing to be particularly salient in developing ensemble poems about race, racial oppression and racial (in)justice.

**Source**: This action was developed as part of the Performing Justice Project.

# What Is (In)Justice?

## Understanding Oppression: Injustice/Justice Creatures

*Using personification is one way to identify specific qualities of a concept or idea and at the same time expose things we know but have not articulated.*

### PJP Connection

Young people may have very different associations with justice and injustice based on their own race and/or incarceration (among other factors). This three-part activity allows youth to take what may be an intangible concept that has real lived experiences and activate it through specific expressions that invite subjective responses.

**Time**: 30–45 minutes

**Materials**: Open playing space, bean bag or light ball (that is easy to throw), large paper, and markers

### Directing the Action

## PART I: SOUND BALL (10 MIN)

1. Invite participants to stand in a circle.
2. Explain to participants that we are going to approach the topic of justice in a different way, using a few different writing techniques. Describe to participants:
    a. We're going to start with sensory language. What are the five senses? When we talk about sensory language, we are talking about language that uses all five senses to paint a vivid picture for an audience member.

    b. To start our action, we are going to toss a ball around the circle, in a particular pattern that we will continue to repeat. Toss the ball—underhand only, please—round the circle. Remember who tosses the ball to you, and who you are tossing it to. Make sure you have eye contact as you toss the ball so that someone is ready to catch it, and please avoid throwing at the head. (Play for 10–12 minutes, until the pattern and rhythm are consistent.)

3. Ask participants to name a familiar animal.

    a. This time, as we toss the ball we are going to describe the animal by what it looks like—just one word when you catch the ball. Then what it feels like if you would touch it. Then what it sounds like.

4. Next, ask participants to name a place or environment. Prompt participants through all five senses in response to the place or environment, still encouraging one-word responses.

5. Explain to participants:

    a. Now we're going to try something a little different. Let's name an emotion. Let's try to personify the emotion by going through each of the five senses.

6. Spend a moment on reflection with participants:

    a. What did we do in this activity?

    b. What was easy? What was difficult?

    c. What was surprising?

7. Explain and describe personification:

    a. So what we just did is called personification. Has anyone heard that word before or know what it means? Personification is a literary device of endowing an inanimate object (in this case a feeling) with attributes of something alive. (If we need an example: The day flew by. The leaves danced in the wind.) We are going to explore this idea in our next activity as well.

## PART II: JUSTICE AND INJUSTICE PERSONIFICATION (10 MIN)

1. Break up into groups—in the group they will personify justice and injustice. There can be multiple groups personifying each concept, or two larger groups. Divide according to how the group works best—larger or smaller groups. Group One will work with the idea of injustice. Group Two will work with the idea of justice. Ask participants to gather around a piece of paper they will use to brainstorm and record their ideas. Pass out paper and writing utensils.

2. Ask each group to choose a scribe. Explain the process to the groups:

    a. Answer the following prompts together in your groups. You can make a list, write in sentences or whatever works best for you. You are making choices to personify in/justice, bringing it to life by assigning lifelike characteristics through sensory language. One group will personify justice and one group will personify injustice. Please write your topic at the top of your page (justice or injustice).

b. As I ask you to respond to these prompts, keep in mind which concept you are writing about—justice or injustice. Feel free to write many words and phrases for each prompt—you do not have to agree on just one word.

 i. Justice/injustice: looks like... (how big/small, tall/short, body shape, skin or hair, facial features)
 ii. Justice/injustice: smells like...
 iii. Justice/injustice: sounds like... (what does its voice sound like? Does it talk? Or just make sounds?)
 iv. Justice/injustice: what does justice/injustice eat?
 v. Justice's/injustice's skin feels like... (temperature, texture)
 vi. Justice/injustice: moves like... (like an animal? Speed?)
 vii. Justice/injustice: has the power to make people feel...

3. Ask participants to go back to the list and circle/underline the most important/vivid words.

## PART III: JUSTICE AND INJUSTICE EMBODIMENT (15 MIN)

1. Explain to participants that they will use their word bank to create a physical representation of the word/creature and all the group members.
a. Using your description, you will create this creature physically in your group, using only your bodies. Everyone must somehow become a different piece of the creature. How does justice/injustice grow? How does it gain power? How can you use your bodies to show this?
2. After you have the shape/physicality of your creature, add sounds.
3. Next, figure out how to move together while making your sounds.
4. Rehearse to share out: How does your sharing begin? Do we see your creature growing? Is your creature entering from another space? How does your sharing end?
5. Share out these performances.
6. Each group offers the other group performers three things they enjoyed.

### Guiding Reflection

- What did you notice in each of the personifications?
- What made you think about each concept differently?
- What mirrored your ideas about justice and injustice, and what pushed you to think differently about the concept?

### In Our Experience

For a group of young people relatively new to theatre this can be a very abstract exercise. Building a creature based on a concept or idea and then embodying it requires some trust in the group. However, if you needed to use this action earlier in a sequence, it could be scaffolded similarly to machines—by creating creatures of concepts that appear to be more concrete and specific.

### Connecting to Performance

The creatures that come out of this action are dynamic and larger than life and provide an interesting counterpart to realistic stories that are likely to show up in the performance. Justice/injustice creatures can provide an interesting opening/closing or transition.

**Source**: Developed by Meg Greene with PJP teaching artists and directors.

# What Is (In)Justice?

## Exposing and Resisting Injustice: Send a Snap

*This action builds energy and connection through sending and catching snaps. It can also be used for word association and is a great energizer at any time in a PJP process.*

### PJP Connection

We love this activity and use it frequently throughout a PJP process. As groups become more familiar with the action and each other, they begin to adapt and add personal flair to the snap catch and send. Here we add on word association to brainstorm ideas of justice and injustice.

**Time**: 5–8 minutes

**Materials**: A large enough space to form a standing circle.

### Directing the Action

1. Invite participants to stand in a circle. Make sure everyone can see each other.

2. Explain to participants:
   a. You will send energy to one another through a snap. It is important to send the snap very clearly across the circle using eye contact and gesture (model examples of this). Whoever receives the snap must catch it before sending a new snap on to another person in the circle (send a snap, catch a snap, send a snap, etc.)
3. Once the snap is clearly established, ask participants to add a word—the first word that comes to mind based on what someone sends them. Start with "injustice" and encourage the group to freely associate. There are no wrong answers; encourage participants to stay focused and on topic in order to thoroughly brainstorm injustice. At any time, re-insert the word "injustice" to begin a new word association thread.
4. When appropriate, shift the focus to "justice" word association.

## Guiding Reflection

- What did you find? Which words surprised you?
- Were you able to relax and freely associate? Or did you feel the need to plan ahead?

## In Our Experience

If the group doesn't snap, we find other ways to pass the energy such as a clap or a swish. We take time in the beginning to establish the pattern of throw and catch before throwing again. Passing a snap is a great warm-up at any time—after a break, before a show, as a group closing. Additionally, we like this to use this action to play with vocal level, tone, rhythm, sound, almost anything that develops a performance language and repertoire. We find this to be a reliable ensemble action.

## Connecting to Performance

We have seen this become a part of performance when youth invited their audience to stand and share a moment of interaction. They used the action as it is described here, and invited their audience to think about justice with them near the end of their performance. This choice created a beautiful, connected group brainstorm around the feelings and actions associated with justice.

**Source**: We learned this game from Sidney Monroe Williams. It has since been adapted by the Performing Justice Project.

# What Is (In)Justice?

# Exposing and Resisting Injustice: Hashtag Activism

*Using hashtags is a form of activism that everyone with access to online information and social trends can participate in.*

## PJP Connection

This action examines the use of hashtags as activism, as a different way to share ideas and speak up. Sharing a pre-written script models how we can use tweets to create a conversation that reflects a current issue. The following information was developed around the #blacklivesmatter movement, but could be updated based on current events or other movements happening during your PJP process.

**Time**: 10–15 minutes

**Materials**: Script created from hashtag tweets; the one included below can be used or a new one can be written with tweets on a current issue.

**PJP Notes (for facilitators and/or participants)**: The following text offers background information for this performance action. We often share quotes (included below, all from the same article) with youth to help them understand the context of the murder of Trayvon Martin and the Black Lives Matter movement. This material can prove challenging and we offer trigger warnings prior to reading the material out loud.

- "In July 2013, after George Zimmerman was acquitted for killing 17-year-old Trayvon Martin, a young woman in California named Alicia Garza wrote an emotional Facebook post that ended with the words 'Our Lives Matter, Black Lives Matter'" (NPR Staff, 2015).
- Her friend, Patrisse Cullors, turned that into a hashtag. "I put a hashtag on it because it just felt so necessary to archive it." Cullors told her friend they should use it "to develop a new narrative around what it means to believe and fight for black life in this moment" (NPR Staff, 2015). This was the first use of #blacklivesmatter hashtag, which started a movement by Alicia Garza, Patrisse Cullors and Opal Tometi; there are now over 20 chapters around the country, and around the world.
- "Black Lives Matter reminds people that black people are human, but more importantly, it reminds black people that we are human," says Alicia Garza (NPR Staff, 2015). #blacklivesmatter is an affirmation and embrace of the resistance and resilience of Black people.

- These women responded to the intersections of race, gender, and sexuality in their work. Among them they had incarcerated family members and black queer identities; these identities and experiences helped to fuel their interest in social justice work.
- #alllivesmatter has been used in opposition to #blacklivesmatter, as a way of stating that one does not see race or color. This hashtag erases differences, rather than celebrating difference and acknowledging and recognizing the way various communities are impacted by systemic discrimination.

## Directing the Action

1. Explain to participants:
   a. We're going to read out some tweets. These are from 2015 and have been put together to form a conversation. Listen to the hashtags that have been used in these conversations.
   b. We will need three volunteers to read this script aloud. You will read all lines, and when you are reading a hashtag, please say "hashtag" and then read the hashtag aloud.
2. Invite volunteers to playing space and give them a moment to look at script.
3. It may be helpful to have volunteers read the script again, or ask for another round of volunteers to read it a second time so that everyone can take the information in clearly. Alternately, create a more current Twitter/hashtag script based on current issues/conversations.
4. Thank participants and take some time to discuss the hashtags and script.
5. If you were to write a hashtag to describe PJP, what would it be?
6. Share out hashtags. Scribe list of hashtags for reference. In the next activity, we are going to write our own scenes using our own ideas about hashtags.

## Guiding Reflection

- What did you hear in this conversation?
- How were the speakers using the hashtags?
- What tweets have you seen or heard about that express strong opinions or speak to social justice and change?
- How are people using tweets? Do you have a twitter handle, and if so, how do you use Twitter?

## SCRIPT SAMPLE GENERATED IN 2015

Person A: We have to teach our kids that their Blackness isn't a crime. That we are human and *worthy* of human responses to injustice. #blacklivesmatter

Person B: Doesn't everyone's life matter though? #alllivesmatter

Person C: I can't believe how long it's been and people still haven't grasped that it's #blacklivesmatter(too) and not #(only)blacklivesmatter

Person A: #blacklivesmatter... Until everyone on Twitter gets bored and moves on.

Person C: We need an intersectional human rights movement. The three queer women who founded #blacklivesmatter understood this.

Person A: Changing it to #alllivesmatter is like going to a cancer fundraiser and going "all diseases are important, why is cancer so special huh?"

Person A: When you change #blacklivesmatter you disrespect Aiyana Jones, Trayvon Martin, Freddie Grey, and so many others that died due to racism.

Person C: All life is sacred, but Black and Brown lives in this country have been stolen. #blacklivesmatter #brownlivesmatter

### In Our Experience

Young people are familiar with hashtags and commonly use them on social media platforms. However, using hashtags for collective action and calling out oppression may be a new idea for them. #blacklivesmatter is an important place to begin, but it is also possible to bring in more recent hashtags that reflect current events and let young people discuss how they are being used for collective action.

### Connecting to Performance

We have found that using and creating hashtags that speak to the work of the Performing Justice Project is a powerful way for young people to crystalize, in their words, what PJP is about for them. These hashtags often become threaded through performance, as titles for or punctuation in scenes, on t-shirts worn in performance, and in transitions between performance moments.

**Source**: Developed by Briana Barner, PJP teaching artist. Hashtags are quoted from Twitter.

# What Is (In)Justice?

# Exposing and Resisting Injustice: Hashtag Stories

*This devising action invites participants to generate scenes using hashtags as a means of naming and speaking back to oppression.*

## PJP Connection

Hashtag Stories invite participants to name an issue that is important to them and play with succinct forms of representation that move into scenes. This action illustrates how "naming" through hashtags can bring various ideas and experiences into conversation with each other, point to systemic injustice, and build movement. These scenes can be performed as they are written. We have also used the hashtags as transitions, titles, and recorded text.

**Time**: 30–35 minutes

**Materials**: Journals, writing utensils, copies of hashtag script

## Directing the Action

1. Invite participants to look at the sample hashtag script from the Hashtag Activism action (or read it aloud if they have not participated in Hashtag Activism action). Reflect as a group:
   a. What do you notice in this script?
   b. What is the difference between a tweet and a conversation? How does this script turn tweets into a dialogue?
2. Building on participants' reflections, identify features of a hashtag story. Scribe the defining features so that all participants can see the list as they prepare to write their own.
3. Next, invite participants to think about experiences of gender and racial injustice in their lives and communities.
4. Brainstorm with the whole group: What makes a hashtag catchy for gender and racial justice? What are the qualities of a hashtag that "sticks" or gains traction?
5. Invite participants to make a list of possible hashtags for their own conversations (hashtags can be in whatever language participants want to use). Ask participants to share their list of hashtags with a partner and together choose one hashtag that they believe people need to pay attention to.
6. After the pairs choose one hashtag, ask them to identify who might get involved in a conversation about this topic or hashtag? Ask participants to choose 2–3 characters or "tweeters."

7. Next, invite the whole group to define what makes a tweet (i.e., short statement of 280 characters or less on the social media platform, Twitter). Tweets often use media-rich images, videos, and links, but for the purposes of creating a dialogue or scene, stick to text and hashtags for this action.

8. Still working in pairs, invite participants to write three to four tweets from each of the "tweeters" they've chosen, and to then put the tweets from each character in order (number them) to develop a conversation. Have the pairs read through the conversation they created and invite them to add or take away lines or tweets to create an interesting hashtag conversation, dialogue, or debate.

9. Ask a few pairs to volunteer to have their hashtag conversations read aloud by other participants. Invite those listening to consider what worked in the conversation and to offer feedback or edits.

10. Finally, invite each pair to take a few minutes to revise their stories.

## SAMPLE SCRIPT WRITTEN BY YOUTH PARTICIPANTS
#trustissues

A: Women should be at home. #trustissues

B: Well, that sounds like personal problem. #trustissues

A: You should be at home, where else would you be at? #trustissues

B: You shouldn't worry about me if you trust me. #trustissues

A: Well apparently if you not at home, prolly y'all out there cheating.

B: It's not always like that, girls should leave the house if they want for any reason. They have their rights. #trustissues

A: You should understand where your partner is coming from. If you really have #trustissues what's the point of being in a relationship?

B: Well I mean obviously y'all want women at home because they the one doing everything around the house. #trustissues #guysshouldclean

A: You deserved better if he really love you but I understand where you coming from. Respect your decisions. #staystrong #trustissues #learntodochores

## Guiding Reflection

- Which hashtags stood out to you and why?
- What do hashtags accomplish? Why are they used in public media?
- How did the hashtags make you think differently about what the characters said to each other?
- How do these hashtag conversations relate to other ideas you are exploring in PJP? How are hashtags part of building a movement for change?

### In Our Experience

Participants form connections between identity, oppression, and storytelling in this action. Performing dialogue that includes the word "hashtag" sometimes brings humor to challenging topics. For some participants though, making these connections can prove vulnerable, so we try to be aware of when or if participants start to shut down or give up. We attempt to offer extra support and options for various types of participation if anyone is feeling overwhelmed or triggered by the content.

**Source**: Developed by Kristen Hogan (PJP co-founder and teaching artist) and Briana Barner (PJP teaching artist) as part of the Performing Justice Project.

# What Is (In)Justice?

# Exposing and Resisting Injustice: Complete the Image—Resistance

*This action is from Augusto Boal's Theatre of the Oppressed and encourages embodiment of words and text. While simple and low-risk, this exercise tends to generate stunning movement sequences.*

### PJP Connection

This round of Complete the Image is used to generate visual representations of resistance in order to consider how to confront and combat oppressions. What does resistance look like? How do we expose, disrupt, and resist sexism and racism? Using our bodies in various and multiple images generates ideas as we work together to build capacity to resist.

**Time**: 12–15 minutes

**Materials**: None

### Directing the Action

1. Invite participants to stand in a circle. Remind participants of this action from Section 2.3.3, What Is Power? Let participants know our focus will be on resistance. Sometimes this may mean the image is very clearly showing a kind of resistance, but encourage them to think abstractly as well. The image can represent a feeling of resistance, or can help brainstorm different ways to resist.

2. Ask for one volunteer to begin in the center with the handshake image from the previous round of this activity.

3. Invite a second volunteer to enter the circle and create an image of resistance. Once they have entered and taken a pose, hold for a moment to allow everyone to really look at the image and move around to take it in from different perspectives if desired. Then, allow the first volunteer to leave the circle and someone new to enter and create a new image of resistance.

4. Volunteers from the circle should continue to step in, filling the negative space with their bodies.

### Guiding Reflection

- What did you notice? How did it feel in different moments?
- What kinds of resistance did you see? What stood out to you?
- What does the idea of resistance make you think about?

### In Our Experience
This action is important for the facilitator to watch from outside of the group. Encourage participants to explore levels and think about facial expressions. Encourage people who have not participated to complete the image.

### Connecting to Performance
This action becomes an interesting way to brainstorm what resistance looks like and this image sequence could also be set to music or text and used in performance.

**Source**: Developed by Augusto Boal and published in *Games for actors and non-actors* (1992, p. 130).

## What Is (In)Justice?

## Exposing and Resisting Injustice: Still I Rise

*Maya Angelou's "Still I Rise" is an inspirational and affirming poem about identity, history, politics and resistance.*

### PJP Connections
Taking time to look at outside sources that are not generated by the youth in the ensemble offers inspiration in both subject and form for their personal writing.

**Time**: 30 minutes

**Materials**: Copies of the poem "Still I Rise" by Maya Angelou.

## Directing the Action

1. Pass out copies of the poem "Still I Rise" by Maya Angelou. Give everyone a moment to read to themselves.
2. Read out loud, chorally. If you have time, have the group read out loud a second time, but this time alter which groups are reading which lines (maybe one triad reads all the "still I rise" lines, etc.).
3. Invite participants to turn to a neighbor and talk about which lines really resonate—which lines reflect something important?
4. Divide into groups of four and find a space in the room to work. Assign each group one stanza. Take five minutes to talk about what this stanza means. Each person will then create one gesture that reflects or responds to the text. Teach this gesture to the rest of the group; repeat until all are clear and you can perform this gesture together.
5. Now decide an order for the gestures to put them all together. How do you move from one gesture to the next? Where does the gesture begin and end? Try performing all four gestures in a row as a group.
6. Now layer the text back onto the gesture sequence that you have created. How will your group speak your text? Will you all speak chorally? Will you take turns with different lines? Will you emphasize different words or phrases by speaking them chorally or repeating them?
7. Rehearse to share with the rest of the ensemble, then share out.

## Guiding Reflection

- What did you notice? Which gestures emphasized the words of the poem?
- How did coming up with a gesture change the way you understood your stanza?

## In Our Experience

Offering text to youth participants validates and echoes their own work on oppression as they discover resonance in what someone else has written. If a group is resistant to activating text, we reinforce that there is no wrong answer, and whatever they put together in terms of gesture and text will create meaning for others. We also find it sometimes helps to model various ways to create gesture and helps for participants to try out gestures that are both realistic and abstract.

### Connecting to Performance

This could become an ensemble performance piece, or could provide inspiration to participants to write their own poem.

**Source**: Developed by Lee Anne Bell and published in *Storytelling for social justice* (2010, p. 71), using Maya Angelou's poem, "Still I Rise" (1978).

# What Is (In)Justice?

## Exposing and Resisting Injustice: The Human Knot

*The Human Knot is a commonly used ensemble or community building activity. It requires that a group work together, communicate, have patience and take care of each other as they attempt to untangle the human knot.*

### PJP Connection

This action offers a physical metaphor for the work of gender and racial justice. Participants experience challenges related to group communication, choosing pathways toward change, and working to untangle webs of oppressions while remaining cognizant of individual experiences. As one area of the knot is untangled, another area gets stuck. This action also demonstrates the ways that groups intersect and collide to consider how we are each necessary in the ongoing challenge to shift oppressions. We conclude with a discussion of this quote, often attributed to Lilla Watson, Aboriginal elder from Australia and Aboriginal activist, Queensland, 1970s:

If you have come here to help me, you are wasting your time. But if you have come because your liberation is bound up with mine, then let us work together.

**Time:** 12–20 minutes

**Materials**: None

### Directing the Action

1.  Divide into groups of 6–8 maximum. Ask participants to form a circle. Begin by putting right hands out and shaking the hand of someone across the circle. Continue to hold this hand and put left hands out and shake the hand of someone different across the circle.
2.  The challenge is to unwind this knot and to return to a circle while holding onto both hands. It can be done. It does take patience and clear

communication. Allow and encourage the group to talk and communicate. This will require stepping over arms, going under arms, and being very close to each other.

3. Give the group time to work it out. Ideally participants will come to a full circle again without disconnecting hands. Some members of the group might be facing backwards, and this is okay. The goal is to remain connected and unwind, back into a full circle. Sometimes the group will find that they have an inner circle and an outer circle.

## Guiding Reflection

- What did you have to do to be successful in this activity?
- What was challenging or frustrating?
- Let's think through this quote together:
  - "If you have come here to help me, you are wasting your time. But if you have come because your liberation is bound up with mine, then let us work together"—attributed to Lilla Watson, Aboriginal elder and Aboriginal activist from Australia, 1970s.
- How does this connect to our knot? How are our different experiences of oppression interconnected and possibly overlapping?
- How is one's own liberation bound up with someone else's? What does this mean?

## In Our Experience

This action takes trust because of proximity to each other and the ways that people have to move under and over each other. It is not a good activity for a group that is struggling to create ensemble unless it seems this might push them through to the other side. This action sometimes requires some side coaching. Groups can get frustrated if they don't seem to be making progress in unwinding. If a group finishes very quickly, ask them to try again, or invite them to discuss what helped them finish so quickly.

## Connecting to Performance

Rather than bring this action into performance, it becomes a metaphor for challenge of addressing racial and gender injustice. The knot becomes one way to imagine our connection to and within interlocking oppressions—the ensemble may also brainstorm other ways to visualize or represent this idea in performance.

**Source**: Developed by Augusto Boal and published in *Games for actors and non-actors* (1992, pp. 67–68).

# What Is (In)Justice?

## Exposing and Resisting Injustice: Justice for Women Means...

*This writing prompt is useful in generating text for performance, and can be worked on for multiple sessions to craft a powerful whole-group performance piece.*

### PJP Connection

This prompt becomes a tangible way for youth to articulate what they actually want and believe should happen for women, or non-binary, gender non-conforming people in our country. Although this builds on the "In society..." prompt, this could be altered to become a brainstorm about justice in relationship to a different identity marker, such as "Justice for trans folks means..." or "Justice for people with disabilities means..." or even "Justice for Black women means..." This prompt can also be altered to respond to a central issue that resonates in the group.

**Time**: 10 minutes for brainstorming, 20 minutes for embodying

**Materials**: Paper or journals and pencils

### Directing the Action

1. Ask participants to find a spot in the room to do some personal writing. Give them four minutes to generate as many responses as they can to the prompt "Justice for women means..."
2. Partner up with someone else in the room and share what you came up with.
3. Choose 4–6 responses that really stand out to you—maybe because you both had them on your list, or maybe because they are very different from each other's lists.
4. Find another pair, and share your lists from each group, and then in your group of four, narrow your group list to 4–6 responses that reflect your group of four.
5. Look at your list together. Underline or circle the words or phrases that feel most important as a group.
6. Your group is going to figure out how to share this list out with the rest of the group. Instead of just reading your list, you are going to perform your list. Think through the following ideas and find a way to follow each direction in your performance:
   a. Everyone must speak at least once
   b. Use repetition and or echo—what do you want to emphasize by repeating, or having other members in your group echo?

    c.   Use at least two gestures. Where to you want to emphasize by adding gesture?

    d.   Use choral text—where might you say something, a line or a word or a phrase, together?

    e.   Vary the group presentation: don't just stand in a line for the entire presentation. Where can you move, change formation, change levels, etc.?

    f.   Pay particular attention to your underlined or circled words/phrases. Find ways to emphasize the importance of these!

    g.   Plan and rehearse to share out.

7.   Share all small group performances with the rest of the group. After each performance, ask audience to reflect back: What things did you notice that made you pay attention? Interesting moments?

8.   Hand in your performances (written on paper).

## Guiding Reflection

- What did you see in other performances that really made you think?
- Which ideas came up multiple times?
- We are going to attempt to put all of these ideas into *one* piece. What do we need to pay attention to in putting them together?

## In Our Experience

There is a fine balance between giving groups enough time to plan a performance and giving too much. We find it is often better to give less time to plan and rehearse so that participants can't overanalyze and must make quick decisions. However, we find that when we are working with new performers, facilitators and directors often need to offer more support and direction. Our goal is to support young people to feel excited and powerful during performance rather than embarrassed and shy. Groups may need some expert direction or support making decisions. Encourage participants to get up on their feet to make decisions and try things out rather than plan everything out on paper.

## Connecting to Performance

We often take all ideas and combine them into one ensemble poem. Before participants hand them in, ask them to put their names next to their favorite lines or lines they wrote, and let them know that the final combination of lines will change as a result of weaving lines together for the ensemble.

**Source**: This action was developed as part of the Performing Justice Project.

# What Is (In)Justice?

# Exposing and Resisting Injustice: Activating Statistics

*This performance action invites participants to work together as a cohesive ensemble to respond to statistics that represent identity-based oppressions such as the wage gap, access to healthcare, and the school-to-prison pipeline.*

## PJP Connection

Using statistics has been a consistent part of every PJP performance. Statistics offer a picture of the real-world impact of identity-based oppressions and help young people connect their own experiences to a larger sense of justice in the world.

**Time**: 30 minutes

**Materials**: List of statistics that reflect, respond to, and challenge work that participants have been doing in the group. We typically use statistics that reflect current local and national concerns.

## Directing the Action

1. Prepare a list of statistics that relate to or reflect conversations and identities in the room (see example in Appendix E).
2. Invite participants to find a partner to work with and spread out around the room. Pass out statistics, giving each pair one to work with.
3. Explain to participants:
    a. With your partner, read your sheet of statistics and talk about them. Which ones stand out to you?
    b. In your pair, choose one statistic that stands out to you, or that you think people need to know about.
    c. For this statistic, please create a frozen image to illustrate your statistic and decide how to perform the text that helps people really hear it.
    d. Think about what this statistic might look like in a frozen picture. What is the context of this statistic, where does this happen? Who is part of that picture? Who is affected by this situation? What role do others play?
    e. Think about how to read/perform your statistic. Should one person read the text? What will help your audience really hear and understand and make sense of the statistic?
4. Come up with a hashtag that goes with your statistic, and share it at the end of your image/text.
5. Share with ensemble.

### Guiding Reflection

- What surprises you? What do you notice when you see all of these statistics together?
- How did you decide which statistic to work with?
- Which statistics represent your truths?

### In Our Experience

We always bring statistics into the PJP process to put youth experiences into context. Be aware of how statistics might bring up emotions for participants. Sometimes statistics represent a reality they are unfamiliar with, sometimes statistics reflect their lived experiences in a way that validates the multiple oppressions they are feeling but may not have named. We attempt to include statistics that reflect intersectional identities and address a variety of issues (such as the wage gap, school-to-prison pipeline, access to health care, etc.).

### Connecting to Performance

Following this action, we choose statistics that connect to performance pieces and that resonate with youth. Youth then record these statistics as sound cues for transitions or as a soundtrack behind a movement performance.

**Source**: This action was developed as part of the Performing Justice Project.

# What Is (In)Justice?

# Exposing and Resisting Injustice: This I Believe

*This writing prompt encourages young people to think about their core beliefs, particularly as related to their own identities and experiences in the world.*

### PJP Connection

This writing has been used to develop performance monologues in many PJP performances. After investigating identities and oppression, young people passionately articulate their own beliefs. The original invitation sent to essayists for the original "This I Believe" series invites essays of a particular type:

> What we want is so intimate that no one can write it for you. You must write it yourself, in the language most natural to you...

We would like you to tell not only what you believe, but how you reached your beliefs, and if they have grown, what made them grow. This necessarily must be highly personal. That is what we anticipate and want...

We are sure the statement we ask from you can have wide and lasting influence. Never has the need for personal philosophies of this kind been so urgent. Your belief, simply and sincerely spoken, is sure to stimulate and help those who hear it.

(This I Believe, 2019)

**Time**: 20–30 minutes for writing and shaping

**Materials**: Writing implements and paper or journals

## Directing the Action

1. Invite participants to reflect in their journals in a quiet space:
   a. Spend some time thinking through what you believe. What do you feel passionate about? What are the things you believe that others might not agree with, things that you defend strongly, or things that would make you angry if someone disagreed or didn't believe you? You might start with a list of beliefs you have about your gender identity, and/or your racial/ethnic identity in the world.
   b. Try to narrow to one belief that you feel is very important in your life—one belief you can express in a single statement.
   c. Take some time to write about this belief and how it plays out in your life and why you believe this. This writing should focus on what you *do* believe, not what you *don't* believe.
   d. Write what is important to you, and use examples from your life to demonstrate why this belief is important to you. Remember that your audience may be someone who doesn't know about or believe in the same things you do. What might they need to hear/know to understand why your belief is important?
2. Each essay should be between 100 and 300 words. Here are some questions to help guide the writing (these could be posted to support the writing process):
   a. Name your belief in a sentence or two. Rather than a list, focus on one core belief.
   b. Why do you believe what you believe?
   c. What is a moment when you realized you believed in this?

    d. Work to include at least one specific example. Be specific. Ground your story in the events that have shaped your core values. Consider moments when belief was formed or tested or changed.

    e. Write in words and phrases that are comfortable for you to speak. Read your essay aloud to yourself several times, and each time edit it and simplify it until you find the words, tone, and story that truly echo your belief and the way you speak.

3. If you have specific examples that you want to include but that might feel too personal to share out loud, you might frame the example as though it happened to a friend or someone you know.

## Guiding Reflection

- What did you learn about yourself and your beliefs?
- What was more difficult or easier than you thought it would be?
- Which beliefs of yours are connected to racial justice and gender justice?

## In Our Experience

It can take some time for young people to articulate their beliefs. Giving ample time to write and reflect is necessary, but offering one-on-one support can also be helpful. We have found it useful to set an expectation from the beginning that participants will do more than one draft (brainstorming, then a rough draft, then a second or final draft) which sets the expectation that they don't have to be finished the first time around, and also invites feedback and questions that help to narrow the essay. This is a time to encourage youth to articulate specific beliefs that are directly related to their own experiences in the world. If they have a hard time beginning, refer them to their six-word stories. What do they want for others? What do they wish was different? What is the world they want to live in?

## Connecting to Performance

This writing often leads to powerful monologues that are included in performance. While only one person may be speaking, others can be using images, statues, 8-Count Movement or complete the image onstage to embody the text.

**Source**: Developed by Edward R. Murrow and aired in the radio segment, *This I believe* (1951–1955).

# What Is (In)Justice?

## Exposing and Resisting Injustice: Imagining Justice

*This action invites youth to imagine their own version of justice and what living in a just world looks, sounds, and feels like.*

### PJP Connection

It is only through analyzing systems of oppression and at the same time imagining what justice can and should look like that we can actually begin to envision what we each want to build in the world. This action offers a chance to answer the question of this entire section of actions, "What is justice?"

**Time:** 30 minutes

**Materials**: Large piece of butcher paper (that will fit all participants sitting around the edges), markers, and background music

### Directing the Action

1. Explain to participants:
   a. We have talked about justice, intersectionality, respectability politics, and power and oppression. Now we are going to think about what a more just future looks like. Questions we want you to think about, and that will be posted for you to see during this activity include:
      i. What does justice look like?
      ii. What does it sound like?
      iii. Who is part of your vision of justice?
      iv. What does justice mean for others?
2. Invite participants to gather around the butcher paper, which can be on the floor or on a large table (or multiple tables end to end). Scatter lots of markers across the paper so that lots of colors are within reach of all sides.
3. Explain to participants:
   a. We are going to play some music, and ask you to brainstorm justice. Imagine that this paper can capture our future and it is full of justice. What needs to be in this mural to help people understand what it looks like and sounds like, what it feels like, what it means? You will begin in once place, drawing or writing. After about ten minutes we will move part way around the paper and you will pick up working on someone else's drawing or writing, and someone else will be adding onto yours. In this mural, we will build on each other's ideas.

b.   This is not about how well you draw, it is about generating ideas, colors, words… it is about picturing justice.

c.   If you can, try to keep your voices low or quiet so that everyone can tune into their own visions of justice.

4.   Rotate 3–4 times, as much as there is time for before this action needs to end.

## Guiding Reflection

- Looking at our Imagining Justice mural, what stands out to you?
- What makes you think about justice in a different way?
- What are you proud of on this mural?
- What do you see in your more just future?

## In Our Experience

It can take a few minutes for people to warm up around this action. Understanding that it is not about drawing skill helps to decrease anxiety for those who do not identify as artists. Typically, what is created collectively is often stunning and provocative. Encourage participants to fill the page as much as possible—building onto each other's images and text, but also filling in any blank spaces.

## Connecting to Performance

This can become a beautiful vision to post in a performance space and could be a backdrop for a performance. Images and text can also be used in shaping performance pieces. This is an excellent transitional action from "What is justice?" into "How do I perform justice?"

**Source**: We have played this game in multiple theatre classes and contexts. The original source is unknown.

## Doing Justice

## Sound Cues

*Tameika L. Hannah*

As the sound designer for the Performing Justice Project, my ambition was to create a space—using music and sound—that would encourage and cultivate a supportive environment for young people to share their personal stories.

Being a participant throughout the entire PJP process allowed me the space and time to become familiar with the personalities of the young people involved in the project. This in turn helped me choose what music would help their performance pieces take form on stage, as well as uplift their spirits throughout the process. Sound was a critical part of our process and product. Music kept the conversation going around what justice was, and at times, without any words needing to be said. All we had to do was listen.

I began the sound design process by choosing a selection of instrumental music and sound cues that I felt made for good background sound but did not overpower the voices of the performers. There was a mixture of up-tempo music as well as songs that had a lighter, more somber feel and tone because everyone's lived experiences had a variation of tempos themselves. Since the young people's stories evoked an array of emotions, I knew the music had to have a similar variety of sounds to help carry their personal narratives. As hoped for, music became a great translator of feelings within each PJP residency.

After a variety of music was selected, I began the process of editing music and creating smaller clips of songs that would be used in our performances. I also recorded the performers' voices during rehearsal and edited them into sound cues that played throughout the performances. Music helped the performers know what part of the performance was coming next and often underscored or supported youths' stories and monologues.

Deciding the exact instrumental music and sound cues for the final performances was a collective effort. The young people took ownership of what music they felt would speak to the personal stories they wrote and performed. If the music I selected did not represent the story the youth were comfortable sharing, they gave me feedback and direction to help me find a better sound for them. The youth set the tone for each PJP performance once given the musical tools to navigate through their original monologues and scenes. Through music and sound, we were able to enact justice. We created a space of honest dialogue about what additions and edits to the script and sound would make for our best work.

The healing property of sound played a crucial role throughout PJP rehearsals. Several PJP projects took place inside a juvenile detention center. The young people were denied access to music, so the excitement surrounding the sound portion of the project was a much-needed therapeutic experience for each of them. I was also incredibly angered knowing that the simple pleasure of listening to music was a luxury that some youth were deemed too criminal to enjoy. Experiencing the joy, laughter, and high spirits displayed by the young people when selecting their songs was exciting, and even more so because of this. Sound offered healing elements for all of us throughout our PJP work. If you are interested in incorporating sound and other musical elements into your creative projects, I encourage you to experiment with as many ideas as you feel inspired to try out. Sound can truly be used to help create the intentional space you have in mind. Trust your vision and see first-hand for yourself.

**Figure 2.4** Tameika L. Hannah (left) and Megan Alrutz (right) place new sound cues based on discussion with the PJP ensemble
Source: Photo by Lynn Hoare.

## 2.3.4 Performance Actions: How Do I Perform Justice?

This section frames the practice of devising performance about gender and racial justice as a form of youth activism. By lifting up, exposing, and performing stories of (in)justice, young people in PJP begin naming what they see around them and what is required to create an equitable and accessible world. The actions in this section invite youth to share their stories and experiences and to create small bits of original performance material that both imagine and enact possibilities for racial and gender justice. Arts educator and scholar Mary Stone Hanley writes, "One of the social justice aspects of this work [the arts] lies in the empowerment that comes with the clarification of the internal voice and the creative agency that then can be used to transform the world through works of expression" (2013, p. 5). The performance actions in this section support project directors and youth participants to create a performance arc that expresses both that clear internal voice and a nuanced vision for justice. This section offers a process for building connective tissue between disparate stories and weaving small bits of performance into a cohesive script and eventually a public performance.

A PJP residency typically results in a montage or collage-style performance that includes a careful arrangement of parts and pieces. Our scripts rarely follow the journey of a single protagonist or a single plot. This type of devised theatre is sometimes referred to as composed theatre, influenced by musical compositions as discussed in *Composed Theatre: Aesthetics, Practices, Processes* edited by Matthias Rebstock and David Roesner (2012), or as a theatrical score, as discussed in *Theatre for Youth Third Space* by Stephani Etheridge Woodson (2015, p. 159). We use Woodson's description of the performance "score" to think about composing a PJP performance, focusing on how a score references rhythm, melody, dynamic choices (not just about sound), texture, duration and gesture and embodiment, among other qualities (2015, p. 159). When creating a PJP performance outline, we ask how various bits of performance complement or contrast each other, as well as what bits of performance might represent multiple points of view and what bits offer something unique to our group. We consider patterns of content and whose voice and identity markers might bring to light a critical idea at an impactful moment in the performance. As project directors, we think deeply about the arc of the score, considering tone and mood, as well as variety throughout the text, movement, vocalization, and overall staging of the performance. In this section of the book, we introduce a number of dramaturgical frames or structures that we use to compose a full performance from the many contributions and bits of material created by the ensemble. We offer considerations for staging performance frames or patterns, as well as activating aesthetic choices, emotionally engaging material, and calls to action.

Section 2.3.4, How Do I Perform Justice?, is organized into four subsections: Refining and Staging Stories, Script Development, Sound/Space/Aesthetics, and Reflection Actions. Refining and Staging Stories includes a collection of performance actions, not unlike earlier sections of Part Two, while the remaining three subsections (Script Development, Sound/Space/Aesthetics, and Reflection Actions) include what we call performance considerations, namely dramaturgical practices and questions that can shape the script development and rehearsal processes. These later subsections offer key considerations and guiding questions for developing a larger script or working toward a produced public performance.

The performance actions in the Refining and Staging Stories subsection offer concrete suggestions for facilitating the movement of participants' creative writing and storytelling work into performance texts, as well as into embodied and vocalized staging. The actions in this subsection support the ensemble's effort to move their stories and experiences into creatively staged and engaging performance pieces for an outside audience. We outline performance actions that help develop character and storyline, as well as activate words and experiences through dynamic vocal and embodied performance.

The next subsection, Script Development, focuses on considerations for the project director(s) and teaching artists. We outline a dramaturgical process for putting together a script; in PJP, this process is led by the project directors and teaching artists, but deeply informed by youth participants. This subsection offers an approach to script development that begins with assessing the text or content already generated by the ensemble and naming what else is needed to complete the full script once a structure or shape for the performance has been established. As part of this process, we begin to think through an opening and closing song or other performance frame, as well as one or more theatrical concepts to help thread together the various pieces of material. During this part of the process, we also consider the visual, physical, and/ or musical transitions that will support a cohesive performance on stage. This subsection raises questions about preparing ensemble members to move their individual, often personal stories into a rehearsal setting with a group, and later into a public performance space with the whole ensemble. Finally, the Script Development subsection offers three dramaturgical models, or organizational structures, for assembling a PJP script. These visual models demonstrate possible ways to organize the ensemble's collection of performance bits into a single, cohesive script, collage, or performance outline.

The third subsection, titled Sound/Space/Aesthetics, offers a list of questions and considerations for thinking through the look and feel of the performance environment. Considering the design of the space and how young performers might use the space is a critical part of supporting youth success within a new and potentially risky performance experience. We ask how youth might be included in and supported by design choices, inviting the ensemble to reflect on the relationship between aesthetics and performing justice.

The final subsection, Reflection Actions, addresses opportunities to weave youth reflection throughout the process of building, rehearsing, and sharing a Performing Justice Project with an audience. Although we emphasize reflection and reflexivity within each of our performance actions, we also include guided reflection with youth as part of the script development process. Reflection Actions also offers frameworks for youth participants to lead reflective and dialogue-based actions with the audience following the performance.

Taken together, the collection of performance actions and considerations in Section 2.3.4, How Do I Perform Justice?, helps bring audience members into conversation with the youth ensemble, inviting all parties to articulate and shift understandings of gender and racial justice individually and with each other.

## Refining and Staging Stories

- From Story to Performance Text
- Role on the Wall
- Creating Character Dialogue
- From 8-Count Movement to Devised Scene
- Activating Text Vocally
- Activating Text with Sound
- Activating Text Physically

## Script Development

- Preparing for Performance
- Collecting and Reviewing Content
- Organizing Content
- Creating a Visual Map
- Dramaturgical Questions
- Text, Groupings, and Transitions
- Three Dramaturgical Models
  - Theme
  - Questions
  - Story

## Sound/Space/Aesthetics

- Sound, Music, and Voiceover
- Setting, Lighting, Costumes, Props, and Scripts

## Reflection Actions

- It Made Me Think
- People to People
- Think, Pair, Share
- Vote from Your Seat
- Spread the Word

## How Do I Perform Justice?

### Refining and Staging Stories: From Story to Performance Text

*These actions invite participants to develop, edit, and activate their writing or stories. They also ask youth to collaborate, supporting them to connect as artists and storytellers and to uplift one another's work.*

### PJP Connection

Participants in a PJP process do a fair amount of writing and brainstorming in response to questions and prompts. This performance action offers one way to take a bit of personal writing and develop it into a detailed story. Youth then refine their stories into a monologue or scene that speaks to or reflects on questions of gender and/or racial justice.

**Time:** 15–20 minutes, including writing and revisions

**Materials:** Journals, writing utensils

### Directing the Action

1. Invite participants to look through their journals to find their six-word stories, a poem, or a bit of writing that could be expanded. Ask them to choose one bit of writing and think about the story or experience that inspired it.
2. Invite participants to free-write or journal about that experience or story for five minutes, focusing on the location, character, and/or action.

3. After participants finish journaling, invite half of the group to stand up and create a circle. Ask each participant to pivot and face outward, while remaining standing in the circle.

4. Invite the remaining students to stand and create an outer circle (around the existing circle) by standing in front of someone in the inner circle. In the outer circle, individuals should face inward, while those standing in the inner circle should face outward. Each participant should end up standing and facing a partner in the other circle.

5. Give participants one minute to share their story with their partners. Explain to participants:
   a. Outer circle, share your story with your partner (the person facing you). *(1 min)*
   b. After one minute, invite listening partners to ask questions: What do you want to know more about? What part of the story do you remember most? What parts of the story were not clear? What kind of details will invite audiences to lean in and listen? *(2–3 mins)*
   c. Now, people standing in the inner circle, share your story with your partner. *(1 min)*
   d. After one minute, invite listening partners to ask questions: What do you want to know more about? What part of the story do you remember most? What parts of the story were not clear? What kind of details will invite audiences to lean in and listen? *(2–3 mins)*

6. Ask the outer circle to rotate clockwise and move over two people to land with a new partner.

7. Invite participants to share their story with their partner, attending to a clear and engaging beginning, middle, and end of their story. Explain to participants:
   a. Share the same story with your new partner, again taking one minute each and allowing both partners to tell an intentionally revised, new version of their story.

8. Invite the group to rotate clockwise, past two people again, to land facing a new partner.

9. For this third and final round, ask participants to choose an opening phrase for their story. Here are some examples:
   a. This I believe…
   b. Once upon a time…
   c. The truth about me is…
   d. The worst/best time was…
   e. I never knew…
   f. What I would tell my younger self is…

10. When participants are ready, ask them to share their story once more with their new partner, beginning with their chosen opening phrase. Again, each partner has one minute each to share.

11. After this round of sharing, bring students back to a single seated circle. Ask them to record changes to their story in their journal.

## Guiding Reflection

- What did you notice about yourself or your story as you engaged in this exercise? What, if anything, surprised you?
- What was your experience of sharing or refining your story? What did you learn or gain from editing your work? What might be lost when we edit our work?
- How is sharing personal stories a part of enacting justice?

## In Our Experience

We believe in being strict timekeepers during this action, inviting participants to making choices and focus on what is most important to them. Participants can get bored with the repetition of retelling the same story, so we provide additional challenges or expectations for each round to help them stay engaged while revising and crafting stories.

## Connecting to Performance

From here, participants' stories could be crafted and staged as monologues, developed into scenes, or shared as narration with tableaux or moving phrases behind the speaker.

**Source:** This action was developed as part of the Performing Justice Project.

# How Do I Perform Justice?

# Refining and Staging Stories: Role on the Wall

*This action helps to develop or analyze characters in Applied Theatre and Theatre in Education settings.*

## PJP Connection

This action helps ensemble members identify what pressures their character(s)—often themselves and each other—might be experiencing and how they respond as a result. This action helps youth add depth and complexity to characters and stories by starting to see how systems shape individuals' beliefs, options, and actions.

**Time:** 10–15 minutes per character in development

**Materials:** Large pieces of butcher paper or printer paper, markers

## Directing the Action

1. Divide into small groups. Assign each group a scene to bring to life. Ask each group to read through their scene and identify the main characters.
2. Ask the group to draw a simple body outline (like a gingerbread person) on a piece of paper (unlined printer paper works fine, although butcher paper allows these to be easily shared with others); this outline will represent the character at hand.
3. Explain to participants:
   a. Discuss the following questions: What are the pressures on this character/person? What are they hearing said about them or to them?
   b. Write down the statements and pressures on the outside of the drawn figure. Include any external factors impacting the thoughts or behaviors of the character: pressures, expectations by others, assumptions from family, friends, and others in their life.
   c. Inside the drawn figure, write down what the character is thinking and feeling, particularly in response to each comment, expectation, or pressure named on the outer parts of the paper.
   d. Inside the head of the figure, write what the character wants.
   e. Repeat this visual brainstorm on a separate piece of paper for other major characters in the scene.
4. Ask participants how this Role on the Wall might shift or support character choices in the scene and/or add complexity and depth to their writing and performance choices.

## Guiding Reflection

- What did you learn about the characters in your scene?
- What might you add or change in your scene now?

## In Our Experience

This action gets to the heart of what is happening internally for a character and can help guide the direction of a scene in development. We often remind youth to play with representing what they know to be true rather than simply trying to reproduce exact details of a story or memory. As the ensemble moves from a single-authored piece of writing to a group-authored scene, we guide the group to determine if the original author has the final say on scene and character choices or not. The original author may or may not take an active role in staging or performing the piece.

### Connecting to Performance

We encourage the ensemble to revise their scene work based on information gained from Role on the Wall. While the scene should remain authentic to the original story or piece of writing, revisions may deepen or clarify the scene for a new audience.

**Source**: Developed by Jonothan Neelands and Tony Goode and published in *Structuring drama work* (1990, p. 22).

# How Do I Perform Justice?

## Refining and Staging Stories: Creating Character Dialogue

*In this action, youth practice writing active dialogue to heighten dramatic action.*

### PJP Connection

Writing character objectives and active dialogue supports scene development. This action encourages youth to work together to tell a cohesive story, and can help activate six-word stories about gender and racial justice by translating and expanding a short piece of text into a multi-character scene. These scenes often demonstrate moments of impact related to racial and gender bias.

**Time:** 10–15 minutes

**Materials:** A chalkboard, markerboard or large piece of poster paper, lined paper, one piece for each pair, writing utensils

### Directing the Action

1. Ask students to think about the fairytale, *Little Red Riding Hood*. To make sure everyone is clear on the plot, ask volunteers to share the beginning, middle, and end of the fairytale. Since there are multiple versions of this fairytale in different cultures, decide on the version you will explore as an ensemble.
2. Explain to participants:
   a. As a group, you are going to explore the moment where Little Red meets the Wolf in the woods on the way to her Grandmother's house.
   b. With your ensemble, decide: What is the conflict between these two characters? What is each character's objective?

    c.   Remind the ensemble that writing character objectives that are in opposition to each other will create a clear conflict.

    d.   Write on the board and gather ideas from the ensemble:

**Conflict:** _____

*(Example: The wolf wants to distract Little Red and beat her to Grandma's House.)*

**Objectives:**

**Wolf: I want** _____

*(Example: Wolf: I want to distract Little Red, so I can eat her.)*

**Little Red Riding Hood: I want** _____

*(Little Red: I want to brush off the Wolf and get to Grandma's.)*

3.   Explain to participants:

    a.   Our goal is to play this conflict out dramatically by writing dialogue between the two characters: Let's work together to develop a definition of dialogue. *(Possible definition for dialogue: When two or more characters have a conversation on stage.)*

4.   Choose a participant from the ensemble to model the exercise with you and decide who will write dialogue for each character.

5.   Decide which character writes first. Silently, this character will write their name, then their line of dialogue on the board (in proper playwriting format, shown below). When the character finishes, the other character responds silently by writing the next line of dialogue in response to the previous line. This continues for 4–6 lines of dialogue.

Dialogue Format:

(Character's name all in capital letters, centered over the line of dialogue)

LITTLE RED RIDING HOOD

*Line of Dialogue Here*

WOLF

*Line of Dialogue Here*

6.   Ask for two new volunteers to read/perform the dialogue for the class.

7.   Ask the ensemble: Who achieved their objective in this dialogue? What tactics did the characters use to achieve their objectives? How did the conflict show up in the dialogue? What made the dialogue interesting to you?

8.   Assign students a partner. Give each pair one blank, lined piece of paper and two writing utensils.

9.   Ask the ensemble to fast-forward the story of *Little Red Riding Hood*, to the moment when Little Red finally gets to her Grandmother's house to find the Wolf dressed as her Grandmother. Ask the partners to explore this moment through dialogue, following the pattern modeled

a moment before. Encourage the pairs to find new ways of communicating this moment in their own language, rather than relying on language they remember from the story (i.e., "Oh, what big eyes you have!").

10. Ask each pair to decide who is playing which character. Invite them to decide what their conflict is and what their characters' objectives are. Ask them to write the conflict and objectives at the top of the paper (see the board for the example).

11. Give the pairs three to five minutes to write their dialogue. Explain to the group:

   a.  One person begins by silently writing a line of dialogue, then passing the paper to their partner.

   b.  Please remain silent throughout the activity and respond to the dialogue your partner has given you only in writing.

   c.  With your partner, read, rehearse and share your dialogue with the whole group.

## Guiding Reflection

- What did you notice about writing dialogue? How is it different from first-person storytelling? What did you notice about the various voices that you all created for Little Red?
- How did dialogue move the action forward?
- How might you use dialogue to turn one of your poems or essays into a scene?

## In Our Experience

This action helps youth understand the difference between a simple conversation and dialogue where something actively happens between characters—where conflict is heightened for an audience. If conflict is not present in the dialogue, we ask partners to introduce new information, play with a new tactic, or add obstacles to characters getting what they want in the scene.

## Connecting to Performance

After participants practice activating conflict and objectives through dialogue, we ask them to revisit their own stories to create or revise dialogue with an eye toward clear conflict and objectives.

**Source**: Adapted by Meg Greene from Young Playwrights' Theater and Arena Stage Student Playwrights Project.

# How Do I Perform Justice?

## Refining and Staging Stories: From 8-Count Movement to Devised Scene

*This action offers a process for to translating 8-Count Movements (see performance action 8-Count Movement in Section 2.3.3) into short scenes on gender and racial justice.*

### PJP Connection

Developing a scene based on an 8-Count Movement allows participants to imagine background information and contexts surrounding their experiences with gender and racial justice. This action allows participants to both name and embody the impact of gendered expectations on their lives. This action can make seemingly hidden, oppressive systems and beliefs visible for the ensemble and the audience.

**Time**: 20–30 minutes

**Materials**: None

### Directing the Action

1. Ask one participant to perform their 8-Count Movement for the ensemble.
2. Ask the participant to then reflect on the following questions about their 8-Count, encouraging them to make quick decisions as they develop a related story:
   a. Who are the other characters in this story?
   b. Where is this event/situation taking place?
   c. What might have happened just before this event in your 8-Count Movement?
   d. What are three emotions your character was feeling right before or during this moment?
   e. What might happen next?
3. Ask additional participants to volunteer to play the main character as well as new characters that have been added or named. Invite the generative artist, the original performer, to step into the role of director and help other participants determine characteristics and conflicts related to their character.
4. Invite the new cast of characters to improvise a quick scene, based on the ideas presented by the generative artist. Encourage the improvisation to carry on for 30–90 seconds.

5.  After the improvisation is over, ask the generative artist: Why does this moment matter to you? Help the generative artist and group name a key concept or theme guiding the scene.
6.  Ask the generative artist and the rest of the ensemble: How can we make the scene more specific or illustrative of the theme or concept?
7.  Invite the performers to revise the scene, adding new staging or lines as needed for clarity. Invite another ensemble member to write down the improvised lines of dialogue to script a short scene with a beginning, middle, and end.

## Guiding Reflection

-   What does this scene tell you about the 8-Count Movement?
-   How is the original prompt for the 8-Count Movement ("Being a woman in society means…") connected to the scene?
-   Why might it be important to write or perform this scene for an audience?

## In Our Experience

This strategy creates short, potent scenes with characters that typically take on an archetypical nature: the controlling partner, the mean bully, the smart, confident protagonist. The situations presented reveal critical thoughts and understandings of oppression in our culture and performing them for an audience often provokes dialogue. Family and community expectations and boundaries related to gender and race are often revealed through this action. This action works well when groups of three or four develop scenes from one person's 8-Count Movement at a time.

## Connecting to Performance

We often use the resulting scenes in performance, sometimes developing three to four different scenes based on 8-Count Movements. These very short scenes work well grouped together, used to illustrate statistics or other content, or as punctuation on a longer set of performance bits.

**Source**: This action was developed as part of the Performing Justice Project.

# How Do I Perform Justice?

## Refining and Staging Stories: Activating Text Vocally

*Practicing vocal performance options in a clearly directed manner helps build confidence with voice, body, and identity-based content.*

### PJP Connection

Vocalizing experiences and truths often requires confidence and bravery. Sharing short poems and six-word stories about experience of (in)justice can become an act of justice and helps build the foundation for youth to perform justice in a longer, ensemble-based performance piece.

**Time:** 15 minutes

**Materials:** Journal, previous writing of six-word stories, or poems collected

### Directing the Action

1. Explain to participants (this can be a solo or small group action):
   a. Choose a short poem or six-word story from your journal to work with.
   b. Read your chosen piece out loud three times to yourself. How does it feel in your mouth? Are there any words you want to change now that you've heard it and said it?
   c. If possible, stand up or change your posture in a significant way. Turn away from the rest of the group, into your own "private studio." Read your words out loud again and see how it feels on your feet or with your new posture.
2. Invite each participant to incorporate the following four elements into the vocal performance of their small bit of text:
   a. One significant pause
   b. One moment where you intentionally speed up or slow down the words
   c. One significant inhale or exhale
   d. One word or phrase that gets repeated (it can be repeated throughout, or just in the first place it appears in your text)
3. Explain to participants:
   a. Take some time to play around with where these might fit and mark them on your paper with a pencil. Once you have them marked in your piece, run through it. Each time you read it, try a new tempo or rhythm. Find a new way to plant your feet or a new place to

focus your shoulders or your eyes. Find where the piece feels right in your body.

    b.    Rehearse this new version so you feel comfortable sharing. It is not the final version; it's just where you are right now.

4.    Invite each participant to vocally share their performance text with the larger group.

5.    Ask the group to share what stood out to them from each performance piece.

6.    Though this action is written for solo text development and performance, it can alternately be led for pairs, small groups, or half the ensemble. Working together, a trio or small group can make similar choices about vocal performance, adding choral speak to the list of elements to play with in rehearsal and performance.

## Guiding Reflection

- What changed as a result of your choices?
- What did you discover about the rhythm or meaning of your text?
- What opportunities do you see for revising, adding to, or further shaping your performance piece?

## In Our Experience

Offering a very specific set of expectations helps new performers follow a plan to create dynamic theatre. Young people are often surprised at the power of their short pieces when they add vocal variation. The invitation to add sound, breath, and repetition may not be familiar and can feel strange. We often model what a finished piece might sound like.

## Connecting to Performance

With the addition of vocal variation, very short pieces can become interesting transitions or repeated text in the larger performance script. We sometimes thread performances of six-word stories together to show multiple points entry points to and experiences of gender and racial justice.

**Source**: This action was developed as part of the Performing Justice Project. A related version of this performance action is also outlined in *The viewpoints book: A practical guide to viewpoints and composition* by Anne Bogart and Tina Landau (2005, pp. 106–109).

# How Do I Perform Justice?

## Refining and Staging Stories: Activating Text with Sound

*Similar to activating text with vocal techniques, this action offers a simple but accessible way to active a short piece of text.*

### PJP Connection

Young people know the sounds of their world. Allowing them to bring these sounds into their writing validates their lived experiences and creates an opportunity to connect with the audience. Sound can support the work of less experienced performers, and creates background and context.

**Time:** 20 minutes

**Materials:** None

### Directing the Action

1.  Invite the ensemble to take inventory of the space and to brainstorm opportunities for creating sound. What things can be used to make sounds that already exist in the space, including everyday objects such as a chair, floor materials, or people's bodies? Brainstorm sounds that can be created with our bodies (give a few examples) and with objects in the room.

2.  Next, invite the group to go on a sound treasure hunt. Explain to participants:

    a.  You have one minute to find a sound on your body. For example: What does it sound like to stomp your feet in our space? What are the different sounds of solo stomping versus choral marching? What are all the different ways we can use our hands on our bodies to make sound? What does it sound like when your hand taps your thigh, your chest, another hand (high five)? Experiment.

    b.  Next, take one minute to find a sound using an object in the room, such as a book with pages fluttering, a light switch turning on and off, a window being raised or lowered, or a door closing. What are the different ways we can use regular objects to make sound? After a minute of exploration, we will each share one sound we have found.

    c.  Let's travel around the space as we share our sounds with the group.

    d.  Now, let's create a sound sequence in pairs. Pair with another participant and experiment with ways to make sound in our space, using only yourselves and found objects in the space. As a pair, find six different sounds: three that are from your bodies, and three using bodies in space (stomping, fast walk, etc.) or objects in space (the window closing/opening, the door shutting, lights turning on and off, etc.).

e.  Finally, string your sounds together in an interesting sequence and share them out with the group.

3.  After the found sounds and sequences are shared out, ask pairs to join together to form a small group of four. Hand out (or invite groups to choose) a piece of text already created by someone in the group. Explain to the groups:

a.  Read your text together: What kinds of sounds are implied in your text? Where are the opportunities to bring these sounds to life? Where might sound support a particular moment in your story? What new sounds might punctuate or draw attention to a moment in your story?

b.  Experiment with creating sound for your text. Find three to five new sounds and decide how these sounds will be performed alongside the vocalization of your text. Decide who will read text and who will share sound, and be sure to give a role to each person in your group.

c.  Let's listen to each group, one at a time, perform what they created. The rest of us will listen for the ways that sound creates an emotional impact or tells what is important in each piece of text.

## Guiding Reflection

• What sounds did you hear in the performances?
• Which sounds were intriguing and made you want to lean in?
• What particular sounds helped tell the story or helped you make meaning?

## In Our Experience

This action offers a low-tech way to add texture to a written piece of text. We offer variations on this action, such as an invitation to perform sound from behind the audience or from behind the main performer. Participants sometimes perform chorally, taking on one sound or one line of text. This action might start out silly but often results in beautiful and unexpected performance.

### Connecting to Performance

Building a soundscape supports further development of a piece of text and helps the ensemble think creatively about what performance sounds like. Soundscapes might be shared live by ensemble members, or recorded and played underneath or alongside a piece of text.

**Source**: Adapted by Performing Justice Project from Tectonic Theater Project's Moment Work Process and published in *Moment work: Tectonic Theater Project's process of devising theater* (Kaufman and McAdams 2018, pp. 91–98).

# How Do I Perform Justice?

## Refining and Staging Stories: Activating Text Physically

*This action focuses on activating text through gesture and embodied images. We share several approaches for inviting youth to use their bodies, not simply their voices, as a tool for creative expression.*

### PJP Connection

Gesture and image sequences are essential components in a PJP process, offering a way to embody text without necessarily presenting a linear narrative or focusing on realism. Expressing ideas through movement and image offers alternatives to the spoken word and acknowledges multiple ways of knowing, making, and expressing what youth know. This action offers five entry points for exploring gender and racial justice through embodied performance.

1. Introduction to Gesture
2. Emotion Gesture Sequence
3. Poem Gesture Sequence
4. Group Tableaux or Stage Pictures
5. Moving Pictures/Complete the Image

**Time:** 15–20 minutes per action

**Materials:** Text (could be a monologue, six-word story, spoken word piece, etc.)

**Directing the Action**

## INTRODUCTION TO GESTURE

1. Invite participants to stand in a circle.
2. Discuss with participants:
   a. What is a gesture?
   b. What are examples of gestures that are common and everyday?
   c. What are examples of gestures that are more abstract and representational?
3. Model everyday gestures such as shaking hands or waving hello, to representational gestures that might physically communicate or suggest a feeling, concept or idea of protective or brave. Ask participants to repeat or mirror these gestures with their own bodies.
4. Next, share one line of a poem or piece of text out loud. Ask the ensemble to face outward in the circle and to create and physicalize their own original gesture in response to the line of text. Give the group a moment to explore and find their gesture, and another moment to finalize and rehearse their choice.
5. Ask the ensemble to face inward in the circle again and share their gestures (either in small groups of three or by moving quickly around the circle one at a time). Notice the variety of gestures created in response to one line of text.

## EMOTION GESTURE SEQUENCE

1. Invite the ensemble to stand in a circle.
2. Choose a piece of writing—a poem or other text—and share it out loud with the ensemble.
3. Ask the group to identify three to six emotions or feelings present in the piece or elicited by the text.
4. Divide the ensemble into groups of three or four and assign each group one of the emotions listed out by the ensemble.
5. Explain to participants:
   a. In your small groups, create one physical movement or repeatable gesture that represents your assigned emotion word. All members of your group should perform the movement or gesture simultaneously.
6. After a few minutes, ask everyone to return to one big circle. Invite each small group to teach their gesture to the ensemble as a whole. Explain to participants:
   a. As each group teaches their gesture to us, we will practice a few times.
   b. Please work toward specificity in your interpretation of each gesture. For example, what is happening with the fingers, the eyebrows, the weight in the body?

    c.   As an ensemble, let's perform this gesture simultaneously, repeating it three times in a row, all together.

7.  After each group has taught their gesture to the ensemble, return to the original text together, and "score" it as a script. Explain to participants:

    a.   Together, we will decide where the emotion shifts in the text.

    b.   Which gestures from the group might line up with specific pieces of the texts?

8.  Invite the ensemble to rehearse the text together with the newly created gestures. Read the text aloud and when the emotion shifts in the text, invite the group to perform the next gesture, repeating each gesture together until the text calls for a change to the next gesture.

9.  Lastly, decide how many participants will vocally perform the text and how. Once these roles are assigned, invite the group to rehearse and perform the text vocally and with gestures. This performance action can be done either as a whole ensemble (all group members perform vocally and physically) or in split halves (one half of the group providing the vocal score and the other providing the physical score).

## POEM GESTURE SEQUENCE

1.  Divide the ensemble into small groups of three, numbering off one to three among the group members. Give each group a four-line poem or a short piece of text that doesn't belong to anyone in the group. We often use the "I Come from a Place" poems for this action.

2.  Explain to participants:

    a.   Person #1 takes line #1 of the poem, #2 takes line #2, etc. Using your body and face, each person will create a physical gesture that represents their line of text. Make sure that the physical gesture can be repeated by others.

    b.   Practice saying your line of text and repeating your chosen gesture.

    c.   #1s: teach your gesture and line of text to your group. Repeat it together three times as a group.

    d.   Next, 2s and 3s teach their line and gesture to the group.

    e.   Finally, put the three gestures together in order of the poem and perform all gestures in order.

    f.   As a group, create a fourth and final gesture to represent the last line of the poem/narrative and to end the short performance.

    g.   Create a strong way to begin and end this short performance, and decide how you will transition from one line of text and gesture to the next.

    h.   If there is time, practice incorporating the words and gestures together, adjusting the physical score, as needed, to go with the length of each spoken line of text.

3.  Give the ensemble a few minutes to refine and rehearse their performance piece, and then ask each group to share their performance with the ensemble as a whole.

## GROUP TABLEAUX OR STAGE PICTURES

1.  Identify pieces of text to develop further, whether from individual journals, collected writing collected from the ensemble, or poems developed in the "I am from" Creative Introductions or similar actions.
2.  Divide the ensemble into small groups of three to five. Give each group a short piece of text.
3.  Explain to participants:
    a.  In your group, your goal is to create a series of stage pictures or tableaux that bring your text or story to life.
    b.  Choose one person to narrate the text. They will remain outside of the stage pictures as a storyteller. The other members of your group will bring the story to life by creating frozen pictures with their bodies.
    c.  Start by reading the story silently. Then read it together and talk about what pictures you see in your mind.
    d.  Use your bodies to create three stage pictures. Think about creating different levels and intentional facial expressions. Consider how to show the action of the story. The pictures do not have to be a realistic portrayal of what happens in the text. You could choose to show the emotional feeling or an abstract representation of what is happening. You could choose to use your bodies as objects in the space rather than people. You could choose to capture the essence of the story or literally show the story with your bodies.
    e.  Once you have your pictures, decide how you will you move from one picture to the next – in slow motion? Abruptly? On a particular word in the text? Practice transitioning clearly from one picture to the next.
    f.  Finally, practice performing your image sequence in time with the narrator's delivery of the text. Be specific about which line of text prompts a transition to the next stage picture.
4.  Close by asking each group to perform their piece for the ensemble. Eventually, the groups might perform their frozen pictures with a live narrator or they might audio record the narration to be played as a voiceover in the space.

## MOVING PICTURES/COMPLETE THE IMAGE

1.  This action begins by identifying a solo text, particularly one which either needs abstract background movement, or in which the performer would benefit from the on-stage support of an ensemble.

2. After identifying the texts for this action, review the action called Complete the Image (as explained in Section 2.3.3). While Complete the Image is often done in pairs, this variation of the action requires small groups.

3. Identify three to five volunteers to embody Complete the Image. Invite the group to letter-off as A, B, C, etc.

4. Explain to participants:

   a. Participant A will begin with the handshake image, and B will add in, filling the negative space. Before A can move out of the image or frozen picture, C will add their body into the negative space of the image. The remaining participants will do the same.

   b. After each performer has added their body into the image, A steps out and finds a different way to add themselves into the negative space of the image in a new way, a new position in the frozen picture. When A freezes in places, B will step out and choose a new place to add themselves back into the negative space of the image, and so on.

5. Invite the groups to practice Complete the Image either in silence or in response to music.

6. After a few minutes, invite the ensemble to identify themes or keywords in their text. Once you collect several keywords, invite the group to begin practicing Complete the Image again. As participants move through the exercise, read or say one of the key words or ideas generated by the group. Invite participants to consider how each key word might impact their images and movement choices.

7. Finally, pair a performative reading of the chosen text with a Complete the Image sequence. Invite groups to think creatively about how to stage a vocal performance of the text with a moving image next to, behind, or surrounding the narrator.

8. Ask the groups to rehearse and then share their performance pieces with the ensemble.

## Guiding Reflection

- How did the image work add to what you heard?
- Which images/movements stood out as interesting and dynamic? Why?
- Which pieces are you interested in developing further?

## In Our Experience

Because image work often relies on abstract movement, some youth find it less comfortable than sharing a more realistic scene. However, actions such as Complete the Image create rich, layered, and complex visual sequences. We find it helpful to practice using image work early in PJP, building capacity for making specific and confident movement choices. Adding movement-based staging behind a monologue can help a solo performer feel supported onstage and offers a dynamic visual landscape that complements or challenges possibly uncomfortable or difficult text.

### Connecting to Performance

These actions lead directly into staged performance material. For this reason, we choose text that the group wants to include in the final performance rather than experimenting with text that an author hasn't agreed to share in performance.

**Source**: These strategies for activating text were adapted from multiple sources, including Boal (1992, pp. 164–172).

# How Do I Perform Justice?

# Script Development: Introduction

This subsection moves away from performance actions and into performance considerations, specifically looking at our approach to developing a PJP script. In this section, we outline our dramaturgical process for moving disparate pieces of devised material (stories, monologues, reflective writing, Six-Word Stories, 8-Count Movements, songs, dances, scenes, etc.), created by many different participants, into a cohesive script that honors a collage of youth voices and intentions and engages an invited and/or public audience. Our dramaturgical process aims to create a performance or public sharing that honors participants' stories, uplifts the knowledge and experience of the group, and calls on audiences to reimagine justice and become youth-allies in their communities.

Dramaturgy can mean many things. Here, we use dramaturgy to refer to the process of composing the PJP script and performance. This includes preparing participants to make choices about their work, collecting, and organizing varied pieces of performance content, looking for patterns and variations in the scripted material, addressing questions and themes, choosing a dramaturgical model or overall shape and intention for the performance, and creating a visual map of the selected performance material. PJP dramaturgy requires continually examining whose stories are being told, how they are activated, and identifying the relationship of each part to the whole composition. The dramaturgical process also includes reflecting on the power of representation and the context of performance: how do performance pieces reify or disrupt systems of power and oppression, and what does it mean for youth to perform their personal stories within particular systems or with particular audiences?

In our experience, the script development process for a PJP residency is largely led by the program director(s) or teaching artist(s). However, the process always includes active input and consent from youth participants. Directors and teaching artists act as playwrights in a sense, making artistic choices about the shape of the script and beginning to order or make sense of the various parts and pieces. The youth ensemble supports the script development process by choosing what materials to include and exclude, and helping to order the devised materials into a dramatic or intentional arc. For example, the directors will often put forward a way to begin the performance, choosing a powerful visual or vocal performance piece as an opening or a lead into a series of monologues or a movement piece. Once a basic arc for the script has been established by the directors, the model or outline is shared with the ensemble for feedback and adjusted as desired by the group. Landing on a dramaturgical model and a draft script often reveals a need for additional devising and the development of specific, new material to solve a structural issue or content gap in the shape of the performance as a whole.

At the end of this subsection, we present multiple ways to frame a performance composed of individual and group performance pieces that are in conversation with each other. We offer three examples of dramaturgical models, or performance and script structures, which grew out of various PJP residencies. Appendix B offers performance outlines from three scripts as an example of some of these models. We encourage directors to borrow from these models as a starting place, but ultimately to play with new and culturally responsive dramaturgical models that spring out of the interests and ideas of their ensemble members.

# How Do I Perform Justice?

## Script Development: Preparing for Performance

About two thirds of the way through a PJP residency, we shift away from generating short bits of performance, such as monologues and group poems, and toward the development of selected materials for the larger performance script. Preparing participants to begin revising and rehearsing key performance pieces requires honest conversations with participants about how decisions are being made and whose artistic vision will drive the process. Shifting from generating material to rehearsing and honing performance can feel jarring and repetitive as participants experience, often for the first time, the discipline and accountability required to work toward a performance for an audience. In our experience, taking time to cast strong working groups and to share decision-making can help create a smooth transition into rehearsal and performance. At this stage in a PJP residency, the adults in the room begin to take on more of a directing role, keeping their eye on the overall cohesion of the production, as well as its clarity and connection for an audience.

We work from the following lists of questions and considerations as a way of centering youth throughout the scripting, rehearsal, and performance process.

## Considerations for the PJP Director(s) and Teaching Artists

- How is each youth participant represented or included within the script or performance piece? Consider script content, stage time, authored text, and areas of risk related to content, staging, and audience.

- How is stage time or story-work evenly distributed or responsive to participants' needs or wishes? Consider ways to find out if participants wish to try something new or remain in their comfort zone.

- How will you check in with each participant to assess their comfort with or willingness to play the characters or perform the stories in the script? Consider having group and individual conversations about how each performance piece will be cast and performed. We often use journal prompts to invite youth to share their ideas, interests, and concerns with us.

- How will you ensure responsible representation of each participant and each performance piece? Ask participants to choose and/or give their consent for which of their stories or performance texts will be included and performed in the public performance. Check in multiple times throughout the rehearsal process, as participants' comfort with sharing their work often changes over time. Sometimes participants feel scared to share their work and gain confidence over time. In other situations, participants begin to understand the consequences or contexts of sharing their work with a public and choose to remove a story or experience from the final script. We have learned to stay unattached to what the youth create; sometimes the most impactful performance pieces are too vulnerable to move into a public performance.

- How will you ensure that participants are comfortable with the way their story is staged, positioned, or shared in the final performance piece? Again, consider checking in throughout the rehearsal process, soliciting feedback from participants verbally but also in a more private process such as reflective journaling or one-on-one conversations.

- How will you give feedback on participants' writing, storytelling, or performance work? Consider asking participants to clarify their intentions and hopes for their performance pieces before offering feedback or language for revision. While we center the participants' intentions as we stage the performance, we also bring our experience as theatre artist into the room. We work to value the knowledge and skills of the youth and the adults in the room; the PJP community of practice grows when everyone's knowledge is shared and adults are listening carefully and responsively.

- How will you help participants understand the potential implications or impacts of performing gender and racial justice? Consider having direct conversations with participants about who their work is for and the intended impacts of the performance or an element of the performance. We ask participants to consider how the form of their performance (what it looks, sounds, and feels like) relates to the content (what it is about), and then how the performance might function (what it will do) in the context of their given site or audience. We check for understanding by asking participants about how power functions in their given site; without censoring youth's effort to impact change, we ask them to name any questions or potential concerns about how the audience will respond to language, images, or content in their work. Performing justice requires youth to have a complete understanding of potential implications and repercussions for performing material that they have written or devised.

- How will you support and uplift participants' experiences through the casting process? We ask participants to consider performing their own stories, while offering them opportunities and options to have their stories, experiences, and writing performed by others in the ensemble. We discuss the ethics and responsibilities of performing someone else's story, offering ways to acknowledge elements of similarity or connection, while honoring the particulars of each participant's identity markers and social locations. We practice color-conscious and gender-conscious casting in PJP, meaning that we pay attention to how the racial and gender identity and expression of each performer impacts how audiences read or understand stories, scenes, and ideas on stage. We believe that bodies and identities are not neutral on stage or off stage.

- How will you support participants who are new to theatre and/or performing? Consider offering a basic introduction to how a rehearsal is structured, what is expected and required of each participant, and where the process is heading. Participants can easily become overwhelmed with a rehearsal or devising process when they cannot imagine or visualize the product they are working toward. We find that devised theatre, non-linear narrative theatre, and collage-style scripts are often new to participants. Consider sharing examples of scripts, bits of performance, and video of ensemble-based, devised theatre.

Working with large groups and ensembles requires PJP directors to imagine a variety of casting arrangements and performance structures. We rely on the following devising, casting, and grouping structures (adapted from Saldaña 1995, pp. 8–10) as we develop a script and organize the flow of rehearsals and work to build participants' investment. PJP participants

become actor-participants at this stage of the process, as we ask all participants to perform in the production.

## Casting and Devising Structures

- Solo performance (one narrator, possibly paired with a small group to provide movement sequences or tableaux)
- Pair performance (two performers work together on a single text)
- Small group performance (three to six performers stage a text together)
- Split halves performance (two large groups perform a single text, diving elements such vocal and physical score or part one and part two of a text)
- Full ensemble performance (full group performs a text together, simultaneously or through assigned lines, images, and/or gestures)

## Staging Structures for Actor-Participants

- Actor-participant(s) vocally and physically perform their own work/story
- Actor-participant(s) physically perform their own work/story, while one or more actor-participant(s) vocally perform their text
- Actor-participant(s) vocally perform their own work, while one or more actor-participant(s) physically perform it
- Actor-participant(s) vocally perform each other's work, live or as a recorded voiceover
- Actor-participant(s) record a voiceover of their work, which is played in the space while they perform a physical score solo or with others
- Whole ensemble performs vocally and physically a piece that was individually or collectively developed

# How Do I Perform Justice?

# Script Development: Collecting and Reviewing Content

Throughout PJP, we ask participants to write and create original performance material. Much of this writing happens in participants' PJP journals,
and we also document and collect pieces of group writing and creative work
by the ensemble. As we move into scripting a performance, we make lists of
and review everything that has been created and completed, noting patterns
and outliers in terms of content and form. In an effort to begin scripting a
performance, we ask each ensemble member to review the content of their
own journals and to indicate what pieces of their work they want to share
or develop further. We also ask them to note any pieces of writing they

want or need to remain private. We remind participants that developing or staging a story does not mean they have to include it in the public performance. Participants often decide they want to include a story in the script, with the caveat that it remain anonymous in the performance. Importantly, participants maintain control over which pieces of their writing get developed, staged, and ultimately included in the script and performance. This process remains fluid; we have learned that building trust and supporting youth agency requires flexibility and a willingness to honor changes and ideas from each participant at any stage in the process.

After participants note which materials they want and do not want to include in performance, the PJP directors review and begin to organize and group all of the possible performance materials. We look for connections across participants' stories, and also pay close attention to pieces of writing that offer a unique experience or provide a counterpoint to other material from the group. This process helps us assess whose and which stories the group is comfortable putting forward and where we might need to encourage and foreground the inclusion of other narratives and experiences. While we will not include material in the performance without explicit consent of the author, enacting gender and racial justice sometimes means offering extra support and encouragement for youth to share experiences, stories, and writing that might question or implicate the very systems supporting PJP, such as our hosting partner or related institutions or stakeholders.

# How Do I Perform Justice?

## Script Development: Organizing Content

The PJP process does not typically build toward a single narrative storyline with a clear protagonist. Rather, we have to imagine how individual and diverse pieces of text and movement-based performance pieces get organized into a constellation or composition that makes sense for an audience. In organizing content for a PJP script, the challenge becomes how to bring different materials together into a single script while simultaneously maintaining the unique voices and perspectives of the ensemble. Knowing that endless options exist for how to organize and order the script, we begin by writing down all of the stories, movement sequences, questions, and pieces of performance generated and approved by the group. We then write the name or title of each bit of performance (questions, song, etc.) onto a single notecard, laying all of the cards out in rows on the floor or a large table, or taping cards to an empty wall. From there, we begin to look for themes or connections among the various pieces. How might different pieces be in conversation with each other? What are some driving questions or overarching themes that speak to multiple pieces? Is there potential for a sequence of stories or pieces to build towards a larger statement? What themes emerge and do they offer a way to create scenes or groups of performance pieces that offer various perspectives on a given idea? With questions like these in mind, we begin to group notecards together, noting where patterns, sequences, and repetition show up. We often name or create titles for groups of notecards that end up together. We also note works that are complete and which pieces might require further development. In organizing content this way, we start to see where repetition offers the potential for a poetic frame and where it invites us to narrow the scope of the performance or let go of material for this particular performance. The process often reveals which performance pieces might anchor a script and which material might serve as touch points or transitions between big ideas. On the whole, this dramaturgical practice of writing, reflecting, and grouping material helps us pay attention to dissonance, as well as resonance, and begin to make sense of the participants' work as an intentional and curated collection.

This way of organizing content also reveals opportunities to consider how various forms of performance show up in the devised content. We often categorize the material by form, looking at what might be considered a movement piece, a text-based piece such as a scene or monologue, a spoken word piece or a poem, a sound piece, or visual art or image-based work. If much of the performance material falls into a single form, such as six-word stories, we return to the performance actions in Staging Stories and diversify the types of material or expand the types of performance structures generated by the group. For example, we might turn six-word stories into scenes or 8-Count Movement pieces. We might develop poems and spoken word pieces from gesture sequences, or we might turn monologues into song. We offer youth the following list of performance actions, categorized by form, as examples for playing with various performance forms and approaches.

## Movement

- 8-Count Movement
- Justice/Hope Machines
- Mapping Geographies
- Flocking
- Complete the Image

## Text

- Individual Poems
- Ensemble poems ("I am from" or poems from story/other text)
- Statistics
- Six-Word Stories
- Scenes developed from six-word stories, "I am from" poems, or other writing/reflection
- Individual stories, monologues, and spoken word poems
- Hashtag Stories

### Sound

- Choral Song
- Solo Song
- Soundscape
- Voiceover

### Images/Visuals

- (In)justice Embodiment—as a monster or machine
- Body Maps
- Illustrated Six-Word Stories
- Identity Pie
- Imagining Justice Mural

# How Do I Perform Justice?

## Script Development: Creating a Visual Map

After collecting, reviewing, and starting to organize the ensemble's devised performance work, we start to visually map out, or storyboard, possible script structures. Our visual mapping process is akin to storyboarding in that we group and move around our notecards to create a picture of the performance timeline, structure, and flow of material. We use various colors and symbols on notecards to denote the type of performance piece (a song, a monologue, a solo piece, and/or a small group performance piece), as well as how music and other materials will help the performers and the audience transition from one piece of performance to the next. Through this process of identifying what kinds of material and storylines have been generated and how they might be threaded together, we also discover where we need to develop existing pieces further and where we need to devise new material to fill a gap in story, arc, or flow of the script and production as a whole.

Generally, the process of determining an outline or flow for performance takes a full day of discussion, deliberation, and visual mapping. The PJP directors, sometimes in conversation with the teaching artists, imagine and try out many possible structures and shapes for the performance. This mapping process happens in conversation with Dramaturgical Questions and goes through multiple iterations as the team considers distribution and diversity of authorship (whose stories are foregrounded) and content (which stories are foregrounded).

This process of visual mapping results in a draft of a performance outline that is then pitched to the youth participants and revised in conversation with the ensemble and the PJP leadership team.

# How Do I Perform Justice?

## Script Development: Dramaturgical Questions

Throughout our script development process, we consider a series of dramaturgical questions that help us see connections and opportunities for pairing materials and sequencing ideas in a provocative, informative, or theatrical way. We pay attention to and seek out places of dissonance as we couple stories that offer multiple perspectives on a similar idea. In this way, our dramaturgical process works to lift up different knowledge of and perspectives about gender and racial justice. Questions we often consider include:

- Which through-lines, themes, or overarching questions might bring these bits of performance into conversation with each other?
- Which stories, questions, words, themes or actions could start the performance and get revisited again at the end of the performance? (Are there any possible book-ends coming up in the process?)
- What pulls the pieces together and/or separates them? What are the similarities and differences across form, content, and intention of the performance pieces?
- Which pieces raise excitement and energy among the ensemble? Among the PJP leadership team? Among staff at the partner-site?
- Which pieces resonate with current events?
- How do performances pieces build on one another to add or change meaning?
- What questions or visions of justice do the bits of performance point to or infer? What questions have been lost, missed, ignored, or forgotten?
- What kind of frames, such as a theme, question, or movement sequence, connect to and lift up individual stories of the group?
- Which pieces present an important spark but need further development?
- What forms or content or feelings are missing from the pool of devised material?
- Where are we headed? What do participants want to say through their performance? What has been important to them in the PJP process? Which pieces of learning have felt significant in the moment and might be relevant to an outside audience? What language from the process has been repeated, highlighted, or exposed?
- What does the pool of material leave us all thinking about and curious about?

# How Do I Perform Justice?

## Script Development: Text, Groupings, and Transitions

While mapping a possible structure for the performance script or outline, we often think about the rhythm, movement, and overall composition of the performance. The following considerations help us make specific choices that serve the ensemble, as well as the performance piece, as a PJP script is developed.

### Variation in Groupings

As we think about the flow of performance, we pay attention to: Who is speaking and how often? Which pieces benefit from more bodies and voices (whole group, small groups) or fewer (pairs and solo)? Which pieces need a single voice for impact? Which pieces or performers need to be accompanied by more ensemble members (through images or tableaux)? How will performers move on and offstage into various pieces and various groupings? As with the process of choosing pieces that will be shared publicly in performance, we approach script-building with the youth in mind first and then shift our attention to the audience. Variation in performer groupings (solo, small group, whole group) and variation in text keep an audience engaged. Similar to our earlier discussion on grouping strategies for rehearsal, we borrow Saldaña's ideas on grouping as a way to think about casting in PJP (Saldaña 1995, pp. 8–10):

- Solo and solo, plus: An individual onstage alone, or an individual who is backed by a small ensemble offering movement or image in relationship or counterpoint to the text.
- Small group: A small group performing a scene, movement piece, or piece of text together
- Split halves: Half of the ensemble does one thing while the other half does another. (For example, one PJP performance opened with the ensemble split in half and entering from behind the audience from house left and house right and meeting together onstage.) Another option is for half of the group to perform text or movement with the other half performing something different (sound, movement, text, shadow).
- Whole group: All participants perform onstage together at the same time, such a song, dance, or movement sequence.

### Variation in Text

When considering the text-based pieces that will be included in performance, we think about ways to diversify the types of texts and performance pieces throughout the script. We try to identify which pieces might be performed as a solo text, which might combine solo text with movement in the background (and why), which pieces might benefit from choral speech, and which pieces might be performed as scenes with dialogue. We often vary performance modes by mixing live performance with pre-recorded audio. Pre-recording a sensitive story can allow a participant to share an experience without the pressure of live performance of a challenging story in a public setting. Using a variety of text arrangements and performance modes informs the way we build a script. Drawing from approaches used by the Tectonic Theater Project and many other devising artists and ensembles, here are some of the ways that we think about using text:

- Dialogue between characters
- Direct address to the audience
- Voiceover or recorded text
- Narrator who is separate from the action
- Narrator who is also a character
- Poetry or verse (heightened language)
- Chanted or intoned text
- Projected text
- Text handed out to the audience
- Text on a set piece or a costume
- Text written in real time onstage

(Kaufman and McAdams 2018, pp. 108–109)

## Opening/Transitions/Closing

As we collect, review, and organize performance content, we continue to think about imaginative ways to weave that material together. Like most performance work, transitions between materials and beats are as important as the main content, communicating meaning and emotion, and contributing to the ways that an audience engages. This does not mean that transitions have to contain content per se, but they might. In PJP, we often use transitions between monologues and scene work to seed or thread an idea that gets introduced in the opening and repeated in the closing. Transitions might also be used to deepen an emotion, give the audience a moment to breathe, or move an argument forward. In PJP, transition techniques include:

- Sharing "facts," statistics, or sound bites of recorded information
- Building in moments of sound or rhythm (live or recorded) as the group changes scenic elements
- Playing a voiceover or recorded sound that repeats or signals something new
- Ensemble singing, humming or choral speech,
- Whole-group movement sequences
- Direct questions to the audience

How might a performance begin? How might this beginning invite an audience into conversation, spark curiosity, or pose a statement or argument that will be supported by the flow of performative moments? Ideally, the opening and closing of a composed piece are somewhat connected, if not by form then by content. If an opening sequence offers the audience an invitation to action, the closing sequence may call for the audience to commit to taking action. If the opening offers a provocation, the closing may repeat the provocation with more voices or less voices to make it stand out or read differently. If the performance begins with information about the US's failure to adopt the Declaration on the Rights of the Child,[5] the closing might bring us to a group of young people asking what it will take to recognize the rights of children in our country. Openings, transitions, and closings become key elements in our script development process.

# How Do I Perform Justice?

# Script Development: Three Dramaturgical Models

In looking at PJP scripts and analyzing how we structured past performances, three general shapes, or dramaturgical models, emerged. We created visual representations of these dramaturgical models as a way of mapping PJP material into a collage-style script. While these models are far from comprehensive (you may curate a model that is quite different), they offer guidance for organizing PJP content and experiences related to racial and gender (in)justice into a performance. Each model includes an overarching frame or entry point, including theme, question, or story. Within each frame, the models organize bits of performance that present core content as well as transitional material that helps thread the core content together and move the audience from one performative moment to the next. Appendix B includes script outlines that demonstrate these dramaturgical models.

## Dramaturgical Model 1: Theme

Our theme-based dramaturgical model begins with a theme or a call to action. For example, one performance opened with a scene in which the characters debated the content of a Beyoncé music video and if/how girls have power in society. The debate revealed themes that run through feminist work, creating a thematic entry point and frame for a performance that explored the racialized nature of political agency and women's rights. The participants wrote scenes and monologues about issues of women's rights in their lives and wove their performance pieces together with statistics on human rights issues and violations. This process of weaving illustrated ways that human rights advocacy work is both critical to the lives of young people and often fails to acknowledge the various needs and contexts of women and girls, LGBTQIA people, and youth of color. Our theme-based dramaturgical model relies on statistics or other short bits of story or historical information to transition between scenes and monologues and to position individual experiences within systemic contexts. For example, a participant's monologue about her right to family planning might be introduced or followed by statistics about a lack of accessibility to women's clinics in the US and the ways that motherhood disproportionately impacts the mortality rate and lifelong income of women of color. Dramaturgically, this theme-based structure offers a balance of contextual information and participants' personal writing and experience. In this way, the thematic model builds an audience's knowledge of particular issues and shares individual and local stories as a way to build momentum around a set of issues.

**Figure 2.5** Dramaturgical Model: Theme

Figure 2.5 demonstrates the way theme becomes the central organizing idea for a PJP performance. The large circle in the center of the figure represents the central theme and suggests that all of the performance material circles the main theme and attempts to show various points of view on the theme. The performance begins by presenting the theme and returns to the theme by the end. The small squares represent scenes, monologues and movement pieces written by the participants and based in their experiences. The bending arrows represent the performance of information that inspired or provides context for the short performance pieces—again, these arrows often represent statistics, current events, or historical facts related to systemic oppression based on beliefs about gender and race. The success of this model lies in the connective tissue (the curved arrows) that help deepen and extend an understanding of the issues at hand and help the audience to make connections between the participants' staged material and their own lives.

## Dramaturgical Model 2: Questions

This dramaturgical model organizes performance material through a series of questions or inquiries related to gender and racial justice. In Figure 2.6, questions are represented by the bulky arrows. The arrows are followed by a series of small circles which represent short performance pieces. Grouped together, the questions and short performance pieces attempt to puzzle out and/or complicate the participants' and the audience's relationship to various areas of racial and gender justice. For example, the first arrow might represent a question such as, "What does it mean to be a woman?" After introducing this question (through a scene, a voiceover, or a direct address to the audience), the participants might then perform a series of six-word stories, a scene about restrictive familial roles and gender-based injustices, or a group poem that addresses a wide of array of meanings and identities associated with "being a woman." The combination of questions and performance bits (represented by an arrow and a group of small circles in Figure 2.6) gets repeated multiple times in a single script, building toward a landing place or a culminating performance piece that attempts to bring all of the questions together and leave the audience with a culminating idea or provocation. The landing place (see the last circle in Figure 2.6) rarely offers neat answers to racial and gender injustice. Instead, this structure ends by sharing the participants' vision for justice or asking the audience reflective questions that may implicate or inspire them to take action.

**Figure 2.6** Dramaturgical Model: Questions

## Dramaturgical Model 3: Story

In this dramaturgical model, the script scaffolds a series of personal stories and experiences, demonstrating connections and questions that come up across shared experiences while building toward an understanding of institutional and systemic oppression. Our story-based structure aims to take the audience on a journey, inviting them to see, empathize with, and possibly relate to participant experiences. This connection then turns into an invitation for audiences to consider how racialized and gendered experiences systemically impact people across society in different ways.

Alternately, the story-based model might begin in the opposite way, first presenting audiences with the larger picture of how society perpetuates systemic oppression before focusing in on individual experiences of injustice. In this model, the script sets up the larger social and political picture before performing possible impacts of oppression on individual people or groups of people.

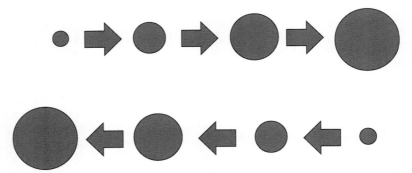

**Figure 2.7** Dramaturgical Model: Story

Both versions of the story-based model demonstrate linear movement of the narrative. The arrows in Figure 2.7 represent transitions between collections of individual experiences, which are represented by the circles. Depending on whether the model is building from individual story to systemic oppression or the reverse, the circles either grow in size as the script moves toward a representation of larger systems of oppression, or shrink in size as the script moves from examining larger systems of oppression to stories that illustrate the impacts of oppression on various individuals.

## How Do I Perform Justice?

## Sound/Space/Aesthetics: Introduction

In each of our PJP residencies, we consider design and aesthetic elements throughout the creative process. Sound, space, and aesthetic considerations become critical elements and practices for supporting novice performers and engaging a public audience. In making devised performance, design choices not only unfold in response to performance material that gets created, they can also inspire text and performance choices. Because we work with youth who tend to be new to performance, we structure learning opportunities alongside opportunities for choice making. In other words, the ensemble develops an understanding of design possibilities while concurrently making choices about and informing the design elements for our particular performance. Designers and PJP directors offer participants opportunities to think about the role of space, lighting, and sound as they devise their performance. Designers help participants make creative choices that reflect the reality of the space (especially non-theatre spaces), sonically support the ethos or feeling of a performance moment, and lift up the expertise of the ensemble and aesthetically respond to the given contexts. In this way, our design process becomes a reciprocal practice in which participants gain a sense of design options and opportunities while coming up with new possibilities. As novice performers try out new skills, the sound, space, and overall aesthetics of a performance can be tailored to support experimentation, respond to various given contexts, and address technical concerns facing novice performers, such as vocal projection and communicating subtext. For these reasons, we invite designers to engage with PJP performers and directors as early and often as possible.

# How Do I Perform Justice?

## Sound/Space/Aesthetics: Sound, Music, and Voiceover

Sound remains the central design element in each of our PJP performances, directed in large part by PJP sound designer Tameika L. Hannah who has been a resident teaching artist in all of the PJP residencies directed by Megan and Lynn. Tameika works with sound as a healing mode as well as a design element. Her approach to sound (see Doing Justice: Sound Cues), and thus the PJP approach to sound, often starts with getting in the room with participants and responding to their ideas and interests. In addition to designing music and sound for PJP productions, Tameika determines where recorded audio, such as a vocal performance of a poem or a reading of statistics, might support the performers in each piece. She coaches participants on vocal recordings and helps them gain comfort in sharing their voice for a digital recording.[6] Importantly, sound design often helps participants track where they are during a performance and what comes next. We use music and sound to underscore performance pieces, but also to signal transitions and to set up a pattern or a change in emotion, story, or context within a performance.

We use the following questions and considerations to help keep sounds and audio design at the center of our creative process:

### Music and Songs

- What songs might open and/or close the performance, offering a powerful frame for engaging audiences?

- Do participants wish to sing and if so, what song and lyrics offer opportunities to provoke and build gender and racial justice?
- How are we lifting up music and songs by artists of color? By artists who identify as LGBTQIA and/or are non-binary?
- What music do participants love and how might we include their musical interests and expertise in the performance?
- What music supports individual participant-devised work and fits within the aesthetics of the production as a whole?
- When/where does music with lyrics support or distract from the performance?

### Recorded Sound and Text

- Where will participants and the audience be served by recorded sound—including music or sound effects? Where will sound create a feeling or an environment, cue a scene change or emotional transition, or communicate beginnings and endings?
- Where might recorded voiceovers help create variation in the performance or draw attention to something important? Where might recorded voiceovers allow the performers to experiment with physical performance choices?
- How might sound, music, or a recorded voiceover support the storytelling? Emphasize a particular action or moment? Challenge or deepen audience expectations?

## How Do I Perform Justice?

## Sound/Space/Aesthetics: Setting, Lighting, Costumes, Props, and Scripts

In addition to sound design, we make intentional and specific choices around setting, lighting, costumes, and props. When possible, we hire designers to collaborate with youth participants to create the look and feel of the visual performance elements (see Figure 0.1). Our performance aesthetic for PJP remains simple and minimalist. The aesthetic often grows out of our short timeframe, budget constraints, and an intentional focus on what the participants want to say. We make design choices that help streamline the visual appearance of the performance and simultaneously create something just beyond the ordinary. We lean heavily on sound (see Sound/Space/Aesthetics: Sound, Music, and Voiceover) to move beyond the ordinary, but we also make intentional choices for the visual setting, basic costumes (often matching pants and a PJP t-shirt or jeans and solid-color t-shirt), lighting, and props.

We use the following questions and considerations to center visual design elements within our creative process:

## Setting

- What words, images, and visual metaphors are present in the devised work? (i.e., freedom and birds, history and books, spiraling or soaring)
- What shapes, images, and objects communicate or evoke a sense of justice?
- How might simple changes to a space make it look and feel just beyond the ordinary? Where does conformity of line, shape, or color help create something beyond the ordinary? Where does difference across line, shape, or color create something beyond the ordinary? (i.e., Does the staging of a song take place in an open space with two matching yellow chairs? Or in an open space with multi-colored chairs—one for each participant?)
- What materials are allowed into the performance space and what options are available for hanging things on the wall or from the ceiling? How might we use shape, line, and color to change the way the space looks or feels? (For example, one year, our set designer, Becca Drew Ramsey, created a backdrop with metal wire and small pieces of paper. Another year, we taped large posters from our "Body Maps" action as a backdrop for the performance.)
- How will the performers move in the space? Do the pieces call for a circular stage or playing space? A square, rectangle, or semi-circle? How can you use materials in the space to create this shape?
- Does the partner or performance site support changes to the space?

## Lighting

- What and how much light exists in the space already?
- What options exist for adding, removing, or controlling light in the performance space?
- How will light shape the mood or feeling of the performance? How will light suggest where and what you want audience or participants to look at?
- How will light create a space that looks and feels just beyond the ordinary?
- What kinds of everyday light, such as the sun setting, a floor lamp, or a flashlight, might help create a particular environment, feeling, or understanding?
- How might lighting communicate or evoke a sense of (in)justice?
- Does the partner or performance site support changes in the lighting? Allow blackouts or other lighting techniques?

## Costumes

- What clothing do participants have access to? What can be provided by PJP? Does the partner or performance site support the use of costumes and changing of clothes?
- What costumes/clothing supports a collage-based performance and the casting of each performer in several roles?
- Where will participants change into costumes and get dressed for the performance?
- How might rules and regulation about gender shape your decisions about costumes and changing rooms?
- If providing costumes, how do the participants decide what the costumes look and feel like? (For example, we invite participants to design a t-shirt for the performance. The group then votes on the final image, as well as the color and shape of the t-shirts.)

## Props

- How will objects and props be negotiated (introduced, used, held, passed, etc.) throughout the performance? We consider how they move on and off stage, as well as where and when props are introduced.
- Which props prove essential to communicating, deepening, or questioning something in the performance? Will props be used to explore gender and racial constructs or communicate hierarchical power dynamics? (i.e., ties, masks, or a cut-out of a thought bubble)
- What props are *not* essential? Less is often more in this area because it is difficult to negotiate props within a short rehearsal timeline, and/or with the PJP script in hand.

## Scripts

- What tools will best support participants to perform their work?
- How will scripts, journals, or performance outlines be necessary and accessed during the performance?
- How might the stage direction of each performance bit and the performance as a whole intentionally include performance scripts or outlines as a prop?
- We do not require PJP participants to memorize text for the performance. The timeline is often too short for both devising original material and memorizing it. Instead, we focus on offering participants a script that is lightweight and easy to hold and which does not draw excessive attention or read as a prop on stage. We format and place scripts into small, black three-ring binders (8.5" × 5.5").

- We also create a performance outline or beat sheet that lists out the order of scenes, monologues, etc. We include the outline in the script binders and often post it to the sides of the staging area as well.
- How are multiple languages included, encouraged, and supported in the scrip? Will languages be translated within the script? How might the storytelling and aesthetics of the performance communicate meaning and reflect participants' cultures?

# How Do I Perform Justice?

## Reflection Actions: Introduction

We facilitate reflection within most of our performance actions and at the end of each PJP daily session plan. Reflection actions become rituals for considering our relationships to past, present and future, and for recognizing that although an action, session, or residency comes to an end, our work around gender and racial justice does not. In addition to building opportunities for youth and audiences to reflect in the moment or at the end of each session, we facilitate a more comprehensive approach to reflection on the last day of each PJP residency. Based on her work with the Storytelling Project, Lee Ann Bell writes:

> The final stage [of social justice work], transforming, happens as the group experience comes to an end. The group moves toward closure and a sense of completion where participants recognize and appreciate what they have accomplished together. Facilitators can help by explicitly inviting participants to comment on the process of their work and give each other feedback and appreciation.
>
> (2010, p. 93)

We, too, build reflection and closure into the final part of each PJP residency. We invite reflective dialogue, individual written reflections, and group appreciations as a way to learn about the participants' experiences, as well as recognize and appreciate their accomplishments. Our closing reflections are also meant to serve as a space for reflecting on naming the work ahead, and noticing the ways that performing justice necessitates ongoing effort.

The actions in this subsection offer frameworks for reflecting at the close of a day or at the end of a PJP residency. We call these *reflection actions* rather than *performance actions* as they mostly live as tools for reflection during and at the end of a PJP process. However, at times they may also be used as performance actions: some PJP performances use the following actions to engage audience members before, during, or after performance, in which case they may be led by youth participants or a teaching artist.

# How Do I Perform Justice?

# Reflection Action: It Made Me Think

*At the end of PJP performance or residency, this action offers a structured way for individuals to share a big idea or something that resonated with them from the performance or the residency at large.*

## PJP Connection

We use this reflection tool with large groups, as a way of getting many ideas and voices into the space in an efficient and poetic way. We use this action frequently at the close of a session as well as at the end of a residency. Participants could also lead this action with the audience following a performance. The structured ritual of responding to a short prompt often proves poetic and beautiful.

## Guiding Reflection

1.  Invite participants to sit or stand in a circle. Ask them to reflect on their experience of the performance or the PJP residency and to think about an idea or moment from the project that feels significant, meaningful, or provocative to them. Ask them to think about the big ideas and questions that will remain with them after this project has ended or when they leave the performance space.
2.  Explain to participants (and/or audience members):
    a.  Boil your significant idea or moment down to a single word or a short phrase.
    b.  In just a minute, we will each share our word or phrase with the group, followed by the statement "it made me think." For example: "Family roles and gender justice, it made me think." Or "Is this the help I need? It made me think." Or "School-to-prison pipeline, it made me think."
3.  Invite individuals to share their distilled reflections out loud, one at a time and without explanation. If participants have more to share, offer time for the group to journal or to turn to a partner and explain their response in more detail.

## In Our Experience

By playing poetically with the phrase "it made me think," this reflection action often shows what participants and audience members pay attention to and what resonates with them on a personal level. Sometimes this prompt simply invites participants to share what is on their mind and other times people express appreciation for someone in the room or an idea that was centered in performance. This open-ended ritual offers a beautiful structure for both bringing closure to a group process and imagining what is next.

**Source**: We learned this action from Michael Rohd.

# How Do I Perform Justice?

# Reflection Action: People to People

*This action moves beyond a typical dialogue structure and offers a physically engaged approach to discussing and reflecting with a partner. (See Section 2.3.1 for additional applications.)*

## PJP Connection

People to People asks participants to connect and talk with different people. As a reflection action, People to People can work as an ice-breaker and give participants and audience members a specific structure for talking with each other for short bits of time. In pairs, participants tackle a physical task while verbally reflecting on a topic together.

**Time**: 5–10 minutes

**Materials**: None

## Guiding Reflection

1. Invite participants (and/or audience members) to stand in the playing space or staging area.
2. Explain to participants:
   a. When I say "people to people," find a partner as quickly as possible and stand back to back with your pair.
   b. Now that everyone is standing with a partner, I am going to give you a prompt such as "palm to palm." Pairs, you are going to work together to make your palms touch. If you would rather not touch, you can simply have your palms facing each other, a few inches apart. Let's try it: Pinkie finger to wrist.
3. Give the group a few more challenges to complete with their current partner (elbow to elbow, wrist to thumb, shoulder to wrist).

4. Next, call out "people to people" and encourage participants to move around the space and find a new partner to stand back to back with. Repeat the same process of offering physical challenges, such as wrist to thumb, and then prompting the group to find new pairs. Depending on the group, you might keep the physical tasks lower risk or increase the difficulty (i.e., wrist to foot, head to knee, shoulder to hip).

5. After practicing a few physical challenges and finding a few new partners, begin to add reflection questions into each round. Invite the group to hold the physical pose, such as shoulder to shoulder, while also discussing the reflection question at hand.

6. Reflection questions might ask the participants or audience members to reflect on something in the performance or to imagine actions in their own lives to support gender and racial justice. Sample questions might include:

   a. What moments from the performance stood out to you and why?
   b. What questions or ideas did the performance raise in your mind?
   c. What surprised you in the performance?
   d. What does gender justice look like or mean to you?
   e. What does racial justice look like or mean to you?
   f. How might you enact gender or racial justice in your daily life?

## In Our Experience

We find that scaffolding risk around touch, personal space, and the use of the body proves central to successful facilitation of this activity. This action requires group members to literally connect to one another with their bodies. Sometimes we work with groups that have restrictions on physical contact; if this is the case, we ask participants to play the game along a taped line on the floor. Partners stand on either side of the line and we ask the pairs to keep some space between their body parts as they complete the physical actions. This activity can build connections among the ensemble and/or the audience members and serves as a way to reflect on the performance, as well as connect and share new stories and ideas.

**Source**: Developed by Augusto Boal and published in *Games for actors and non-actors* (1992, p. 78).

# How Do I Perform Justice?

# Reflection Action: Think, Pair, Share

*This action slowly builds from individual reflection toward a group discussion.*

## PJP Connection

This reflection process helps build and cement knowledge and understanding about complex ideas and topics. Participants or audience members are invited to reflect silently on their own before dialoguing with a partner and eventually sharing with and listening to ideas in the larger group. These steps bring multiple voices and perspectives into the room and reinforce experience as knowledge.

## Guiding Reflection

1. Offer participants or audience members a question or topic to consider. For example:
   a. How are gender and racial justice connected?
   b. How can storytelling and performance help make change?
   c. What have you learned from other participants in this project?
   d. What are you taking away from the PJP process or the performance?
2. Give them 20 to 30 seconds to think about the question or topic silently.
3. Next, invite audience members turn to a partner or a small group near them in the space.
4. Ask the pairs to share some of their ideas with each other.
5. Finally, invite each pair or a handful of pairs to share one big idea from their discussion with the larger group.
6. Synthesize some of the connections and questions coming up in the room.

## In Our Experience

This action helps bring new voices into the space. The three-step process supports individuals who need time to think and process information before sharing ideas out loud or in front of a group. If the question or topic is particularly challenging, we offer time for individuals to journal in response to the prompt before pairing up and bringing ideas to the full group. Journaling after a Think, Pair, Share sequence can further cement ideas and help assess what the group thinks and cares about. This is a useful reflection action with an audience after a PJP performance as a way to allow many people a chance to share their thoughts before sharing out to the larger group or asking questions of performers.

**Source**: We have played this game in multiple contexts. The original source is unknown.

# How Do I Perform Justice?

# Reflection Action: Vote from Your Seat

*Participants express their opinion or point of view by raising their hands to express agreement, lowering their hands to express disagreement, and holding their hand at shoulder height to signal an in-between response. (See Vote with Your Feet and Exploding Atom in Section 2.3.2 for variations on this action.)*

## PJP Connection

Sharing opinions and experiences related to gender and race, particularly in public settings, might be new to participants or audience members. This action invites everyone to share a point of view without necessarily talking. PJP emphasizes embodied approaches to critical conversations and Vote from Your Seat offers a low-risk participatory structure for inviting audience perspectives into the space in a short period of time.

## Guiding Reflection

1. Read a statement or a question to the group and invite participants to vote, or demonstrate their response, with their arm or hand. Build statements from easy or low-risk to more thought-provoking and complex. Some of the statements should result in varied responses and encourage participants to reflect on what they know or believe.

2. Explain to participants as they are seated:

    a. I am going to read a statement. If you agree with the statement, raise your hand high in the air. If you disagree with the statement, put your hand on your knees. If you are somewhere in the middle, put your hand up to chest height.

    b. The statements are open to interpretation. I might invite people to volunteer to share why they are voting a particular way, but you do not have to talk during this action or explain your vote. You will essentially vote from your seat.

    c. I am going to read the first statement. "When I was in school, my teachers talked about identity in the classroom."

    d. Now, I invite you all to vote from your seat. If you agree with the statement, raise your hand up high. If you disagree with this statement, place your hand on your knees. If you are somewhere between yes and no, raise your hand to about chest height.

    e. Here is the first statement again: "When I was in school, my teachers talked about identity in the classroom."

    f. Keeping your arm or hand in place, please take a look around the room and notice who is answering similarly to you.

3. Some additional prompts that invite the participants/audience to bring their lived experiences into a group reflection include:
   a. I grew up talking opening about race.
   b. I grew up talking openly about gender.
   c. The color of my skin impacts my experiences in public.
4. If time permits, invite a few participants to explain their vote or point of view to the group. Encourage audience members to share their reasoning in two sentences or in "one breath" to keep the conversation flowing. Think, Pair, Share can also be used here as a way for participants to share why they voted the way they did.

### In Our Experience

The audience generally takes a few statements to warm up, but this action gets everyone involved in a discussion—without having to talk. Vote from Your Seat can help take the temperature of the room and reveal places of divergence and convergence in the room. This action helps participants or audience members build connections between their own lived experiences and the performance they just witnessed or are about to watch.

**Source**: We have played this exercise in multiple contexts. The original source is unknown.

# How Do I Perform Justice?

# Reflection Action: Spread the Word

*This action offers a simple but often profound way to have the audience perform a personal statement of justice.*

### PJP Connection

Participants "spread the word" by sharing their own statements about why justice matters or what justice looks like to them. Describing and naming justice is one step toward action. Moreover, the collective witnessing of multiple ideas on a given topic can deepen a group's relationship to or understanding of a given idea.

### Guiding Reflection

1. This action begins with finishing a prompt or filling in a blank template and ends with statements about justice and justice-building. Spread the

Word can be led as a written or verbal reflection, and often results in declarative statements, beliefs, actions, or commitments.

2. Offer the group a simple reflection prompt, inviting each individual to come up with their own response. Example prompts might include:
   a. Justice looks like...
   b. Justice is important because...
   c. Gender and racial justice matter because...
   d. Gender and racial justice require...
   e. Today, I will perform justice by...

3. Give participants a minute to come with their responses. Invite the group to share their responses out loud as a popcorn call-out, or in a written poster format.

4. With permission, record or photograph these responses and share them on social media to amplify the performance and resulting actions.

5. End the sharing by reminding the group to spread the word—to keep talking about gender and racial justice.

### In Our Experience

Spread the Word offers a way for the ensemble and audience members to take a small action in the room. In some ways, this action mirrors a public post on social media, inviting short statements or "posts" that are publicly shared. This action can provide a first social justice action for some people and might offer affirmation or a challenge to others. There are a lot of creative ways to share the statements and ultimately "spread the word."

**Source**: This action was developed as part of the Performing Justice Project.

## Doing Justice

## Leaning into Difference

*Briana Barner and Cortney McEniry*

As co-facilitators of a PJP residency, we (Briana and Cortney) carry different identities, backgrounds, and fields of expertise from one another. Briana is Black and grew up in a low-income area on the Southside of Chicago. Cortney is a white, straight, cisgender, Christian woman who grew up in an upper-middle class home in suburban South Florida. Our different identities and perspectives sparked a rich, dynamic collaboration and provided us with an opportunity to model an appreciation of difference—specifically for the young people in PJP who are often taught in school and detention centers to be "colorblind," to ignore the different identities of those around them.

I (Briana) remember that just after devising a "Justice Machine," towards the beginning of our residency, the young artists in our group devised a short scene to honor a friend who had been killed. While watching the artists devise the scene, eventually titled "Hands Up, Don't Shoot," my heart was both full and heavy. It was powerful to see the youth truly stepping into the role of artists with an investment in this particular scene. Quite literally, they were performing justice. But it was also difficult to see the scene enacted, as gun violence played a pivotal role in my upbringing. The scene was triggering for me, but its connection to my life also made the scene powerful. Although only one of the young artists knew the victim honored in the scene, I recall thinking that the larger topics we had been discussing—namely justice and intersectionality—finally became real for our group.

I (Cortney) remember that after sharing the scene with us, one of the artists asked if they could have a gunshot sound cue for the performance. My dramaturgical instincts came to the forefront, and I asked the group if they wanted to avoid using gunshot sounds that may prove "triggering or over-the-top" for their audience. I didn't realize the gravity of my question until Briana raised a point of disagreement, offering that we should not be afraid of the visceral power of the scene. She didn't take me aside or wait until after the session was over to offer her opinion; rather, she voiced it clearly and openly in front of the ensemble. I listened clearly and openly, too, and recognized that I have never lost a loved one to gun violence. In that moment, I understood that gunshots feel over-the-top to me because gun violence is not a part of my everyday reality. As Briana and I shared our differing perspectives, the young artists saw an honest, thoughtful disagreement between two adults carrying different racial identities and backgrounds. The youth quickly added their own thoughts to the conversation. The more I listened, I understood that my dramaturgical lens was not ultimately the most informed lens for the experiences, knowledge and impulses of the group.

In hindsight, we (Briana and Cortney) both believe that this moment added value to our process. We moved forward with a greater clarity of intention and an even more communicative ensemble, one that recognized and named the power of difference., If Cortney had framed her question as a statement—"No, gunshots would be triggering" —we may have lost out on the opportunity to establish learning from difference as a norm for our process. Asking the question also provided an opportunity for the ensemble to articulate the desired outcomes from their envisioned relationship between intended audience, aesthetic choices, and affect. Particularly around topics where we lack lived experience because of our privilege, white facilitators must balance participation and humility, acknowledging that our identities may place us in the role of learner and listener more often than not. For me (Briana), it was important to center the experiences of the young people, particularly in a moment where they were connecting to the inequalities they've experienced in their lives because of their marginalized identities. There is power in identifying lived experiences—in this way they were co-creating knowledge with each other, for facilitators and, later, the audience. This also shifts the perspective of the performance piece from the center to those who stand outside of it on the margins. Additionally, when Briana discussed the use of the gunshot with Cortney, the conversation modeled an opportunity to speak openly about how diverse identities inform our distinctive experiences.

We believe it is important to lean into difference, rather than shy away. This PJP residency and our collaboration invited us to think through the many meanings that we drew from the sound of a gunshot. Cortney's distance from gun violence helped acknowledge how some audience members might experience the piece if they had not lost someone to gun violence. Briana's experience with gun violence helped validate the young people's feelings and experiences, and possibly those of some audience members as well. Leaning into difference means having difficult conversations about how systemic inequalities impact the lived experiences of those most affected. This also means acknowledging the invisible ways that difference impacts those who do not hold marginalized identities. Leaning into difference helps reshape how we view our own identities and those around us.

**Figure 2.8** PJP participants perform justice by naming their identities and honoring their differences
Source: Photo by Lynn Hoare.

## Notes

1    We first came across the term *youth-allied adult* in Shelley Goldman, Angela Booker, and Meghan McDermott's essay "Mixing the digital, social, and cultural: Learning, identity, and agency in youth participation" (2008, p. 202).

2    Most activities listed in both sections are interchangeable. This category includes a few strategies we have found useful to examine the impact of gender identity and sex on our experiences in the world. As with race, it is impossible

to fully extricate our experiences of gender from our racialized experiences. We use the idea of gender and birth-assigned sex as one way into building critical consciousness, and although we ask young people to think specifically about gender, we attempt to acknowledge that their experiences of gender are indelibly linked to experiences of race (and other markers of difference). In the first few actions in this section, we refer exclusively to gender as a way into the conversation. As we get into Alphabet Relay and then into naming and explaining vocabulary, we separate birth assigned sex from gender identity and gender expression.

In many of our Performing Justice Project programs, we have worked in separated sex units in juvenile justice systems. We are aware that not everyone in the unit identifies as female; youth have been placed in units depending on sex assigned at birth, regardless of gender identity and/or expression. Systems often don't account for gender fluidity or non-conformity, making it difficult and often unsafe for young people in these systems to share frankly or honestly about their own identities. We have worked most commonly with the female units in juvenile justice systems, and we have a number of exercises that ask youth to reflect on the cultural and societal messages about being a woman and the behaviors they perceive as required for young women. Whether or not the youth in our PJP groups identify as female in the world, if they are in the female unit, it is likely they are familiar with the overwhelming amount of messages directed to women in our country as well as the often conflicting directives contained in these messages. We find the same thing is true of people of all gender identities—we have all been well schooled in messages related to gender roles and supposed "acceptable" ways to perform and inhabit gender.

3   The video covers the origin of racial categories by a European scientist, Johann Friedrich Blumenbach, in 1776. He created five racial categories based on physical appearance and geographic origin of their ancestors. Americans of European descent embraced these ideas it helped them resolve the contradiction between freedom for all and slavery. The video further discusses the ways racial categories have been in flux over the years, categorizing and re-categorizing people based on shifting US political and financial priorities. While racial categories have been constructed by people over time, it still doesn't diminish the impact race has on everyday rights and freedoms.

4   The term "respectability politics" was coined by Evelyn Brooks Higginbotham in her book *Righteous Discontent: The Women's Movement in the Black Baptist Church, 1880–1920*. She discusses racial uplift in her book as well, in terms of the Black women's club movement and how they were developed as racial uplift organizations.

5   See the Declaration on the Rights of the Child (Committee on the Rights of the Child 1990).

6   Expectations around gender identity and expression are often linked to expectations around voice and vocal qualities. In navigating expectations and desires around voice in this performance program, we strive to support and learn from how participants wish to represent themselves and/or be represented.

# References for Part Two

Alrutz, M. (2015) *Digital storytelling, applied theatre, & youth: Performing possibility*, New York: Routledge.

Angelou, M. (1978) *And still I rise*, New York: Random House.

Bell, L. A. (2010) *Storytelling for social justice: Connecting narrative and the arts in antiracist teaching*, New York: Routledge.

Boal, A. (2002) *Games for actors and non-actors*, 2nd ed., trans. A. Jackson, London: Routledge.

Blackless, M., Charuvastra, A., Derryck, A., Fausto-Sterling, A., Lauzanne, K., et al. (2000) 'How sexually dimorphic are we? Review and synthesis,' *American Journal of Human Biology*, vol. 12, pp. 151–166.

Boal, A. (1992) *Games for actors and non-actors*, trans. A. Jackson, London: Routledge.

Bogart, A. and Landau, T. (2005) *The viewpoints book: A practical guide to viewpoints and composition*, New York: Theatre Communications Group.

Brown, A. C. and Ojalvo, H. E. (2010) 'Express yourself: Crafting social location maps and identity monologues,' *The New York Times*, February 11, viewed July 5, 2019, https://learning.blogs.nytimes.com/2010/02/11/express-yourself-crafting-social-location-maps-and-identity-monologues/

Butler, A. (2010) 'Ethnic and racial identity development,' ACT for Youth Center of Excellence, viewed June 19, 2019, www.actforyouth.net/adolescence/identity/ethnic_racial.cfm

Cahnmann-Taylor, M. and Souto-Manning, M. (2010) *Teachers act up! Creating multicultural learning communities through theatre*, New York: Teachers College Press.

Cissna, K. and Anderson, R. (2002) *Moments of meeting: Buber, Rodgers and the potential for public dialogue*, Albany: State University of New York Press.

Committee on the Rights of the Child (1990) *Convention of the rights of the child*, viewed July 6, 2019, www.ohchr.org/en/professionalinterest/pages/crc.aspx

Cox, T. and Beale, R. L. (1997) *Developing competency to manage diversity: Readings, cases & activities*, San Francisco: Berrett-Koehler Publishers, Inc.

Davis, A., Beatrice, Peacock, E., Fatimah, Short, S., et al. (2018) *DRESS CODED: Black girls, bodies, and bias in D.C. schools*, National Women's Law Center, viewed July 5, 2019, https://nwlc-ciw49tixgw5lbab.stackpathdns.com/wp-content/uploads/2018/04/5.1web_Final_nwlc_DressCodeReport.pdf

Dawson, K. and Lee, B. (2018) *Drama-based pedagogy: Activating learning across the curriculum*, Bristol: Intellect.

DBI Network (2019) 'Name + adjective + movement,' viewed June 19, 2019, https://dbp.theatredance.utexas.edu/teaching-strategies/name-adjective-movement

Desmond-Harris, J. (2014a) '11 ways race isn't real,' *Vox Media*, October 10, viewed June 19, 2019, www.vox.com/2014/10/10/6943461/race-social-construct-origins-census

Desmond-Harris, J. (2014b) *The myth of race, debunked in 3 minutes*, viewed June 19, 2019, www.youtube.com/watch?time_continue=68&v=VnfKgffCZ7U

Epstein, R., Blake, J., and González, T. (2017) *Girlhood interrupted: The erasure of black girls' childhood*, Center on Poverty and Inequality Georgetown Law, viewed June 20, 2019, www.law.georgetown.edu/news/black-girls-viewed-as-less-innocent-than-white-girls-georgetown-law-research-finds/

Ginwright, S. (2018) 'The future of healing: Shifting from trauma informed care to healing centered engagement', *Medium Psychology*, May 31, viewed June 10, 2019, https://medium.com/@ginwright/the-future-of-healing-shifting-from-trauma-informed-care-to-healing-centered-engagement-634f557ce69c

Goldman, S., Booker, A., and McDermott, M. (2008) 'Mixing the digital, social, and cultural: Learning, identity, and agency in youth participation,' in D. Buckingham (ed.), *Youth, identity, and digital media*, Cambridge: MIT Press, pp. 185–206.

Hamilton, G. (2003) 'English in the city: Responding to literature in the city,' *The English Journal*, vol. 93, no. 1, pp. 100–104.

Hanley, M. S. (2013) 'Introduction: Culturally relevant arts education for social justice,' in M. S. Hanley, G. Noblit, G. Sheppard, and T. Barone (eds.), *Culturally relevant arts education for social justice: A way out of no way*, New York: Routledge, pp. 1–11.

Higginbotham, E. B. (1994) *Righteous discontent: The women's movement in the black Baptist church, 1880–1920*, revised ed., Cambridge, MA: Harvard University Press.

hooks, b. (1994) *Teaching to transgress: Education as the practice of freedom*, New York: Routledge.

Johnston C. and Brownrigg, C. P. (2019) *Ensemble-made Chicago: A guide to devised theater*, Evanston: Northwestern University Press.

Kaufman, M. and McAdams, B. P. (2018) *Moment work: Tectonic Theater Project's process of devising theater*, New York: Vintage Books.

Koppett, K. (2001) *Training to imagine: Practical improvisational theatre techniques to enhance creativity, teamwork, leadership and learning*, Sterling: Stylus Publishing.

Lyon, G. (1999) *Where I'm from: Where poems come from*, Spring: Absey & Co., Inc.

Lyon, G. and Landsman, J. (2017) *I am from project*, viewed May 15, 2019, https://iamfromproject.com

Morrow, E. (1951–1955) *This I believe*, radio program, CBS Radio Network.

Neelands, J. and Goode, T. (1990) *Structuring drama work*, Cambridge: Cambridge University Press.

Norris, M. (2010) *The race card project*, viewed May 15, 2019, https://theracecardproject.com

NPR Staff (2015) 'The #blacklivesmatter movement: Marches and tweets for healing,' *National Public Radio*, June 9, viewed July 5, 2019, www.npr.org/2015/06/09/412862459/the-blacklivesmatter-movement-marches-and-tweets-for-healing

Performing Justice Project (2011) *Gonzalo Garza Independence High School performing justice project*, devised performance, Central Texas.

Performing Justice Project (2015) *The good in me/In my skin*, devised performance, Central Texas.

Race Forward (2014) 'Moving the race conversation forward: How the media covers racism, and other barriers to productive racial discourse, part 1,' viewed June 9, 2019, http://act.colorlines.com/acton/attachment/1069/f-0114/1/-/-/-/-/Racial_Discourse_Part_1.PDF

Rebstock, M. and Roesner, D. (eds.) (2012), *Composed theatre: Aesthetics, practices, processes*, Bristol: Intellect.

Rohd, M. (1998) *Theatre for community, conflict & dialogue: The hope is vital training manual*, Portsmouth: Heinemann.

Saldaña, J. (1995) *Drama of color: Improvisation with multiethnic folklore*, Portsmouth: Heinemann.

Sensoy, Ö. and DiAngelo, R. (2012) *Is everyone really equal? An introduction to key concepts in social justice education*, New York: Teachers College Press.

Spolin, V. (1986) *Theater games for the classroom: A teacher's handbook*, Evanston, IL: Northwestern University Press.

This I Believe (2019) viewed July 5, 2019, https://thisibelieve.org

Watson, R. (2019) viewed July 5, 2019, www.reneewatson.net/

Weinstein, M. and Goodman, J. (1980) *Playfair: Everybody's guide to noncompetitive play*, San Luis Obispo: Impact Publishers.

Woodson, S.E. (2015) *Theatre for youth third space: Performance, democracy, and community cultural development*, Chicago: Intellect Ltd.

# Part Three

# Producing a Performing Justice Project

## 3.0 Introduction

Racial and gender injustice show up in the lives of young people on a daily basis. These injustices become important frames of reference as PJP participants devise theatre from their own life experiences. Given the prevalence of racism and sexism in the US, PJP residencies intersect directly with horrific acts of racialized and gendered violence on a national scale. During our 2015 PJP residency, Dylann Roof, a 21-year-old white supremacist entered the Emanuel African Methodist Episcopal Church, one of the oldest historic Black churches in the South. Roof sat in a prayer meeting with nine other people for almost an hour before he murdered all of them, including the pastor. We learned about this act of terror and white supremacy as we began a dress rehearsal of our PJP performance. The performance text was already set and we needed to find a way to acknowledge the connections between the racially motivated massacre in Charleston, SC and the work we were asking youth to do around systemic racism and sexism. Below is the Directors' Note that we wrote for the performance:

> "The Good In Me/In My Skin"
> 2015 PJP Performance
> Director's Note

> The work of PJP feels essential at this moment in time—racial and gender injustice are unfolding around us every day. The Charleston shootings—murders—happened while we were building "The Good in Me/In My Skin." We dedicate this performance to the nine people who were killed, and hold them in our hearts along with the many other victims of racial and gender violence every day. PJP asks young people to reflect upon and write stories about their experiences of injustice, and then to take the very brave step of performing their stories in public. You are going to see the work of youth who are thinking actively about gender and racial in/justice in their lives and our world—this is courageous and risky work. Thank you, PJP 2015

performers and creators—for your courage, patience, strength, intelligence, creativity, and your support for each other.

With love and support, Megan and Lynn
#YouAreTheOnesWeveBeenWaitingFor
#YouthRise
#PJP2015

As outlined by this performance and the surrounding events, PJP is woven directly from participants' experiences and understandings, and the current contexts in which we are all living. What happens in the world and in the lives of the participants is considered and reflected as part of the residency and devising process, as well as the performance itself. This means planning ahead but also remaining flexible and responsive to what is happening around us.

To support participants as they create theatre from life, from ideation to performance, we rely on some systems and checklists to help us produce a Performing Justice Project. A fair amount of pre-work happens before the workshop and outside of the devising space in order to pull off a critically engaged public performance. In Part Three, we outline some of the logistics involved in designing, planning, and producing a PJP performance—from finding a site partner and recruiting a group of participants, to ordering t-shirts, administering evaluations, and maintaining partnerships. In Section 3.1, Director/Facilitator Preparation, we discuss the importance of preparation on the part of the director/facilitator/teaching artists, sharing practices and reflection questions for preparing oneself to do racial and gender justice work with others. Section 3.2, Finding and Working with a Community Partner, addresses the importance of finding a community or site partner and our processes for inviting youth participants into a PJP residency. In Section 3.3, Assembling a Team, we outline the makeup of a PJP artistic team, explaining the varied and necessary tasks for producing a PJP performance for a public audience. Section 3.4, Sample Plans and Scripts, offers sample session plans and script outlines. Section 3.5, Program Development and Documentation, discusses steps we take to record, document, evaluate, and fund projects.

# 3.1 Director/Facilitator Preparation

Producing a PJP performance and engaging with youth around issues of gender and racial justice requires constant and ongoing diligence and reflexivity on the part of the project director(s), facilitators, and teaching artists. As discussed in Section 2.1, How We Work, self-actualization is a core and necessary practice for directors/facilitators engaged in a PJP process. Coupled with the frameworks offered in Section 2.1, we offer specific questions here for reflecting on one's own positionality and relationships to power, privilege, and oppression prior to and during a residency.

As project directors, and more specifically as white, cisgender adults, we (Megan and Lynn) must continually examine how our own power and privilege show up in the world—in our design of PJP residencies, and in our relationships and interactions with youth participants. DRWorks, an organization that provides resources for dismantling racism, dives deeply into ways to resist oppression and take action. The authors of the *Dismantling Racism Workbook* remind us that preparing to do racial justice work with others requires self-awareness around our identities, skills, and areas of challenge:

> Taking action for racial justice requires a level of self-awareness that allows us to be clear about what we are called to do, what we know how to do, and where we need to develop. Another way of thinking about this is to know our strengths, our weaknesses, our opportunities for growth, and our challenges. Knowing ourselves means that we can show up more appropriately and effectively in whatever the work is, avoid taking on tasks we are not equipped to do well, ask for help when needed, and admit when we don't know what we're doing or claim our skills gracefully when we do.
>
> (Jones et al. 2016, p. 57)

While practicing self-awareness is lifelong work, we borrow frameworks from artist, writer, and activist Sharon Bridgforth for considering personal identity and power in relationship to facilitating creative work with multi-racial ensembles. In her co-edited and authored book, *Experiments in a Jazz Aesthetic: Art, Activism, Academia and the Austin Project*,[1] Bridgforth writes about facilitator preparation. In her chapter "Finding voice: Anchoring the Austin Project's artistic process" she offers a series of critical questions to help facilitators self-reflect before leading a group process (Bridgforth 2010). She outlines a list of questions for "checking yourself" (Bridgforth 2010, p. 19) before leading a creative process with others, encouraging facilitators to articulate how and why they plan to engage in a given creative process with a group. Bridgforth's facilitator questions prove critical for preparing to lead a PJP residency as well:

- Why am I creating this circle [PJP process]?
- Whom will this [PJP] circle serve?
- How will the organization that sponsors the [PJP] circle affect, inform, and support the process?

(Bridgforth 2010, p. 19)

- What does internalized oppression look like in your life, and how might that affect your work as a facilitator?
- What control issues do you have? How might they affect you as a facilitator?
- What are your triggers?
- What work have you done to dismantle oppression in your personal life?

(Bridgforth 2010, p. 18)

Building on Bridgforth's Finding Voice facilitation method, we ask ourselves and those working in PJP to consider additional questions about systemic oppression and personal accountability. We recognize that privilege and power look different for every person who works with PJP; many of these questions are designed to support reflection and action around privilege, as well as to examine intention and impact in our actions. These questions encourage facilitators to consider adult and other privileges, although they grow out of our experiences of grappling with our own white cisgender privilege.

- Where do you see institutional and structural oppression at work in your life and in the systems with which you engage (both positively and negatively)? How and where have you benefited from or been impacted by institutional oppression?
- How do you recover and take care of yourself when the realization you have benefited from, relied on, used, or been oblivious to your privilege arises? What do you do if and when the realization of your access and power results in feelings of guilt or shame? How do you practice self-accountability and healing without burdening those around you (particularly peers and colleagues of color if you are white) with your process of learning and un-learning?
- How do you recover and take care of yourself when you are upset or triggered by a response, action, an aggression or a microaggression that is connected to one of your identity markers?
- When you realize you have acted on bias or committed a microaggression, how do you hold yourself accountable for the *impact* of your action rather than focus on and justify your intent?
- How do you actively work to accept responsibility and reconcile or restore relationships that may be impacted by your microaggression?
- In what ways can and do young people act as agents of change? What is your role in this?

We know that we do our best work in PJP when we lead with curiosity and remain open to learning—about ourselves, the world, and the youth engaged in PJP. As co-collaborators and co-directors, we work to hold each other accountable—to PJP participants, to dismantling systems that keep racism and sexism in place, and to continually questioning our lens, our words, and our actions. Working in collaboration towards racial and gender justice requires an openness to authentic and courageous learning. It requires that we question each other and ourselves and take steps to reconcile or restore relationships and actions when we find ourselves, or others find us, in moments of enacting oppression. For these reasons, we recommend co-facilitating and co-directing this work as one way to hold each other accountable, and to debrief in community about the ongoing work of developing a heightened awareness of race, gender, power, privilege, and oppression. When a PJP teaching artist leads a residency on their own, we encourage them to name who they will turn to outside of the residency to debrief, process, and question their own lens, language, and actions.

We try to facilitate and direct PJP as a collaborative, reciprocal process with each other and with participants; this requires continued self-reflection and awareness about who we are in the world and why we do the work of PJP. We ask the question, "Why am I creating this PJP residency?" again and again as a way to check our intentions and name potential impacts. This work of self-reflection and reflexivity helps us move away from traditional adult-led frameworks that minimize possibilities for youth to act as agents of change. Our answers to this question have changed over time and include: a desire to know what young people see and think about in their communities, a commitment to the practice of working alongside young people to develop multi-age and multi-racial communities of love and resistance, an understanding of youth as necessary members of a connected, healthy, joyful, and equitable community, and the recognition that our own liberation is tightly bound to the freedom of Black and Brown women and girls, trans people of color, and gender non-binary folks. The guiding questions in this section offer a starting place for facilitator reflection and preparation, and, this work requires ongoing learning about and connections to histories, contexts, and issues related to gender and racial justice.

# 3.2 Finding and Working With a Community Partner

We lead and support PJP residencies in a variety of sites, including middle and high schools, juvenile justice centers, and residential foster care sites. These sites are often state-mandated for young people in some way, making them critical places to collaborate with youth to better understand and shift the systems shaping their lives. Every site has advantages, challenges, and priorities—all of which impact the process of choosing and nurturing a community partnership in PJP. In this section, we detail our process of finding a community partner and collaborating to create a PJP residency. For a more extensive examination of building project partnerships, we appreciate the depth and breadth of Stephani Etheridge Woodson's thinking and recommendations in "Section Three: Partnering, Project Management, Planning and Evaluating" in her book, *Theatre for Youth Third Space* (2015, pp. 161–236). Her book offers approachable and thorough frameworks for thinking through community partnerships, including barriers to partnering, possibilities for change-making, proposal writing, evaluation, and project management (Woodson 2015).

Table 3.1 lays out steps and questions we ask when finding and developing a PJP partnership, from looking for a partner to engaging youth to maintaining open lines of communication.

## Finding a Community Partner

Our first step in finding a community partner is to identify and research a variety of sites that work with youth ages 14 to 21 years old and whose mission or programming could align with that of PJP. Sites that already engage young people, such as schools, juvenile justice centers, residential foster care sites, youth support or drop-in centers, recreation centers, arts programs, and leadership or service programs for youth, often have support systems in place for youth and understand what is required to offer youth programs (such as time for snacks, access to youth counselors, transportation, alignment with school schedules, etc.). After identifying potential partners for gender and racial justice work—through internet searches, recommendations, and previous contacts—we send an email with a descriptive PJP flyer to a contact whose position or biography suggests alignment with youth programming or justice-based programming in some way. In our initial emails or cold calls, we offer a clear, concise overview

**Table 3.1** PJP steps for partnership development

| | Questions that guide PJP partnership development | |
|---|---|---|
| **Finding a community partner** | Research possible partners/sites | • Which organizations serve youth?<br>• Which organizations have justice-based missions?<br>• Which organizations do we have relationships with?<br>• Which organizations would we like to have relationships with?<br>• Which organizations of staff are potential allies for youth, us, or our organizations? |
| | Contact site staff with interest | • Who on staff might be a good contact for partnership development?<br>• What can we offer to get the conversation started?<br>• What does the organization need to know about PJP? About the PJP staff?<br>• Why are we interested to partner with this organization or staff person? |
| **Assessing and building a partnership** | Informational meeting | • What can we share about PJP to help an organization imagine partnering?<br>• What collateral, history, or vision will assist a potential partner to get on board?<br>• What questions do we have about the organization or the staff?<br>• What information will help us envision a possible partnership? |
| | Assess potential for partnership and reciprocity | • What are the strengths, challenges, and questions that came out of the information meeting?<br>• What kind of support and compromises would need to be made to partner on delivering a PJP residency?<br>• What kind of staffing, space, and other resources are needed to support a project with this partner? |
| | Memorandum of understanding | • What are the goals and deliverables of the PJP residency?<br>• What roles and responsibilities will each partner hold?<br>• What will communication look like?<br>• How will families, guardians, and supportive communities be engaged in PJP?<br>• What will the final performance look like? |
| **Youth recruitment and participation** | Interactive Workshop "invitation" with youth participants | • What information do youth need in order to determine if/how they will participate in PJP?<br>• How will we invite youth to a pitch session?<br>• How will we give participants and partners a sense of our process and approach to performing gender and racial justice?<br>• How will we learn about our partner and participants in a short workshop/pitch session? |

**Table 3.1** Cont.

| | Permissions | • What kind of permissions are needed? Youth, guardian, site, copyright?<br>• How will permission forms both give information about PJP and gain consent from guardians and youth participants?<br>• How much time is needed to gather consent and from whom?<br>• Who will hold permission forms?<br>• What kinds of permissions are needed—participation, video-taping, photography, audio, travel? |
|---|---|---|
| **Maintaining open communication** | Ongoing communication | • What systems of communication are in place prior to the start of PJP residency?<br>• Who are the main points of contact on each side of the partnership?<br>• How much involvement will a partner have in the residency?<br>• What information needs to be communicated or approved throughout the residency?<br>• What will communications with the partner and the participant youth look like? |

of PJP and ask to follow up in person or by phone. Our goal with any initial reach out is to find the best contact and to work with that contact to assess the possibility of a productive partnership. Whenever possible, we aim to meet with a potential partner for an informational meeting, where we get to know a staff contact, learn more about their organization, explain the work of PJP, and respond to any concerns or questions. We often begin looking for a community partner three to nine months before we wish to begin a residency with youth participants. Finding a compatible partner can take several months, and the process of building necessary relationships, setting up a PJP residency, and finalizing funding and logistics can take another few months.

## Assessing and Building a Partnership

We show up at an initial partnership meeting with a lot to offer and a lot to learn. We also "pitch" the idea of a PJP residency again, sharing the basic structure and goals of the program, as well areas of flexibility and potential for meeting the needs of a partner site. Through conversation with a potential partner, we assess the feasibility of running an intensive performance-making process with a group of youth at this site. We gather information about if and how the site already structures opportunities for youth participation and where we could build on existing infrastructure and/or fill some gaps:

- How regularly and for what reasons do youth show up to this location?
- What kinds of programs does the site already offer for 14–19-year-olds, and is there value and opportunity to weave PJP into an existing program or structure?

- Does the organization have the capacity to support a PJP residency? We consider staffing, space, materials and supplies, organizational stability and track record in youth programming, theatre programming, and social justice work, and philosophical buy-in.
- What are the expectations of the site in terms of youth participation, behavior, and attendance? What incentives exist for youth to participate? How does the site support youth, and are staff available to be involved in this process?
- How would the site support a public or invited performance for community members? Does the site have rehearsal space and/or a performance space?
- See Table 3.1 and Appendix C for further questions that we use to assess the potential for a community partnership.

Importantly, at this informational meeting, we also aim to be clear and direct about the goals of PJP and our direct engagement with youth around personal stories and topics of gender and racial justice. The words *gender and racial justice* alone can prove threatening to some staff and organizations, and sharing this information early on helps us assess the support levels and challenges of doing any kind of politically charged change-work in the organization. Through this process, we seek out partners who are excited about this opportunity for the young people in their lives and communities, who are invested in youth development and willing to support the sometimes risky and brave work of examining internalized and structural power and oppression. Although the project is shaped in response to needs and conditions of the site (including number and length of sessions), the goals of moving through a structured process of naming identities, considering (in)justice, and rehearsing and performing justice remain constant. Understanding that race and gender are political constructs, we want site partners to know that we intend to dig into power-laden topics that may implicate individuals and institutions holding power or privilege. As part of our efforts to be transparent about our goals, we often bring print copies of a PJP flyer with us to the first meeting. We leave the flyers with the potential partner as a way of assisting in their effort to share the project with additional administration or staff who may need to sign off on the project or become involved with PJP in some way. Hard copies encourage site partners to meet in person with each other rather than simply communicate over email around a potential project. (See Appendix C, PJP Informational Flyer for a sample one-page overview we have shared with youth, families, and partner institutions.)

We also go into every site prepared to make compromises, while remaining aware of our own bottom lines. We pay attention to where our processes may need to change to meet the scheduling, logistical, and individual needs of a partner, a partner site, or the youth served by the site. We commonly negotiate the number of youth participants and how the youth will be recruited into or required to participate in PJP. We always discuss behavior expectations for young people, working to understand if and how participating in PJP might impact a young persons' relationship to the site. (For example, if we are asking youth to freely share their experiences, will there be consequences for swearing or addressing certain topics at the given site? If youth aren't allowed to touch each other at this site, does flexibility exist for touching within our theatre/performance context?) We often negotiate longer program times, moving away from the typical 50-minute programs of many sites and toward two- or three-hour sessions whenever possible. At this time, we also try to understand parameters around or challenges related to holding a public performance and/or inviting families and guardians. During these informational meetings, we pay close attention to a site partners' relationship and response to these logistics, as well as their willingness to dialogue and practice flexibility. We use these first meetings to assess if and how a partnership will serve the PJP process and, more importantly, the youth involved.

When we find a strong community partner and both parties agree to move forward, we draft a Memorandum of Understanding (MOU) as an official step in negotiating specific details of a partnership and confirming timelines, roles, and responsibilities. Before signing an MOU, we work with the partner to agree on session times and dates, the number of youth participants and staff who will be involved, and the roles and expectations for both site partner staff and PJP staff. The process of drafting and revising an MOU with partners creates a structure for detailing expectations and communication practices before issues arise. It also invites everyone to document who will be responsible for which components of the project, an area where potential challenges arise when things are not figured out prior to the start of a residency. (See Appendix C for a sample PJP MOU.)

## Youth Recruitment and Participation

Creating original performance material based on personal experiences of racial and gender injustice can be a vulnerable process. In early iterations of PJP, we worried that requiring anyone, particularly young people, to participate in PJP would negatively impact the youth, the residency, and performance. Instead, we found that when PJP took place in sites where youth are required to participate (due to a previously organized course or a state-mandated support group), the participants often surprised themselves. Youth who would not otherwise have chosen to engage in a theatre project, or in gender and racial justice work, or with people outside of their "friend" group, developed new and unexpected relationships, particularly across markers of difference. Moreover, youth ultimately felt proud of their accomplishments in PJP and were surprised by how much they enjoyed the process and learned from each other.[2] Partnering with organizations that have existing structures for bringing together and supporting youth groups can make the process of recruiting participants both possible and efficient. While we always talk with partners about mandatory versus elective youth participation in PJP, we are aware that initially reluctant participants often find PJP the most rewarding.

Prior to starting a residency, we host a short meeting or workshop with youth to offer participants a taste of what PJP entails. During this "invitation" workshop (see Appendix A for sample session plan), we facilitate introductory performance actions, provide an overview of our devising and performance process, and introduce our focus on gender and racial justice. The pitch session introduces potential participants to our on-your feet facilitation style and lets them know what they can expect as a participant in PJP. Our pitch sessions are designed to be playful and to communicate the physical and participatory nature of PJP. With this session, we begin to build relationships in the room and pique youth's interest around performing justice.

## Maintaining Open Communication

After determining a site partner and pitching to youth participants, we set up a process for regular and ongoing communications between PJP staff and our site partner. Knowing that issues and questions often come up in the rehearsal room, we ask for scheduled check-ins prior to the rise of any issues. We structure time to share and receive updates, including specific plans to support individual participants and to keep the project moving forward. We know that PJP is often an added program to staffs' already busy schedules; we make a concerted effort to maintain meaningful relationships with staff, keep communication open between all entities, and build on what already exists in each organization.

In addition to collaborating with staff, we see our work at any given site as a collaboration with youth and their larger systems of support. We often provide an informational note on PJP for parents, family, teachers, and caretakers with an explanation of the project and an invitation to the final performance. Early on in the residency, we often invite larger community circles to attend PJP performances as well, reaching out to people who are actively involved in youth services, arts, and activism. Whenever possible, we talk with the ensemble about who needs to see their work and who they would like to invite.[3]

Our community and school partners have shaped the structure of PJP in ways that are difficult to fully identify. The ideas, identities, and systems that come with each partner are woven tightly into the what, how, and why of PJP residencies, session plans, and performance structures. We know that our strongest partnerships have resulted from reciprocal relationships, those in which the PJP process reflects and responds to the contexts, assets, and needs of the site and the participants. What stands out from past partnerships is the commitment and enthusiasm of at least one staff person who repeatedly said yes and supported young people to reflect on and perform justice. Many site partners help create culturally responsive PJP programming, while others help negotiate institutional boundaries, court sentencing, and the impacts of trauma on youth. The commitment of a community or site partner remains a linchpin in making spaces for lifting up youth voices and performing justice.

# 3.3 Assembling a Team

Building a PJP residency offers an exciting opportunity to bring together people with diverse skill sets, identities, and perspectives. Co-directing PJP residencies can also bring an important depth and diversity of creative tools and content to a PJP residency. In assembling a team, we think about the various roles and skill sets that make a performance project happen, but equally important, we think specifically about how a multi-racial and gender-diverse team of project directors, teaching artists, and guest artists might serve the diverse identities of the ensemble. We also think about assembling a group of individuals who are committed to social justice efforts and interested in diverse approaches to and goals around gender and racial justice. While it may not be possible for every residency to include a team of people, everyone benefits from honest and ongoing dialogue about how power and privilege play out in the form and content of PJP.[4] This dialogue requires at least two project staff and often deepens when the artist teams are collaborating and learning across different identities. For us, this dialogue happens most often in the car (to and from a PJP site) among the PJP team members as we plan for and reflect on the work in the room, its relationship to our lives and the way it intersects with local, national, and global events. It also happens in the room, in the moment, as we navigate, open up to, and remain accountable to each other's different viewpoints, perspectives, and identities. Working with multi-racial and gender-diverse teams makes it possible to model discussions and performance-making that acknowledges many of the gender and racial differences in youth groups, differences that tend to get erased or marginalized in traditional school or youth program settings. It also means that our decision-making includes an accountability to varied experiences, interests, and knowledge. For example, having a multi-racial group of artists facilitating a PJP residency has inspired youth participants to try out new language around race and gender identity with each other, and to practice naming the systemic and individual impacts of racial and gender differences within the lives of the ensemble members and our communities at large.

When we co-direct a PJP process, we also hire resident teaching artists to be in the room for the duration of the process. Much of the program planning, script-creation, and performance prep, along with directing small bits of performance, and running the technical elements of the performance are shared among members of this artistic leadership team. We also invite guest artists to lead workshops and share their skills, expertise, and knowledge with the group on a more short-term basis. Guest artists often include poets, designers, or experts in a particular style of theatre (spoken word, solo performance, performance art) or gender and racial justice work. For a number of years, we invited poets to perform their work and lead workshops about creative writing as a tool to lift up often marginalized identities and disrupt oppressive systems. One year guest artists Emily Aguilar and Megan Nevels led a workshop on writing and performing spoken word ("I Am/Yo Estoy" spoken word outline included in Appendix A). Many of the spoken word pieces from this workshop moved into the PJP performance, significantly shaping the style and rhythm of that particular script. Another year, a performance artist introduced the history of performance art and several performance tools which later sparked non-linear approaches to writing, as well as the use of slow motion in the performance. For every PJP process, we attempt to build an artistic team that is diverse in a myriad of ways that both reflects and expands upon the identities and skills of the youth participants.

Within the PJP team, including individuals organizing the PJP residency, those directing the production, and resident teaching artists—those individuals hired to help facilitate the program, handle logistics, and support creative youth practices—we assign or choose specific roles and tasks for each team member. Tasks vary depending on program context, residency length, and support already in place at a partner site, but typically include coordinating communications such as press releases, emails, invitations to the performance; guest artist schedules, payment, and logistics; ordering and organizing supplies and food; documenting, tracking, and recording changes to and printing scripts; archiving PJP materials; and writing and disseminating evaluations for participants, teaching artists, site partners, and audience members. We include a detailed list of PJP roles, tasks, supplies and logistics in Appendix D.

# 3.4 Sample Plans and Scripts

## Session Plans

In Appendix A, we offer a sample program outline and session plans from past PJP residencies. We encourage directors and teaching artists to choose performance actions and create session structures that fit their own approach to devising and facilitating, as well as their specific contexts, goals, and aesthetics. We use the term "session plan" to describe a daily agenda or plan for each meeting with participants. The length of each session is largely dictated by parameters at our partner sites, but usually ranges from one to three hours. Appendix A also includes an overview of a PJP residency over 14 three-hour sessions. In our experience, the structure of a PJP residency varies with each project. We might meet with participants every day for three weeks or once a week over the course of four or five months. The length and frequency of face time with participants greatly impacts what can be achieved in a PJP residency and may also dictate how many sessions are necessary to build a script and ready the ensemble for a public performance. Time with participants greatly influences how "produced" the performance is, shaping how much movement or staging gets created, as well as the possibility of working toward memorized text and realizing design elements.

As artists and educators, we tend to write highly structured session plans that follow a particular rhythm and form, including specific goals for each session, carefully scripted transitions, and time lengths for each action (see Section 2.1, How We Work, and 2.2, How We Devise). Despite our structured approach, we remain flexible and adaptable, ready to let go of an action or revise an entire session plan when something isn't working or if the opportunity arises for deeper or more connected and responsive work. We rely on daily session plans to help us hold the big picture, including where we are headed on a daily and weekly basis, as well as to think through how we respond to youth work, skills, and questions. Because we often share facilitation between several team members, our session plans also offer a road map for who is facilitating and who is supporting any given action and what comes next. Session plans also serve as a communication tool for connecting with site partners, many of whom are responsible for PJP within their organization but are not usually in the room with us. Sharing our daily session plans with a site partner prior to showing up on site each day offers an opportunity for our partners to ask questions, add insights, and let us know if any of our material or actions might require special considerations. Special considerations might involve getting approval to play music or bring technology into a space, or grouping strategies that help avoid interpersonal tensions on any given day. Appendix A offers samples of detailed daily session plans, providing a sense of our overall structure for a session plan, but also showing the "connective tissue"—the transitions, questions, ending points that help weave individual performance actions into a full session plan. Appendix A also includes a sample "invitation" session plan which we use to introduce PJP to a group of youth and invite them to participate. This invitation session is often our best informational and recruitment tool because it offers an experiential taste of the program.

## Script Outlines

We discuss our scripting process in more detail in Section 2.2, How We Devise, and in Script Development within Section 2.3.4. Each PJP residency results in a collage-based performance, meaning that we weave together small bits of performance that might include different characters, locations, plots, and stories. Performances are often organized by themes, questions, or relationships between individuals and systems. Appendix B includes three script outlines from past PJP performances. Taken together, these three samples show a variety of ways to structure a PJP performance, including beginnings and endings, transitions between bits of performance, and possible structures for grouping and organizing devised materials, such as monologues, scenes, movement or dance pieces, songs, and recorded bits of text.

Many of our partner sites require a level of anonymity for youth participants when sharing their performance work. Our script pieces rarely attribute bits of performance directly to any particular individual; rather, the group works collectively to script and share out the performance material created by the ensemble as a whole. While authors sometimes choose to perform their own stories, they always have a choice about whether or not to include their stories in a script and whether or not they want to be involved in the performance of their own stories. Individual stories often represent collective experiences, or experiences shared by several people in the ensemble. In these cases, the script and the performance text are often performed by multiple voices, maintaining the anonymity of the main writer and/or making a statement about the larger systems at play in any given experience. The sample script outlines included in the Appendix do not include all of the text from each performance, but rather provide a sense of the structure and the types of performance material that makes up a PJP script and performance.

# 3.5 Program Development and Documentation

During our eight years of running and supporting PJP residencies, our team developed a handful of living documents that help us sustain and maintain the PJP model. (See Appendix C for source documents that we use to promote, document, evaluate and assess, and fund PJP.) While creating ongoing and sustainable partnerships and programs is an exciting goal, we have also learned the value of offering programs one time and of moving away from expectations that a single residency will turn into a long-term or ongoing partnership.[5] This section offers a series of considerations and documents to support PJP programs, partnerships, residencies, and workshops.

## Documentation

From the beginning of our PJP process, Kristen Hogan (co-founder and a PJP resident teaching artist) consistently directed our attention to the documentation of PJP and practices of justice-based archiving. She encouraged us to consider: How might we capture and share what was happening in PJP? How could others learn from what was created in the room? How might the process and products of PJP be recorded, preserved, and shared? Who does our documentation and archive lift up? How might an archive of PJP work to *perform justice*? As practitioners of theatre, an ephemeral art, we struggled to imagine effective ways to capture and archive our process or products, particularly since recorded theatre often offers an inadequate (and hard to watch) representation of art meant to be witnessed in person. However, Kristen's early focus on and support around documenting and archiving PJP pushed us all to imagine different ways to record what was happening. We now have reflective writing and text about the program, as well as photography, recorded audio, and video. In the context of partnering with state institutions, we have had to get creative about documentation, as filming or photographing the faces of state-involved youth is prohibited. We have approached this challenge in two ways, both of which involve obtaining permissions: audio-recording the voice and performance work of youth participants and capturing photos or video that do not include youths' faces or other identifying information. In one case, we audio-recorded a PJP performance and then hired a visual artist/animator to create a visual score to accompany the recorded audio;[6] in another case, we audio-recorded voices and hired a filmmaker to put the recording to photos from the performance that didn't include faces. This focus on documenting PJP has resulted in a variety of videos that illustrate the content and aesthetics of the work. It has also enabled us to share both the processes and products of various Performing Justice Projects more widely, giving youth participants and the wider public a sense of what the work can look or feel like. In her book *Theatre for Youth Third Space*, author, academic, and community-based artist Stephani Etheridge Woodson, confirms: "Documentation captures the essence of a project to communicate scope and sequence to project partners, participants, funders, and stakeholders... In addition, documentation of past projects becomes work samples for future projects and/or funding requests" (2015, p. 221). Documentation provides evidence and information that a project actually happened and provides a way into witnessing *what* happened. Early documentation of our process and daily lessons also helped us notice our own errors and capture our successes as we explored what it looked like to devise performance with youth about racial and gender justice. As we tried new actions, repeated and refined them, we recorded these changes and shared them with PJP teaching artists so that the model could be continually improved and eventually replicated. Overall, documentation provides many benefits to a program and its many stakeholders.

## Assessment and Evaluation

We believe that the process of creating and performing an original piece of theatre can be a significant experience for young people. As a way to better understand and learn from their experiences in PJP, we ask participants to share thoughts, reflections, and self-assessments about their experience in the project and their relationships to gender and racial justice and to performance. Rather than producing formal research, these assessment and evaluation efforts help youth make meaning of or cement their own experiences of performing justice, and offer information that shapes future residencies and program development.

In each residency, we ask stakeholders close to the process—from audience members to site partners to teaching artists, youth participants, and ourselves—to reflect on individual and collective experiences in PJP. During our closing session with the ensemble, which takes place after the final performance, we celebrate the performance with food and festivity. We also lead a group reflection on the process, asking the participants to reflect on what remains for them now that the performance and project is coming to a close. We also provide more specific reflection prompts for participants to articulate their experiences with PJP both verbally and through written evaluations. During these closing sections, we often learn about the impacts of completing a performance project, including feelings of pride, new relationships, and changes in perspective about gender, race, and justice. Immediately following a performance, we often ask audience members to respond to the work through talk-backs and a brief written evaluation form. The forms (see Appendix C) help PJP staff assess the impact of the performance on attendees, while the talk-back often garners accolades and encouragement for youth performers, as well as some critical reflections and dialogue from audience members. We also ask teaching artists to complete a written reflection and an evaluation form at the end of each residency so that we can learn from their experiences and perspectives as facilitators of PJP. Finally, we like to close each PJP residency by meeting with our site partners to reflect on what went well, what challenges came up, and what we might shift in future collaborations. Each of these program assessments provides critical information for building and maintaining successful PJP residencies.

Appendix C includes some sample forms that we've used to assess the program and shape future residencies. In addition, we often use the information gathered in informal assessments to report back to funders and strategize around future partnerships and funding opportunities. We see program assessment and evaluation as a valuable tool in working toward gender and racial justice.

## Funding

In our experience, PJP residencies and performance budgets range anywhere from $250 to $20,000 and typically engage 5 to 30 youth participants and public audiences of varying sizes. This budget range is dictated largely by our ability to raise money for the PJP and our salary needs for staff at any given site. However, the PJP budget is also determined by the number of youth served, availability of space, and the level of residency and production support needed. Our staff teams vary in size from one core director to teams of six directors and teaching artists and some partner sites provide space, materials, and/or food. In addition, larger budgets usually include designers, videographers/photographers, and significant transportation budgets. In laying out funding priorities for any given residency, we think through funding in the following areas:

- Core program staff: directors, teaching artists, and community partners
- Support staff: administrative/logistics, designers, community partners
- Guest artists: workshop facilitators, vocal coaching, etc.
- Travel: staff transportation, participant transportation
- Materials/supplies: journals, pencils, paper, t-shirts, printing, etc.
- Food/snacks: daily snacks and drinks for participants, celebration food
- Documentation: labor and materials for video, audio, photography, animation, etc.

Understanding that each residency benefits from a different set of funding priorities, we try to budget in conversation with our site partners. Knowing the needs and resources of each site help us make decisions about where to channel resources. The following considerations often shape our budgeting decisions:

- How are the funding priorities lifting up gender and racial justice? Who is being hired and who benefits from any given funding decision? How can funding priorities help remove barriers to participation?
- How will staff and guest artists support the project? How can funding and other resources help diversify the skills, experiences, and identities that get foregrounded in the residency? What staff time will be in-kind and what additional staff needs to be hired or supported?
- How much time do we have to garner project resources?
- What resources do we bring to each residency? What kinds of support can the community partner provide?
- What additional organizations in the community might support and participate in this project?
- How can we leverage past projects to garner support for future projects?

As discussed in Part One, PJP was developed with the generous financial support of the Embrey Family Foundation and the Center for Women's and Gender Studies at the University of Texas at Austin. Having university and foundation support for the research and development of this work has been a significant privilege that puts us in a position to investigate and shape this set of practices, to hire and engage teams of artists and scholars to collaborate toward racial and gender justice performance practices, and to publicly share this model through conference presentations, articles, and now this book. We realize that a funding situation such as this is not only rare, it is also a benefit of being situated within a university network, which is itself reliant on privilege in many forms—educational privilege, socioeconomic privilege, white cisgender privilege, and privilege of time and space. We know that our identities as white women come with significant privileges that directly shape our access to support required to build this program.[7] Remaining aware of and working to disrupt how our funding systems are born out of and contribute to gender and racial oppression is part of performing justice. This can happen by attending to how funding decisions are made, how funding is distributed, and who decides what gets funded.

PJP program development remains deeply connected to documentation, assessment, and funding systems. These systems require attention throughout a residency, not simply at the start or finish of a project. In Appendix C, we include several sample documents that we use to keep an eye on documentation, assessment, and funding as we build support for current and future residencies.

# Notes

1    This book is "both an anthology of new writing and a sourcebook for those who would like to use creative writing and performance to energize their artistic, scholarly, and activist practices" (University of Texas Press 2019).

2　At our first PJP site, the staff's expectation that their entire class would take PJP for credit and finish with a performance for their classmates ended up mirroring what we hoped to create: a committed group of racially, economically, age-diverse young women, primarily non-performers, working together towards a public performance about women's human rights. Through partnering with this school, we learned the value of strongly encouraging, if not requiring youth to at least try a few days of PJP.

3　In some cases, we work with youth who are prohibited from seeing/performing for other court-involved youth. In other cases, the site has restrictions on minors and has prohibited other youth from attending the performance.

4　We have run and supervised PJP projects with various levels of support from a large team of directors, resident teaching artists and guest artists, to one or two resident teaching artists and a community partner. We believe this project can be run by one person, although we find the quality of the performance often deepens with the additional of a designer, project manager, stage manager, and/or a producer. When partnering with a high school theatre class or youth who have theatre experience, some of these roles might be shared between youth ensemble members in the program.

5　Year after year, we return to several of the same partner sites, both on a regular basis and intermittently, to facilitate PJP. We also have highly successful programs and productions that grew out of one-time residencies and partnerships. In this way, our experiences with PJP have taught us to challenge the often-held ideal that teaching artists and community-based theatre artists should always aim to create "intentional, ongoing, sustainable" partnerships in educational settings (for more information on professional development with teachers, see Gursky 2000). We acknowledge the value of ongoing and sustainable partnerships, and we believe that PJP is most successful when we remain open to what a residency or partnership needs, even when this could be a one-time or short-term experience. Various factors influence the length, location, goals and outcomes of a PJP residency. For example, working in juvenile justice contexts with court-involved youth means working with an ensemble of young people who we hope will not be in this system long-term. It also means choosing to work with youth who may transition out as the project is being developed. Similarly, when we have worked in a high school context, we may interface with youth who want a temporary community or who may transition out of a class before a residency ends.

6　Visit the Performing Justice Project Gallery to see examples of documented performance work, as well as interviews with participants about their experiences in the project: https://performingjusticeproject.org/project-category/gallery/.

7　We acknowledge that as white women, we have privileges within the university system; we are not subject to the same scrutiny as faculty and staff of color about how we spend our time, and what kind of creative work is considered publishable, reportable, and valid in a system of higher education. Unfortunately, youth-related arts work and gender and racial justice work is rarely valued within most higher education systems, as demonstrated by the lack of faculty positions and promotions in this area, as well as the limited funding for those that focus their research in these areas. Given this systemic oppression in higher education, we know that our whiteness has often given us access to support for this project and research.

# References for Part Three

Bridgforth, S (2010) 'Finding voice: Anchoring the Austin Project's artistic process,' in O. O. J. L. Jones, L. Moore, and S. Bridgforth (eds.), *Experiments in a jazz aesthetic: Art, activism, academia, and the Austin Project*, Austin: University of Texas Press, pp. 12–25.

Gusky, T. R. (2000) *Evaluating professional development*, Thousand Oaks: Corwin Press, Inc.

Jones, K., Okun, T., Brown, C., Jeffries-Logan, V., Johnson, M., Henderson, J., Kelley, J., and Chapman, C. R. (2016) *Dismantling racism workbook*, viewed July 7, 2019, https://resourcegeneration.org/wp-content/uploads/2018/01/2016-dRworks-workbook.pdf

Okun, T. (2006) 'From white racist to white anti-racist: The life-long journey,' *dRworks*, viewed June 24, 2019 www.dismantlingracism.org/uploads/4/3/5/7/43579015/white_identity_ladder_2013.pdf

Performing Justice Project (2019) *PJP Performance Gallery*, viewed June 26, 2019, https://performingjusticeproject.org/project-category/gallery/

University of Texas Press (2019) 'Description,' viewed June 24, 2019, https://utpress.utexas.edu/books/jonexe

Woodson, S. E. (2015) *Theater for youth third space: Performance, democracy and community cultural development*, Intellect: Chicago.

# Epilogue

# Belonging and Accountability: Doing Justice

As we finish writing this book, horrifying, ugly events continue to unfold all around us—from the daily images on the news of Black, Brown, and trans bodies murdered at the hands of white men to white nationalist marches and published hate speech; from families torn apart and children kept in cages on the border to the ongoing assault on women's bodies and their access to healthcare—events that are both difficult to turn away from and equally difficult to witness. Our work with young people in PJP and with this book reminds us that we must continue to turn toward—towards the

**Figure 4.1** The PJP ensemble faces the audience with a call to accountability. Set design by Becca Drew Ramsey with PJP ensemble. Lighting design by Tameika L. Hannah
Source: Photo by Lynn Hoare.

horrific images of real bodies, real people, real experiences, but also towards each other and the work of doing justice.

How do we develop resilience in the face of such ugliness to continue to turn toward accountability and belonging?[1] adrienne maree brown, in *Pleasure Activism: The Politics of Feeling Good*, reminds us that our greatest sense of belonging is in the spaces of our accountability to and with each other. "It must become an incredible pleasure to be able to be honest, expect to be whole, and to know that we are in a community that will hold us accountable and change with us" (brown 2019, p. 11). We know that making theatre is a site of deep joy and often becomes a space of powerful belonging. It is also a site that calls us to be accountable to each other while simultaneously expanding our sense of what and who we belong to. Through this book and the ongoing work of PJP, we call on each other, we call on you, we call on our collective, radical imagination to create a sense of belonging and accountability that both dreams and enacts justice. We may not fully arrive in this lifetime, we may never be finished with the work. But you and I will know that we belong, we will feel whole for a moment, listening deeply, sharing stories, and practicing loving accountability across difference. All of this is now. All of this is performing justice.

## Note

1    Our ideas of belonging are deeply influenced by the writing of A. C. Rowe. See her article "Moving Relations: On the limits of belonging' for a deeper discussion on this topic (Rowe 2009).

## References

brown, a. m. (2019) *Pleasure activism: The politics of feeling good*, Chico, CA: AK Press.
Rowe, A. C. (2009) 'Moving relations: On the limits of belonging,' *Liminalities: A Journal of Performance Studies*, vol. 5, no. 4, pp. 1–10, viewed July 3, 2019, http://liminalities.net/5-4/movingrelations.pdf

# Appendix A

# Program and Session Plans

## A.1 Performing Justice Project: Pre-Program Invitation Workshop

*This workshop introduces the PJP program to potential youth participants and partners. It is intended to offer a low-risk introduction to the ways we work, as well as the goals and content of a PJP residency.*

**Time**: 45 Minutes
**Materials:** PJP sample video if possible (from the performance gallery at performingjusticeproject.org), butcher paper and marker or blackboard/whiteboard for scribing, PJP materials and paperwork necessary to sign up for PJP

**Performance Action: Creative Introductions** (10 min)
*See Creative Introductions in Section 2.3.1.*

Please introduce your name and your pronouns (share examples: she/her/hers, he/him/his, they/them, ze/hir). Then introduce where you are from by describing a sound, smell, or sight. For example: I am from loud sirens on Saturday night; I am from the smell of wood fire in my clothes; or, I am from rain drizzling outside my window.

**Performance Action: Vote from Your Seat** (10 min)
*See Vote from Your Seat in Section 2.3.2.*

Respond to each statement by standing or sitting. Notice where you are located (sitting or standing) in comparison to others in the group. Please sit down after each statement to reset for the next statement.

- Stand up if you wish were still in bed.
- Stand up if ice cream is one of your favorite things to eat. (If you are standing, share your favorite flavor with a neighbor also standing; if you are sitting, tell a sitting neighbor about one of your favorite foods.)
- Stand up you like to perform—whether or not you have had experience.

- Stand up if you're willing to try some kind of performance.

Thanks to all of you who stood up. This performance project is focused on inviting people to express themselves and to try new things, and our process is open to folks with and without performance experience. Part of our work in PJP is figuring out how performance work might become an act of standing up for your vision of justice.

- Stand up if you ever think that sometimes things aren't fair or just.
- Stand up if you ever feel pressure to behave a specific way because of messages you receive from friends, family or society.
- Stand up if you've ever wished you had the power to change something.

In PJP we think about the experiences we have in the world related to our identities—who we are. We will create performance related to ideas of fairness, justice, power, and what we think needs to be changed. We will stand up with and for each other. Please join us in a circle.

## Performance Action: Thumb Grab (5 min)
*See Thumb Grab in Section 2.3.1.*

## Performance Action: Heads Up (10 min)
*See Heads Up in Section 2.3.1.*

## Guiding reflection

- What do you have to do to be successful in either of these actions?
- How might these skills be related to or helpful in theatre and performance?
- What do you think of when we talk about performance?
- What are different kinds of performance?
- Whether or not you're a performer, or have experience in theatre/performance, these are the kinds of skills that we will use to collaboratively create a performance piece around gender and racial justice. We will work toward a performance piece that we can all feel proud of, but the emphasis will be on a developing a critically engaged, supportive, and collaborative process. As you return to your seats, think about what performance means to you.

## Introduce the Performing Justice Project (5 min)
In this project, we will work with a group, or an ensemble, to create an original performance. We will weave together stories from your lives and experiences with stories and ideas about gender justice and racial justice. There is no story or script that exists yet. That is something we will create together through different exercises. You may have done something like that before, or this might be something completely new for you—either way is okay. You don't need to know how to do this to join PJP.
    Please let us know what questions you have!

## Performance Action: It Made Me Think (5 min)
*See It Made Me Think in Section 2.3.4.*

# A.2 A 90-minute PJP Workshop

*This 90-minute workshop is for groups that are ready to dive into content around racial and gender justice. Rather than opening a devising process, this mini-PJP workshop offers an experience of PJP performance actions in one brief session.*

**Time:** 90 minutes to 2 hours
**Materials:** Notecards and pens, information and/or website for PJP

**Performance Action: Creative Introductions** (10 min)
*See Creative Introductions in Section 2.3.1.*

Please introduce your name, the pronouns you use (share examples: she/her/hers, he/him/his, they/them, ze/hir), and one thing we can't tell by looking at you.

**Performance Action: Group Agreements** (5 min)
*See Group Agreements in Section 2.3.1.*

Take care of yourself and get what you need, speak for yourself rather than others or groups, allow yourself to work in new ways and challenge yourself as you can. Anything else that you would like to add to some basic agreements for our work together?

**Introduction to PJP** (10 min)
PJP directors and/or teaching artist share out overview and goals of PJP, what the performance devising process typically looks like. If possible, share a sample video of a PJP youth performance (see the performance gallery at PerformingJusticeProject. org.).

**Transition**: Today we plan to take you through a very short taste of some performance actions used in the Performing Justice Project.

**Performance Actions** (10 min)

- Thumb Grab (see Section 2.3.1.)
- People, Shelter, Storm (see Section 2.3.1.)
- Round of Applause (see Section 2.3.1)

**Performance Action: Exploding Atom** (10 min)
*See Exploding Atom in Section 2.3.2.*

With each statement, invite participants to notice where they are located in comparison to others in the group.

- I grew up talking openly about race.
  *Ask participants to share with a neighbor why they are standing where they are standing.*

- I grew up talking openly about gender.
  *Ask for volunteers to share why they are standing where they are standing.*

- I have experienced injustice related to an identity I hold.
  *Ask participants to notice where they are standing in reference to others, just notice, don't discuss.*

- My identities impact what I am able to get done (in my life, or where I work or study).
  *Ask participants to notice where they are standing in reference to others, just notice, don't discuss.*

- I can create a more just world.
  *Ask for volunteers to share why they are standing where they are standing.*

The Performing Justice Project is about creating original performance about experiences of race and gender, and using performance to build individual and ensemble awareness of racial justice and gender justice. In this next performance action, we encourage you to think about your personal experiences of race and/ or gender.

### Performance Action: Six-Word Stories About Race/Gender (15 min)
*See Six-Word Stories in Section 2.3.2.*

The Race Card Project by Michele Norris, has inspired this next action, which is to write your own very short story or experience through six words. Although the original Race Card Project addresses race, we are going to invite you to respond to experiences of race or gender for this next action. We will share some samples, but you can find many more—and submit your own—at TheRaceCardProject.com. After we share some examples we will guide you through quickly writing and activating some of your own six-word stories about race or gender.

Gender (examples written by our PJP directors and teaching artists):

- Shutup! My body isn't your business.
- Little girls are more than dolls.
- woman, girl, no. who am I?
- Lately, I love my body hair.

Race (from the Race Card Project website):

- Black male in hoodie equals trouble.
- You don't look like a Latina.
- Only black woman in the room, again!
- Borderlands born. Always illegal. Always home
- Native American. We are still here.

On a notecard, write a six-word story about your experience with gender or race. You may write as many six-word stories as you want, but only include one per notecard.

**Performance Action: Activating Text Through Image** (20 min)
*See Activating Text Through Image in Section 2.3.2.*

- Choose only one story from the group to focus on staging as a triad.
- Use your bodies to create a frozen image, or a picture, that represents something new about the story.
- Practice sharing the text out loud in combination with the frozen image. Where will you add the text? How many people will speak the text? Will the text repeat?
- Rehearse how you will share this with the rest of the group.
- Each group performs the image and text for the rest of the group.

**Performance Action: It Made Me Think** (10 min)
*See It Made Me Think in Section 2.3.4.*

Thank you for your work and for playing with us today. If you want to find out more about PJP, please see the website for information and videos of past productions with youth: performingjusticeproject.org.

# A.3 PJP Residency Overview

*This chart shares one way to scaffold and combine performance actions over the course of 14 sessions, including performance and closing reflection.*

**Table A.1** PJP residency overview: session plan outlines for 14 three-hour sessions.

| Session One: Ensemble | Session Two: Ensemble | Session Three: Who Am I? |
| --- | --- | --- |
| Thumb Grab | Check In with Thumbs | Check in With Thumbs |
| Round of Applause | Ta-Da-Da | Name and Gesture |
| Creative Introductions | Group Rhythms | Round of Applause |
| PJP Overview and | Group Agreements | "I Am" Spoken Word |
| Participation | Heads Up | Snack Break |
| Number Up | Mapping Geographies | Rehearse and Perform |
| Keep 'Em Standing | Who Am I? Word Web | Spoken Word |
| Snack Break | Snack Break | Brainstorm Performance Title |
| Name and Gesture | Journal Writing: Reflection | Costume Check In: t-shirt |
| Cover the Space | on Ensemble and Justice | design and size request |
| On the Line | Check Out | Journal Reflection on |
| Machines as Warm Up | | "Who Am I?" |
| What is Ensemble? | | Check Out |
| Check Out | | |

**Table A.1** Cont.

| Session Four: Who Am I? | Session Five: Who Am I? | Session Six: What Is Justice? |
|---|---|---|
| Check In With Thumbs | Check In | Check In with Creative |
| Hey! | People to People | Introductions |
| Exploding Atom: Gender | Guest Artist: Poetry | Number Up |
| Journal Writing: Gender | Performance | Columbian Hypnosis |
| Gender Cards: Six Word | Go-Stop/Name-Jump/ | The Great Game of Power |
| Stories | Knees-Arms | Snack Break |
| Image Work: Gender | Vote with Your Feet: Race | In Society… with 8-Count |
| Snack Break | Defining Race and Ethnicity | Movement |
| Alphabet Relay: Gender | Snack Break | Rehearse: |
| Defining and Identifying | Round of Applause | • Mapping Geographies |
| Gender, Sex, and Attraction | Race Cards: Six-Word | • Spoken Word |
| Activate Gender | Stories | • Gender Cards |
| Cards: Scene Work | Activate Race Cards: Image | • Race Cards |
| In Society… Brainstorm | Work, Scenes, or | • 8-Count Movement |
| Check Out | Monologues | Check Out |
| | Check Out | |

| Session Seven: What Is Justice? | Session Eight: How Do I Perform Justice? | Session Nine: How Do I Perform Justice? |
|---|---|---|
| Check In | Check In | Check In |
| Your Greatest Fan | Everyone's It Tag | Send a Snap |
| Flocking | Human Knot | Carnival in Rio |
| Hashtag Activism | Justice for Women Means… | Rehearse Song for Opening |
| Hash Stories | Activate with Complete | Learn Song for Closing |
| Snack Break | the Image | This I Believe |
| Activate Statistics | Snack Break | Snack Break |
| Rehearse Bits of Material | Song for Script Opening | Collecting and Reviewing |
| Check Out | Refining and Staging Stories: | Content |
| | • From Story to | Refining and Staging Stories |
| | Performance Text | Check Out |
| | • Creating Character | *Directors: Script |
| | Dialogue | Development on Your Own |
| | • Activating Text Vocally | |
| | • Activating Text Physically | |
| | Check Out | |

| Session 10: How Do I Perform Justice? | Session 11: How Do I Perform Justice? | Session 12: How Do I Perform Justice? |
|---|---|---|
| Check In | Check In | Check In |
| Zip, Zap, Zop | Everyone's It Tag | Dress Rehearsal |
| Overview of Performance | Devise New Material | Check Out |
| Script/Outline | As Needed | |
| Rehearse Material | Rehearse with Attention to | |
| Record Voiceovers | Groupings | |
| Sound/Space/Aesthetics | Costumes: distribute/try on | |
| Check Out | t-shirts | |
| | Check Out | |

| Session 13: Performance! | Session 14: Reflection, Closing, Celebration! | Follow Up: Return journals and other personal items to youth. |
|---|---|---|

# Daily Session Plan: Week 1, Day 2 (Three-Hour Sessions)

This example of a three-hour session plan from the first week of a PJP residency models how PJP performance actions move participants quickly into exploring identity and devising small bits of performance material.

## Focus: Developing Ensemble, Listening, and Who Am I?

**Time**: three hours

**Materials**: five chairs and a water bottle, notecards, butcher paper (hang on the wall for group agreements), extra pieces of butcher paper for social location maps, sample social location maps, tape, markers, pencils, journals

### 8:30–8:35 Performance Action: Check-in Circle

*See Check-in Circle in Section 2.3.1.*

Check-In with Thumbs: To begin, let us know how your day is going with a thumbs up, sideways or down.

Today, we are going to focus on *listening* and *who am I?* Part of being in an ensemble and creating performance together means that we have to listen carefully to each other. A lot of our performance actions require you to listen carefully, so bring your attention and your best listening self.

### 8:35–8:45 Performance Action: Ta-da-da (see Section 2.3.1)
### 8:45–8:55 Performance Action: Group Rhythms (see Section 2.3.1)

Transition to semi-circle sitting in front of paper on wall.

### 8:55–9:10 Performance Action: Group Agreements

*See Group Agreements in Section 2.3.1.*

Record ideas on poster to sign on Wednesday when our group is finalized.

### 9:10–9:45 Performance Action: Mapping Geographies

*See Mapping Geographies in Section 2.3.2.*

String a series of images and movements together. Rehearse them. If time, have half the group perform while the other half witnesses. If time, play with adding different music.

### 9:45–10:15 Performance Action: Who Am I? Word Web

*See Who Am I? Word Web in Section 2.3.2.*

10:15–10:35 Snack break

### 10:35–11:00 Performance Action: The Great Game of Power

*See The Great Game of Power in Section 2.3.3.*

### 11:00–11:10 Journals/Reflection

As a part of PJP, we will be asking you to write your thoughts in response to different questions. This will also be a place where you might do some writing that will become part of our performance. The PJP team will be reading your journals and your counselor might also see them, but your journals will not go back to your dorms and you will get to choose what gets shared out in our group or for a public audience. When our residency is over, you will get to hold onto your journals.

We are going to pass out journals and give you a few minutes to write your name inside and you are welcome to decorate the cover. Please write your name clearly so that we know who each journal belongs to. We will be using them regularly and will make sure you get yours back.

**Performance Action: What is Ensemble?** (revised for journal reflection)
In your journal, take a few minutes to reflect on and answer the following questions:

1.    What is one thing you bring to the ensemble, that you are committed to bringing, even when things feel difficult?
2.    What is one thing you learned about yourself or someone else today that surprised you?
3.    One question you have about the things we worked on today—a question (that maybe could become a title?) related to the Great Game of Power or the Social Location Mapping.

11:10–11:15 **Closing reflection**
**One word/phrase check-out.** What are you thinking about as you leave today?


# Daily Session Plan: Week 2, Day 3 (Three-Hour Sessions)

*This example of a three-hour session plan from the second week of a residency models how "small bits" created in earlier PJP sessions are developed into performance pieces.*

### Focus: Developing story and performance pieces
**Time**: 3 hours
**Materials**: Stack of white typing paper, journals, pieces of paper from butcher roll, three half-page posters and markers, ten sheets of printer paper for writing final copy, four printouts of sample hashtag story

### 8:30–8:45 Performance Actions: Check-in Circle and Keep 'Em Standing
*See Check-in Circle and Keep 'Em Standing in Section 2.3.1.*
Today we are focusing on finishing spoken word pieces, developing some new writing, and moving some ideas into brief scenes. We are also going to learn a song that we think might work as an opening for the performance—something we could all sing together as we move into the theatre.

### 8:45–9:15 Vocal Warm-up and Song
Begin with a vocal warm-up such as breathing together and face massage. Breathe into different parts of face.
    Lip trills
    Sirens

## Teach and Rehearse Song
We Rise, written by Rhiannon Giddens

> Song lyrics for chorus (which is all we will use)
> Sister of my tears
> Sister of my cries
> Hand in hand, we take a stand
> We push, we reach, we rise
> We rise, we rise, we rise
> Hand in hand, we take a stand
> We push, we reach, we rise

Reflect with the group: What does this song mean to you? How is this song related to performing gender and racial justice?

### 9:15–9:20 Transition into Devising Stations
We are going to spend the rest of our time today developing pieces you have started and creating some new work. We will do this by visiting three different "stations" where you will get to work on something different at each station.

- **Station Purple:** Writing Hashtag Stories
- **Station Orange:** From 8-Count Movement to Devised Scene
- **Station Green:** From Story to Performance Text

You will visit all three stations. At the end of today, you will have created more bits of performance that will move into the script. You will have 25 minutes at each station to write or revise some material.

## Divide into Rotation Groups
9:20–9:45 **Stations Round 1**
9:50–10:20 **Stations Round 2**
10:20–10:35 **Snack break**
10:35–11:05 **Stations Round 3**
11:05–11:10 **Guided Journal Writing**

What was devised today that you hope gets used in our performance? Take a moment to look through your entire journal and star the things you would like to have included in the performance if possible, and put an X next to the things that you do *not* want included in the performance. Let us know if you want to talk through any of these pieces as you are making your decisions.

### 11:10–11:15 Closing Performance Action: It Made Me Think
*See It Made Me Think in Section 2.3.4.*

Share a word or phrase from today—something that stuck with you in a significant way, and follow it by saying "It made me think." Example: "Hashtag, It made me think."

## Daily Session Plan: Rehearsal: Week 3, Day 1 (Three-Hour Sessions)

*This example of a three-hour session plan from the final week of a PJP residency models an early rehearsal as a transitional step, rehearsing the sequence of already-developed pieces while continuing to support the development of solo and ensemble pieces.*

### 8:30–9:00 **Performance Actions**

- Check-in Circle (see Section 2.3.1)
- Columbian Hypnosis (see Section 2.3.3)
- Flocking (see Section 2.3.1)
- Vocal Warm-up and Sing Opening Song (see Section 2.3.4)

### 9:00–9:20 **Share and Discuss Script/Performance Sequence:**

- Opening: We Are the Ones
- Act 1: Group Spoken Word, My Name Is, A Baby is Born, In Society Women Are Expected To…, 8-Count Movements
- Act 2: Three Short Scenes
- Act 3: Hashtag Scene, Monologue, Scene
- Act 4: Activated Statistics: Scene, Monologue, Scene
- Act 5: Hashtag Scene, Hashtag Scene, Hashtag Scene
- Act 6: Group Poem and Justice Machine
- Closing: We Rise, Invite the Audience to Sing

### 9:20–9:45 **Performance Action: Rehearse 8 Count Movement** (see Section 2.3.3)
### 9:45–10:20 **Performance Action: Activating Text with Sound** (see Section 2.3.4)
*Read, Record Statistics*

Divide into three groups with PJP Teaching Artists supporting the work in each group. We are going to move into small groups and hand out the gender and racial justice statistics you have been working with. Each group will have 3–4 different statistics. Read the statistic with your small group, decide what it means or makes you think about, and decide how you might perform it vocally. We will audio record your group performing the statistic vocally and the voiceover will be woven throughout the performance at different times. Think about how to use your voices, repeat words or emphasize words, or speak together to help your audience members know what to listen to and what is important in the statistic. Lastly, decide on a hashtag that describes this statistic. Let's end each recording with the hashtag that you create.

### 10:20–10:35 **Break**
### 10:35–10:50 **Performance Action: Activating Text Vocally**
*See Activating Text Vocally in Section 2.3.4.*

Introduce Group Poems curated from lines of text that each participants wrote separately in their journals:

- Group Poem: My Name Is
- Group Poem: Justice for Women Looks Like…

## 10:50–11:05 **Script Approval**
Bring copies of everyone's pieces for them to read and approve. Hand them out, invite participants work on their own, supporting as necessary.

## 11:05–11:15 **Closing Circle**
What is one thing you are excited about? What is one thing you are feeling nervous about?

# A.4 "I Am" Spoken Word Outline in English

Emily Aguilar and Megan Nevels, PJP Guest Artists

I AM…
Line 1: My name is…
Line 2: My skin looks like…
Line 3: My body feels like…
Line 4: My voice tells me…

Repeat (from above) line 2
Line 5: My mind thinks…
Repeat (from above) line 4
Line 6: You should know…

Repeat (from above) line 5
Line 7: My hands want…
Repeat (from above) line 6
Line 8: My feet want…

Repeat (from above) line 7
Line 9: The world says…
Repeat (from above) line 8
Line 10: I say…

Repeat (from above) line 9
Line 11: Today I am…
Repeat (from above) line 10
Line 12: Tomorrow I will be…

Create your final line with three words from the poem.
Give your piece a title.

## A.5 "Yo Estoy" Spoken Word Outline in Spanish

Emily Aguilar and Megan Nevels, PJP Guest Artists

YO ESTOY...

Línea 1: Mi nombre es...
Línea 2: Mi piel parece...
Línea 3: Mi cuerpo se siente como...
Línea 4: Mi voz me dice...

Repita la línea 2
Línea 5: Mi mente piensa...
Repita la línea 4
Línea 6: Usted debe saber...

Repita la línea 5
Línea 7: Mis manos quieren...
Repita la línea 6
Línea 8: Mis pies quieren...

Repita la línea 7
Línea 9: El mundo dice...
Repita la línea 8
Línea 10: Digo...

Repita la línea 9
Línea 11: Hoy estoy...
Repita la línea 10
Línea 12: Mañana estaré...

Cree su línea final con 3 palabras del poema.

# Appendix B

# Script Outlines

## B.1 Performance Outline: "The Good In Me/In My Skin"

*Devised with youth in juvenile justice facility and performed for a public audience at a local theatre.*

### Act 1: Opening

1.  **We Are the Ones** (song); *whole group, divided in halves, enters from both sides to meet center onstage*
2.  **The Good In Me...** (group spoken word piece with movement); *whole group*
3.  **A Baby is Born—Is it a Boy?** (audio recorded scene with movement); *small group*
4.  **Women Are Supposed To...** (voiceover of a poem into music); *text recorded, played over next action*
5.  **8-Count Movement**; *ensemble movement pieces with half of the group*

### Act 2: Short Scenes

6.  **Mom Home from Hospital with Baby**; *small group*
    Stat: single motherhood and income levels (recorded)
7.  **Wife Gets Promotion**; *small group*
    Stat on leadership and income levels (recorded)
8.  **Dress to Impress**; *small group*

**Transition:** Stats on self-worth related to gender, race, and youth (recorded)

## Act 3: I Am Enough (Personal Pieces)

9. **We Were Here First**; *solo piece*
   #Whyamltreateddifferently?
10. **No sabes nada de me**; *solo piece*
    #Whyamltreateddifferently?
    STAT on Suicide (Recorded)
11. **Dust to Dust**; *solo spoken word*
    #Whyamltreateddifferently?
12. **Tia's Morning Rules**; *solo piece*
    #Whyamltreateddifferently?
13. **I Do Know How to Swim**; *solo piece*

**Transition:** Stat on sexual assault (recorded)

## Act 4: Trust Issues

14. **Princes Get Your S\*\*\* Together**; *small group*
    Stat: street harassment (recorded)
15. **Group Hashtag Stories: #Trust Issues**; *small group*
    Stat: sexual violence (recorded)
16. **Group Poem: Yours Truly, a Letter from Your Daughter**; *small group*
    #trustissues
17. **Dear Mom**; *small group*
    #trustissues

**Transition:** Stat on education (recorded) and prison (recorded)

## Act 5: The System

18. **Once Upon a Time**; *solo piece with group movement*
    #thisiswhathappened
    #shewasaminor
    #howlgotintothesystem
19. **Every Girl Should Be Safe**; *solo piece with group choral support*
    #hesnotinthesystem
20. **Because I'm Black. Because I'm Latino**, *solo piece*
    #don'tjudgemysexuality
    #changetheSystem
    Stat: incarceration and LGBTQ identities (recorded)

**Transition**
**Dance**: Queen

## Act 6: We Rise

21. **Speak Up: From My Voice**; (group poem), *whole group*
    Stat: young people rise: teen involvement in community (recorded)
22. **Justice for Women Looks Like** (group poem); *whole group*
23. **We are the Ones We've Been Waiting For** (song); *whole group*

*This script was devised by youth participants and put together by PJP directors and teaching artists Megan Alrutz, Lynn Hoare, Kristen Hogan, Briana Barner, Tamara Carroll, Cortney McEniry.*

# B.2 Performance Outline: "Imagining a Just World"

*This performance was created with eighth graders at a public middle school and was performed for peers and family through two performances.*

## Act 1: Questions
Can you imagine what a just world would look like? *(Whole group movement and text)*

## Act 2: Facts
Individual actors step up to share their fact and once finished, mix back into the collective, which shifts ritualistically between the different statements.

## Act 3: Power
The evolution of power.
*The actors perform eight-count movements that represent the evolution of power in society.*

## Act 4: Stories of Injustice
Actors shift to sit in front of the audience facing individuals who share stories of injustice.

**Collective**: If you saw injustice would you speak up and try to stop it?
Personal Story
**Collective**: Can you imagine a world without stereotypes?
Personal story
**Collective**: Can you imagine a world without racism?
Personal Story
**Collective**: Can you imagine a world without violence?

## Act 5: Group Poem

*Actors move to their final positions for group poem:* Is Equality Enough?

*This script was devised by youth participants and put together by PJP teaching artists and performance directors: Emily Freeman and Victoria Dominguez.*

# B.3 Performance Outline: "(I Am) More Than Society Thinks"

*This performance was created with youth in a juvenile justice facility, and performed in the facility for staff and families.*

OPENING

Audience hears recording of a personal journal entry. Actors enter and sit while the journal entry plays. One actor stands and looks at the audience.

**Scene 1: Justice for Women** (solo performance)

**Scene 2: Justice for Women** (group poem)
Being a woman means…
Ends on "to be honest" as ALL get in place on stage for the 8-Count Movement.

**Scene 3: 8-Count Movement** (whole group movement piece to recorded music)
Song: "I Decided" by Solange

**Scene 4: Respectability and Judgment Scene** (whole group scene)

**Scene 5: Mapping Geographies** (whole group movement piece to recorded music)
Song: "Beautiful" by India.Arie
Some actors sit where they are at the end of Mapping Geographies. Some move to the other side of the stage.

**Scene 6: My Name Is…** (solo spoken word)

**Scene 7: Cumbia Dance Scene** (small group scene)

**Scene 8: Hands Up, Don't Shoot Scene** (solo spoken word)
Individual actor sings "Lay Me Down" behind solo spoken word.

**Scene 9: Snap Scene** (actors invite audience to participate)
**Actor:** For our last scene, we want to invite anyone who would like to join us to come stand in a circle with us, open to the audience.
Actors demonstrate passing a snap with audience members, and then add in word association.

- peace
- hope
- love
- justice

Thank you. You may return to your seats.

"To Be Honest" spoken word pieces support transitions as actors get in place for final song.

Closing Song: "Everyday People" (whole group sings)

*This script was devised by youth participants and put together by PJP teaching artists and performance directors: Briana Barner and Cortney McEniry.*

# Appendix C

## Performing Justice Project Support Documents

# C.1 Performing Justice Project Informational Flyer, 2014

## Performing Justice Project 2014

**PJP Model**
The Performing Justice Project (PJP)
* generates performance workshops with youth to explore their relationship to gender and racial justice,
* engages high school youth, many of whom have little to no theatre experience, in the devising of original performance materials imagining justice, and
* draws on live performance and digital storytelling to activate awareness and dialogue around personal and community change.

The PJP draws on personal story, creative writing, and a variety of performance-based skills and techniques to engage the experience and wisdom of young people. Based on our 2011, 2012 and 2013 pilot programs, this model is in development as a national performance project for schools and community-based sites that work with under-served and underrepresented populations.

**PJP People and Support**
PJP was founded in 2011 with the support of The Center for Women's & Gender Studies, UT Austin, and the Embrey Family Foundation, to develop a model for facilitating socially and critically engaged performing arts with young people.

Founding co-directors of the program are:
* Megan Alrutz, PhD, Assistant Professor, Department of Theatre & Dance, UT Austin
* Lynn Hoare, MFA, Theatre for Dialogue Specialist, Voices Against Violence, UT Austin

**What to Expect**
The PJP facilitators engage youth in performance workshops to explore the vocabulary and embodiment of imagining gender and racial justice.
* The PJP works in collaboration with teachers and community partners.
* Spring programs take place over approximately 12 sessions and usually run 6 to 12 weeks.
* The PJP culminates with a sharing of youth work with peers and/or an invited audience.
* In support of the PJP model, we conduct pre- and post-project evaluations with participants.

**PJP Video of Past Programs**
PJP 2012 Ann Richards School: http://www.youtube.com/watch?v=7iOugSQeyS4&feature=plcp
PJP 2011 Garza HS: http://www.youtube.com/watch?v=CiqfhQboAls&feature=plcp

*The Performing Justice Project is a project of the Center for Women's & Gender Studies Embrey Critical Human Rights Initiative at The University of Texas at Austin.*

*For more information, contact:* Mollie Marchione, PhD, Associate Director, Center for Women's & Gender Studies, UT Austin  mmarchione@austin.utexas.edu  512-471-5666.

# C.2 Partnership Assessment

*We have come to rely on the following list of questions to assess the fit of a community partner/location (either to guide a discussion with a potential site partner, or to use to assess a fit for a particular project).*

## Youth

- Who does this site serve? Where do youth come from and what brings them here?
- What kind of arts experiences do the youth have at this site and what are they interested in?
- What do we need to know about the youth involved, including specific learning styles, individual needs, site expectations about participation and/or behavior, and how they participate in group processes?
- How might youth at this site engage with the project? Is there a need or desire for the work?
- Is there an incentive for youth to participate? Will they have a choice whether or not to take part? Or will we work with a specific group—such as a class or program?
- What are the identity markers of the group, including racial and ethnic identities and gender identities?

## Site Partner

- In what ways can staff/administration/leaders at this site support this project?
- Will staff from the site be in the room during the project?
- What would the site need from our PJP teaching artists and directors, in terms of paperwork, background checks, training or orientation?
- What are community partner/site expectations for a PJP process (goals, number of youth participating, hours, supplies, performance opportunities, etc.)?
- What kind of expectations or completion requirements are there for youth involved?
- How would the site recommend inviting youth into this project? Does the site have a structure in place for deciding who will be involved?
- How does the site handle challenges and conflict? What rules, expectations, or boundaries do we need to be aware of?
- How does this system/institution meet the needs of young people and what support systems are in place already?
- What kind of arts do youth at this site already have access to, if any?
- What is important to this site in partnerships and collaborations?
- Who might attend a public performance and how is this site connected to the community?

- What kind of room/space is available to dedicate to the project, and will it work for a performance devising process?
- What are the options for performance at the site? Are youth able to travel to a performance location? If so, do we have access to transportation for youth?

## PJP Fit

- Do schedules align between teaching artists/directors and when youth are available?
- How will the PJP process need to adapt to work with this partner and the youth associated with the site (including number of sessions, timing, distance, number of students, make up of group, content development, etc.)?

# C.3 Memorandum of Understanding

## The Performing Justice Project (at Site Partner Name)
## (DATE)

This Memorandum of Agreement is between (Site Partner Contact) and (Site Partner/Location), the Performing Justice Project through the Center for Women's and Gender Studies at The University of Texas at Austin and funded by the Embrey Foundation and graduate student teaching artists: (Names of Teaching Artists). The Performing Justice Project (PJP) is an ongoing model created by Megan Alrutz, Lynn Hoare and Kristen Hogan.

The purpose of this agreement is to outline the expectations between both parties as we enter into a residency partnership at (Name of Site Partner/Location). The Performing Justice Project addresses topics of contemporary social justice, including race and gender justice, using drama, theatre, and feminist pedagogies.

**Scope of Project:** The Performing Justice Project facilitates the creation of performanceprojects with youth to explore their relationship to gender and racial justice. This project assists high school youth in devising a performance piece that imagines social justice, making social change relevant and important in their lives.

**Services Provided:** During the X-week residency, teaching artists, (Name) and (Name), will facilitate a total of X dates (plus performance date). (Teaching Artists) will develop the session plans and curriculum on their own, while consulting (Contact) with any questions. Session plans will be provided the week of facilitation via email. The final performance will be the week of (Date) during the session time (or alternate performance time, if possible). This memorandum of agreement outlines this specific residency. Future collaborations with the Performing Justice Project will be discussed as needed.

**Copyright:** After the completion of the Performing Justice Project residency, (Contact) has the privilege to use any and all written and developed materials created by (Teaching Artists) but we request that these materials are not shared beyond (Contact). If the Performance Justice Project session plans are used in the future, (Teaching Artists) and the Performing Justice Project should be cited as follows: All materials are created by (Teaching Artist Names) while working with the Performing Justice Project through the Center for Women's and Gender Studies at the University of Texas at Austin. Use of the Performing Justice Project name requires permission from Lynn Hoare and Megan Alrutz. As part of developing the Performing Justice Project model, Lynn Hoare and Megan Alrutz may quote from experiences of and narratives from the Performing Justice Project in published work that discusses the Performing Justice Project.

**Communication Expectations:** Most communication will take place over email, but we are open to phone conversations as needed (e.g., last-minute schedule changes, emergency situations, stuck in traffic).

- (Include all relevant phone numbers and email addresses for all primary contacts, including Teaching Artists, Site Contact and PJP Directors/staff)

Scheduled Dates and Times for PJP Residency:

List of Dates in Residence:
List of Times in Residence:

Performing Justice Project agreements specific to this project:

- (Teaching Artists) will provide (Contact) with advanced notice on potential use of library resources, ensuring that (Contact) has enough time to contact the librarian to reserve use of resources.
- All photos, videos, recordings, and student writing collected during the X week residency are subject to use by the Center for Women's and Gender Studies at the University of Texas at Austin, (Teaching Artists), and other representatives of The Performing Justice Project and the Embrey Family Foundation. Photos and video may be used for evaluation, publicity, and grant funding.
- Student participants/Guardian in PJP will be asked to sign media releases. Those students who do not sign a media release will not be featured in any public documentation.
- The performance will occur during the agreed upon session time, and may include outside audiences.
- Prior to the start of the residency (Teaching Artists) will visit youth and provide a pre-evaluation form. After the residency (Teaching Artists) will provide a post evaluation, either in the form of an informal sharing, or in the form of a written reflection.
- (Contact) will be responsible for any required or necessary student evaluation (and grading, if applicable) throughout the residency.
- Throughout the residency, students will write in notebooks that remain (at the site with Contact).

# C.4 PJP Press Release Sample

(Contact)                                            FOR IMMEDIATE RELEASE: (DATE)
Performing Justice Project
(phone number)
(email)

### Young People Create Theatre to Enact Racial and Gender Justice

**Austin, TX:** The Performing Justice Project (PJP), a signature project of UT-Austin's Center for Women's and Gender Studies, presents a dynamic original performance, written by and about the lived experiences of young women. In collaboration with Teatro Vivo, the performance will take place on Saturday, June 27, 2015 at 1:00 p.m. at the Emma S. Barrientos Mexican American Community Center on 600 River Street, in Austin, TX.

With guidance from artists and allies in the Performing Justice Project, a group youth have grappled with often difficult topics, including economic injustice, feminism, race, gender, and sexuality, in the making of their latest performance. Through a month-long summer intensive these young women, ages 13–18, collaborate with graduate students, faculty, and staff from the University of Texas at Austin to perform personal stories and experiences that speak back to a society that often ignores and excludes their voices.

During the devising process for their current performance, *The Good in Me/In My Skin,* the participants have collaborated with spoken word and performance artists Emily Aguilar Thomas and Megan Nevels, as well as poet Morgan Collado and performance artist Hayley Morgenstern. They have also discussed how their race and gender impacts the way they move through the world. This latest performance includes original writings from the participants, along with movement, dance, and song.

The Performing Justice Project was created by Dr. Megan Alrutz and Lynn Hoare, MFA, with support and collaboration from Dr. Kristen Hogan. This year's production was devised with the support of three dynamic graduate students from UT Austin, Briana Barner (Women's and Gender Studies), Tamara Carroll (Theatre and Dance), and Cortney McEniry (Theatre and Dance), as well as designers Tameika L. Hannah and Becca Drew Ramsey. The program, now in its fourth year and in development as a national performance model, generates theatre with youth to explore their relationship to gender and racial justice, and engages young participants with little or no theatre experience in creating theatre.

PJP prepares students, audience members, and teachers to understand, talk about, and enact gender and racial justice. The Performing Justice Project is a signature project of the Center for Women's and Gender Studies at the University of Texas at Austin, and is generously supported by the Embrey Family Foundation.

For more information, please contact:

# C.5 Video/Photo Media Release

### Performing Justice Project at (Site Partner/Location)

I hereby agree that representatives from the Center for Women's & Gender Studies, UT Austin, and (Site Partner/Location) have the right to take or use photographs or record video of me (and/or my property) during rehearsal and performances of the Performing Justice Project and to use these in any and all media including online for any educational purpose.

I waive any rights, claims or interest I may have to control the use of my identity or likeness in the photographs and agree that any educational uses may be made without compensation or notification to me.

Initial one of the following:

_____ I consent that my name and identity may be revealed therein or by descriptive text or commentary.

_____ I require that my name and identity be anonymous in descriptive text or commentary.

_____ I do not give consent to be audio/visually recorded.

I have read and understand the above statement and am competent to execute this agreement.

Student
Name_____Date_____

Student
Signature_____Date_____

Parent/Guardian
Signature_____Date_____

# C.6  Participant Evaluation for Performing Justice Project

*Please rate yourself on the following items both <u>before PJP</u> (on the left)*
*and <u>right now</u> (on the right):*

| Before PJP began | | | | Statement | Now (at the present time) | | | |
|---|---|---|---|---|---|---|---|---|
| Not at all | Kind Of | Yes | I'm really good at this | | Not at all | Kind Of | Yes | I'm really good at this |
| | | | | I can identify <u>gender injustice</u> in my life and my community. | | | | |
| | | | | I can identify <u>racial injustice</u> in my life and my community. | | | | |
| | | | | I feel confident about talking with other people about gender and racial justice. | | | | |
| | | | | I listen to and respect others while working together. | | | | |
| | | | | I identify as an activist, as someone who will speak up against racial and gender injustice. | | | | |

What have you learned about gender and racial justice? Be as specific as possible.

If you could describe PJP to other people, what would you say?

How have you changed from being part of PJP?

Would you participate in this project again? Why or why not?

What do you imagine a world with more justice looks like?

What are some specific actions you will take to help make the world a better place?

# C.7 Audience Evaluation for Performing Justice Project

*Please take a few minutes to complete this survey.*
*Your feedback helps support future performances. Thank you!*

| Please check the appropriate box on the right: | Very | Moderately | Slightly | Not at All |
|---|---|---|---|---|
| How much has this performance raised your awareness of gender and racial justice? | | | | |
| How much did this performance raise your awareness of gender and racial justice in Austin? | | | | |
| How likely are you to talk the information presented in this performance in discussions with your family, friends, communities, or work? | | | | |

1. Was there any information that changed your perspective on racial and gender justice? If so, what?

2. What is the most important piece of information you are taking away with you today?

3. What was your favorite part of the performance? Why or how so?

4. How has this performance affected how you think about gender or racial justice?

*Thank you for your feedback!*

# Appendix D

# Roles, Tasks, and Supplies

## D.1 Team Roles and Tasks

**Communications:** Write and disseminate project overview for partners/families, save the date announcement for performance, create invitation and cultivate audience, write and send press release, write thank you notes to partners and other important stakeholders after program ends.

**Space/Schedule/Transportation Logistics:** Coordinate rehearsal needs and location, coordinate or book performance space, communicate site needs and plans with partnering organization, coordinate transportation needs (on a daily basis or as needed for performance location); coordinate and communicate schedules with site partner, youth, and directors/teaching artists as well as guest artists.

**Purchase Supplies:** Purchase and distribute supplies, design, coordinate, order, and distribute t-shirts, research, order necessary performance props/supplies (such as notebooks to hold scripts).

**Design, Order, and Purchase T-shirts:** Work with team to design shirts that are related to PJP process. Multiple designs may be voted on by ensemble. Allow youth to choose sizes, order shirts for youth, PJP artists/directors, program site staff, various stakeholders.

**Budget Management:** Oversee budget and track and manage expenses, including: food (both daily snacks as well as food for a performance reception), t-shirts for performance, musicians, guest artists, designers, space, performance programs, daily workshop supplies.

**Guest Artist Logistics:** Contact artists, handle logistics of timing and pay, find artists that complement PJP teaching artist skill set. Communicate schedule, send reminders and thank-you notes after visit.

**Performance Action Session Plans and Residency Plans:** Track and record daily updates of session plans as they change, print out as necessary for team, track what is written by youth in journals as potential performance material.

**Capture Residency and Archive Material:** Support production of promotional and archival video or audio (and photos if allowed at the site). Capture material produced for performance, either through audio track, video/photo or script/text.

**Script Writing:** Track "small bits" for potential inclusion in performance, track original authors along with performers, update script daily, dramaturg script/performance, organize and coordinate layout and printing of script in format that supports performance, update as necessary.

**Permissions, Evaluation, Reporting:** Produce, distribute, and collect necessary permission forms prior to project start date, including permission to participate (if necessary), Photographic and Video Consent and Release Form, create, conduct, and synthesize evaluations for all participants, including youth performers, audience members and resident teaching artists prior to close of project.

**Stage Management (throughout process and through performance):** Coordinate prep for daily program needs including snacks, materials and space, review daily materials consistency and quality), manage all production elements, handle schedules of visiting artists and support people.

**Production Management:** Produce performance program (includes collecting information, designing and producing the program digitally), develop or coordinate development of logo for program and t-shirts, print and distribute program, coordinate with designers (set, costume, lighting).

**Event Management:** Coordinate and produce final event/celebration, including any food purchase, set the agenda and flow of events, procure gifts for participants and partners, make sure appropriate people are invited to both performance and any closing events.

# D.2 Supply List

1.  Journals, 3.5" × 5.5", plain colored, no staples or wire allowed (for a juvenile justice location); enough for one per participant with a few extras (always have extras on hand for those that get lost during the process). We look for small journals that can be decorated on the outside, and journals that are desirable and special rather than common spiral bound notebooks or composition books. We put time into finding the right journal so that participants feel that this place they will do some personal writing is special.
2.  Name Labels—at least for the first five sessions until all directors/artists know the names of participants
3.  Scented marker boxes × 4, or regular markers (scented are more fun)
4.  Masking tape × 3 rolls
5.  One box of quart-sized zip-top bags
6.  One battery operated pencil sharpener
7.  One box of sharpened pencils × 50

8. Index cards and sticky notes (lots and a variety of colors of sticky notes)
9. A large roll of butcher paper
10. Daily snacks (individually wrapped small bags)
11. Small black binders for performance (we prefer 5.5" × 8.5" so that performers can hold them with one hand onstage without blocking their faces)

# Appendix E

# Sample Infographic: Systemic Oppression Through Statistics

## WHAT DOES *Injustice* LOOK LIKE?

### LEADERSHIP

Only **1 out of 10** governors are women. Only **4 out of 100** governors are women of color.

The United States ranks **60th** globally for women's political empowerment.

**16 AND 17-YEAR-OLDS** are the only age group of women in which a majority are involved in their communities.

### VIOLENCE

In the US, **1 in 3** girls is a victim of physical, emotional or verbal abuse from a dating partner.

**70%** of LGBTQ people, **41%** people of color, and **99%** of women with disabilities suffer street harassment regularly.

**About 3** women are killed by a current or former lover **every day.**

### MONEY

For every **$1.00** a White male makes, a White woman makes **78¢,** an African American woman makes **64¢,** and a Hispanic or Latina woman makes **54¢.**

Of the **1.7 million** youth who experience homelessness every year, **20% - 40%** identify as LGBTQ.

People who live in poverty are **more likely** to suffer from mental illness.

People who are mentally ill are **more likely** to live in poverty.

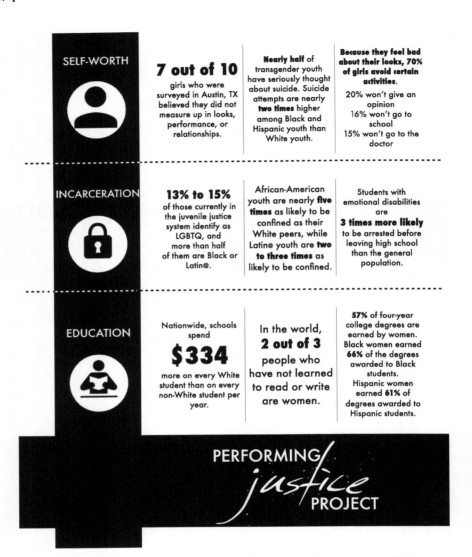

**SELF-WORTH**

**7 out of 10** girls who were surveyed in Austin, TX believed they did not measure up in looks, performance, or relationships.

**Nearly half** of transgender youth have seriously thought about suicide. Suicide attempts are nearly **two times** higher among Black and Hispanic youth than White youth.

**Because they feel bad about their looks, 70% of girls avoid certain activities.**
20% won't give an opinion
16% won't go to school
15% won't go to the doctor

**INCARCERATION**

**13% to 15%** of those currently in the juvenile justice system identify as LGBTQ, and more than half of them are Black or Latin@.

African-American youth are nearly **five times** as likely to be confined as their White peers, while Latin@ youth are **two to three times** as likely to be confined.

Students with emotional disabilities are **3 times more likely** to be arrested before leaving high school than the general population.

**EDUCATION**

Nationwide, schools spend **$334** more on every White student than on every non-White student per year.

In the world, **2 out of 3** people who have not learned to read or write are women.

**57%** of four-year college degrees are earned by women. Black women earned **66%** of the degrees awarded to Black students. Hispanic women earned **61%** of degrees awarded to Hispanic students.

PERFORMING *justice* PROJECT

**Figure E.1** PJP infographic exploring systemic oppression through statistics, created for youth participants by PJP teaching artists

# Appendix F

# Glossary of Related Terms

It is impossible to create a comprehensive list of terms because language around race and gender is continually changing. Terms included below have been discussed elsewhere in this book or are ideas that we feel are essential to building a Performing Justice Project with youth. We include the source list at the bottom of this document because these sources reference the definitions included here and are recommended for staying updated on terminology that sometimes changes rapidly. It is inevitable that new terms will arise when working with youth—we honor this as a way to learn from and lift up youth voices which are often at the forefront of language and culture change.

**Agency:** A person's capacity to make their own choices, independent of outside pressures or influences.

**Ally:** Someone who believes in and stands with others who face oppression.

**Asexual:** Someone who does not experience sexual attraction.

**Biphobia:** Fear, hatred, resentment, prejudice, or other negative responses towards people who identify as bisexual. Biphobia can originate from within the LGBTQIA community or from society at large.

**Bisexual:** A person who is attracted to at least two genders although not always at the same time or in equal amounts.

**Cisgender:** Someone whose birth-assigned sex and gender identity are the same; for example, someone assigned female sex who identifies as a woman.

**Colorblind:** The belief that race should not impact how one is perceived or what one has access to in our country. The result of colorblindness is to deny the continuing existence of structural or institutional racism and the fact that racism continues to be a significant negative factor in the lives of people of color.

**Gender:** A set of social constructs that have been used to define and reinforce ideas of masculinity and femininity. This can impact how a person views their body, physical presentation and societal role. Gender is not determined by the sex that someone is assigned at birth.

**Gender Expression:** The outward presentation of a person's gender identity that may or may not align with pre-existing societal expectations.

| | |
|---|---|
| **Gender-Fluid:** | A person whose gender identity is not fixed along the gender binary (male and female), but is rather changing or fluid. They may go through periods of identifying as more female or male, or may not choose binary labels for gender. |
| **Gender Identity:** | The way a person identifies on the gender spectrum. These identities include, but are not limited to: female, male, transgender, non-binary, genderqueer, or gender-fluid. Gender identity may impact pronoun choice and physical presentation. A person's gender identity may not match their sex assigned at birth. |
| **Gender Justice:** | An intersectional effort to ensure equity for people across lines of gender, race, and class. |
| **Gender Non-Binary:** | A person who does not identify within the gender binary of male and female. |
| **Gender Non-Conforming:** | A person whose gender expression or gender identity does not conform to the gender binary. |
| **Genderqueer:** | A person who does not align themselves with expected ideas of binary gender roles or gender identification. A genderqueer person may also identify as non-binary or gender-fluid. |
| **Heteronormative/ Heterosexism:** | The reinforcement of a worldview that believes that a heterosexual identity is the typical or normal identity. Heterosexism refers to a system of oppression that gives institutional power and privilege to those identified as heterosexual at the expense of those who identify as gay, lesbian, bisexual, transgender, and queer. |
| **Homophobia:** | Fear, hatred, resentment, prejudice, or other negative responses towards the LGBTQIA community. |
| **Institutional Oppression:** | Refers to the policies and practices within and across institutions that, intentionally or not, produce outcomes that chronically favor one group over another. |
| **Internalized Oppression/ Dominance:** | Internalized oppression refers to messages that members of a target group take in and internalize about themselves. Internalized dominance refers to messages received and actions taken that reify one's superiority based on membership to a dominant group. |
| **Interpersonal Oppression:** | Includes ways in which one acts with others based upon the idea that one identity is inherently better and others are inherently inferior. |
| **Intersectional/ Intersectionality:** | Terms coined by Kimberlé Williams Crenshaw in her 1989 paper, "Demarginalizing the intersection of race and sex: A Black feminist critique of |

antidiscrimination doctrine, feminist theory and anti-racist politics," refers to the ways different identities, such as race and gender, as well as systems of power and oppression simultaneously intersect and impact marginalized groups.

**Intersex:** A person who has a combination of chromosomes, anatomy or hormonal makeup that don't fit the typical definitions of male and female biology.

**Justice:** The idea that all members of a society have equitable access to social, political and economic opportunities and privileges.

**LGBTQIA:** Umbrella term to describe those who identify as lesbian, gay, bisexual, transgender, queer or questioning, intersex, and agender. Often shortened to LGBTQ, which reflects sexual orientation and gender identity. Other letters are sometimes added to the acronym to acknowledge specific identities.

**Microaggressions:** Microaggressions are everyday slights directed towards someone of a different identity marker. They can be verbal, behavioral, or environmental indignities and are often unnoticed or minimized by the person enacting the microaggressions. Although originally used to describe racial microaggressions, this term can be used to describe microaggressions against any identity based on membership to an oppressed group (women, trans folks, people with disabilities, etc.).

**Misgender:** To misgender someone is to use the wrong pronouns to refer to them.

**Myth of Meritocracy:** The belief that achievements are based solely on one's own efforts, abilities, or merits. Relies on the idea of equal opportunity—that in today's world everyone has the same opportunities—and on the idea of individualism—the belief that group memberships are irrelevant. Reinforces the belief that gaps between dominant and target groups (education, wealth, etc.) are the result of individual strengths or weaknesses.

**Oppression:** A set of policies, practices, traditions, norms, definitions and explanations which function to systematically exploit one social group to the benefit of another social group. The group that benefits is the dominant group, while the target group is exploited. *See also* Structural Oppression, Institutional Oppression, Interpersonal Oppression, *and* Internalized Oppression/Dominance.

**Pansexual:** Someone who is attracted to all gender identities.

**Power:** Includes access to resources, the ability to influence others, access to decision-makers to reinforce or implement what one wants done, the ability to define reality for oneself and others.

**Prejudice/bias:** Bias is a tendency to favor one thing over another. Prejudice is the act of making a judgment about someone before having knowledge of them.

**Privilege:** Through a social justice lens, privilege is about the rights, advantages, and protections enjoyed by some at the expense of the rights, advantages and protections available to others. Although privilege is often assumed to be something that can be earned, racial or gender privilege is unearned, systemic privilege.

**Pronouns:** Pronouns are used to identify someone's gender identity and may include they/them/theirs, ze/hir/hirs, she/her/hers, he/him/his. Pronouns cannot be assumed by looking at someone; it is appropriate to ask for someone's pronouns rather than assume or misgender them.

**Queer:** Used to describe individuals who do not identify as heterosexual/straight and/or cisgender. Originally used as a slur against those who identify as LGBTQ, and because of this the term queer is not used uniformly within the community.

**Race:** A socially constructed system for dividing people based on the color of their skin and other physical features.

**Racial Justice:** The creation and maintenance of political, social, and economic systems that guarantee equitable opportunities for everyone regardless of race, gender and class.

**Racism:** A form of oppression in which one racial group dominates over others. Although often thought of as racist actions or personal prejudices, racism describes complex systems of racial hierarchies and inequities. **Why not reverse racism?** The critical element that differentiates racism from racial prejudice and discrimination is the historical accumulation and ongoing use of institutional power and authority that supports discriminatory behaviors in systemic and far-reaching ways. People of color may hold beliefs or prejudices that discriminate against white people, but do not have social and institutional power or backing—the impact of their prejudice on whites is temporary and contextual.

**Respectability Politics:** The process by which members of a marginalized group attempt to monitor and influence the behaviors of other group members to conform to the expectations of those in power in order to receive better treatment. The idea was first articulated by Evelyn Brooks Higginbotham in her book *Righteous Discontent: The Women's Movement in the Black Baptist Church, 1880–1920.*

**Same Gender Loving (SGL):** Term used to describe attraction between people who identify as the same gender. The phrase was coined by Cleo Manago as a way for people of color to identify as queer without aligning themselves with European or white definitions of queerness. More information on the history of this term can be found in the essay "'In the life' in diaspora: Autonomy/desire/community" by Jafari Sinclaire Allen in the book *Routledge handbook of sexuality, health and rights* (Aggleton and Parker 2010).

**Sex/Sex Assigned at Birth:** The sex that is assigned to a person at the time of their birth. A person is generally assigned according to the gender binary, which may or may not correspond with their gender identity.

**Sexism:** A system of oppression in which one sex—male—dominates over all other sex and gender identities. Also tied to a gender binary system (male/female).

**Sexual Orientation:** Describes romantic/sexual attraction. Includes lesbian, gay, heterosexual, bisexual, queer, pansexual, among other orientations.

**Structural Oppression:** Structural oppression refers to the historical, cultural, social and psychological aspects of a society that keep inequity in place.

**Third Gender:** A person who identifies as another gender besides man or woman. This identification is utilized in societies whose ideas of gender go beyond the gender binary.

**Toxic Masculinity:** Rigid societal definitions of masculinity based in dominance and aggression that result in microaggressions, dangerous behavior, violence towards others and oneself.

**Transgender/Trans:** Someone whose birth assigned sex does not correspond with their gender identity or cultural expectations and expressions of sex assigned at birth. Can be used by someone who is transitioning from one sex/gender identity to another, as well as by someone who has already transitioned.

**Transphobia:** Fear, hatred, resentment, prejudice, or other negative responses towards people who identify as trans. Transphobia can originate from within the LGBTQIA community or from society at large.

**White Nationalism:** The belief that there should be a white national identity and that white people should have social, political and economic control of a nation. While white nationalists are white supremacists, not all white supremacists are white nationalists.

**White Supremacy:** The conviction that white people are superior to people of color and should occupy the dominant position in society.

# Source List

Aggleton, P. and Parker, R. (eds.) (2010) *Routledge handbook of sexuality, health and rights*, New York: Routledge.

DiAngelo, R. (2018) *White fragility: Why it's so hard for white people to talk about racism*, Boston: Beacon Press.

Crenshaw, K. W. (1989) 'Demarginalizing the intersection of race and sex: A Black feminist critique of antidiscrimination doctrine, feminist theory and antiracist politics,' *University of Chicago Legal Forum*, vol. 1989: no. 1, pp. 139–167, viewed June 9, 2019, https://chicagounbound.uchicago.edu/cgi/viewcontent.cgi?article=1052&context=uclf

Dismantling Racism Works (2019) *Dismantling racism works web workbook*, viewed June 28, 2019, www.dismantlingracism.org/

Gender Spectrum (2019) *Understanding gender*, viewed June 28, 2019, www.genderspectrum.org/quick-links/understanding-gender/

GLSEN (2019) *Gender terminology: Discussion guide*, viewed June 28, 2019, www.glsen.org/sites/default/files/Gender%20Terminology%20Guide.pdf

Higginbotham, E. B. (1993) *Righteous discontent: The women's movement in the Black baptist church, 1880-1920*, Cambridge, MA: Harvard University Press.

Human Rights Campaign (2019) *Glossary of terms*, viewed June 28, 2019, www.hrc.org/resources/glossary-of-terms

National Education Association (2018) *Racial justice in education*, viewed June 28, 2019, https://neaedjustice.org/wp-content/uploads/2018/11/Racial-Justice-in-Education.pdf

Racial Equity Tools (2019) *Glossary*, viewed June 28, 2019, http://racialequitytools.org/glossary

Safe Zone Project (2019) *LGBTQ+ vocabulary glossary of terms*, viewed June 28, 2019, https://thesafezoneproject.com/resources/vocabulary/

Sensoy, Ö. and DiAngelo, R. (2012) *Is everyone really equal? An introduction to key concepts in social justice education*, New York: Teachers College Press.

Showing Up for Racial Justice (2019) viewed June 28, 2019, www.showingupforracialjustice.org/

Sue, D. W. (2015) *Race talk and the conspiracy of silence: Understanding and facilitating difficult dialogues on race*, Hoboken: John Wiley & Sons Inc.

Trans Student Educational Resources (2019) *LGBTQ+ definitions*, viewed June 28, 2019, www.transstudent.org/definitions/

# Index of PJP Performance Actions

# Index

# Belonging Is Political

**Figure 6.1** Belonging in PJP
Source: Photo by Lynn Hoare.

As we begin and end each Performing Justice Project, Aimee Carrillo Rowe reminds us of the critical—as in important *and* power-laden—nature of belonging and becoming.

> Belonging is political ... Whose lives matter to us? Whose well-being is essential to our own? And, alternatively, whose survival must we overlook in order to connect to power in the ways we do? ... The sites of our belonging constitute how we see the world, what we value, who we are becoming.
>
> (Rowe 2009, p. 3)

## Reference

Rowe, A. C. (2009) 'Moving relations: On the limits of belonging,' *Liminalities: A Journal of Performance Studies*, vol. 5, no. 5, p. 3.